COMMENTARY FOR BENEDICTINE OBLATES
ON THE RULE OF ST. BENEDICT

By
Canon G.-A. Simon
Priest Oblate of St. Wandrille's Abbey

Translated from the second French edition by

Leonard J. Doyle
Oblate of St. John's Abbey

Reprinted and re-typeset from
the 1950 St. John's Abbey Press edition by:

MEDIATRIX PRESS

MMXVI

Commentary For Oblates on the Rule of St. Benedict
Originally published by:
St. John's Abbey Press, 1950

ISBN: 978-1-953746-26-9

Nihil obstat:

BASILIUS STEGMANN, O.S.B. Censor Librorum
Imprimi potest:
+ALCUINUS DEUTSCH, O.S.B. Abbas S. Joannis Bapt. January 5, 1947
Imprimatur:
JOSEPHUS P. BUSCH Episcopus S. Clodoaldi January 8, 1947

©Mediatrix Press 2016
Post Falls, ID
http://www.mediatrixpress.com/

TABLE OF CONTENTS

FOREWORD. i

INTRODUCTION. iii

TRANSLATOR'S PREFACE. xv

PROLOGUE. 1

CHAPTER 1
On the Kinds of Monks. 23

CHAPTER 2
What Kind of Man the Abbot Ought to Be. 31

CHAPTER 3
On Calling the Brethren for Counsel. 51

CHAPTER 4
What Are the Instruments of Good Works. 57

CHAPTER 5
On Obedience. 73

CHAPTER 6
On the Spirit of Silence. 81

CHAPTER 7
On Humility. 89

CHAPTER 8
On the Divine Office During the Night. 135

CHAPTER 9
How Many Psalms Are to Be Said at the Night Office. 145

CHAPTER 10
How the Night Office Is to Be Said in Summer Time. 153

CHAPTER 11
How the Night Office Is to Be Said on Sundays.............. 155

CHAPTER 12
How the Morning Office Is to Be Said. 160

CHAPTER 13
How the Morning Office Is to Be Said on Weekdays.......... 163

CHAPTER 14
How the Night Office Is to Be Said on the Feasts of the Saints.. 167

CHAPTER 15
At What Times "Alleluia" Is to Be Said. 170

CHAPTER 16
How the Work of God Is to Be Performed During the Day..... 172

CHAPTER 17
How Many Psalms Are to Be Said at These Hours. 175

CHAPTER 18
In What Order the Psalms Are to Be Said. 179

CHAPTER 19
On the Manner of Saying the Divine Office.................. 187

CHAPTER 20
On Reverence in Prayer.................................. 192

CHAPTER 21
On the Deans of the Monastery. 197

CHAPTER 22
How the Monks Are to Sleep............................. 201

CHAPTER 23
On Excommunication for Faults........................... 205

CHAPTER 24
  What the Measure of Excommunication Should Be. 208

CHAPTER 25
  On Weightier Faults. 212

CHAPTER 26
  On Those Who Without an Order Associate With the Excommunicated. 215

CHAPTER 27
  How Solicitous the Abbot Should Be for the Excommunicated. . . 217

CHAPTER 28
  On Those Who Will Not Amend After Repeated Corrections. . . . 221

CHAPTER 29
  Whether Brethren Who Leave the Monastery Should Be Received Again. 224

CHAPTER 30
  How Boys Are to Be Corrected. 227

CHAPTER 31
  What Kind of Man the Cellarer of the Monastery Should Be. . . . 229

CHAPTER 32
  On the Tools and Property of the Monastery. 237

CHAPTER 33
  Whether Monks Ought to Have Anything of Their Own. 240

CHAPTER 34
  Whether All Should Receive in Equal Measure What Is Necessary 246

CHAPTER 35
  On the Weekly Servers in the Kitchen. 249

CHAPTER 36
    On the Sick Brethren. 255

CHAPTER 37
    On Old Men and Children. 259

CHAPTER 38
    On the Weekly Reader. 261

CHAPTER 39
    On the Measure of Food. 266

CHAPTER 40
    On the Measure of Drink. 269

CHAPTER 41
    At What Hours the Meals Should Be Taken. 272

CHAPTER 42
    That No One Speak After Compline. 276

CHAPTER 43
    On Those Who Come Late to the Work of God or to Table. 281

CHAPTER 44
    How the Excommunicated Are to Make Satisfaction. 288

CHAPTER 45
    On Those Who Make Mistakes in the Oratory. 292

CHAPTER 46
    On Those Who Fail in Any Other Matters. 294

CHAPTER 47
    On Giving the Signal for the Time of the Work of God. 297

CHAPTER 48
    On the Daily Manual Labor. 300

CHAPTER 49
    On the Observance of Lent. 310

CHAPTER 50
    On Brethren Who Are Working Far From the Oratory or Are on a
    Journey. 313

CHAPTER 51
    On Brethren Who Go Not Very Far Away. 316

CHAPTER 52
    On the Oratory of the Monastery. 318

CHAPTER 53
    On the Reception of Guests. 321

CHAPTER 54
    Whether a Monk Should Receive Letters or Anything Else. 329

CHAPTER 55
    On the Clothes and Shoes of the Brethren. 332

CHAPTER 56
    On the Abbot's Table. 341

CHAPTER 57
    On the Craftsmen of the Monastery. 345

CHAPTER 58
    On the Manner of Receiving Brethren. 349

CHAPTER 59
    On the Sons of Nobles and of the Poor Who Are Offered. 364

CHAPTER 60
    On Priests Who May Wish to Live in the Monastery. 368

CHAPTER 61
    How Pilgrim Monks Are to Be Received. 371

CHAPTER 62
    On the Priests of the Monastery. 377

CHAPTER 63
    On the Order of the Community.. 381

CHAPTER 64
    On Constituting an Abbot. 389

CHAPTER 65
    On the Prior of the Monastery.. 395

CHAPTER 66
    On the Porters of the Monastery. 401

CHAPTER 67
    On Brethren Who Are Sent on a Journey. 405

CHAPTER 68
    If a Brother Is Commanded to Do Impossible Things. 409

CHAPTER 69
    That the Monks Presume Not to Defend One Another. 411

CHAPTER 71
    That the Brethren Be Obedient to One Another.. 417

CHAPTER 72
    On the Good Zeal Which Monks Ought to Have. 421

EPILOGUE
    *On the Fact That the Full Observance of Justice Is Not Established in
    This Rule.* 425

FOREWORD

DURING the fourteen centuries that have elapsed since the death of St. Benedict, the Rule which he wrote, and which has always been known as "the Holy Rule," has continued to make the monks who followed it a living and a life-giving force in the Church and in Western civilization and has kept them near, in the measure in which they follow their Holy Rule, to the spirit of the Gospels, of the Apostles and of the early Fathers. But it has influenced not only monks and nuns, living in religious communities. From the very beginning the Rule of St. Benedict has extended its influence over men and women in the world who want to live in the spirit of Christ. Indeed, it is only because the Rule is of interest to Christians in general that it is suitable for monks; for St. Benedict's whole aim was to make his monks perfect Christians.

For many centuries during which books were handwritten and consequently scarce, the Holy Rule exerted its influence on the laity through the good example of the monks and nuns who conformed their lives to it. Even long after the invention of the printing press, the text of the Rule and the many commentaries which had been written on it through the centuries were still directed to men and women in the religious life. Only recently has literacy become so widespread that the need was felt for translations and commentaries prepared especially for the Christian living in the world.

Several commentaries have now appeared in English, some of them directed particularly to the laity. Canon G.-A. Simon's commentary is the first book, however, which comments on the Rule systematically, neglecting no chapter or paragraph, with practical applications for Christians in the world, especially those who have become affiliated with the Order of St. Benedict as Oblates. I am therefore especially pleased to introduce this commentary in English translation, and to commend the translator, an Oblate of St. John's Abbey, for his splendid work in faithfully rendering the French idiom into English.

Canon Simon's work should prove singularly interesting and valuable to several classes of readers: to those outside the Order of St. Benedict, even outside the Church, as an introduction to Benedictine spirituality; to lay Oblates, who will learn to know their Order better through the

i

commentaries on each day's reading of the Rule, and to live the Benedictine life through the applications following each commentary; to priest Oblates, for whom very little has been written in English, and whom the author, himself a priest Oblate, has always in mind; to priest monks doing parish or mission work away from the communal life of the monastery and therefore finding themselves in somewhat the same situation as priest Oblates; to directors of Oblates; even to monks and nuns living in community, who will find here, as the testimonials on the French editions prove, a compendium of the best commentaries on their Rule down through the ages.

In commending this work, it is my hope and prayer that it will serve the purpose for which it was written and translated, that of intensifying in many souls the desire to model their lives in accord with the principle of our Holy Father Benedict—"to seek God alone." May He, in His loving goodness, bless and fructify the seed that is sown in these pages.

✠ Alcuin Deutsch, O.S.B.

Abbot

INTRODUCTION

HIS commentary makes no pretense of doing any more than helping our brothers and sisters in St. Benedict, the Oblates, to read and meditate the Holy Rule and to draw practical conclusions from it. Thus the author has not tried to be erudite. If he has ventured sometimes to enter into some details of textual or historical criticism, the reason is that he thought he could thus provide a better grasp of the meaning of the text, and also that he wanted his work to be a sort of compendium of the principal problems posed by the study of the Holy Rule, for the use of those who would have neither the time nor the means to devote themselves to a more personal or more extensive study. If here and there he has multiplied the quotations, the reason is that, being simply an Oblate himself, he needed to feel himself always supported by authentic interpreters.

It is with the same purpose of furnishing the Oblates a body of knowledge indispensable for them or nearly so, that by way of introduction the author proposes to say here a few words on the history of the Benedictine Oblature and to follow this summary with brief notes on the principal commentaries.

1. The Benedictine Oblature

It has sometimes been asked whether there were Oblates in St. Benedict's time. It is certain that the term "Oblate" was originally reserved for the children offered to the monastery, as we learn from Chapter 59. But it is no less certain that from the beginning there were in the vicinity of the monasteries persons desirous of perfection, united to the cenobitic groups by a more or less definite manner of affiliation.

Some of these Christian men and women belonged to the ancient institution of the "ascetics," faithful living in the world, often with their families, in conformity with that ideal of the primitive Church whose close relation to the monastic ideal has been shown by Dom Germain Morin. There were still some ascetics of this first type, as Dom Ursmer Berlière has observed, in the seventh century.

Thus the Life of St. Benedict, by St. Gregory the Great, shows us, not far from Monte Cassino, "two religious women of distinguished origin, who lived in a place apart" with their nurse, and whose temporal affairs were administered by a very religious man. They belonged to a secular church, where they received Communion; and yet St. Benedict excommunicates them for a lack of charity towards their benefactor, as if he had a certain authority over them.

In another chapter it is the brother of the monk Valentinian, "a layman and very devout," who comes to the monastery every year to renew his spiritual strength. He is compared to the "servant" of the Prophet Eliseus; and St. Gregory informs us that "from his place he came every year, fasting, to the monastery of the man of God." Evidently this custom had been prescribed for him by the Saint himself; for one day when he had failed to observe it, "the holy man rebuked him for eating on the way," and he in confusion "fell at Benedict's feet and was ashamed for his sin, the more so when he had learnt that the venerable man had seen him commit the fault though not present."

Moreover, around the monastery there lived workmen employed in the labor of the fields. St. Benedict implies their presence when he says in Chapter 48 that in poor monasteries the monks may have to gather the harvest themselves, a proof that in the more fortunate monasteries this task was entrusted to others.

Now the monks were far from being indifferent to the religious formation of these modest co-workers, for in imitation of their holy Father they strove to lead the neighboring peasants to God. If the faithful felt an attraction towards the monastery, surely the monks for their part felt a need of assimilating them, and the assimilation is already a form of apostolate.

In his substantial study on the Origins of the Oblature, a scholarly Oblate, the Abbe Deroux, has shown that with the evolution of the monastic labor the workmen of the monastery became *famuli* and ended by being progressively transformed into religious under the name of *fratres conversi* or Lay Brothers. But their original situation was really that of Secular Oblates, living in the atmosphere of the monks and under their spiritual direction, under Statutes varying from place to place.

Beginning with the seventh century, we see alongside of these *famuli* laymen and laywomen joining the monasteries under certain conditions as permanent guests. They submit to the Abbot and occupy themselves with carrying out his plans outside of the monastery. They usually make a partial or total donation of their property into his hands in return for their room, clothing and board. When they renounce their freedom they take the name of Oblates and wear a habit resembling that of the monks.

Not all, however, live in the monastery. Some remain in the world, kept there by their circumstances. These two categories, resident and non-resident, appear clearly in the ninth century. We know how William, Abbot of Hirschau, in the 11th century organized the Oblates of his Abbey and gave them Constitutions which provoked the admiration of his contemporaries.

But alongside of these numerous cases of union we find others in which the bonds of brotherhood seem to be mostly spiritual. This is the case with the *fratres* or *sorores familiares*. Princes, Bishops, knights, inscribed in the register of the monasteries, are united by a religious bond to the monks, who consider them as "brothers" and "sisters." But, according to the persons and the places, the affiliation appears more or less close and involves more or less of obligations.

In certain cases, evidently, it is scarcely more than a simple union of prayers and of merits; but in others it is more than that. Sometimes the reception takes place in chapter. The Oblate is "received as a brother." Sometimes he is given a monastic habit, which he will wear under his clothes or which he will put on for certain occasions. Guichard, Abbot of Pontigny, clothed St. Thomas á Becket, Archbishop of Canterbury, in a cowl with a reduced hood and narrowed sleeves, so made that he might wear it constantly without its being seen. To William Longsword, Duke of Normandy, who would have liked to become a monk, Martin, Abbot of Jumièges, also gave a cowl and a tunic, which the prince put away in a chest of which he always carried the key; and undoubtedly the Duke put them on for certain occasions. The Abbé Dubois, relating the history of the Abbey of Morimond in the middle of the 12th century, tells us that many priests, impressed by the life of the monks and unable to resist such touching examples, regarded it as the greatest good fortune to be affiliated with the Order, had their heads shaved, took the monastic habit and followed the Benedictine Rule as best they could in their own houses.

No doubt the already ancient custom of giving the monastic habit or a part of it to the Christians affiliated with the Order but unable to enter the monastery, was what inspired St. Norbert when he invested with a white woolen scapular the Count Thibaut of Champagne, the first of his

Tertiaries. Later, St. Francis of Assisi did not consider himself an innovator in giving the Franciscan serge to Luchesio and to Bona Donna, but rather in giving them a Rule which constituted an Order, complete in itself and living in the world.

In the ninth century we have in the person of Géraud d'Aurillac the example of a lay nobleman leading the religious life in the world, under the direction of the Bishop Walbert. If there is no question of a habit for him, we learn at least that he had the monastic tonsure given him, which he concealed "under the rest of his flowing hair," and that he recited the Office every day with the clergy.

The history of St. Henry, Emperor, is well known. When he asked Richard, Abbot of St. Vannes, to receive him as a monk, the Abbot had him come to Chapter and put this question to him: "Will you, following the Rule and following the example of Jesus Christ, be obedient until death?" Upon the affirmative reply of the "postulant," the Abbot continued: "I hereby receive you as a monk and from this day I charge myself with the care of your soul. For that reason I want you to do, with the fear of God, everything that I shall order you to do." The Emperor having acquiesced once more, the Abbot declared: "I want you, therefore, to return and govern the empire which God has entrusted to you, and by your constancy in administering justice to procure in so far as you are able the welfare of the whole state."

During his life the Oblate remained, as much as he could, under the direction of the monks. St. Henry frequently consulted Abbot Richard.

Certain Oblates, like Bouchard the Venerable, Count of Vendome, at Saint-Maur-des-Fossés, came to live near the Abbey so that they could take part in the psalmody of the monks. For the women this was rather common. Living in cells near the monastery, they spent the intervals between the Offices in mending or washing the monks' clothes or in making ornaments for the church. This was done at the Abbéy of Le Bee in Normandy by the mother of Blessed Herluin, the founder, and later by Basilis, widow of Hugh, Amfride, her niece, and Eve, widow of William Crespin. We may cite, at the priory of Le Desert, a dependancy of Notre-Dame de Lyre, Hélisende, wife of Gilbert de Terray; at Lessies, Ada, widow of Thierry d'Avesnes, Petronilla, widow of Raoul, Count of Viesville, and others. The list could be considerably lengthened. These holy women received "the habit of religion" or at least the veil. Some were virgins, others widows, some married women, such as Helisende, cited above, for whom her husband endowed Masses, recalling that she had lived "as a sister," near the priory of Le Désert. The influence of these Oblate women was sometimes profound. The monk Chronicler of Lessies tells us that the Oblate Ada was "the guardian of the Abbey's religious fervor."

At the hour of death the Secular Oblate was often clothed in the monastic habit and, following the example of the monks, he expired on ashes. Still more often, he was clothed in it after his death and was buried in the cloister, as he had stipulated at the time of his reception. An obit was made for him and he was accorded suffrages like the members of the community.

Thanks to St. Frances of Rome, a group of Oblate women became famous in the 15th century, namely the group which was formed at Rome around the monastery of St. Mary of the Snows, served by the Benedictine Congregation of Mount Olivet. After having been a model wife and mother, Frances, who had been a Secular Oblate since 1425 and had become a widow in 1436, retired with some pious ladies to the house of Tor' di Specchi, which she had rented while her husband was living. The "sisters," without any vow, followed the Rule of St. Benedict, adapted to their situation by Dom Antonello di Monte-Savelli. They wore a white woolen veil over a modest black dress.

"Frances", writes Dom Bernard Maréchaux, "directed her little flock admirably. Hers was a soul all of a piece, having no end but God and going straight to Him like an arrow. Living in constant contact with God and His Saints, the admirable mystic was none the less an ardent apostle. She carried on a battle without truce against licentious fashions. She devoted herself to the sick and the poor; and amid manifold works of mercy and sowing miracles in her footsteps, she went down to the bottom of that abyss of humility and obedience dug by St. Benedict. She was filled to the brim with that spirit of compunction which is the strength of Benedictine prayer. . ."

The monastic decadence of the 15th and 16th centuries necessarily involved a decadence of the Oblature. Yet the latter was not wholly forgotten in the 17th century. Writing at that time the life of the Venerable Mechtilde of the Blessed Sacrament, the Abbé Duquesne made this observation: "Formerly it was quite a common practice to take the habit of a certain religious Order to which one had some attraction.

"One did not give up one's state in life nor even the clothes proper to that state, but was content to wear under the ordinary clothes some mark or symbol of the Order one had chosen." But, he continued, "this devotion, formerly so esteemed and so revered, is no longer anything but the object of the censure and the mockery of the world."

The 17th century saw some great Oblate women. The most celebrated was Helena Lucretia Cornaro-Piscopia, of one of the most illustrious families of Venice. A prodigy of learning, but also of piety and of mortification, she consecrated herself secretly to the Lord at the age of 11. In love with the liturgy, she assisted at the Office every day in the Abbey of St. James. A little later she renewed her vow and received as an Oblate the large Benedictine scapular, which she always wore under her secular clothes. Dom Mabillon did not fail to go and visit her on his way through Italy. Death took her at the age of 32. Her body, clothed in the habit of the Order, rests at St. Justina of Padua in the chapel reserved for the burial of the monks.

During the same era Mother Mechtilde of the Blessed Sacrament received into the Oblature the Countess of Chateauvieux. Through the Abbé Duquesne we know the details of the investiture, which took place during the night, after Matins; and the same author has preserved for us the little allocution addressed by the "Venerable Mother" to the new Oblate when she had put on the tunic, the leather belt, the scapular and the veil.

In the 18th century the Oblature necessarily followed the destinies of the monastic Order and suffered its agony. It was revived in the 19th century by the great monk who restored the Order of St. Benedict in France, Dom Prosper Guéranger, first Abbot of Solesmes. His thoughts on this subject have been collected in a little work entitled *The Church or the Society of the Divine Praise.* Later on, the Oblature was revealed to the public at large by a celebrated Oblate of Ligugè, the writer Huysmans, whose book *The Oblate* has not been without influence on the progress of the Oblature. Since then it has not stopped prospering and being an effective instrument of Christian renewal in a society three-fourths paganized.

In 1898 His Holiness Pope Leo XIII in a Brief dated June 17 established the privileges of the Benedictine Oblates. In July, 1904, His Holiness Pope Pius X, at the request of the Right Reverend Abbot Primate of the Order, Dom Hildebrand de Hemptinne, approved and confirmed the Statutes of the Oblates. Henceforth the Benedictine Oblates have a juridical status in their Order and in the Church.

2. Principal Commentaries on the Holy Rule

Our purpose in giving some notes here on the principal commentaries on the Holy Rule is not so much to outline a chapter of literary history which could not be complete in so few pages, as to allow the reader to identify the commentators whose names will recur most often. Moreover, we shall limit ourselves in general to the Latin and French commentaries, these being the ones with which the majority of our readers have some chance of coming in contact.

To Dom Ursmer Berlière's excellent book, *Benedictine Asceticism*, we owe some scholarly and interesting pages on the commentaries on the Rule composed from the beginning up to the end of the 12th century. The first and best known was that of Paul Warnefrid, called Paul the Deacon, written about 770 for the monks of Civate, near Milan. "Rich in precise details on the Benedictine observance of the eighth century, it served as a basis for the works of Hildemar and Basile," both belonging to the ninth century.

To St. Benedict of Aniane, who died in 821, we owe the *Codex Regularum* and the *Concordia Regularum*, the latter being particularly useful for studying the sources of the Benedictine Rule.

A little after 817 and before 820 a commentary was published by Smaragdus, Abbot of St. Michael. This commentary, which was above all literal and moral, was much used in the Middle Ages.

About 820 the pupils of Hildemar, monk of Civate, collected their teacher's conferences under the title of *Tractatus in Regulam Sancti Benedicti.*

Hucbald of St. Amandus, who died in 930, wrote the *Glose de Diversis Doctoribus Collecte, in Regulam Sancti Benedicti.*

In the 12th century appeared the works of Rupert of Deutz, Peter the Deacon, St. Hildegard, Stephen of Paris, as also an *Expositio in Regulam Sancti Benedicti* attributed without proof to the Cistercian Radulph, Abbot of Vaucelles, who died in 1151.

The principal commentator of the 13th century was Bernard, Abbot of Monte Cassino, whose *Expositio in Regulam*, although inspired by the works of Paul the Deacon and Smaragdus, has nevertheless, in Dom Butler's opinion, "a great value" as a picture of the life and the ideas prevailing at Monte Cassino in the 13th century, in the heyday of that monastery's prosperity and influence.

In the 14th century Peter Boherius, a French monk who became Bishop of Civita-Vecchia in 1364, wrote his *In Regulam S. Benedicti Apparatus*. In his explanation of the Rule he followed especially Cassian and St. Jerome. He owed much to Bernard, but was not equal to him.

In the 15th century the Dominican Juan de Torquemada, whose name is sometimes latinized into "Turrecremata" (1388-1468), composed an *Expositio in Regulam S. Benedicti* "of great excellence" according to Dom Butler; a commentary which felt the effects of the endeavors at reform begun in the Councils of Basle and Constance.

At the end of the same century, John Tritheim (Trithemius), Abbot of Spannheim, undertook a commentary which he brought only as far as Chapter 14, of a preeminently ascetical and mystical character.

With the 17th century and the great reforms of St. Vannes and St. Maur there appeared a whole host of scholarly commentators whose works are a veritable gold mine from the point of view of monastic history but with whom, as Dom L'Huillier observes, the method of exposition word by word has the disadvantage "of preventing any view of the whole, any general pattern," or at least of making them hard to discover.

In 1638 Dom Hugh Menard wrote some imposing *Notae et Observationes* on the *Concordia Regularum* of St. Benedict of Aniane.

To Dom Benedict van Haeften, prior of Afflighem, we owe a scholarly work published in 1644 under the title of *Disquisitionum Monasticarum Libri XII*. It is not a literal commentary, but the material in it is grouped by subjects and the whole is preceded by an explanation of the life of St. Benedict according to the *Dialogs* of St. Gregory.

The *Commentaire sur la Règle de S. Benoist* (1687) of Dom Joseph Mège enjoyed its hour of fame in the 17th century. It had its polemical aspect, since it was aimed at the *Traité de la Sainteté et des Devoirs de la Vie Monastique* published by Dom Armand Jean Le Bouthillier de Rancé, Abbot and reformer of La Trappe; but it is much more than a weapon of argument. The commentary of Dom Mége was regarded as "laxist"; still on the whole it is excellent and reflects well the "discretion" of St. Benedict.

The *Règle de S. Benoist Expliquée selon son Véritable Esprit*, which the Abbé de Rancé brought out in 1689, is a sort of justification of the ideas set forth in the *Devoirs de la Vie Monastique*. This commentary enjoyed a very great vogue in its time, and from it were drawn some *Meditations sur la*

Règle de S. Benoist (4th ed. 1713). One may find in it some explanations of detail which are not without interest, but the whole of the book is dominated by the personal notions of the reformer, who allowed himself to be swayed by an unbalanced admiration for the practices of the desert Fathers and accentuated the penitential note immoderately. As a consequence the work reflects the spirit of the Abbé de Rancé much more than the spirit of St. Benedict and, despite real merits, it would not be a sure guide in Benedictine spirituality.

The scholarly commentary of Dom Martène, *Commentarius in Regulam S.P. Benedicti* (1690), was intended as a mean between Dom Mège and the Abbé de Rancé. The learned Maurist took advantage of his immense erudition to clarify the text with the help of the monastic customs of all times. The whole appears heavy, but quite rich in information for anyone who has a taste for monastic history.

To Dom Louis Quinet, Abbot of Barbery, we owe the *Éclaircissements sur la Règle de S. Benoist* in the form of dialogs between an Abbot and a woman in religion, which are above all of a practical character.

Alongside of these great works we may appropriately cite some mystical writings having the Rule as object, such as the meditations or various treatises of Dom Philippe Frangois of the Congregation of St. Vannes, Dom Robert Morel, Dom Simon Bougis, Dom Claude Martin and others of the Congregation of St. Maur.

The great commentator of the 18th century was Dom Augustin Calmet, Abbot of Senones, of the Congregation of St. Vannes. It was in 1732 that he published his *Commentaire sur la Règle de S. Benoist*, of which a Latin translation appeared in 1750. In Dom Butler's opinion this commentary is "really learned, but less archaeological than Martène's, and seems to bring out better the spirit and meaning of the Rule." It is preceded by a preface treating of the Rule and of monastic history which Dom Butler describes as admirable and which in his opinion is "so good as to merit being printed by itself as an Introduction to the Rule."

La Traduction et Explication Littérale et Morale de la Règle de S. Benoist, published at Rouen in 1714 without any author's name by M. de Gournay, Abbé du Tronchet, is all but forgotten today. Perhaps it does not deserve this oblivion. The commentary is rather well thought out. Historical explanation and textual criticism are not neglected in this work, but its character is above all ascetical. We have made rather frequent use of it.

The 19th century produced no French commentary. It was a time of restoration, and sometimes of difficult restoration. More pressing needs had to be met, and the works of the old writers could suffice.

The 20th century will undoubtedly be more fertile.

The *Explication Ascétique et Historique de la Règle de S. Benoist* brought out in 1901 without any author's name by Dom L'Huillier is far from being a negligible work. It is a very personal work, sometimes out of proportion, but one which will never be consulted without profit. It was certainly the best commentary before that of Dom Delatte.

In 1908 Dom Étienne Salasc, Abbot of La Grande Trappe, gave us, likewise without author's name, *La Règle de S. Benoît Traduite et Commentée*. The translation is that of Dom Gueranger. "We would not have been capable of doing better," says the author modestly. As for the spirit which presided over his work, he tells us that he was "inspired above all by the original monuments of Cîteaux, erected by Saints and, thanks be to God, still in force in our day." The quotations are numerous, but they often consist of glosses on the text rather than being a literal commentary properly so called.

In the following year, 1909, Dom Symphorien, definitor of the Order of Reformed Cistercians, gave us *La Règle de S. Benoît Meditée*. It is not a commentary properly speaking, but a series of meditations on the text, or rather on a choice of more inspirational passages. It is a work at once practical and profound, which a person can utilize with profit for meditating the Holy Rule.

The *Commentaire sur la Règle de Saint Benoît*, by the Right Rev. Dom Paul Delatte, former Abbot of Solesmes, which appeared in 1913,[1] is, beyond contradiction, a work of the first rank. "For an understanding, not only intellectual but spiritual, of the Rule," declares Dom Butler, "it is, I think, the best of all. The element of learning, monastic history and archaeology is there in sufficient proportion, but it does not overload the work; there is also an element of theology in explaining the principles of the Rule. It is highly practical both in details of the life and their application to modern conditions, and also in regard to the spiritual and religious side of the life. It is clear, sane, full. . and satisfying. I do not hesitate to pronounce it, for general purposes of instruction, the best of

---

[1] English translation by Dom Justin McCann, monk of Ampleforth, *Commentary on the Rule of St. Benedict* (Latrobe, Pa.: The ArchAbbey Press, 1950).

the commentaries." It will be seen that we have followed this commentary almost step by step, in order to make the essence of it accessible to the greatest number of our fellow Oblates. We shall be happy if in doing this we have responded to the thought of the venerable author, who dedicated his work "in love and devotedness, to all those, whether in monasteries or in the world, who belong to the great family of St. Benedict."

More recently, in 1925, the Right Rev. Dom Bernard Laure, Abbot of Hautecombe, brought out, especially for the Oblates, the *Règle du Patriarche Saint Benoît, Texte, Traduction, Commentaire*. The Latin text and the translation, which is Dom Gueranger's, are divided into sections according to the daily readings followed in the French Congregation. This arrangement makes the book very practical for Oblates who want to unite themselves each day "in thoughts and sentiments with those who make the Benedictine Rule the norm of their life in the cloister." The commentary, succinct but adequate, is almost always followed by a few words of practical application.

We have no intention whatsoever of making a needless duplication of this excellent little book, which it will always be good to reread. The reading public we have in mind is perhaps more limited than that of the "pious persons deeply attached to the Benedictine Order" to whom the author addressed himself. We have in mind especially those Oblates who desire to know the Holy Rule with a knowledge somewhat more than elementary, so as to draw the greatest possible profit from it for their interior life, but who have not the leisure to consult the great commentaries directly. That is why, without pretending to do a work of scholarship, we have not neglected the manifold problems on the subject of the text and its meaning. That is also why we have developed the practical applications, separating them, however, from the commentary properly so called, since these applications sometimes consider situations which had not been directly envisaged by St. Benedict.

3. Texts and Translations

As to the translation, we have not ventured to undertake one ourself. There are several in existence on the choice of which we hesitated. We followed the counsels given us in adopting the translation of the "received text" made by Dom Guéranger, which is used for the readings in the refectory in the French Congregation and hence has a sort of privileged position.

The "received text," utilized by Dom Guéranger and generally followed since the 11th century, goes back certainly at least to the eighth century, for it is the one which Paul Warnefrid used in his commentary composed about 735. It is the result of a combination of two more ancient versions. The one, represented especially by an Oxford manuscript, was in current usage in the seventh and eighth centuries in the monasteries of Italy, France, England and Germany.

The other version, in circulation especially at the beginning of the ninth century, came from an exemplar preserved at Monte Cassino; and the representative of it closest to the original is the manuscript of St. Gall transcribed from a copy sent to Charlemagne by Theodemar, Abbot of Monte Cassino. It is this last, judged the most authentic, which served as a basis for the works of Dom Butler, for the translation made by the Reverend Fathers of Farnborough and for the one published in 1933 in the Collection *Pax*, made by the nuns of Sainte-Croix de Poitiers.

The differences among these three texts, says Dom Butler, "are not, in the majority of cases, great, and seldom affect the substance of the Rule." In our explanations we have ignored the insignificant variations, but we have been careful to note in passing all those which might have some interest for the comprehension of the text.

May this humble work help the children of St. Benedict living in the world to become permeated with the spirit of him whom they have the good fortune of being able to call their holy Father. It has no other reason for being.

Ut in omnibus glorificetur Deus.

Montreuil-en-Auge
On the Feast of St. Wandrille
July 22, 1934

TRANSLATOR'S PREFACE

FOUR of the most widely known English translations of the Rule of St. Benedict made in modern times are based on the "received text." The translation by Dom Oswald Hunter-Blair, monk of Fort-Augustus, published in 1886 and revised in 1906, includes the Latin text and some explanatory notes. The version by Aidan Cardinal Gasquet, O.S.B., published in 1925 as a volume of *The Medieval Library* by Chatto and Windus, London, is a rather free translation in a very pleasing English style. The volume contains an introduction by the Cardinal. An American "popular edition" of the Holy Rule is the translation by the Rev. Boniface Verheyen, O.S.B., of St. Benedict's Abbey, Atchison, Kansas. This translation, in an inexpensive format, without footnotes or Scriptural references, has proved its popularity by running as high as an eighth edition in 1935. Another American edition, likewise without notes or references, was published in 1937 by the Benedictines of St. Meinrad's Abbey, St. Meinrad, Indiana.

Abandoning the received text, the English translation made by Dom Justin McCann and published in 1937 at Stanbrook Abbey follows the text as edited by Abbot Cuthbert Butler, now regarded as more authentic and adopted as official by the English Congregation and the American-Cassinese Congregation of the Order of St. Benedict. Dom McCann also takes cognizance of the text as edited by Dom Benno Linderbauer of Metten (Bonn: Peter Hanstein, 1928), which he regards as "the only perfect edition of the authentic text," being practically the equivalent of Abbot Butler's for purposes of translation but closer to the original of St. Benedict in that it keeps to the non-classical Latin forms which Abbot Butler changed. Dom McCann's notes, in general, are on the language rather than on the subject matter of the Rule.

All of these translations preserve the "thee" and "thou" and other archaic forms which have long been traditional in English translations of religious works. Convinced that those forms detract from the understanding and the appeal which the Rule of St. Benedict ought to have for the modern reader, the translator of this present volume undertook a new translation of the Rule. This new translation is based on the text of Dom Linderbauer, and of course owes much to the English versions mentioned above, as well as to the French version of Dom Prosper Guéranger. It is printed herein as the text preceding the commentary for each day. Within the commentaries, however, the translator has followed the commentator in varying the translation according to different interpretations of the Latin or different synonyms or turns of expression. The commentator presumes that any reader who is interested in points of textual criticism will consult one of the available editions of the Latin text.

Acknowledgment is due for the constructive criticisms offered by the Right Reverend Abbot of St. John's Abbey, who entrusted this work to the translator, and by the Reverend *censor librorum*.

L. J. D.
St. John's University
Collegeville, Minnesota
December 1, 1946

COMMENTARY FOR OBLATES
ON THE RULE OF ST. BENEDICT

PROLOGUE

January 1—May 2—September 1

ISTEN, my son, to your master's precepts, and incline the ear of your heart (*Proverbs* 4:20). Receive willingly and carry out effectively your loving father's advice, that by the labor of obedience you may return to Him from whom you had departed by the sloth of disobedience.

To you, therefore, my words are now addressed, whoever you may be, who are renouncing your own will to do battle under the Lord Christ, the true King, and are taking up the strong, bright weapons of obedience.

And first of all, whatever good work you begin to do, beg of Him with most earnest prayer to perfect it, that He who has now deigned to count us among His sons may not at any time be grieved by our evil deeds. For we must always so serve Him with the good things He has given us, that He will never as an angry Father disinherit His children, nor ever as a dread Lord, provoked by our evil actions, deliver us to everlasting punishment as wicked servants who would not follow Him to glory.

COMMENTARY

If we undertake to study the Holy Rule, this is not out of mere curiosity. We wish to reform ourselves, and to attain that end we are looking for a sure guide. And here it is that we find ourselves face to face with St. Benedict.

Indeed, from the first lines of his Rule the holy Father presents himself to us and truly welcomes us. This guide, this "master" who is going to give us "precepts" is also and above all a "loving father" who addresses himself to his children. *Ausculta, fili.* His spiritual fatherhood, the noblest of all fatherhoods, is offered to "whoever, renouncing his own will," wants to "do battle under the Lord." To such a one Benedict will give his soul's best.

What are the Patriarch's sons to be? Soldiers. Their commander? Christ, the true King. Their arms? The best and the strongest: obedience. The end of their effort, the object of their conquest? God. We are going towards God, and we shall reach Him by an unending struggle, under the guidance of Christ our Lord. That is the whole program to be realized.

It will be noticed that from the very first lines St. Benedict repeatedly

1

speaks of obedience. He understands it here in its most general meaning. Obedience is opposed to sin, which is a disobedience to God's law and which thereby alienates us from Him. It is a constant docility—a readiness to learn—the object of which comprises at the same time the commandments of God and of His Church, the duties of our state of life, our rules, our particular regulations, and so forth. In fact, the Christian's whole activity encounters obedience at every moment. Obedience assures in his life a continual triumph over his own will in favor of the divine will. It is truly "the strong, bright weapon" with which he will do battle under Christ the King.

St. Benedict addresses himself, therefore, to whoever has the firm will to obey Christ as the soldier obeys his commander. He does not even conceive that the one to whom his invitation comes can refuse an appeal as tender as his, and decline to enlist in the holy militia. Is it not our most loving father who invites us, and this in order to conduct us to a Father infinitely more loving still, since it is He in whom everything, and consequently love, is infinite, and who "has deigned to count us among His sons"?

The matter is settled, then. We are "volunteers in the service of Christ."[1] Under the aegis of our holy Father, we are going to begin the forward march.

But this is a supernatural work, and for it we need grace. Let us pray, therefore, from now on "with most earnest prayer." God will certainly hear us. He will work in us at the same time that we are working. For He has deposited treasures of grace in our soul since the day of our Baptism. With these treasures which are His and which are ours (*de bonis suis in nobis*), we are strong enough to fight the good fight to victory.

Too bad for us if, despite everything, we were to be deaf or too little attentive to so much tenderness! The heavenly Father, "angry," would no longer recognize us as His children; we should be forever disinherited; and, having been unwilling to follow Christ into glory, we should have nothing for our portion but eternal suffering.

APPLICATION

By our Oblation we have truly become the sons of St. Benedict. He is for us the most loving Father, who shelters us under his mantle. And what

---

[1] "La Sainte Règle ," in Bulletin de S. Martin et S. Benoît, January, 1922, p. 7.

does he ask of us? That which he asks of all his children, those of the cloister and those of the world: to make themselves soldiers of Christ, in other words to work at becoming perfect Christians. If we align ourselves under the Holy Rule, it will offer us the means of attaining that goal. Let us be most attentive to his "advice," therefore; and let us force ourselves, after having fully grasped its spirit by meditation, to "carry it out effectively."

To that end, let us first of all read our Rule regularly and attentively. "In order to have all the attention and all the docility which St. Benedict demands of us with regard to his Rule," said an old commentator, "we must have this Rule always before our eyes; we must meditate it day and night, so to speak; after the Scriptures we must love nothing so much, study nothing so much . . . ; and our principal study must be to penetrate its meaning, to grasp its spirit, to follow its maxims and to conform to it our sentiments, our inclinations and our life."[2] We shall not be truly Benedictine except by this laborious assimilation of our Rule.

The "Statutes of the Oblates" tell us the same thing: "They shall often read and ponder over the Rule of our holy Father Benedict."[3]

The simplest and easiest way to make a practice of this reading of our Rule is to conform to the customs of our Order. The Holy Rule has been divided into sections which are to be read every day of the year. Among some Congregations, the text is read in Latin at the morning Office of Prime, in the final part, which is ordinarily recited in the Chapter. It is read in the vernacular at noon or evening, in the refectory. Could we not likewise place this reading either immediately after Prime or at the end of that one of the exercises of our day which we are most likely to perform regularly? At any rate, let us hold fast to this practice which puts us in daily contact with our holy Father, helps us penetrate his mind more and more, and unites us with our brethren of the cloister.[4]

---

[2] Dom Robert Morel, *Meditations sur la Règle de S. Benoît*, (Lophem- lez-Bruges: Apostolat Liturgique, Abbaye de S. Andr6, 1923), p. 2.

[3] In *Manual for Oblates of St. Benedict*, 3rd ed., by the Rt. Rev. Alcuin Deutsch, O.S.B. (Collegeville, Minn.: St. John's Abbey Press, 1948), p. 44, §18.

[4] Dom Oswald Hunter-Blair's edition (*The Rule of St. Benedict*, 2nd ed., St. Louis: B. Herder, 1907) contains the Latin text and an English translation divided for daily readings. Dom Justin McCann's translation (*The Rule of St. Benedict*, Stanbrook Abbey Press, 1937) also indicates the divisions, as does the translation used in this commentary, which is published separately (St. Benedict's Rule for

January 2—May 3—September 2

Let us arise then, at last, for the Scripture stirs us up, saying, "Now is the hour for us to rise from sleep" (*Romans* 13:11). Let us open our eyes to the deifying light, let us hear with attentive ears the warning which the divine voice cries daily to us, "Today if you hear His voice, harden not your hearts" (*Psalm* 94:8). And again, "He who has ears to hear, let him hear what the Spirit says to the churches" (*Matthew* 11:15; *Apocalypse* 2:7). And what does He say? "Come, My children, listen to Me; I will teach you the fear of the Lord" (*Psalm* 33:12). "Run while you have the light of life, lest the darkness of death overtake you" (*John* 12:35).

COMMENTARY

St. Benedict considers the one addressed as a man lying asleep. The idea is that as long as we do not work at our reformation and do not seek God, we live in the midst of the light, but without seeing it; for our eyes are closed and our mind is fixed on the things of earth. Alas, what we instinctively take for reality is only a dream; it is but the fashion of this world, which is passing away. There is only one reality that matters: God.

"Let us arise, then, at last!" It is not only St. Benedict, it is God Himself who says it: Here and now is the hour to tear ourselves away from our sleep. That hour is always the very one in which we are living. At every instant, indeed, the divine voice addresses us and cries its urgent appeal, "Today if you hear His voice, harden not your hearts." This word of the Scripture rings out every night at the Invitatory. It is truly the echo of the Lord's unceasing call.

We must open our eyes, therefore, and strain our ears. Then shall we see "the deifying light." We shall verify in many ways that "we are ever

---

Monasteries, St. John's Abbey Press, 1948).

The reading in Latin, where it is customary, is recited as a Lesson of the Office. The Prologue is announced by the formula: *Incipit Prologue Sanctissimi Patris Nostri Benedicti in Regulam suam,* its divisions, by: *Sequitur in prologo Smi. P. N. Benedicti in Regulam suam.* On the day the Prologue is finished, there is added at the end: *Explicit Prologus.* Chapter 1: *Incipit Regula Smi. P. N. Benedicti, Caput primum,* then the title. The other chapters: *Sequitur in Regula Smi. P.N. Benedicti caput...,* then the title. The divisions are announced: *Sequitur in capite... Regulae Smi. P. N. Benedicti.* The lesson is always ended with the *Tu autem, Domine, miserere nobis.* At the end of Chapter 73 is added: *Explicit Regula.*

enveloped by the divine light and that God speaks to us every moment."[5] And the more we turn toward this unique reality, the more we shall be enlightened by it. The Holy Spirit will speak to us; He will become our Teacher; He will "teach us the fear of the Lord," that fear which is the beginning of holiness.

Let us profit for our reformation, then, by the present instant in which God is speaking to us, and by that light with which He is surrounding us. Let us run while it shines; for if we were to be sluggish and intractable, the light would disappear, perhaps forever, and we should be seized by the darkness of death.

APPLICATION

We live, therefore, in the midst of a world which is nothing but falsehood and illusion. As long as the divine voice had not, so to speak, forced the entry of our soul, as long as it had not jolted our torpor by one of those graces which change the orientation of a life, we were truly blind men. To be sure, we were baptized persons, but we were not sufficiently putting to account the spiritual treasures deposited in us by Baptism. We were unconscious. We knew that we were "sons of God," but with a knowledge too theoretical.

"Want of reflection, levity, routine, inadvertence to the truths of faith, that milder form of forgetfulness which makes such havoc . . ." kept us in our torpor. "While faith sleeps, fear, hope and love, which should carry us to God, slacken their course, and wander about aimlessly. Hope is without desire, charity without fervor; the other virtues lose their activity; torpor reigns everywhere; the sleep which deadens faith gains upon our whole supernatural life, and the enemy profits of it to sow cockle in the field of our soul.

"We sleep and we dream; and while our eyes are closed towards God, our imagination is taken up with a thousand foolish fancies as in a dream, our memory is filled with a thousand frivolous recollections, our intellect exhausts itself in useless thoughts and in the preoccupations of our work and office."[6]

---

[5] Rt. Rev. Dom Paul Delatte, *Commentary on the Rule of St. Benedict*, translated from the French by Dom Justin McCann. (Latrobe, Pa.: The ArchAbbey Press, 1950), p. 8.

[6] Dom Vitalis Lehodey, *The Ways of Mental Prayer*, translated from the French by a monk of Mount Melleray (Dublin: M. H. Gill & Son Ltd., 1944), pp. 18-19.

But now the voice of God has made itself heard. On that day we arose resolutely. And we asked St. Benedict to guide us to the light. Happy day, on which the monastic Order admitted us into its fraternity, on which we resolved to imitate in the greatest possible measure our brethren of the cloister!

Have we been really faithful? Would not our heart, after having been touched, have some tendency to fall back into its sleep? Little by little, would we not return to our former illusions?

Each day, at the Invitatory, when we read again that same appeal which so moved our holy Father, could we but be moved by it ourselves, and each day renew from a fervent heart our resolution to belong to God!

January 3—May 4—September 3

And the Lord, seeking His laborer in the multitude to whom He thus cries out, says again, "Who is the man who will have life, and desires to see good days?" (*Psalm* 33:13). And if, hearing Him, you answer, "I am he," God says to you, "If you will have true and everlasting life, keep your tongue from evil and your lips that they speak no guile. Turn away from evil and do good; seek after peace and pursue it" (*Psalm* 33:14-15). "And when you have done these things, My eyes shall be upon you and My ears open to your prayers; and before you call upon Me, I will say to you, 'Behold, here I am.'" (*Psalm* 33:16; *Isaias* 65:24; 58:9).

What can be sweeter to us, dear brethren, than this voice of the Lord inviting us? Behold, in His loving kindness the Lord shows us the way of life.

Having our loins girded, therefore, with faith and the performance of good works (Ephesians 6:14), let us walk in His paths by the guidance of the Gospel, that we may deserve to see Him who has called us to His kingdom (*1 Thessalonians* 2:12).

COMMENTARY

St. Benedict has asked us to shake off our torpor, to look at the light, to turn our ear to the divine voice. Now he is going to specify the object of that appeal and the attitude which he requires of us.

He presents the Lord under the Gospel figure of the Master of the Vineyard, who has come to the public square in search of laborers (*Matthew* 20:1-16). He looks over the crowd. And what He proposes to the workmen of good will is not a mercenary employment, but life and happiness eternal. And this so tempting proposition is addressed to all in general and to each of us in particular. Are we going to let it go without a response? God forbid! The Master cries, "Who will follow Me?" Let us present ourselves without hesitation, saying, "I will follow, Lord."

But under what precise conditions is the engagement to be made? Here are the Master's conditions: If you will live the true life, you must first of all keep your tongue from evil; your lips must utter no deceitful word. It is a preliminary cleansing, therefore, which is enjoined, a cleansing which should not be understood in too restricted a sense.[7] What God requires is that our life be not a perpetual falsehood, that our actions belie not our faith, and that, as St. Benedict will say later on, we be not of those "who lie to God by the tonsure" (Chapter 1). There is to be no duplicity, then, but unity and simplicity in our life.

Having once understood this, let us pass on to the positive element: "*Fac bonum—Do good.*" To be sure, the formula seems vague; but it will be developed in the whole course of the Holy Rule. To do good is to seek peace in a positive way. And peace is found where there is not the dissension of falsehood, where one seeks God alone. That is what the Master demands.

And now, the salary. It is of inestimable value. As soon as the laborer turns away from evil, as soon as he begins his forward march, he will actually be living in the friendship of his Lord.

St. Benedict had spoken above of the disciple's eyes opened to the deifying light, of his ears attentive to the divine voice. And here is the reply, in a sort of parallelism: "My eyes shall be upon you and My ears attentive to your prayers." What a touching bounty is that of our divine Master! What delicate attentions! Not only will He hear the desires of His child (for indeed there is no longer question of a workman), but He will anticipate them: "Before you call upon Me, I will say to you, 'Behold, here I am.' " At the thought of this touching divine friendship, which he himself had experienced, our holy Father feels his heart moved. The flight from Rome, the grotto of Subiaco, all the recollections of his youth come back to his memory: "What can be sweeter to us, dear brethren, than this voice of the Lord inviting us? Behold, in His loving kindness the Lord Himself shows us the way of life."

Who would deprive himself of such sweetness and turn away from such a future?

---

[7] Dom Paul Delatte, *Commentary*, p. 10.

APPLICATION

The appeal so full of sweetness of which our holy Father speaks, we have undoubtedly heard several times. And the day that we asked for the Oblature, was it not in reality because we wanted thus to follow better the Lord's invitation and, aided by His grace, to "do good" and "seek after peace"? We should be strangely mistaken indeed if we saw in the Oblature only a sort of snobbery, only the satisfaction of a certain taste for a famous Order, but without any concern for our reformation. It is not that. The Oblate is a Christian who, like his brother the monk, aspires to perfection because he has felt the divine call, has understood it and wants to answer it. "The Oblates," it has rightly been said, "are Christians who desire, for a more secure realization of their personal perfection, to draw near the monks, participate in their life and be pervaded with their spirit."[8] If they are affiliated and incorporated with the monastic Order, is not the purpose indeed to take on its spirit, which, as Dom Guéranger said, "is entirely in a deeper penetration of the Gospel and of the life of Holy Church"?[9] The Oblature, then, was our way of replying "I will follow, Lord" to the Master's call.

And so, how sweet it is for us to remember the circumstances of that call and of our answer! How appealing the voice of the Lord seemed to us! *Quid dulcius nobis, fratres carissimi.* ... Starting from that moment, if we have been faithful, have we not felt ourselves invaded, as it were, by that ineffable peace which was promised us, that Benedictine peace which is one of the characteristics of our Order? How right it is that in conformity with our Statutes we have adopted and loved the motto "*Pax*," which is that of all the sons of St. Benedict,[10] and which expresses so well the profound and lasting sentiment residing in every soul that seeks God sincerely.

January 4.—May 5—September 4

For if we wish to dwell in the tent of that kingdom, we must run to it by good deeds or we shall never reach it.

But let us ask the Lord, with the Prophet, "Lord, who shall dwell in Your tent, or who shall rest upon Your holy mountain?" (*Psalm* 14:1).

---

[8]   Dom Paul Chauvin, L'Oblature dans l'Ordre deSaint-Benoil (Paris: Prieur6 Sainte-Marie, 1921), p. 30.

[9]   *L'Église ou la Société de la Louange Divine*, p. 30.

[10]   *Manual for Oblates*, p. 50, §41.

After this question, brethren, let us listen to the Lord as He answers and shows us the way to that tent, saying, "He who walks without stain and practices justice; he who speaks truth from his heart; he who has not used his tongue for deceit; he who has done no evil to his neighbor; he who has given no place to slander against his neighbor" (*Psalm* 14:2-3).

It is he who, under any temptation from the malicious devil, has brought him to naught (Psalm 14:4) by casting him and his temptation from the sight of his heart; and who has laid hold of his thoughts while they were still young and dashed them against Christ (*Psalm* 136:9).

It is they who, fearing the Lord (*Psalm* 14:4), do not pride themselves on their good observance; but, convinced that the good which is in them cannot come from themselves and must be from the Lord, they glorify the Lord's work in them (*Psalm* 14:4), using the words of the Prophet, "Not to us, O Lord, not to us, but to Your name give the glory" (*Psalm* 113, 2nd part:l). Thus also the Apostle Paul attributed nothing of the success of his preaching to himself, but said, "By the grace of God I am what I am" (*1 Corinthians* 15:10). And again he says, "He who glories, let him glory in the Lord" (*2 Corinthians* 10:17).

COMMENTARY

The sweetness of the voice of God, the magnificence of His promises and the fear of His judgments have decided us, then, to arise and to march, our loins girded, under the guidance of the Gospel. Following the footsteps of Christ, we take the way to the "tent of that kingdom where we wish to dwell." We are concerned with a real forward march. We must not be like those stage characters who say with vehemence "Let's go, let's go!" and do not budge. We must start out and never halt. "In the way of perfection," says St. Bernard, "he who halts, goes back." St. Benedict even wants this march to be really strenuous; in reality, it is a running. "Unless a man runs by means of good works, he surely will not arrive." He must suffer no illusion, then; he must not stop in his unceasing effort.

And St. Benedict proceeds to develop what he had already said about the conditions of victory and about the possible obstacles, paraphrasing broadly Psalm 14, *Domine, quis habitabit....* One must "be without stain," "practice justice," "speak truth," "do no evil to his neighbor," and so forth.

Then, continuing the paraphrase, our holy Father dwells on the obstacles. The first is the devil, who worms his way into us and suggests objections to us. A verse of the Psalm referring to him who "has reduced the devil to naught" calls up to St. Benedict's memory a passage of Psalm 136. The way to reduce to nothing our invisible enemy is to crush his offspring, namely the evil thoughts, against the rock which is Christ.

The other obstacle is ourselves. As soon as we have done a little good, self-love flatters us; we are tempted to attribute this good to ourselves, to pride ourselves on it. And if we abandon ourselves to pride, everything is compromised. In reality, the good which is in us comes from God. Our perfection is His work, and we are nothing but poor collaborators. We ought to say to Him again and again, with the Prophet: It is not to us, Lord, not to us, but to Your name that the glory must be given.

APPLICATION

From the fact that we have made the first step, put on the Benedictine scapular, and even made our final Oblation, we should not think that we have arrived at perfection. We have simply placed ourselves in conditions more favorable for advancing in that direction. But we are still very far from the goal. The habit does not make the monk . . . nor the Oblate.

We must run, therefore; and we must expect our course to be strewn with obstacles. Our holy Father has pointed them out to us.

The demon, the spirit of darkness, desires our doom. He lies in wait for us, he knows the weak point of our temperament. At the moment when we consider ourselves secure, when we even abandon ourselves to tranquil satisfaction in the progress we think we have made, he will suddenly revive old memories, former temptations which we thought were surely dead, and which all at once, at the contact of a word, of a look, of a tiny circumstance, will gather before us and burst in a storm on our poor disabled soul. The fight will be rugged then. If we succumb, it seems that all will have to be begun again.

Let us not forget our holy Father's warning. Let us be on guard. He who foresees temptation is much stronger. When it presents itself, let us cry to the Lord, let us cry with the whole force of our faith and our love. Let us cry also, as St. Bernard advises us, to Mary.[11] And "let us dash the cursed offspring against Christ."

But there is another enemy: ourselves. The beginner scarcely notices this enemy. His heart is filled with sensible favors. *Quid dulcius nobis. . . . . The Lord overwhelms him with delights....* He is tempted to take himself

---

[11] Sermon *Super missus est.*

for a saint. At every moment, vain complacence comes to lay siege to him. It inspires him readily to comparisons with others. He admires himself in his good actions and in his progress.

Here also, our holy Father puts us on guard. Alone, we are nothing; alone, we can do nothing. The truly saintly souls recognize this: "The good things in them cannot come from themselves, but are the Lord's work."

To be sure, God does not ordinarily act without us. But if it were given us to compare our part with His in the work of our sanctification, how astonished we should be at the misery of our efforts. Let us be willing, then, to testify in all humility to the good which works in us, and "let us boast of it in the Lord." As Dom Delatte observes, "God loves to be thanked, and we can only give thanks for a benefit which we know and which we allow ourselves to contemplate."[12]

But a rather serious examination of conscience will show us all the evil that we have done and are still doing, despite such great graces. That will put us back in our place.

Now we know the obstacles. Our holy Father has duly warned us. Let us profit from the warning.

January 5—May 6—September 5

Hence the Lord says in the Gospel, "Whoever listens to these words of Mine and acts upon them, I will liken him to a wise man who built his house on rock. The floods came, the winds blew and beat against that house, and it did not fall, because it was founded on rock" (*Matthew* 7:24-25).

Having given us these assurances, the Lord is waiting every day for us to respond by our deeds to His holy admonitions. And the days of this life are lengthened and a truce granted us for this very reason, that we may amend our evil ways. As the Apostle says, "Do you not know that God's patience is inviting you to repent?" (*Romans* 2:4). For the merciful Lord tells us, "I desire not the death of the sinner, but that he should be converted and live" (*Ezechiel* 33:11).

COMMENTARY

Our holy Father had forewarned us of the obstacles to be encountered on our course. Borrowing a text from St. Matthew, Chapter 24, he sums up those obstacles by a comparison which shows us in a striking manner how imprudent it would be to disregard them.

---

[12] *Commentary*, pp. 15-16.

It is a regular conspiracy of the elements that rises against the edifice of perfection we wish to complete: "The floods came, the winds blew and beat against that house." If our piety is not solid, if we trust too much in ourselves, we have no chance of withstanding such great attacks. But if, "like the wise man, we have built our house on the solid rock" which is Christ, we shall withstand everything.

The formula *Haec complens*, which connects this passage with the following, has been translated in very diverse ways.[13] The Abbé de Rancé and the translation in use with the Maurists (1755) paraphrase: "While the Lord labors to bring all these truths home to us" (*Pendant que le Seigneur travaille à nous faire entrer dans toutes ces vérités*). The author of the *Traduction el Explication Littérale* (1714): "It is for this purpose, namely to show the truth of these words" (*C'est pour cet effet, c'est-à-dire voulant faire voir la vérité de cette parole*). Dom Philippe François in his *Considerations sur la Règle de S. Benoist* (1664): "To fulfil this" (*Pour accomplir cecy*). Dom L'Huillier: "For a finishing touch" (*Pour comble*). Dom Guéranger: "To complete" (*Pour achever*). Dom Delatte: "Having said this" (*Cela dit*). The Benedictines of Farnborough: "Fulfilling these things" (*Accomplissant ces choses*).[14]

It is evident that grammatically *complens* modifies *Dominus*; it is the Lord who "accomplishes" or "fulfils," who "realizes completely," who "goes to the very end." *Haec* can only refer to what precedes, namely to the assurances given by the Lord in the Gospel. The meaning seems to us to be this: The Lord, for His part, promises true life, under certain conditions, and He insures it against every attack. He will go to the very end of His promise: *Haec complens.*—But He waits for us, on our part, to fulfil the conditions laid down, and to respond by actions to the holy counsels He gives us.

This thought, that the Lord, laden with promises, is waiting for us, is dear to St. Benedict. It arouses in him touching sentiments on the divine

---

[13] Translator's note: The "translations of translations" which follow, although they may not give the exact shade of meaning intended by the authors of the French versions quoted, will at least show the variety of the interpretations of *Haec complens.*

[14] Translator's note: A similar variety of interpretations is found in the translations into English. Dom Oswald Hunter-Blair: "...in fulfilment of these His words." Dom Justin McCann: "Having given us these instructions." Rev. Boniface Verheyen, O.S.B., in *The Holy Rule of Our Most Holy Father Benedict*, 8th ed. (Atchison, Kansas: The Abbey Student Press, 1935): ". . . fulfilling these words."

goodness and mercy. The Lord is waiting for us "every day," calls us "every day," "prolongs like a truce" the days of our life, in order that we may finally amend our conduct and come back resolutely to Him. He desires not the death of the sinner, but that he be converted and live.

APPLICATION

When we made our Oblation, we promised in the presence of our Abbot or of his delegate "the reformation of our life,"[15] which means a turning away from the world in order to live in Jesus Christ. The Lord appeared to us then as the solid rock on which we wanted to "build our house." We knew that He alone has the promises of eternal life and that none of those promises is empty.

That is why, "kneeling on the floor (before the altar) with hands folded," as the Ritual has it,[16] we uttered this confident formula of petition, which opened for us the entrance into the monastic family: *"Suscipe me, Domine...* Uphold me, O Lord, according to Thy word, and I shall live: and let me not be confounded in my hope."

We may be sure that the Lord who was waiting each day for us received us with open arms; we may be sure that He who desired not the death of the sinner but his life, will not confound us in our hope. He will make real what the celebrant wishes for us in a last Oration,[17] which is like a reply to the *Suscipe*: "Suscipiat te Deus... May the Lord receive thee into the number of His elect, may He grant thee final perseverance, may He protect thee against the snares of the enemy and conduct thee to His eternal kingdom." But as for us, have we persevered since that time? If we have gone back, if we have fallen again into a torpor like that of earlier days and perhaps worse, if we have let ourselves be overcome by the winds and the storms, let us make no mistake: it is not the Lord who has failed us, it is we who have failed Him, it is we who have withdrawn ourselves from His arms, into which He had received us. But let us be well aware that at the very time when we were sinning, He was always waiting for us, His heart filled with its divine promises, and that He waits for us still. We may have been ungrateful children, lukewarm, negligent; He is

---

[15] *Manual for Oblates*, p. 236.

[16] *Manual for Oblates*, p. 239. In the French Congregation, the Ritual is somewhat different: "kneeling before the altar with the arms crossed over the breast."

[17] This Oration is not found in the Rituals of all the Congregations.

always the *pius Dominus*, the merciful Lord; just as St. Benedict, who intercedes for us with Him, is always the *pius pater*, the "father full of tenderness."

Let us recall to mind often the promises of our Oblation, in order to maintain or to reestablish the harmony between our actions and the divine will. *Dominus exspectat quotidie* . . . "The Lord is waiting every day for us to respond by our works to His holy lessons."

January 6 May 7—September 6

So, brethren, we have asked the Lord who is to dwell in His tent, and we have heard His commands to anyone who would dwell there; it remains for us to fulfil those duties.

Therefore we must prepare our hearts and our bodies to do battle under the holy obedience of His commands; and let us ask God that He be pleased to give us the help of His grace for anything which our nature finds hardly possible. And if we want to escape the pains of hell and attain life everlasting, then, while there is still time, while we are still in the body and are able to fulfil all these things by the light of this life, we must hasten to do now what will profit us for eternity.

COMMENTARY

Critical scholars point out that the most ancient manuscripts ended the first sentence of this section with the words *Sed si compleamus habitatoris officium.* The word *si*, then, must be given the meaning "on condition that," and we must translate "but on condition that we fulfil the duty which procures this happy dwelling-place," omitting the words that follow.[18] This reading is admitted as definitive by Dom Butler and by the Benedictines of Farnborough. A copyist who did not grasp the meaning of *si* and believed that he was confronted with an unfinished sentence, thought he ought to complete it with the words *erimus haeredes regni coelorum*, "we shall become heirs of the kingdom of heaven."

The three most ancient manuscripts bring the Prologue to an end here. It would be a mistake to conclude, as some have done, that the Prologue originally ended at this sentence. It is probable that our three manuscripts had as their common source a text from which the last page was accidentally missing.

Now we know, says St. Benedict, what the Lord wants of us. It is up to

---

[18]   That is, the interpolated words of the "received text."

us to fulfil the conditions.

In order that we may successfully "do battle under holy obedience," we must "prepare our hearts and our bodies." Our hearts, that is to say the immaterial element of our being, whence come thoughts, acts of will and affections.—Our bodies, which will have to become tractable and accustomed to the observances. It is with our whole selves, with all our faculties, moral and physical, that we shall fight.

In this fight there will be difficult periods, there will be painful efforts, moments of fatigue, of lassitude, observances or obediences which will be more or less repugnant to nature. St. Benedict knows this, he has to admit it; but in order not to frighten us unduly, he designates all those obstacles by a term which attenuates the fear of them: "that which nature has less possible in us," that which nature "would find less easy." Whatever be the euphemism which designates them, those moments will come and they will be unpleasant.

This prospect should not make us draw back. Let us remember the Lord's goodness. He has His grace under His command; it awaits only a word from us and from Him, to be granted us. Let us ask Him, then, from this moment "that He order His grace to lend us aid."[19] Moreover, what are these difficulties in face of the "pains of Gehenna" on the one hand and "eternal life" on the other? Come, no hesitation; let us profit from the life which is still given us, and from this time on "let us run" in the way of the commandments.

APPLICATION

When we made our Oblation we answered in the affirmative to these three questions:[20]

"Do you renounce the vanities and pomps of the world?" "Will you undertake the reformation of your life according to the spirit of the Rule

---

[19] Translator's note: This interpretation of *ut gratiae suae jubeat nobis adjutorium ministrare* agrees with Dom Guéranger's translation. The English version given above, however, agrees rather with Dom Justin McCann's translation, taking *jubeat* in the sense that the imperative of the same verb has in the familiar liturgical formula, *Jube, domne, benedicere.* The rest of the clause can agree grammatically with either interpretation.

[20] *Manual for Oblates*, p. 236.

of our holy Father Benedict, and observe the Statutes of the Oblates?"

"Will you persevere in your holy resolution until death?" Such is the object of the battle: to renounce, to reform oneself, to persevere. That is what we have promised. Those promises were not empty words, pure formality. What would be the use of our being Oblates in that case?

It is a struggle without truce and without letup that we have undertaken. Let us have no illusions. More or less often we shall meet on our path "that which our nature finds hardly possible." Did not our holy Father himself encounter temptation within him; and around him did he not encounter hatreds, ambushes, betrayals? Why should we be more favored than he?

Besides the temptations common to all men, we shall meet some peculiar to our religious "profession." That is the "hardship of being good" of which St. Francis de Sales spoke, the fatigue of sustained effort. There are times when our program of Benedictine religious life, with the obligations it entails, seems tiresome to us, when we are weary of "doing battle under the holy obedience of the commands." No doubt we have known those moments, and they will come again.

But lest all of that frighten us, let us reflect well on three things in particular, and keep them in mind. First, the hell which awaits us if we are unfaithful. In the spiritual life he who does not advance goes back, and he who has begun to go back passes quickly from lukewarmness to unrepented venial sin, and from venial sin to mortal sin. Let us not offer the excuse that our Rule and our Statutes do not bind us under pain of sin. To forsake them, after having taken them upon oneself as one undertakes a way of perfection, is certainly to fall into lukewarmness; and lukewarmness, as we have said, is the first step on the road to hell. Let us consider, therefore, the hell which threatens us.

On the other hand, let us look at the happiness of heaven. If the toil frightens us, let the vision of the recompense sustain us. What we are enduring is such a little thing compared to the vision of God, of His Christ and of His Saints, in eternity.

Let us remember finally and above all that we are not alone. The Lord Jesus is very near to us, with the treasures of His grace. We have only to speak to Him in our distress, and He will aid us; and, as St. Paul said, "We will be able to do all things in Him who strengthens us."

So "let us make haste to accomplish, by the light of this life, all the good works that we shall in heaven congratulate ourselves on having done. What does St. Paul think now of his scourgings, or St. Lawrence of his gridiron, or St. Benedict of his rolling amid the thorns, or St. Benedict Labre of his poverty? It is enough to cut short our procrastination, if we but ponder for an instant this weighty advice of our holy Father."[21]

January 7—May 8—September 7

And so we are going to establish a school for the service of the Lord. In founding it we hope to introduce nothing harsh or burdensome. But if a certain strictness results from the dictates of equity for the amendment of vices or the preservation of charity, do not be at once dismayed and fly from the way of salvation, whose entrance cannot but be narrow (*Matthew* 7:14). For as we advance in the religious life and in faith, our hearts expand and we run the way of God's commandments with unspeakable sweetness of love (*Psalm* 118:32). Thus, never departing from His school, but persevering in the monastery according to His teaching until death, we may by patience share in the sufferings of Christ (*1 Peter* 4:13) and deserve to have a share also in His kingdom.

COMMENTARY

We know our goal now, we know the indispensable conditions for attaining it, we know the difficulties. Still, that is not enough. To assure a successful result, we need a method, a training; and St. Benedict has provided for it. He is going to set up, by means of his Rule, "a school for the service of the Lord."

"The ancients," says Dom Calmet, "gave the name of *schola* to the places where people learned literature, science, the liberal arts, military training." A school, then, is a place of formation, whether of the mind or of the body. For Cicero, Quintilian and others, the school is also the whole of the teachings of a master, or again a collection of practical lessons methodically arranged on a definite subject.

There have been the schools of Aristotle, of Epicurus, etc.; there will be the Thomistic School, the Scotistic School, etc.; St. Benedict also is going to set up a methodic and practical teaching, having for its object the service of the Lord. His precepts, His ascetics or drill will permit the pupils to be trained in this divine service and to progress in it.

The Fathers of the desert, whom St. Benedict held in veneration, had also their methods of ascetics. They had established before his time

---

[21] Dom Paul Delatte, *Commentary*, p. 18.

"schools of the divine service," of which Cassian made himself the panegyrist. But those "schools" were often very arduous; they exacted from nature a series of extraordinary sacrifices which fill us at once with dismay and with admiration.

Certainly our holy Father had not exactly the intention of reacting against the spirituality of the Eastern deserts; but, having meditated at length and having gathered the fruits of a profound experience of souls, with an admirable discretion he made his choice among those rich treasures.

His own school will present "nothing harsh, nothing burdensome." A violent asceticism might drive souls away. St. Benedict wants to win over as many of them as possible, counting on what they can give right now in order to raise them gently to the very heights of perfection.

Let us have no illusions, however. Our holy Father knows that we are the disciples of Him who said, "If anyone will come after Me, let him deny himself and take up his cross and follow Me." We shall at times encounter, therefore, "something just a little rigorous," even something at which we might be, at first glance, "thrown into consternation."

We must remember that beginnings are often difficult and that we can get into the way of salvation only "by a narrow entrance." True, it is said that the enthusiasm of beginnings sustains, *initia fervent*. But this "novice fervor" generally does not last; and a person very soon finds himself again, with all his weaknesses, confronted by a life which exacts a constant self-denial and continual renouncements of his own will. When the ardor of the beginning has disappeared—and that happens very quickly—many things become tiresome to poor nature, and a person needs a certain heroism to keep himself faithful to those things. It is thus that we shall carry our cross and "share in the sufferings of Christ."

But the sufferings have their compensation even here below. Our mores, that is to say our exterior activities, become more and more tractable, our faith brightens, our heart expands and we "run in the way of the commandments with an unspeakable sweetness of love."

The fact is that the cross we embrace has its attractions. It is not the bare cross: we find Jesus there. We love Him for whom we suffer. He in turn pours into the souls which renounce themselves for Him an abundance of love, and love makes all things light.[22]

We no longer drag our-self along painfully; we are sustained and drawn by love. And if we are faithful, if we never withdraw from the divine teaching, if we persevere in the doctrine and attach our-self to a monastery where it is practiced, we are taking the sure course to the perfection which will flower in eternity.

APPLICATION

The supposition is that we have rightly entered the Benedictine family with a real desire for perfection. Let us consider what St. Benedict presents to us in his Rule: a school of divine service. We have enrolled in this school, then; and his Rule, applied literally or adapted as the case may be, remains the guide we are to follow. It is by meditating the Rule, by observing it according to our opportunities, by becoming impregnated with its spirit, that we shall accomplish what our holy Father has a right to expect of us.

And for what does he want to form us? For the divine service. We are Oblates of St. Benedict not for the sake of science or of art, we are Oblates only to learn how to serve God. If the sciences and the arts enter into the compass of our activities, they will be for us not an end, but a means of raising ourselves to God. We want to be not just somewhat, not just especially, but only, men "who are seeking God." Has He not created us for Himself? Is He not our only end? If we are not for Him entirely, if we want to belong to Him and to science, to Him and to art, to Him and to social works, to Him and to the world, we are not for Him at all; for it is our whole being that He has created for Himself. To want to hold back anything from Him is to give Him nothing, since we do not give Him what He wants, namely our whole selves. We are to be completely at His "service," therefore. In our Rule we shall find the method and the school to bring us to that goal.

We shall see in practice that St. Benedict is a very gentle and sympathetic father. He presents to us a spirituality extremely simple, without complications, without extraordinary procedures.

He cannot, however, dispense us from the cross. To be sure, nothing will be too harsh, nothing too burdensome. He will not require of us the

---

[22] Madame Cécile J. Bruyère, *Spiritual Life and Prayer*, translated from the French by the Benedictines of Stanbrook, 2nd ed. (New York: Benziger Brothers, 1906), p. 30.

fasts of the desert Fathers, nor their silence, nor their frightful scourgings. Every precept of his school is in itself adjusted to what the average man can bear. But not all temperaments are the same. That which is easy in itself is not always so in practice. What is easy for one is repugnant to another. It will certainly happen, therefore, that such and such precept of the Holy Rule which is opposed to such and such stubborn tendency of our nature will seem rather hard to us and sometimes will even frighten us. Our holy Father expects this. We must have confidence in him. This precept was dictated by "a reason of equity." It was necessary "for the amendment of vices and the conservation of charity."

We shall find crosses, then, in the observance, even the adapted observance, of the Holy Rule. These crosses will be met particularly in the fidelity to those little things, the repetition of which so often annoys us; in the effort to mold our character to obedience, to humility, to patience; in the fact that every day at the proper hour we must, with or without attraction but moved by a constant desire to please the divine Master, bring Him our tribute of praise; in the forgetfulness of ourself for the souls that have a claim on us; in putting up with the faults or the whims of those with whom we must live; and so forth—little crosses which sometimes become heavy by their number, heavy enough even to inspire in us the temptation to give it all up. After all, we might say, I have made only a promise, I have made no vow; this and that do not oblige me in conscience.

True enough, but if we reject these crosses we have promised to carry, we shall not be carrying any. And how can we follow Jesus without the Cross? *Amor duris probatur.* Love is proved by hardships. Where is our love if we shrink back? Shall we turn to another Master, another school? If we do not find suffering there, assuredly that school and that Master are not of Jesus Christ. Our holy Father has told us this: One cannot get into the way of salvation except by a narrow entrance.

Let us set forth, then, with courage. Let us not forget that we are seeking perfection. That is our goal; there can be no other. And it offers us unlimited prospects: "The holy Patriarch," says the Abbess of Solesmes,[23] "has no distinctions among his children; in his view the career is open to all, and nothing remains but to run for the prize. To aspire after the highest reach of the spiritual life, which is union, is the normal state

---

[23] Madame Cecile J. Bruyere, *Spiritual Life and Prayer*, p. 30.

for the Christian, and especially for the religious. The soul which has entered the *status perfectionis acquirendae* (the state which aims at perfection) must, however, take heed lest a want of generosity and energy in overcoming herself should hinder the carrying out of this divine program."

Moreover, we shall have divine compensations. The Lord will make the arid desert of our heart flourish. "The unspeakable sweetness of love" will lift up the soul, will make it embrace the Cross because the Beloved has carried it before us and because it makes us take an active part in His work of Redemption. "Let us share by patience in the sufferings of Christ."

Let us enroll, therefore, in the school of St. Benedict; let us listen to the wise, affectionate advice of our Father and Teacher. If we are faithful we will surely attain the goal of every resolutely Christian life: perfection.

CHAPTER 1
On the Kinds of Monks

January 8—May 9—September 8

I T is well known that there are four kinds of monks. The first kind are the Cenobites: those who live in monasteries and serve under a rule and an Abbot.

The second kind are the Anchorites or Hermits: those who, no longer in the first fervor of their reformation, but after long probation in a monastery, having learned by the help of many brethren how to fight against the devil, go out well armed from the ranks of the community to the solitary combat of the desert. They are able now, with no help save from God, to fight single-handed against the vices of the flesh and their own evil thoughts.

The third kind of monks, a detestable kind, are the Sarabaites. These, not having been tested, as gold in the furnace (Wisdom 3:6), by any rule or by the lessons of experience, are as soft as lead. In their works they still keep faith with the world, so that their tonsure marks them as liars before God. They live in twos or threes, or even singly, without a shepherd, in their own sheepfolds and not in the Lord's. Their law is the desire for self-gratification: whatever enters their mind or appeals to them, that they call holy; what they dislike, they regard as unlawful.

The fourth kind of monks are those called Gyrovagues. These spend their whole lives tramping from province to province, staying as guests in different monasteries for three or four days at a time. Always on the move, with no stability, they indulge their own wills and succumb to the allurements of gluttony, and are in every way worse than the Sarabaites. Of the miserable conduct of all such men it is better to be silent than to speak.

Passing these over, therefore, let us proceed, with God's help, to lay down a rule for the strongest kind of monks, the Cenobites.

COMMENTARY

In the Prologue, St. Benedict had not yet designated his disciples by a generic name. From the first sentence of the first chapter we learn that they are *monks.* Etymologically, the word *monachos, monachus,* means alone.

Historically, the name of monks was first given to certain of the faithful who, while remaining in the world, isolated themselves from the conditions of ordinary life in order to devote themselves to the practices of the perfect life. They were also called *ascetics*. Practicing perfect chastity, living in voluntary poverty, given to fast and abstinence, often wearing a particular habit, they dwelt sometimes alone, sometimes in their families, sometimes in little groups.[1] Their manner of living separated them from the world, even though they dwelt there materially; they were solitaries.

But in the course of time the word *monk* assumed a more restricted sense. To explain its meaning, the idea of unity was insisted upon, connected with that of solitude. This word *monk*, as the Pseudo-Dionysius explains,[2] comes from the word *monas*, which means *unit*, for in vowing himself purely to the service of God, in renouncing the multiplicity of the things of the world, the monk "should be made one with the One, and should be gathered up into a divine unit."

Even if the etymology is forced, the definition is accurate: "That is the monk," says Dom L'Huillier, commenting on this passage; "be he hermit or cenobite, he is the man of a single goal, and the goal is that union with God about which theology teaches us." He may be employed, according to the needs of Holy Church, in the apostolate, in sacred studies, in works, his single goal remains always the same: to seek God.

The term *monk*, therefore, applies, properly speaking, only to the sons of St. Benedict and of St. Bruno. In France it is attributed also by extension to the Franciscans and to the Dominicans. But regularly, the members of all the Orders and Congregations devoted to the apostolate ought rather to receive the name of religious.

St. Benedict distinguishes four kinds of monks.

The first kind are the Cenobites. Those are so named "who live together in a monastery and serve under a rule and an Abbot."[3] Our holy Father mentions at the same time the rule and the Abbot, because the latter is the necessary interpreter of the former, which, without him, would be too often a dead letter and an object of controversy. He feels no

---

[1] Dom Jean Martial Besse, *Les Moines d'Orient* (Paris: Oudin, 1900), p. 22.

[2] *De Ecclesiastica Hierarchia*, Cap. VI, 1st part, No. Ill, and 3rd part, No. II; in J.-P. Migne, *Patrologia Graeca*, Tome 3, col. 533 A and D.

[3] Dom Guéranger translates slavishly: "under a rule or under an Abbot" (*sous une Règle ou (Vel) sous un Abbé*). We know that with St. Benedict the word *vel* has the copulative sense of *et*.

need to say any more about the Cenobites, since his whole Rule is the explanation, as it were, of these simple words.

The second kind of monks are the Anchorites or Hermits. Those are so named who withdraw into solitude to live alone with God. St. Benedict holds the Anchorites in esteem, but he thinks that their state of life is not without dangers and that it needs a long preparation. That preparation is the cenobitic life itself. No one should become a hermit under the influence of a "novice fervor";[4] one must have learned how to fight, "thanks to the support of a great number"; one must already have been trained "in the fraternal army for the single-handed battle of the desert."

St. Benedict has known, in the grotto of Subiaco, the delights and the dangers of the solitary life. He can speak of it, therefore, from experience. The hermit has not in his afflictions the "consolation of anyone else"; he has not, in the weariness of soul, the reenforcement of examples; and the temptations of the flesh and of thoughts which come to besiege him find him unfortified by that safeguard which is the presence of witnesses. One must be well proven, then, to risk the life of a hermit. With these reservations, it remains evidently the life of exceptionally hardy souls.

On the subject of the desert, we may repeat the impassioned sentences addressed by St. Jerome to Heliodorus: "O desert, bright with the flowers of Christ! O solitude, whence come the stones of which, in the Apocalypse, the city of the great king is built! O wilderness, gladdened with God's especial presence! What keeps you in the world, my brother, you who are above the world? How long shall gloomy roofs oppress you?"[5]

The third kind of monks, says St. Benedict, is "a detestable kind, the Sarabaites." The meaning of the word sarabaite is not known exactly.

---

[4] The "received text" of the Latin reads *conversionis fervore novitio*, which Dom Guéranger translates "the fervor of a recent conversion" (*la ferveur d'une conversion récente*). Dom Butler will have us read *conversationis* here in place of *conversionis*. In the name of textual criticism he suppresses *conversio* irrevocably wherever it is found. See below, commentary on Chapter 58. Here, however, the description *novitio* agrees better with *conversio* than with *conversatio*. Notice that to indicate the entrance into the monastic life, St. Benedict uses, not the verb *conversari*, but *converti* (Chapters 2 and 63), which is the root of *conversio*.

[5] Letter XIV, 10; in J.-P. Migne, *Patrologia Latina*, Tome 22, cols. 353-354; translated by W. H. Fremantle in *A Select Library of Nicene and Post-Nicene Fathers of the Christian Church*, 2nd series, Vol. 6 (New York: The Christian Literature Company, 1893), p. 17.

According to Dom Calmet, Dom L'Huillier, Dom Delatte and others, it would come from the Aramaic *sarab*, which means rebel. According to Cassian the word would have an Egyptian origin.[6] Whatever be the origin, for St. Benedict the Sarabaites are monks who "live in twos or threes or even alone, without a shepherd." St. Jerome[7] completes the picture by saying that they are great fasters: "they compete with each other in fasting." They affect extraordinary costumes: "their sleeves are loose, their boots bulge, their garb is of the coarsest." They love to show off their pretended compunction by "always sighing." They work with their hands, but they make the product of their labor pay more dearly than do other workmen. They have only the outward affectations of holiness.

The thing for which St. Benedict reproaches them above all is that they have no rule. They live to suit their fancies: "Whatever enters their mind or appeals to them, that they call holy; what they dislike, they regard as unlawful." Thus their little monasteries are certainly not "the Lord's sheepfolds"; they are "their own sheepfolds." Under their outward monastic appearance they are of the world, and "they are known to lie to God by their tonsure."

The fourth kind of monks are "Gyrovagues." They are the monks of the highways. They spend their whole life traveling about the provinces, "taking the hospitality of different cells for three of four days at a time, always wandering and never stable." Our holy Father reproaches them, like the Sarabaites, for having no rule, "for being subject to their own wills." But they have other vices which are not ordinarily found among the Sarabaites. These were great fasters; the Gyrovagues give themselves over "to the pleasures of gluttony." And there are even other things besides. But our holy Father judges that he has said enough about them already: "Of the miserable conduct of these monks it is better to keep silent than to say any more."

APPLICATION

Because of their affiliation with the monastic Order, the Oblates could be called "the monks of the outside," "the prolongation and the radiation

---

[6] Conference 18, Chapter 7; in *Corpus Scriptorum Ecclesiasticorum Latinorum*, Vol. 13 (Vienna: apud C. Geroldi *filium Bibliopolam Academiae*, 1886), p. 513; translated by Edgar C. S. Gibson in *Nicene and Post-Nicene Fathers*, 2nd series, Vol. 11, p. 482.

[7] *Letter XXII*, 34; in *P.L.*, Tome 22, col. 419; translated in *Nicene and Post-Nicene Fathers*, 2nd series, Vol. 6, p. 37.

into the world of the monastic spirit."[8] The Abbé Gellé, in his little work on *Solitary Pastors*, even found it possible to compare certain Oblates, namely those who exercise the parochial ministry in the country, to hermits, and to apply to them the beginning of the present chapter. One might very well compare them also to the ancient *ascetics*, who were, as we have seen, the ancestors of the monks.

Be that as it may, the ideal of the Oblate, of every Oblate, is monastic perfection, which he ought to approach as nearly as possible. "The Oblates," wrote Dom Besse,[9] "who hold the place (in the monastery) of an external family, imitate the life of the monks, in the measure in which their situation permits, by conforming their life to the fundamental maxims of the Rule of St. Benedict, and by observing certain practices of the cloister compatible with the life they must live."

The monk separates himself from the world to seek God. The Oblate ought to remember that he is not of the world,[10] and that he is to live for God. We have said this in explaining the Prologue, and we need not dwell on it here. Let us make our soul truly monastic, therefore, and let us apply ourselves, with the help of God, of Our Lady and of St. Benedict, to being not too unworthy of the splendid line to which we belong.

That which ordinarily resists the reign of God in a soul is the reign of the ego, "self-will." It is from self-will that the vices of the Sarabaites and of the Gyrovagues arise. The former declare holy that which pleases them, unlawful that which they do not want. The latter do not even give themselves that illusion. They are "enslaved to their own wills." What both lack is a shepherd and a rule which represent the divine will.

If we do not want to become like them, therefore, we must guard ourselves against self-will. To do this, we have our Rule, which, with the advice of our directors, we shall adapt to our particular situation. Our docility in observing it, sometimes to the letter, always in its spirit, will be the measure of our progress towards perfection, and consequently of our love of God. We shall see that St. Benedict has no other end than to make perfect Christians of all his children. The monk is a perfect Christian; the Oblate does not want to be anything else.

---

[8] Dom Prosper Guéranger, *L'Église ou la Société de la Louange Divine*, Foreword, pp. 5 and 6.

[9] *Les Oblats de Saint-Benoît* (Paris: Librairie de l'Art Catholique, 1918), p. 6.

[10] "*Statutes of the Oblates*," §12, in Manual for Oblales, p. 43.

Another thing for which St. Benedict reproaches the bad monks is "vagrancy," to which he is going to oppose *stability*. There is a real spiritual vagrancy, which consists in continually changing rule and guide, under the pretext that we do not find where we are that which is suitable to us. A person turns successively to St. Francis, to St. Dominic, to St. Benedict. He tries, without ever persevering, all the activities, confraternities or archconfraternities. And so many fruitless trials leave his soul just as imperfect as it was in the beginning. He flatters himself by imagining that it is the desire for perfection which prompts him; in reality it is caprice, that is to say, self-will.

We are the children of St. Benedict; we have attached ourselves to a monastery. Let us have a filial love for our holy Father, and let us be unfailingly faithful to the monastery which has been so kind as to receive us. This stability will be for us a real safeguard. Having become the brothers of the "strongest kind, Cenobites," we shall try, "the Lord helping," to model ourselves on them.

And since we are speaking of stability, let us conclude with this page from Dom Chauvin, on the stability of the Oblates:

"The Church ... requires of the Oblates a sort of stability, for the reason that the Oblation, in a real and concrete sense, makes one enter a family: it is an adoption. A person does not leave a family at will. When he is born into it, he remains in it until death, unless particular circumstances lead to the enlargement of the family circle. He takes part, whether he wants to or not, in the trials and the joys of the family to which he belongs. That is a social law.

"So it is with the Oblate and the Tertiary. From the moment he enters into the religious family he has decided to join. . .he promises a stability much like that which the religious himself has vowed to God. Religious and Oblate are members of the family: only the degree of relationship differs, one may say. The one, like the other, can forget his obligations, deny them, fulfil them slothfully. It makes no difference: prodigal child or faithful child, he remains a child.

"For this reason the Church forbids even an Oblate to belong at the same time to two religious families, except in cases which are extremely rare and in which the Holy See reserves the right to intervene."[11]

---

[11] Dom Paul Chauvin, *L'Oblature dans l'Ordre de Saint-Benoît*, pp. 38-39. Let us note, however, that if the Oblate promises, on the day of his profession, to "persevere until death," he is not obliged to this by a vow. His step is the result of

Let us add that the Church does not authorize except "for serious reasons" the passage of an Oblate from the obedience of one monastery to that of another. A reminder of this was contained in the decree of the Sacred Congregation of Rites dated March 24, 1927, which declared likewise that this transfer could take place only after agreement between the Abbots of the said monasteries.[12]

---

a "deliberate resolve of the will"; it "is worthy of high respect," and on this account there would be serious loss in disengaging himself from it. "Stability" is the normal consequence of it.

[12] "Statutes of the Oblates," §10, in *Manual for Oblates*, p. 42.

CHAPTER 2
What Kind of Man the Abbot Ought to Be

AN Abbot who is worthy to be over a monastery should always remember what he is called, and live up to the name of Superior. For he is believed to hold the place of Christ in the monastery, being called by a name of His, which is taken from the words of the Apostle: "You have received a Spirit of adoption as sons, by virtue of which we cry, 'Abba— Father!'" (*Romans* 8:15).

Therefore the Abbot ought not to teach or ordain or command anything which is against the Lord's precepts; on the contrary, his commands and his teaching should be a leaven of divine justice kneaded into the minds of his disciples.

COMMENTARY

St. Benedict, therefore, wants his monks to be "of the very strong race of Cenobites." But he does not conceive of their groupings as a simple juxtaposition of individuals, ruled by a constitutional charter which is designed to safeguard the real or pretended rights of the human person. His monastery is a family, and a family strongly constituted, in the Roman manner. The paternal power, the *patria potestas*, will be its keystone, and the father will be the Abbot. St. Benedict will speak to him at length here, and he will come back to him in what follows.

The very name of Abbot, Abba, means Father. "The Abbot," says Dom Bernard Maréchaux,[1] "is head because he is father; the monastery is his family."

This word Abba brings to our holy Father's mind a passage from the Epistle to the Romans: "You have received a Spirit of adoption as sons, by virtue of which we cry, 'Abba—Father!' " In the mind of St. Paul, it is not exactly Christ whom we call "Abba," but God the Father, whose children we are by our union with His Son Jesus. But St. Benedict has not any intention of giving us a strict exegesis. It is enough for him that one may, in certain relations, attribute that same name to the Savior, whom the prophet had already announced as "Father of the world to come" (Isaias

---

[1] *S. Benoît, Sa Vie, Sa Règle , Sa Doctrine Spirituelle*, 3rd ed. (Paris, 1928), p. 103.

9:6).

"Even though, considered as Son of God," says an old commentator,[2] "He be our Brother and do us the honor of calling us His brothers, as having the same Father. . . nevertheless, in the role of Redeemer, of life-giver, or of author of our holiness, He is truly our Father and the Father of all the Saints." And as the Abbot "is supposed to hold the place of Christ in the monastery," the same name applies perfectly to the one and the other.

It is a spiritual paternity, therefore, which presides in the monastic family. Being father, the Abbot "has the mission of begetting his disciples into the perfect Christian life."[3] But, being Christ's representative, he can do this only in spreading the teaching of Christ Himself. He is to "teach nothing, establish or prescribe nothing which is contrary to the Lord's precepts."

APPLICATION

The monastery, then, as St. Benedict conceived it, is a family. It is worth-while for us Oblates to consider what our situation is in that family, and this will undoubtedly help us form an exact idea of what the Oblature ought to be.

St. Benedict wants a family solidly constituted. Everything rests on the Abbot, who is the father and the representative of Jesus Christ. It is to the Abbot that the obedience and the affection of all is directed; it is from him alone that the doctrine of life comes authentically. In consequence, the monastic group can be conceived only as very homogeneous. From the monastic point of view, therefore, the Oblates attached to that group cannot have existence outside of it. It would certainly be going against the spirit of the Holy Rule to imagine "fraternities of Oblates" forming, as it were, little "cells" around the big one, and possessing, even under the surveillance of the latter, a sort of autonomous existence, in the fashion of the Third Orders. It is thus, to be sure, that the Franciscan fraternities, for example, are constituted. But St. Benedict did not found a Third Order. We are not Franciscans but Benedictines, and our duty is to conform ourselves to the spirit and the traditions of the Benedictine Rule.

---

[2] *La Traduction et Explication Littérale et Morale de la Règle de S. Benoît* (Rouen: M. de Gournay, 1714), p. 66.

[3] Dom Bernard Maréchaux, *S. Benoît, Sa Vie, Sa Règle, Sa Doctrine Spirtuelle*, p. 103.

The Oblate, therefore, is not attached to a fraternity of Oblates; it is by an individual bond that he belongs to his monastic family. Thus the Abbot is really the "father" of his Oblates. Their monastic existence itself depends upon him. Like a father of a family with regard to his children, he can ask more of one and less of another. "Each Abbot," says Dom Besse,[4] "can complete, with regulations which adapt them better to a determined end," the Statutes of the Oblates.

From the foregoing it can be seen that groupings of Oblates of diverse obediences can only be arrangements of convenience, and that even groupings of Oblates belonging to the same monastery but living at a distance from it can have a right to existence only in the measure in which the Abbot permits it, and in the measure also in which they receive their spiritual direction from him or from those delegated by him. It can even be said that on this point no initiative, properly speaking, is permitted them as Oblates, but only a suggestion proposed respectfully to the Abbot, who alone can give approval.

But aside from these consequences of a disciplinary order, this passage can carry very personal applications, varying with each one of us according to our situation and the duties of our state. How many Christians have not in their hands a greater or less part of that authority which, according to St. Paul, always comes from God? Besides this divine basis common to all forms of authority, is there not even a strict resemblance between the function of the Abbot and that of the shepherds of souls at all degrees of the hierarchy? Between the function of the Abbot and that of the parents in the Christian family? Is not each church a community of which the priest is the father; and moreover, has not the sacrament of Matrimony made the family a complete spiritual society?

What responsibility, then, is ours if God has entrusted to us more or less of His authority! To tell us that we hold the place of Christ! That we are to think as He would, act as He would, speak as He would!

And so what profit we shall have from meditating this chapter of the Rule of our holy Father! Not only will it tell us our duties of affection and docility as Oblates towards our Abbot or his representatives, but it will further show us our duties towards the souls which, despite our weakness, the Lord has deigned to entrust to us under various titles.

---

[4] *Le Moine Bénédictin*, ed. 1920. p. 41.

January 10—May 11—September 10

Let the Abbot always bear in mind that at the dread Judgment of God there will be an examination of these two matters: his teaching and the obedience of his disciples. And let the Abbot be sure that any lack of profit the master of the house may find in the sheep will be laid to the blame of the shepherd. On the other hand, if the shepherd has bestowed all his pastoral diligence on a restless, unruly flock and tried every remedy for their unhealthy behavior, then he will be acquitted at the Lord's Judgment and may say to the Lord with the Prophet: "I have not concealed Your justice within my heart; Your truth and Your salvation I have declared" {Psalm 39:11). "But they have despised and rejected me" (Isaias 1:2; Ezechiel 20:27). And then finally let death itself, irresistible, punish those disobedient sheep under his charge.

COMMENTARY

The Abbot, therefore, is the representative of Christ. As such, he must account to Christ for the sheep with which He has entrusted him. This is a leading thought for St. Benedict, that an account must one day be rendered at the dread tribunal of God. He wants this thought to be habitual with the Abbot: *Memor sit semper*—let him remember always. The Abbot, therefore, will frequently, in thought, stand before the tribunal of Jesus Christ.

The account to be rendered will bear upon two objects: the teaching given by the Abbot and the obedience of the disciples.

Of the teaching our holy Father has already spoken. It is to be that of Jesus Christ, presented to the "sheep" in conformity with their needs. If the teaching is good, the sheep have every chance of being good; if it is bad, they are almost sure to perish. The Abbot ought to meditate his doctrine in the light of Christ, therefore, in order to be assured that it answers both to the divine will and to the necessities of souls.

The obedience of the disciples is in a broad sense not only their outward docility, but also and especially their inward docility to the Abbot's instructions.

If the sheep have been lost, even if they have not borne all the profit which the Master of the house had a right to expect of them, the Abbot will be held responsible before Him. "The default of the sheep will weigh upon the shepherd."

There is one case, and only one, in which he will be able to clear himself; that is when the flock, "restless and disobedient," will have shown itself stubbornly resistant to the counsels and rebukes of its shepherd. It is when the latter in all sincerity will be able to say to God with the Prophet, "Your justice I have not hidden in my heart; Your truth and Your salvation I have announced; but they paid no attention to them, and they scorned me." Woe to the rebellious sheep then, for eternal death will be their punishment!

APPLICATION

This is a celebrated page of St. Benedict. It founds authority on its only solid basis: the responsibility of the head before the Sovereign Master. Historically, this conception of the responsibilities of authority ennobled and strengthened the royal power in the societies of another day. The idea of having to render an account to the Sovereign Judge appeared still very profound in the Memoires of Louis XIV. Our contemporary societies, unhinged and going off on a tangent, surely will not find their equilibrium again until, having been re-Christianized, they return to the great principle affirmed by St. Benedict. We have often heard of the social import of the Holy Rule. Here we have an example of it.

But for us Oblates it is less a question of the government of societies than of our own governing. What holds for the abbatial authority holds also for every parcel of authority which may have been given us, whether by Providence or by the will of our Superiors. The father of a family will have to account to God for the souls of his children. From him to whom the Church has entrusted the care of her faithful, an account will be required even of the least among them, for all souls are precious in the eyes of Him who died for them. Let us be attentive, therefore, to the voice of our holy Father.

The eyes of the Lord, he tells us over and over, are fixed on you at every instant with that same penetrating look which unsettled the Apostle Peter after his sin and made him burst into tears. May it please heaven that we also may not cease to look towards Christ, to seek the light of the true doctrine in Him and not in our caprices, in our human preferences, in our too personal notions. Holding His place, we ought to be nothing other than the echo of Him. If it is ourselves that we preach, we are lost and we lose others. It is not our dominating personality but the Christ acting in us which will bring forth docility and obedience in those entrusted to us.

Let us meditate this truth often, *memor sit semper*, if we do not want
to be condemned when the day of reckoning comes. We are forgetful, the
Lord remembers; and it is soul by soul that we must justify ourselves.

But, observes Dom L'Huillier, if this chapter has for its title "What
Kind of Man the Abbot Ought to Be," it could also be entitled "What Kind
of Persons the Disciples Ought to Be." As Christians we are the disciples
of the Church; as Oblates we are the disciples of St. Benedict, represented
by our Abbot and by those whom he has appointed to guide us; as the
faithful we are the disciples of our pastors. The doctrine of salvation
reaches us by way of all these authorities. And we shall owe an account
also, at the divine tribunal, of the manner in which we have been docile
and in which we have obeyed.

Too bad for us if our restless and indocile spirit, our "unwholesome
behavior" render useless or less efficacious the efforts of those who have
charge of our souls! Who knows whether the Divine Master will not end
by abandoning us to our misery and treating us as "rebellious sheep" who,
little by little, from infidelity to infidelity, arrive at eternal death?

January 11—May 12—September 11

Therefore, when anyone receives the name of Abbot, he ought to
govern his disciples with a twofold teaching. That is to say, he should
show them all that is good and holy by his deeds even more than by
his words, expounding the Lord's commandments in words to the
intelligent among his disciples, but demonstrating the divine precepts
by his actions for those of harder hearts and ruder minds. And
whatever he has taught his disciples to be contrary to God's law, let
him indicate by his example that it is not to be done, lest while
preaching to others he himself be found reprobate (1 *Corinthians* 9:27),
and lest God one day say to him in his sin, "Why do you declare My
statutes and profess My covenant with your lips, whereas you hate
discipline and have cast My words behind you?" (*Psalm* 49:16-17). And
again, "You were looking at the speck in your brother's eye, and did
not see the beam in your own" (*Matthew* 7:3).

COMMENTARY

The dignity of Abbot, therefore, is a formidable charge. St. Benedict has
already told us in what it consists. He comes back to the subject with a
still greater insistence and precision. The Abbot owes his disciples a
twofold teaching: that of doctrine and that of example.

The Abbot is to have a doctrine, therefore. But the concern here is not with "human knowledge" nor even with "dry theological or scriptural speculation."[5] "A man may possess all the treasures of human knowledge, even in theological matters, and yet produce no fruit for souls." [6] The concern is rather with a practical teaching based on "the commandments of the Lord." This teaching may be very personal, and it will be so if it is truly assimilated by meditation and by experience. It will determine the Superior's "tendency, his spirit, the deep motive of his actions. It is a sort of secret magnetism, an impulse which souls do not resist; and it is in this way that little by little a monastery takes the character of its Abbot."[7]

This teaching will reach the "apt disciples," the refined, sensitive, just souls who go joyfully without hesitation wherever the divine will is shown to them.

But one may find, even in a monastery, disciples who are rather simple and "hard of heart," that is to say, of intelligence. These will hardly be impressed by doctrine. They will not retain much from reasonings and explanations. They must have something more striking, namely deeds. If the Abbot truly lives what he teaches, his life itself becomes a lesson within everyone's reach. And if he touches the simple hearts, so much the more will he impress the good, by adding the persuasive force of his example to that of his reasonings. That is why St. Benedict says, in a general way, that the Abbot "ought to show all that is good and holy by his deeds even more than by words."

The Abbot will fulfil what he teaches, then, and avoid what he forbids. He will harmonize his teaching and his life, "for fear that while preaching to others, he himself will be found reprobate." He knows that God will not fail to punish the odious discrepancy that might occur between the severities of the moralist and the laxity of his private life.[8]

APPLICATION

One of the purposes of the Oblature is to propagate in a bewildered world the monastic spirit, which is really the spirit of the Gospel. The

---

[5] Dom Paul Delatte, *Commentary*, p. 41.

[6] Dom Columba Marmion, *Christ, the Ideal of the Monk*, translated from the French by a nun of Tyburn Convent, 2nd ed. (St. Louis: B. Herder Book Company, 1935), p. 45.

[7] Dom Paul Delatte, *Commentary*, p. 42.

[8] *Ibid.*

Oblate will attain this end especially by taking on the character of his monastery. Is it not natural that he acquire the spirit of the family to which he belongs?

But above all in his apostolic life the Oblate will apply to himself what our holy Father prescribes for the Abbot. He will always remember "that we teach more by our life than by our preaching."[9]

In the milieu of the world, the "simple" and the "hard of heart" are legion. Even many of those who consider themselves learned and intellectual are to be placed in this category.

Are there not too many, alas, who are tempted to see nothing in what we priests preach but fine theories, the teaching of which is part of our function, but which have no other importance? If, unfortunately, they think that they perceive the least discrepancy between our life and our doctrine, what a triumph for them! And if they are sincere, is it not something still worse, for these poor people are scandalized and turned away not only from us, but from Jesus Christ?

On the other hand, if they see that we preach what we live, as did our holy Father, of whom it has been said that "He taught not otherwise than he lived," ah, then how much more willingly they will let themselves be affected, for in reality it is not we who preach ourselves, but it is Jesus Christ who preaches in us. We cannot live a life of evangelical perfection and impregnate ourselves with it without being impregnated with Jesus Himself. It has been said of the Saints that they are chalices overflowing with Jesus.[10] To possess Jesus Christ abundantly and to impart Him as we possess Him—what an ideal for our apostolate!

Has not the Lord bidden us to hate that hypocrisy which would make us tell others to "Be holy, avoid sin!" while we would not seek holiness and take care to correct ourselves?[11]

January 12—May 13—September 12
Let him make no distinction of persons in the monastery. Let him

---

[9] *Ibid., p. 41.*

[10] Rev. Mateo Crawley-Boevey, SS.CC., *Jesus King of Love*, 4th ed. (Brookland, D.C.: National Center of the Enthronement, 1945), p. 227.

[11] Is it necessary to dwell on showing that these reflections have their application in the family, in one's activities, in the workshop? Especially with little ones, with children, the best preaching is that of a Christian life intensely lived.

not love one more than another, unless it be one whom he finds better in good works or in obedience. Let him not advance one of noble birth ahead of one who was formerly a slave, unless there be some other reasonable ground for it. But if the Abbot for just reason think fit to do so, let him advance one of any rank whatever. Otherwise let them keep their due places; because, whether slaves or freemen, we are all one in Christ (Galatians 3:28) and bear an equal burden of service in the army of the same Lord. For with God there is no respect of persons (Romans 2:11). Only for one reason are we preferred in His sight: if we be found better than others in good works and humility. Therefore let the Abbot show equal love to all and impose the same discipline on all according to their deserts.

COMMENTARY

St. Benedict passes now to the qualities of the abbatial government. Inspired by the words of St. Paul, he forbids the Abbot to "make distinction of persons in the monastery." Not that he would wish to make everyone pass under the equalitarian level. He will soon tell us the contrary. Not even that he would wish to disapprove of social inequalities; this is outside of his point of view. He is concerned here with equality in supernatural affection: "Slave or freeman, we are all one in Christ; we do battle under one Lord alone, bearing an equal yoke of servitude."

Let us recall that the Abbot holds the place of Christ. Now Christ loves all His own. He does not neglect some to occupy Himself only with the others. Has He not even special solicitude for the poor sinners? The Abbot is to follow His example. He is not to consider natural compatibility, relationship, nobility and the like as being titles to any distinction or special affection. What makes a religious worthy is his love of the Rule; his obedience, which inspires him to "good actions"; above all, his humility.

The fervent, supernatural charity of the Abbot will guide him in his choices, and will make him find that which is most conducive to the good of each and most useful for the monastery. His charity indeed will be basically equal for all, but it will not show itself in the same way for all. In confiding a charge or an obedience to one religious, in taking it away from another, in withdrawing a third from all function, he will be practicing no favoritism at all, but an attentive and enlightened charity. In truth, "the one is not more loved than the other," but "whoever is found to be better is given distinction" by him as he is by the Lord.

A superficial reading might lead a person to think that the last part of the paragraph contradicts the first. It will be noticed that wherever St. Benedict forbids the distinction of persons, he immediately makes a reservation in favor of virtue. "This," says a commentator,[12] "does not in any way contradict what was said above, namely that the Abbot shall be authorized to love more that one in whom he sees more sanctity and humility. In this case the love has as its object the virtues of the religious rather than the religious himself; this sentiment of affectionate esteem is imposed by the qualities of the subject, and becomes the possession of anyone who knows how to discern merit."

Moreover, the affection of the Abbot, as Dom L'Huillier remarks, will not be shown by dispensations, by exceptions to discipline, not even by more attention to the one who is its object, for the sinners and the weak need much more attention; but by more confidence, more requirements in the service of God, and sometimes even by more trials.

APPLICATION

St. Benedict appeals to a general principle: "With God there is no respect of persons." And the consequence is that whoever, under any title whatsoever, represents the Lord, ought to behave in the same way.

Chapter 2 of the Holy Rule is really an admirable treatise on Pastoral Theology. The shepherd of souls ought to love all his sheep. He loves them because they are the Lord's, because they are of His mystical body, because "we are all one in Him." If he treats with diverse shades of manner the noble and the poor man, the master and the servant, the employer and the workman, he does not, however, love the one more than the other; he devotes himself equally to the one and the other. He is not one of those who consider themselves more evangelical because they flatter one social class at the expense of another. The base practices of demagogy have no place in the house of God. Class struggle is unknown there.

The true shepherd of souls will not ignore certain sinners, certain unruly or naturally repugnant souls. They are loved by God, and that is enough. He will avoid favoritism; he will take no account of fortune, natural sympathies, connections of worldly advantage, but will have regard for virtue alone. To those souls under his care who distinguish themselves by their piety, their docility, their humility, he will be able to

---

[12] Dom Étienne Salasc, *La Règle de. S. Benoît Traduite et Commentée* (1908), p. 87.

give his trust; he will be able, with all the necessary prudence, to make them his devoted collaborators; he will be able to push them farther ahead in the ways of perfection and renouncement, and try them on occasion, that they may always belong more and more to God.

There are preferences which are unjust, and sometimes do much evil; they are those which are not directed to a true merit, or those which are shown by favors or by inadmissible dispensations.

But when the one who is the object of preferences really merits them, when he responds to them by more supernatural devotion and more piety, the preferences cannot but have the approval of good Christians and be blessed by God.

It is felt that they go less to the person than to the virtues that are in the person.

January 13—May 14—September 13

In his teaching the Abbot should always follow the Apostle's formula: "Reprove, entreat, rebuke" (*2 Timothy* 4:2); threatening at one time and coaxing at another as the occasion may require, showing now the stern countenance of a master, now the loving affection of a father. That is to say, it is the undisciplined and restless whom he must reprove rather sharply; it is the obedient, meek and patient whom he must entreat to advance in virtue; while as for the negligent and disdainful, these we charge him to rebuke and to correct.

And let him not shut his eyes to the faults of offenders; but, since he has the authority, let him cut out those faults by the roots as soon as they begin to appear, remembering the fate of Heli, the priest of Silo (*1 Kings* 2-4). The well-disposed and those of good understanding let him correct with verbal admonition the first and second time. But bold, hard, proud and disobedient characters he should curb at the very beginning of their ill-doing by stripes and other bodily punishments, knowing that it is written, "The fool is not corrected with words" (*Proverbs* 18:2; 29:19), and again, "Beat your son with the rod and you will deliver his soul from death" (*Proverbs* 23:13-14).

COMMENTARY

St. Benedict continues his remarks on the "doctrine" of the Abbot. We see that for him the meaning of the word doctrine is eminently practical. It does not mean only speculative thought, but besides that and above all a method of action which is the putting into practice of the theory.

The fact is that the Abbot has not been chosen to do the work of a theorist; he is a shepherd of souls. Now as Dom L'Huillier observes, "in the supernatural world there is never identical resemblance between two souls, and the Holy Spirit never leads any two by exactly the same way. In like manner will the Savior's representative act in the monastery."

He will observe the rule of St. Paul the Apostle: "Reprove, entreat, rebuke." And our holy Father proceeds to explain the Scriptural counsel with the help of a series of examples. According to the text, word for word, the Abbot will know how "to mix the times with the times," *miscens tempora temporibus*. Literally the formula is not clear, but the context indicates the sense of it perfectly. He will act, as Dom Guéranger translates, "according to the times and the circumstances" (*selon les moments et les circonstances*). "It is not impossible," note the translators of Farnborough,[13] that "the formula had the value of a proverb, but it is still better explained by recalling the development of Ecclesiastes, Chapter 3, verses 1 to 8: 'All things have their season .... A time to be born and a time to die, a time to plant and a time to pluck up . ....' " There is also, according to our holy Father, a time for kindnesses and a time for threats, a time for showing the tenderness of a father and a time for displaying the authority of a master. Even for a single soul, so changeable are we, these different times may succeed one another according to the circumstances. But they vary most of all from one person to another.

There are not only saints in the monastery. St. Benedict distinguishes three principal classes of characters: the undisciplined, restless spirits; the obedient, meek, patient spirits; the negligent, contemptuous spirits.

The first class are not necessarily rebels. Rather, like children, they are thoughtless, turbulent spirits. Their impulses will carry them as easily to revolt as to enthusiasm. These have frequent need of sharp remonstrances. One must speak to them "loud and clear,"[14] and even go further if necessary, as we shall see.

With the obedient, the meek and the patient, the task will be easier. They need to be encouraged in a fatherly way. There will be occasion, however, to spur them on energetically to do still better.

The negligent, the contemptuous are those who are hardened in the

---

[13] *La Règle de Saint Benoît*, Nouvelle Traduction Littérale (Paris: Art Catholique, 1924), p. 135, n. 2.

[14] Dom Paul Delatte, *Commentary*, p. 46.

habit of non-observance. They have come to disdain, as being far below them, what they have so long neglected. The whole detail of observances is, in their eyes, a good thing only for novices. Judging everything from the lofty pinnacle of their minds, they think that the orders and advice of the Abbot are not justified, are not the best, that they would know how to do much better. These in particular need to be reprimanded and corrected.

The Abbot must never shut his eyes to faults. He will remedy them from the beginning and cut out the evil by the roots. He will remember the calamity of Heli, priest of Silo, so severely punished for not having dared to correct his sons while there was still time.

Up to now St. Benedict has spoken only of counsels, warnings, reprimands. These purely verbal corrections will bear weight with souls that are sensitive and capable of reflection. But there are others—at least there were in St. Benedict's time—there are others whose spirit is bold and hard, proud and disobedient, to such a degree that words alone are not enough. Then recourse must be had to more impressive arguments: corporal punishments, and in particular the rod.

The use of such chastisements was long permitted in the monasteries. It has disappeared today, with the changing of the monastic personnel. "This study of the morals of the monks in the 6th century," says a commentator,[15] "is anything but flattering, we must admit. One would not speak otherwise to an educator of schoolboys. Would the Saint today use less severe maxims? We have reason for believing so. The truth is that monasteries at that time used to admit applicants of any age; and manners less polite than ours justify the severity of discipline in the Lawgiver."

APPLICATION

It is with a very sound psychology that St. Benedict develops his pastoral treatise. The penetrating mystic, P. Surin, wrote in the 17th century: "The prudence necessary for a director . . . consists ... in conforming his conduct to the character of those whom he is directing and in knowing how to vary it according to their needs; for to presume to subject all types of persons to one and the same method would be not to conduct them along God's way but to oblige them to follow one's own imagination and to prefer one's own ideas to the movements of grace. There are directors who could be compared to a doctor who would

---

[15] Dom Étienne Salase, *La Règle de S. Benoît*, p. 91.

prescribe only one remedy for all sorts of ills; they have certain practices which they prescribe to everyone, taking no notice that what is good for one is not good for another and that God leads souls by quite different ways."[16]

St. Benedict had long since said the same thing in other words; His method of direction is to have no single method. The method varies with the characters, whose variety is unlimited. Our holy Father knows that we must not "treat a living being as an abstraction" and that "men are not the proper subject of experiments."[17] What succeeds for one may be harmful for another. The counsels which our holy Father gives are always timely, always practical for anyone who has souls to direct.

A duty particularly painful for a director is that of correcting, especially certain difficult natures. Our holy Father's soul was really paternal, wholly permeated with divine charity. And yet, how he insists on the duty of correction!

How much easier it would be to close one's eyes! Dom Delatte, commenting on the forceful *neque dissimulet* of St. Benedict, has written this remarkable passage: "It is so pleasant not to make oneself trouble and to have a quiet life. And then one may say: It will do no good. I have spoken before. To speak again is only to play the part of a Cassandra. There will be a scene, tears, a week of obstinate ill-humor, a violent ferment of rebellious thoughts, perhaps even the wish to break with a life which has become unbearable. Then is created this terrible situation: on one side timidity and reserve, on the other an attitude of defense and defiance and the disposition of the 'deaf asp that stoppeth her ears' for fear of hearing. There is no worse misfortune for a soul than this of having forced truth to be silent, of having as it were discouraged God. Henceforth He keeps an awful silence and is provoked no more."[18]

One must have the courage, therefore, to reprove and to censure, hard though it may be. One must have that courage for the love of souls. God wills it thus. He has shown this in the Scriptures by punishing the high

---

[16] *Catéchisme Spirituel*, in Migne, *Catéchisme*, Tome 2, col. 1202-1203.

[17] Dom Paul Delatte, *Commentary*, p. 45.

[18] *Ibid.*, pp. 47-48.

priest Heli for the misdeeds of his sons.[19] And St. Benedict could tell us again here what he has already declared elsewhere: If you do not correct that soul, if you are "a dumb dog," and if the soul dies as a result of your weakness, you will have to render an account of it to the Sovereign Judge; and woe to the shepherd who, through an illusory charity, which at bottom was only selfishness and lazy love of ease, has lost any one of the sheep whom he had charge of keeping!

January 14—May 15—September 14

The Abbot should always remember what he is and what he is called, and should know that to whom more is committed, from him more is required (Luke 12:48). Let him understand also what a difficult and arduous task he has undertaken: ruling souls and adapting himself to a variety of characters. One he must coax, another scold, another persuade, according to each one's character and understanding. Thus he must adjust and adapt himself to all in such a way that he may not only suffer no loss in the flock committed to his care, but may even rejoice in the increase of a good flock.

COMMENTARY

St. Benedict comes back to what he had already said, so much does he have the matter at heart, namely that the Abbot is not simply an administrator or executive, as we say in our modern constitutional style. He is a teacher and a father and the representative of Christ. He will always remember, therefore, what he is and what name he bears.

To be sure, his prelature constitutes a dignity; he represents an authority. But how fraught with responsibilities are that dignity and that authority! St. Benedict reminds him of them unsparingly: "He must know that from him to whom more has been entrusted, more will be required." This is an austere truth. But just as truly is it "a difficult and arduous task to direct souls and to adapt oneself to the ways of behavior of a great number." It is a hard procedure to make oneself all things to all men, to know how to use kindness, reprimand, persuasion at the right time and never at the wrong time!

What constant attention is required, what understanding of different characters and of their needs! What supernatural light also in order not to

---

[19] Does not this example of a father punished for his weakness in reprimanding show us also to what degree these principles apply to parents with regard to their children?

make a mistake! For when the concern is with souls and with supernatural life, one error or one false move is often a very grave matter.

And the Abbot must be attentive lest his flock suffer any harm. Will he not have to render an account to the Lord? Moreover, he may not even content himself with maintaining the flock just as it is. He must take joy in augmenting it. Indeed, if he is zealous, can he do other than desire the salvation of the greatest possible number of souls? Can he have a more profound consolation than that of seeing them come to him? This goal he will attain by supernatural means above all. The sight of a fervent monastery is attractive; the virtues shine forth and exert an influence; the prayer makes its invisible power felt.

Sometimes the Lord, for a time, lets us believe that He neither sees nor hears; but when a St. Stephen has prayed and mortified himself, a St. Bernard comes with his companions to people the house of God with new children.

APPLICATION

From this short lesson those who have "the difficult and arduous charge of guiding souls" will retain these words of our holy Father: "From him to whom more has been given, more will be required." Let us not lose sight of the greatness of our responsibility. To be sure, it is heavy, but God does not require much of us without also giving us much. His grace never fails us, and it is more abundant in proportion as we are more supernatural. His grace alone can guide us, enlighten us, strengthen us. May we on our part not fail His grace.

The consciousness of our own responsibilities will help us understand better those of our Superiors and in particular those of our Abbot. Remembering that we also are the sheep of his fold, we shall pray for him each day, as we pray for our Bishop and for the Sovereign Pontiff. And our piety can help obtain for him a little of that joy which, according to the words of St. Benedict, he must experience in seeing the fervor of his flock increase.

January 15—May 16—September 15

Above all let him not neglect or undervalue the welfare of the souls committed to him, in a greater concern for fleeting, earthly, perishable things; but let him always bear in mind that he has undertaken the government of souls and that he will have to give an account of them. And if he be tempted to allege a lack of earthly means, let him remember what is written: "First seek the kingdom of God and His justice, and all these things shall be given you besides" (*Matthew* 6:33). And again: "Nothing is wanting to those who fear Him" (*Psalm* 33:10).

Let him know, then, that he who has undertaken the government of souls must prepare himself to render an account of them. Whatever number of brethren he knows he has under his care, he may be sure beyond doubt that on Judgment Day he will have to give the Lord an account of all these souls, as well as of his own soul.

Thus the constant apprehension about his coming examination as shepherd concerning the sheep entrusted to him, and his anxiety over the account that must be given for others, make him careful of his own record. And while by his admonitions he is helping others to amend, he himself is cleansed of his faults.

COMMENTARY

As father of the monastery the Abbot, like the father of a family, will have to take care of material interests, for he must provide well for the life of his children. This concern will be not the least of the crosses in the life of one who had renounced earthly preoccupations.

He must not be uninterested, then, in the temporal subsistence of the monastery. But it is important that he put everything in its place, and consequently that he occupy himself much more with the salvation of souls than with things that are fleeting, earthly and perishable. The point is that our cares ought to be proportioned to the value of their objects. The goods of this world are of interest only in the measure in which they safeguard the normal conditions for giving oneself peacefully to the things of eternity.

It may happen that in a poor monastery the Abbot is tempted to argue from "the insufficiency of the resources" to excuse himself for placing the care of the temporal ahead of that of the spiritual. That is not what Our Lord wants: "Seek first the kingdom of God and His justice" and "all these things" which legitimately preoccupy you "will be given you besides," for, as the Psalmist says, "nothing is wanting to those who fear Him." Should we not trust in Providence? Let us say plainly that the only labor truly blessed is that which is fulfilled in the spirit of the Gospel.

And now St. Benedict has reached the end of his chapter. That which concerns the Abbot is of such capital importance in his eyes that he will come back to it later on. But before concluding, he is going to repeat once more what he has already told us several times: A terrible day will come, the day for the rendering of accounts. Whatever may have been the number of the souls entrusted to the Abbot's care, he will have to answer for every one of them and for his own besides. He can save himself, therefore, only by saving the others or at least by laboring sincerely for their salvation. If he does not seek to "correct his own faults," he will do nothing of merit. Let him therefore ardently desire holiness and, so radiant is that quality, he will produce an abundance of spiritual fruits. And then without fear he will be able to face the dread examination "which the shepherd will undergo on the subject of the sheep lent to him."

APPLICATION

The Rule of St. Benedict is nothing but an application of the Gospel. The holy Patriarch seeks only to make us perfect Christians. Now the perfect Christian lives for heaven, works for heaven, and, if he has charge over souls, seeks to save those souls with his own. *Quae sursum sunt sapite*, says the Apostle. Have no relish but for the things above, seek only the things above, and not that which is on earth.

Having entered by Baptism into the supernatural life, the Christian by vocation ought to seek first the kingdom of God and His justice. What are the things here below if not those "vanities of the world" which we promised to renounce on the day of our baptismal profession, as also on the day of our profession as Oblates? What a forfeiture it would be if those vanities were again to take a place in our heart and our mind which belongs only to the things of God!

It is important, then, that we have not an absorbing anxiety for the goods of this world. Unfortunately there are too many Christians who have, in practice, only a halfhearted trust in Providence, and who willingly sacrifice their religious duties to the desire of amassing money. Sometimes there are shepherds of souls whom the fear of poverty or even of mediocrity prompts to more or less lucrative labors which cause them to neglect the salvation of their flock. If we are tempted in that direction, let us listen to St. Benedict's advice: "Let him not neglect or esteem of little importance the salvation of the souls entrusted to him, giving more care to things which are fleeting, earthly and perishable."

But someone will say, must not a person make proper provision for his future? Our resources are so small; sickness may come; old age may surprise us very suddenly. What shall we do? What will become of us? And this thought becomes an obsession. It makes one forget heaven and

Providence and the care of souls. And while one is giving to these poor goods of no value the time which belongs to God, one remains empty of spiritual goods, and souls are dying for want of nourishment.

Let us not, of course, tempt Providence; but let us prefer nothing to the things of God. On the day when we must render our accounts, the Sovereign Judge will not preoccupy Himself with the riches amassed at the expense of souls, except to turn them back against us. Let us rather listen to the Lord, who repeats to us that we ought first to seek His kingdom, and that He Himself will undertake to give us the rest over and above.

In the explanation of this remarkable second chapter, we have been led to two kinds of considerations: one kind concerning the person who has charge of the monastery, the Abbot; the other kind applying the same principles of St. Benedict to our own role in so far as it also is a service to souls. We shall conclude by summing them up.

Since our Abbot has received from God the grave function of leading to heaven all the members of his monastic family, is it not part of our duty to help him in this by our prayers and by our docility? It is said in the "Statutes of the Oblates" that our goal, along with our personal sanctification, is "to promote, as far as lies in our power, the good of the monastery to which we are attached, and of the entire Benedictine Order."[20] Now the person through whom Providence works for the good of the monastery is our Abbot; it is by him that "the leaven of divine justice is diffused in the minds." As affectionate children, therefore, let us give him the help of our prayers, of our good works and of our sacrifices. And since in our position as members of the family we "share in the spiritual goods of the monastery,"[21] we shall be paid a hundredfold for our efforts. Is it not readily seen that it is to our spiritual advantage for our monastery to be fervent and for our Abbot to be sustained by the prayers of all his children in his weighty task?

But, as we have seen, Chapter 2 is also an admirable pastoral treatise. Every word carries home. The holy Patriarch's deliberate repetitions have only the purpose of inculcating in our minds the principles which are to guide us in every apostolate.

---

[20] *Manual for Oblates*, p. 40, § 1.

[21] Ceremonial of the Profession of Oblates, in *Manual for Oblates*, p. 240.

Those of us who are priest Oblates or Oblates charged with the cares of a family will learn from our holy Father to put in first place the care of the souls entrusted to us; not to listen too much to our natural affections; not to shrink, even occasionally, from the necessary correctives which it will sometimes be painful for us to give, especially if there is question of the little souls of children; always to put the indispensable care of the things of heaven before the care, however legitimate, of material things. Following his example, we shall have our eyes fixed on the Father of heaven, who will sustain us with His grace and work with us to save those souls for which we must render Him an account.

Let us conclude with this observation often made by the commentators. St. Benedict's life, according to the words of St. Gregory in his *Dialogs*,[22] "could not have differed from his teaching." It is he himself, then, who, unwittingly in his humility,[23] is pictured in these pages. Do we not know also from those same Dialogs his tender solicitude not only for his monks, but for the herdsmen of Subiaco whom he instructed, for the pagans of Cassino whom he converted? Let us admire him, pray to him, permeate ourselves with his spirit; and, like him, we shall give souls to God.

---

[22] Book 2, Chapter 36; in *P.L.*, Tome 66, col. 200; translated by the Rev. Odo J. Zimmermann, O.S.B., and the Rev. Benedict R. Avery, O.S.B., in *Life and Miracles of St. Benedict* (Collegeville, Minn.: St. John's Abbey Press, 1949), p. 74.

[23] Dom Columba Marmion, *Christ, the Ideal of the Monk*, p. 42.

CHAPTER 3
On Calling the Brethren for Counsel

 HENEVER any important business has to be done in the monastery, let the Abbot call together the whole community and state the matter to be acted upon. Then, having heard the brethren's advice, let him turn the matter over in his own mind and do what he shall judge to be most expedient. The reason we have said that all should be called for counsel is that the Lord often reveals to the younger what is best.

Let the brethren give their advice with all the deference required by humility, and not presume stubbornly to defend their opinions; but let the decision rather depend on the Abbot's judgment, and all submit to whatever he shall decide for their welfare.

However, just as it is proper for the disciples to obey their master, so also it is his function to dispose all things with prudence and justice.

COMMENTARY

The commentators point out the close bond which ties this chapter to the preceding one. It completes the preceding chapter, says Dom L'Huillier, and "one may say without exaggerating that the monastery could live with these two chapters of the Rule alone; at least in the way of fundamental principles, everything necessary for the religious life was found there, aside from the traditional customs which formed the basic practices observed more or less by the different aggregations of monks."

St. Benedict has established, therefore, that the father and teacher is the Abbot. Here there is no intention of reducing his power, of making him a constitutional head. St. Benedict "never dreamt," says Dom Delatte, "of introducing into his work the forms of democracy or parliamentary government."[1] It is a question of helping the Abbot, of informing him, of enlightening him, while still leaving him the entire freedom of weighing and deciding.

When "any important business has to be done," therefore, the Abbot will call together the whole community, omnem congregationem. It is the first time that we meet the word congregatio in the Holy Rule. It is not to

---

[1] *Commentary*, p. 56.

be understood in the modem sense of the word "Congregation," but in its etymological sense. For St. Benedict the "congregation" is, as Dom Guéranger translates, the "community," that is to say, "all the monks living in one monastery," and not a grouping of communities submitting to the same Rule.[2]

The Abbot, then, will gather together all his monks. In those days there were no Lay Brothers, but simply monks and little Oblates, who were real monks also. These youths themselves are called into the council, and the Abbot can question any one of them, for "often it is to the youngest that the Lord reveals what is best to do." Our holy Father knew the Biblical examples of Samuel and Daniel, but he was instructed above all by his experience with the young Maurus and the little Placidus.

It is the Abbot himself who sets forth the agenda of the council. He questions the brethren, he solicits opinions. The brethren for their part should answer "with all the submission of humility," and "they shall not be permitted to uphold their point of view insolently."

After the council the Abbot, "by himself," will reflect on what has been said. This will be prudence on his part. Does he not know that he is to "dispose all things with foresight and justice"? Then, when he has judged "what is most useful," he will command, he will act.

After that, the brethren have nothing more to do but obey, for "it is fitting that the disciples obey the master." They will do so with humility and with affection, convinced that their Abbot has been guided by prudence and charity.

In our day Holy Church has somewhat modified the application of this chapter. In certain cases canon law has given a value no longer advisory but deliberative to the decision of the majority in Chapter. But the spirit which animates the members of the "congregation" should always be the one which the Holy Rule calls for. And in point of fact, says Dom Delatte, "in communities which are wisely governed and which have a good spirit, things go on always much as they did in the days of St. Benedict: a feeling of filial trust causes matters which he knows better than anyone else to be left to the decision of the Abbot; conflicts between an Abbot and his council are unknown, and all is done in harmonious concord."[3]

---

[2] *La Règle de S. Benoît,* translated by the Benedictines of Farnborough, p. 135.

[3] *Commentary,* p. 60.

APPLICATION

It is evident that a chapter which applies neither to Lay Brothers nor to Regular Oblates cannot in any case have a literal application for us. It is enough for us to be members of the family.

But it carries, nevertheless, a useful lesson. To be ranged with those who give their advice without humility and without respect are those who give it when it is not asked of them. And often they are the very ones for whom a certain tact and the consciousness of their situation would counsel silence.

There are thousands of citizens who set out every day, in a peremptory manner, to reform the State. During wars there is no lack of parlor strategists who, from their cozy fireside, pronounce on the conduct of the generals. One finds numerous Christians who know that they would have done if they had been in the place of the Sovereign Pontiff and the Bishops, and who do not hesitate to inform anyone who will listen.

Are there perhaps Oblates who think they know better than the Church, better than the Abbots, better than the monks, what their Order or their monastery ought to be? They are parlor reformers, who would like to be able to subject to their private, narrow views something that they know insufficiently or understand badly. Perhaps it even happens that they "uphold their point of view insolently" and forget that "submission of humility" which our holy Father demands.

Such an attitude as that is neither truly Christian nor truly monastic. Our spiritual Superiors, of whatever kind they be, are better placed than we to judge what is fitting. Our role is to consider that God is assisting them, that they have graces of their state which we have not and, as far as our monastery is concerned, that we have been accepted into the family to take on its spirit and not to give it ours. Our role is to guard humility, and also to pray for our Superiors and our brethren.

January 17—May 18—September 17

In all things, therefore, let all follow the Rule as guide, and let no one be so rash as to deviate from it. Let no one in the monastery follow his own heart's fancy; and let no one presume to contend with his Abbot in an insolent way or even outside of the monastery. But if anyone should presume to do so, let him undergo the discipline of the Rule. At the same time, the Abbot himself should do all things in the fear of God and in observance of the Rule, knowing that beyond a doubt he will have to render an account of all his decisions to God, the most just

Judge.

But. if the business to be done in the interests of the monastery be of lesser importance, let him take counsel with the seniors only. It is written, "Do everything with counsel, and you will not repent when you have done it" (*Ecclesiasticus* 32:24).

COMMENTARY

St. Benedict had just spoken to us of obedience, he had just told us that no one should become too attached to his own opinion and uphold his point of view insolently. The point is that the monk may not govern himself to suit his fancy. The different phases of his activity have been determined by a Rule, and it is to that Rule that he must always have recourse: "In all things, therefore, let all follow the Rule as the instructor, and let no one have the temerity to turn aside from it." Even when the Rule is silent on a particular point, we always have its spirit at least to guide us. And above all, there is the Abbot, who is the living Rule.

Nothing is to escape the Rule. "In all things," says St. Benedict, it is the instructor. It is above criticism; and the Abbot himself, in so far as he is the authorized interpreter, shares that prerogative. Thus no one should have the audacity to "argue insolently with his Abbot." Above all, no one should cause scandal by carrying his recriminations "outside of the monastery." The original text, which Dom Butler restored by suppressing one word,[4] names two forms of resistance. One is the bold hostility displayed face to face with the Abbot, and the other is the hypocritical struggle carried on from without. The one and the other are to be punished by the "regular discipline."

Disciplina regularis. It is the first time we meet these words. Exactly what do they mean? According to Dom Mège and Dom Calmet they would designate the whole ensemble of the various penalties St. Benedict describes in different chapters. Dom Martène, Dom L'Huillier and others think the words have a more restricted meaning. The principal penalties prescribed by St. Benedict are admonitions, excommunication, bodily chastisements. Now the *disciplina regularis* is distinct from admonitions; for in Chapter 65 St. Benedict tells us that if admonitions are fruitless

---

[4] The common text has "neque praesumat quisquam cum Abbate suo proterve *intus* aut foris monasterium contendere." According to Dom Butler the primitive text did not have the word intus, "inside," but only "cum Abbate suo proterve aut foris monasterium contendere." A copyist is supposed to have inserted the word *intus*, which he thought was called for by foris.

against a rebellious Prior, recourse shall be had "to the regular discipline."
It is just as surely distinct from excommunication; for in Chapter 24 St.
Benedict reminds the Abbot that he should proportion to the fault "the
measure of the ex-communication or of the regular discipline." It remains,
therefore, that the regular discipline must be the equivalent of bodily
chastisement, and more precisely of the rod. And this explains the present
meaning of the word "discipline."

"When the custom of mortification by the whip had spread," says Dom
L'Huillier, "about the 11th century, it seems that the thing simply passed
into the domain of the usual mortifications with the name it had borne in
the monastic penal code." A person took, or gave himself, the discipline;
the discipline became the name of the instrument of penance with which
he imposed the voluntary penalty on himself.

In the present case the delinquents are to be punished with the whip
or with the rod.

In conclusion St. Benedict reminds the Abbot that he himself must not
lay himself open to protests, but should remember that he is the living
Rule and that all expect of him the example of a perfect observance. Will
he not one day have to "render account of all his judgments to the
sovereignly equitable Judge"?

From the beginning of the chapter there has been question only of
important matters. But much more frequently there are "lesser things"
which must be regulated. In these cases there is no need to call together
the whole community. The Abbot may content himself with the counsel
of the "seniors" or elders.

APPLICATION

One sentence above all ought to attract our attention in this passage.
It is the one with which the reading begins: "Let all follow the Rule in
everything as the instructor, and let no one have the temerity to turn aside
from it." Even for the Oblates this is to be taken literally.

Let us recall what happened on the day of our profession.[5] When we
asked the celebrant for the "brotherhood" of the Order, he answered us:
"You have already sufficiently learned the Rule under which you wish to
serve, not only by reading but also by a whole year of practice and
experience as an Oblate Novice. You are, therefore, aware, under what

---

[5]   Manual for Oblates, pp. 234-235.

conditions you are about to be accepted as an Oblate of St. Benedict. If, then, you are ready and willing to observe the salutary teachings of our holy Father Benedict, . . . you may now make your final Oblation; if not, then you may still freely depart."

We have freely chosen, therefore, the yoke of the Holy Rule. Consequently it has become for us, as for our brethren of the cloister, the *regula magistra*, the master Rule; and it is to the Rule that we shall have recourse on every occasion. Sometimes it will be the letter which applies, sometimes the spirit. But in any case we shall not want to escape it. From the daily meditation of its precepts, made with a humble and docile mind, will follow a comprehension always more profound, an assimilation always more intimate. And, confronted with a problem to solve, an attitude to assume, a step to take, very seldom shall we fail to find in some one of its chapters the proper solution. The more familiar we become with it, the more sweetly but surely shall we feel this yoke impose itself on us at every moment. And if, in spite of everything, we remain undecided as to what is most in conformity with its spirit, we shall recall then that the Holy Rule has its living interpreters, whether in our Abbot or in the one whom he has charged to watch over us, or again in our director, whom St. Benedict calls the "spiritual father" (Chapter 4, No. 51).

We shall remember above all that it is the love of the Holy Rule, the preoccupation of assimilating ourself to it and of making it the guide of our life, which will make us true Benedictines. We shall be careful not to forget that this is what we have freely promised to God, to St. Benedict and to the monastery which received us, and that only on this condition were we adopted.

CHAPTER 4
What Are the Instruments of Good Works

January 18—May 19—September 18

1. In the first place, to love the Lord God with the whole heart, the whole soul, the whole strength (Deuteronomy 6:5).

2. Then, one's neighbor as oneself (Luke 10:27).

3. Then not to murder (Luke 18:20).

4. Not to commit adultery (Matthew 19:18).

5. Not to steal (Exodus 20:15).

6. Not to covet (Deuteronomy 5:21).

7. Not to bear false witness (Mark 10:19).

8. To respect all men (1 Peter 2:17).

9. And not to do to another what one would not have done to oneself (Tobias 4:16).

10. To deny oneself in order to follow Christ (Matthew 16:24).

11. To chastise the body (1 Corinthians 9:27).

12. Not to become attached to pleasures (2 Peter 2:13).

13. To love fasting (Joel 1:14).

14. To relieve the poor (Tobias 4:7).

15. To clothe the naked (Isaias 58:7).

16. To visit the sick (Matthew 25:36).

17. To bury the dead (Tobias 1:21).

18. To help in trouble (Isaias 1:17).

19. To console the sorrowing (1 Thessalonians 5:14).

20. To become a stranger to the world's ways (James 1:27).

21. To prefer nothing to the love of Christ (Matthew 10:37-38).

COMMENTARY

Together with the Prologue and the chapter on the degrees of humility, this chapter is one of those which best show forth Benedictine spirituality. Thus our Statutes invite us to meditate it particularly, when they advise us to "employ the tools of the spiritual craft" indicated in the Holy Rule.[1]

The commentators have asked precisely what is meant by the word instruments, instruments. We shall indicate only the two most probable opinions. For some, like Dom Mège and Dom L'Huillier, with but shades of difference, the instruments "are the authentic texts on which one can

---

[1] *Manual for Oblates*, p. 44, §18.

base oneself and to which one can refer" or, if you wish, "the documentary evidence" of our spiritual activity. For Dom Calmet, Dom Delatte and others, whose opinion seems to be the better, they are the "tools" which a person will use in "the workshop" of the monastery to practice "the spiritual craft." These latter expressions are from St. Benedict and proceed from the same comparison.

The ancients liked to group the rules of the spiritual life under the form of mottoes, proverbs, short, concise sentences. Thus it has been asked whether St. Benedict used some source. No one has been able to prove that supposition up to now, and we may well believe that this chapter is strictly personal, even though each of its elements is borrowed, whether from the Scriptures or from the Fathers or from the ordinary rudiments of the monastic tradition. It has been possible, in fact, for the commentators to give a reference for each instrument.

Must the enumeration of the instruments of good works be reduced to a precise plan? This is very doubtful. At the most, there are natural groups in this chapter, one maxim calling to mind another, so to speak.

In looking over this first section, one is not a little astonished, at first, to see included in a monastic code such precepts as: not to kill, not to commit adultery, not to steal, and so forth. The fact is that St. Benedict here views Christian perfection as a whole and from its humblest beginnings.

The monk is a perfect Christian; but he who comes back to God may set out from a very low estate, like the thief converted by St. Wandrille; and it is well to inspire in him who has departed from crime to set himself to the search for God, a horror of the sins he has committed, by reminding him of the divine prohibitions.

And then, will it not keep us truly humble to recall the things of which we would be capable, left to our own weakness? The faults against a virtue may vary greatly in kind and in gravity; but, however harmless they appear, they always constitute one step more towards the abyss. How many have fallen very low, who commenced by yielding on a very small matter! The Saints always had a lively sentiment of the evil of which they would have been capable if left to themselves. It is not without advantage for us, therefore, to recall from time to time the disasters into which too many Christians have fallen, in order to put ourselves on guard against every slight fault, which is always a first step towards a more serious evil.

The first instrument, the one in which all the others are summed up, was given us by the Lord. It is the greatest commandment of the Law: "In the first place, before all, to love the Lord God with one's whole heart, with one's whole soul, with one's whole strength."

We know that God is our end, that He has created us for Himself, and that there is nothing sure and steadfast outside of Him. We ought, therefore, to place Him "in the first place, before all" in our concerns. But the service of God is not slavery; it is a service of love. That is why it is said "Thou shalt love," and in that love we must spend all the forces of our mind, of our will, of our heart. God must be our all.

At bottom, for the faith, there is nothing but God. Creatures are a reflection of God, they are full of God, they sing the glory of God. And when those creatures are rational beings, when they are called to supernatural destinies, the "Word who enlightens every man coming into this world" and who gives Himself abundantly by His grace to the baptized, manifests Himself the more in them. We love them in God, and we love Him in them. And so the second commandment is like the first: "Thou shalt love thy neighbor." But love him how? "As ourselves." If we have a truly supernatural spirit, what we love in ourselves is God working there, God lifting us up to Himself, God transforming by His grace and His intimate union a soul created to His image and likeness. That is also what we ought to love in our neighbor; and this love is naturally transformed into an apostolate, for how can we help wanting our God to live always more abundantly in our brethren as we want Him to live abundantly in us?

We shall avoid, therefore, whatever may harm our neighbor or do him wrong in the rightful enjoyment of his goods, his family, his reputation. But we shall not content ourselves with that wholly negative attitude. We shall respect him, and we shall exclude no man from our love, for all are created in the image of God. St. Benedict is going to return further on to the positive evidences of love towards our neighbor. For now, he seems to conclude a first series of precepts with this maxim inspired by the Book of Tobias: "Not to do to another what one would not want done to oneself."

We are now going to enter into a series of instruments which are related properly to Christian asceticism.

First, here is a group of four which support one another:

To renounce oneself in order to follow Christ

  To chastise one's body

Not to seek pleasures
    To love fasting.

God is our end. To save us, He united Himself to our humanity; and we have the consolation of finding our God under the brotherly aspect of Christ. But because our nature has been wounded by original sin, instead of going naturally towards its divine goal, it resists and excites in us the pride of the ego. This ego it excites in its intellectual faculties and in its sensual faculties, and makes of it a sort of idol which wants for itself that which is due only to God. The proud, carnal creature becomes its own god; it forgets the infinite love of Christ. And who can escape this tendency? We must fight it. We must annihilate in ourselves the idol of our ego and renounce ourselves in order to turn all the powers of our being towards Christ.

We know too well, alas, that original sin, aggravated with the weight of our actual sins, has destroyed the primitive equilibrium and harmony of our nature. The lower faculties seek to prevail over the spiritual faculties. The senses want to command. It is necessary, therefore, to chastise the body and reduce it to servitude.

This goal will be approached first by spurning pleasures. The sensual man seeks his ease, he "embraces" that which pleases his eyes, his taste, his touch and so forth. He is obsessed with the idea of living comfortably. All that, in reality, ought to be foreign to us. We should render ourselves as indifferent as possible to comfort and ease of life.

More than that, we ought to chastise our body in a positive way with the help of those mortifications of which fasting is the most traditional form. We must "love fasting." The Church, in the Preface for Masses during Lent, tells us why: It is by fasting that the Lord stifles vice, uplifts the mind, generously bestows virtue and its rewards.[2] To be sure, the Benedictine does not have penance and expiation as his special vocation, as do some congregations. His duty is above all the divine praise. But he cannot escape the great law of mortification. He knows that mortification purifies and lightens the soul; and he loves it as a means without equal for offering to God a praise more agreeable because it comes from a soul

---

[2] *Corporali jejunio vitia comprimis, mentem elevas, virtutem largiris et praemia.* The English wording is from the translation by the Rev. James A. Kleist, S.J., in *Orate Fratres* (Collegeville, Minn.: The Liturgical Press), Vol. 18, No. 4, Feb. 20, 1944, p. 158.

purified by sacrifice.

St. Benedict returns again to the love of neighbor. Just as the love of Christ will prove itself by the mortifications of penance, so the love of neighbor will manifest itself by a meritorious service. It is necessary to "relieve the poor, clothe the naked, visit the sick, bury the dead, help those in tribulation, comfort the afflicted." For the monk some of these works of mercy will be more collective than personal. For the Oblate they will be an excellent means of bridling egoism and practicing detachment.

Our reading ends with two precepts which truly echo the Benedictine soul and which one never tires of repeating and meditating:

To keep oneself from the ways of the world To prefer nothing to the love of Christ.

We can never repeat it too often: we are no longer of the world. The world and time, it is all one. It is the love of the ego, it is the search for pleasures, it is a state of mind, a fashion of thinking and of acting, determined by a conception of the goal of life which is practically atheistic. To all that we are and must remain strangers. The world is preoccupied with a multitude of useless things. And how many Christians, and perhaps priests, are the same way! Do not too many newspapers and magazines, for example, encumber our mind with their futilities? Do we not become excessively preoccupied with being in the current of what is said and done in the world of which we are not—with the latest invention, the latest performance, the latest feat, the dernier cri? And we profess to belong to Jesus Christ! Let us be, then, what we ought to be, what our Baptism, our vocation, our profession have made us. Let us neglect everything that could distract us from Christ. Let us prefer nothing to the love of Christ.

APPLICATION

Chapter 4, as has been remarked, is one of those which impose themselves literally on the Oblate as well as on the monk. Thus we may look back to what precedes for the application. To keep to our plan, however, we shall indicate here some practical and particular applications which could not find place elsewhere.

St. Benedict orders us, with the Scriptures, to "chastise the body." He distinguishes between fasting and this voluntary chastisement. Thus we are concerned here actually with a penitential practice. Now the practice adopted currently in our Benedictine cloisters, a practice formerly followed also by many pious persons and one which, it seems, can preferably be adopted by Oblates, yet without being an obligation, is the "discipline" whose origins we have indicated in commenting on the *disciplina regularis* of Chapter 3. The discipline is generally more troublesome than painful. Its common practice does not expose one to that vanity which might arise from some other, extraordinary mortification. On the other hand, it is truly painful to subject oneself to it regularly. According to the Constitutions of the French Congregation, the discipline is taken Friday evenings, and is accompanied by prayers which will be found in the Monastic Breviary, of which the principal ones are the Psalms *Miserere* and *De Profundis* and the Oration of the Passion: *Respice, quaesumus, Domine, super hanc familiam tuam*, etc.

As we have seen, St. Benedict recommends likewise the love of fasting. With the sacred liturgy we have told the spiritual advantages of it, so that it is unnecessary to return to this point. If we cannot readily subject ourselves to the monastic fasts, at least let us avoid the indifference of too many Christians towards the fasts which the Church imposes on us.[3] Let us remember that the divine Master Himself fasted, and that He taught us that certain devils cannot be driven out except by prayer and fasting, *in oratione et jejunio.*

January 19—May 20—September 19

22. Not to give way to anger (Matthew 5:22).
23. Not to nurse a grudge (Ephesians 4:26).
24. Not to entertain deceit in one's heart (Psalm 4:3).
25. Not to give a false peace (Romans 12:9).
26. Not to forsake charity (1 Peter 4:8).
27. Not to swear, for fear of perjuring oneself (Matthew 5:33-37).
28. To utter truth from heart and mouth (Psalm 14:3).
29. Not to return evil for evil (1 Thessalonians 5:15).
30. To do no wrong to anyone, and to bear patiently wrongs done to oneself (1 Corinthians 6:7).
31. To love one's enemies (Luke 6:27-35).

---

[3] If there are legitimate reasons for being dispensed from fasting, reasons which should be explained to our spiritual father, the fact remains that we should at least hold in high esteem this form of penance commanded by the Church. It is evident that there are much fewer reasons for being dispensed from the law of abstinence. (Cf. "Statutes of the Oblates," 516, in *Manual for Oblates*, p. 43.)

32. Not to curse those who curse us, but rather to bless them (1 Peter 3:9).
33. To bear persecution for justice' sake (Matthew 5:10).
34. Not to be proud (Tobias 4:14).
35. Not addicted to wine (1 Timothy 3:3).
36. Not a great eater (Ecclesiasticus 37:32).
37. Not drowsy (Proverbs 20:13).
38. Not lazy (Romans 12:11).
39. Not a grumbler (1 Corinthians 10:10).
40. Not a detractor (Wisdom 1:11).
41. To put one's hope in God (Psalm 72:28).
42. To attribute to God, and not to self, whatever good one sees in oneself (1 Corinthians 4:7).
43. But to recognize always that the evil is one's own doing, and to impute it to oneself (Osee 13:9).

COMMENTARY

St. Benedict continues the enumeration of the instruments whose use assures charity with regard to one's neighbor. It is not simply on the lips, in the look and the gesture that he wants to see true charity, but in the depths of the heart. It is there that everything capable of wounding charity must be extinguished. There must be no anger, however interior, no anger fostered and dissimulated, no projects of vengeance, none of those ruses which hide "falsity in the heart" under polite exteriors, none of these worldly compliments whose expression by no means answers to what one is thinking. The holy Patriarch does not wish to separate charity from truth. One must "utter truth from the heart as well as from the mouth."

But does it not sometimes happen that a person finds himself faced with implacable enemies, with persecutors who do not disarm? St. Benedict knew that. Let us recall the monks of Vicovaro and the persecutions of the priest Florentius.[4] And yet he never cursed anyone. He retired and wept over the eternal loss of his persecutors. It can be said that he practiced in an eminent degree these principles which he teaches us:

Not to return evil for evil To do injustice to no one But to sustain patiently the injustice done to us To love one's enemies Not to curse those who curse us But rather to bless them To suffer persecution for justice'

---

[4] *Dialogs of St. Gregory*, Book 2, Chapters 3 and 8; in Pit., Tome 66, cols. 134-136 and 146-150; in *Life and Miracles of St. Benedict*, pp. 9-11 and 22-24.

sake.

If necessary, then, charity will go even to the point of heroism and even to the realization of the supreme beatitude announced by Jesus, to suffer persecution for the sake of justice, that is to say, actually for the sake of God.

St. Benedict carries refinement in charity even to the extent of forbidding an oath. He who swears engages himself in an absolute way towards God and towards his neighbor. If he perjures himself—and human weakness exposes him to this—his injustice becomes more serious towards the one and the other. But of what good is an oath? Ought we not to be absolutely sincere, to promise only what we will give and to affirm only what we know to be true? And so we shall not expose ourselves to frustrating our neighbor in his right to the truth and to the fidelity of the given word.

Up to here St. Benedict has occupied himself above all with our life in relation to others, save in the four instruments relative to mortification. Now he is going to consider especially our strictly personal life. He attacks capital sins of which he had not yet spoken. We have seen him, at the beginning of the chapter, condemn lust; he will come back to that subject later on. He has already branded anger likewise. He devotes only one line to pride; we shall find it again in the chapter on humility. Gluttony in drinking and eating has only two lines. St. Benedict will have occasion to speak of it at greater length when he comes to the question of the nourishment of the monks; and he has already recommended fasting to us. Finally he condemns laziness, along with those two dispositions of mind customary to the lazy: grumbling and detraction. Our holy Father will come back to all those matters in different chapters of the Holy Rule. But it was indeed necessary, in this collection of the instruments of good works, to enumerate principles as essential as these.

Our reading ends with three instruments extremely important:

 To put one's hope in God
 Whatever good one sees in oneself
 to ascribe to God and not to oneself

As for the evil, to understand always that one has done it oneself and to consider it one's own.

The edifice of our perfection rests on trust in God. Alone, we are weakness itself. But God wants to save us. That is why He has adopted us by Baptism, that is why He has deposited in us the treasures of His grace.

Are we not "grievously insulting God when we ignore His merciful intentions and obstinately persist in fearing, in spite of this law of confidence? Are we not wounding Our Lord to the quick?"[5]

We shall have a total confidence, then, in Our Heavenly Father. In return for this perfect docility, He will work in us "the willing and the doing," *velle et perficere*. But we shall also know how to discern our acts and their merits. That the good is working in us, that we are progressing, we can by no means deny. St. Benedict had already told us that at the end of the Prologue. But let us not be lured by the illusions of pride. All this good is the work of the Lord in us. Let us not, therefore, assign the glory for it to ourselves. If we want to render justice to ourselves, let us rather consider the evil which we still do, in spite of so many graces; let us consider the slow rate of our progress. That is indeed our work, and we should deplore it.

APPLICATION

As we have already said, the Holy Rule in this whole chapter is to be taken literally. The concern is with Christian perfection; and both the monk and the Oblate are striving for nothing else than to become perfect Christians. Let us content ourselves, therefore, with transcribing here by way of conclusion some lines from Dom Delatte which make most evident the quality of justice and sincerity which will characterize our charity towards God and men: "It is the glory of the monastic life to be founded in loyalty and absolute sincerity, to be delivered from all the diplomacy and shiftiness of the world. Happy those who have nothing to hide, who know nothing of tortuous or subterranean maneuvers, who live full in the day. Happy those who have brought all their being to a perfect simplicity, and who, before God and before men, are what they are, without duality, stiffness, or effort, but with flexibility and ease."[6]

January 20—May 21—September 20

44. To fear the Day of Judgment (Job 31:14ff.).
45. To be in dread of hell (Matthew 10:28).

---

[5] Madame Cecile J. Bruyere, *Spiritual Life and Prayer*, p. 85.

[6] *Commentary*, p. 71.

46. To desire eternal life with all the passion of the spirit (*Philippians* 1:23).
47. To keep death daily before one's eyes (Matthew 24:42ff.).
48. To keep constant guard over the actions of one's life (*Deuteronomy* 4:9).
49. To know for certain that God sees one everywhere (*Proverbs* 5:21).
50. When evil thoughts come into one's heart, to dash them against Christ immediately (*Psalm* 136:9).
51. And to manifest them to one's spiritual father (*Ecclesiasticus* 8:11).
52. To guard one's tongue against evil and depraved speech (*Psalm* 33:13-14).
53. Not to love much talking (*Proverbs* 10:19).
54. Not to speak useless words or words that move to laughter (*Matthew* 12:36).
55. Not to love much or boisterous laughter (*Ecclesiasticus* 21:23).
56. To listen willingly to holy reading {Luke 11:28).
57. To devote oneself frequently to prayer (*Colossians* 4:2).
58. Daily in one's prayer, with tears and sighs, to confess one's past sins to God, and to amend them for the future (*Psalms* 6:7),
59. Not to fulfil the desires of the flesh; to hate one's own will (*Galatians* 5:16).
60. To obey in all things the commands of the Abbot, even though he himself (which God forbid) should act otherwise, mindful of the Lord's precept, "Do what they say, but not what they do" (*Matthew* 23:3).
61. Not to wish to be called holy before one is holy; but first to be holy, that one may be truly so called (*Matthew* 6:1).

COMMENTARY

We are going towards a goal and we are preparing for it. Our life here below will end in something positive. If there are moments when that goal fills us with enthusiasm, when the beauty of God draws us on, when love sustains and prompts us, there are also other moments, alas, when we feel our indigence too much, and when it is the earth that attracts us. Reason with ourselves and arouse ourselves as we will, the feeling which had sustained us seems to have abandoned us.

Then indeed must we turn towards fear. Let us consider the Judgment Day, that day which the Church calls the Day of Wrath, *dies irae*. Do we want it to be that for us? Let us consider hell and the eternity of its sufferings. Is it not terrifying? Is that the lot we have chosen? This fear of the Judgment, this dread of hell are really beneficial. They inspire a horror of sin by the horror of the punishment.

But our holy Father asks us to make a comparison at the same time: Let us look at heaven, all filled with the infinite beauty of God, let us look at the Angels and the Saints in the "deifying light." Is there not something there to inspire in us "a supernatural longing"?

All the things of earth will pass. Of ephemeral beauties there will remain for us nothing but regret for having been attached to them. And the hour when we shall leave them is perhaps very near. Let us have this imminence of death before our eyes, not to trouble us but to keep us ready. There is nothing more conducive to peace than to feel oneself thus prepared to welcome without danger the hour of death and that of judgment.

But in order to have that peace, it is necessary to watch over oneself, to watch over one's thoughts, words, actions. And is not the best means of assuring the effectiveness of this "looking" at our heart, to think that God is looking at us at every hour and in every place?

Our too earthbound preoccupations, our passions still poorly controlled too often prevent us from seeing that which is. There is, in fact, a reality more present than the sun which shines on us, than the beings which surround us, than the very air we breathe: the reality of God, in whom we live, in whom we move, by whom we are. *In ipso vivimus, movemur et sumus.* The thought of this divine reality should accompany us everywhere, not only in prayer, but in work, and even in recreation.

St. Benedict next indicates what ordinarily turns us away from the presence of God.

There is first of all temptation, "the bad thoughts that come to the soul." Using a Scriptural comparison which he had already employed in the Prologue, our holy Father bids us "dash" those thoughts against Christ. As long as those ghosts torment you, look well on Him who is looking at you. Christ encourages you. He gives you His grace. Everything in Him speaks to you of love. He deserves indeed that you annihilate at His feet all those bad imaginings which are highly displeasing to Him.

Do you feel yourself too weak to repulse them alone? Go find your spiritual advisor, your director. The remedy is a proven one; its efficacy is certain.

But distraction from the divine presence can come to us also from our own dissipation. And the dissipation of the mind often arises from our talking too much. Not only does St. Benedict turn us away "from bad and perverse language," but also from vain babbling. He does not like his children to waste their time in frivolous conversations, which amuse the gallery and feed their vanity. The sentiment of the presence of God, the fear of the Judgment and the desire of heaven do not fit in with buffoonery and "too frequent and too noisy laughter." There is a certain brand of joy that indicates a vain soul; there is a peaceful and mild joy which indicates a fervent, recollected soul.

It is not enough, however, to push back obstacles. One must still seek the means to entertain in oneself the thought of the presence of God and of His judgments. There are, says St. Benedict, the "holy readings" which we must learn to love; there is the taste for frequent prayer; there is the compunction which puts us face to face with our sins, makes us weep for them, makes us correct them.

Those sins come "from the desires of the flesh and from one's own will." By these procedures, a person gets into the habit of not fulfilling the former and of hating the latter, and thus of driving all trouble from his soul. The sins come also from disobedience. Let us be obedient. We should not busy ourselves with finding out whether those who command us are themselves doing what they teach. It should be enough for us to know that they are right in their teaching.

And if we make some progress, let us not proceed to draw vanity from it. Let us not take ourselves for Saints. He who thinks he is a Saint may be assured that he is not. The true Saints always consider themselves great sinners. Let us not "wish to be called holy before being such," says our holy Father; "let us be holy first, that we may more truthfully be so called."

APPLICATION

Each of these precepts of St. Benedict could be made the object of a long meditation. They are of capital importance, and they support one another. It is by the practice of them that we can assure that inner recollection without which it would be impossible for us to achieve the progress we have promised. The spirit of silence, "spiritual reading" done each day, frequent prayer, and the rest, separate the soul from the things of the world and maintain it in a supernatural atmosphere. Would not the ideal be never to leave the divine presence, and to remain in spirit, like Mary Magdalen, at the feet of the Savior? Our holy Father furnishes us at least the indispensable instruments for approaching that ideal. They are good instruments. Let us not fail to make a trial of them.

January 21—May 22—September 21

62. To fulfil God's commandments daily in one's deeds (*Ecclesiasticus* 6:37).
63. To love chastity (*Judith* 15:11).
64. To hate no one (*Leviticus* 19:17).
65. Not to be jealous, not to harbor envy (*James* 3:14, *Galatians* 5:19ff.).
66. Not to love contention (2 *Timothy* 2:14).
67. To beware of haughtiness (*Psalm* 130:1).
68. And to respect the seniors (*Leviticus* 19:32).
69. To love the juniors (1 *Timothy* 5:1).
70. To pray for one's enemies in the love of Christ (*Matthew* 5:44).
71. To make peace with one's adversary before the sun sets (*Ephesians* 4:26).
72. And never to despair of God's mercy (*Psalm* 51:10).

These, then, are the tools of the spiritual craft. If we employ them unceasingly day and night, and return them on the Day of Judgment, our compensation from the Lord will be that wage He has promised: "Eye has not seen, nor ear heard, what God has prepared for those who love Him" (1 Corinthians 2:9).

Now the workshop in which we shall diligently execute all these tasks is the enclosure of the monastery and stability in the community.

COMMENTARY

The last maxims of Chapter 4, says Dom L'Huillier, "do not appear to have any very definite connection with what precedes, nor even among themselves: they seem intended rather to make up for the omissions."

Our holy Father reminds us that virtue consists not in theories but in acts, and that those acts are not to be isolated and intermittent, but repeated every day.

For the first and only time he names chastity, and proposes it to our love. It is so much a part of the religious life that it was not necessary to dwell on it any more. Chastity indeed effects a separation more total and a gift more entire. "For priest and for monk," says Dom Delatte, "chastity is a part of charity, its fine flower and perfection. With it the holocaust is complete and our body contributes its share to the work of the adoration of God and union with Him."[7]

The duties with respect to neighbor are completed by the forbidding to hate, to be jealous and envious, and to love contention; by the advice to become reconciled before the setting of the sun; and by the formal precept to venerate the elders, to love the young and to pray for one's enemies in the love of Christ.

St. Benedict has humility so much at heart that he bids us once more not only to lower ourselves, but to "flee haughtiness." And the holy Patriarch concludes with this final advice: Never to despair of God's mercy.

We have just passed in review all that we have to do to separate ourselves from the world, to destroy our own will, to "prefer nothing to the love of Christ." In all this there were necessarily dura et aspera, hard and bitter things; for the ways that lead to God are narrow. We shall sometimes have moments of discouragement, of weakness, perhaps of failure. At such moments it seems as if everything is lost or about to be lost, as if what we have done thus far is vain, as if we would never reach any goal.

"It is a painful thing," says Dom Delatte, "to be always running on the same rock, or always cleaning up the same dirt; it would be far sweeter to unite oneself to Our Lord for ever by a single act, like the Angels. However, there is a good side even to these perpetual jerks and oscillations. For when all is said, to return to God when one has been misled, to make it up with Him, to put our whole soul back at His feet, this is an act of perfect charity. It is not impossible that these falls have contributed much to our progress. In any case they invite us to greater watchfulness and teach us the little or nothing that we are. Whatever our weakness may have been, God has not changed, His arms are always open. Let us remember the father of the Prodigal Son, and the Good Samaritan, and other Gospel parables, in which is enshrined for ever the

---

[7] *Commentary*, p. 79. Is there any need to recall, with the "statutes of the Oblates," that there is a chastity in accord with the state of Christian marriage? (Cf. *Manual for Oblates*, p. 43, §15.)

form of divine mercy."[8]

And now St. Benedict concludes: "There are the instruments of the spiritual art."

The words *artis spiritualis* justify well enough the meaning of tool given to *instrumentum*. Art is "a work which is learned and not improvised, which has its rules and its procedures."[9]

And here is what confirms the interpretation. This art is learned in a workshop, *officina*, which is the monastery. It is there that the monk will work "day and night," and will merit that ineffable reward which God reserves for those who love Him.

APPLICATION

St. Benedict has put into our hands all the instruments necessary for the work of our sanctification. As we have already remarked, these instruments are adapted to a certain end, perfection. The latter is realized in that charity required absolutely and unconditionally by the greatest of the commandments: Before all, to love the Lord God with one's whole heart, with one's whole soul, with one's whole strength. And St. Benedict wants us so to love God and His Christ that we prefer nothing to Them. To assure that exclusive love, our holy Father will preach to us the separation from everything which turns us from God, the adherence to everything which leads to Him.

That which turns us from God is attachment to the goods of the earth, the concupiscences of the flesh, self-will. We must therefore renounce all that, detach ourselves, free ourselves.

Then in the measure in which our soul rids itself of the useless and the harmful, it must become penetrated with this great and sanctifying truth, that the Lord is omnipresent. It must live, so to speak, in the reflected light of the divine countenance, it must feel at the same time the infinite justice and the infinite charity of Him who does not stop looking for us and calling us in order that nothing may separate us from Him.

Let us examine well each instrument, and we shall see that it has for its end either to destroy to the last stronghold the spirit of the world, or

---

[8] *Commentary*, pp. 80-81.

[9] Dom L'Huillier, *Explication Ascétique et Historique de la Règle de S.Benoist (1901)*, Tom3 1, p. 171.

to produce in us always more of the divine life. We shall see in particular that this little code is not an artificial assemblage of edifying maxims, jotted down at random on the parchment, but that it truly represents a spirit, the monastic spirit, the Benedictine spirit. That spirit ought to be our own. It is to impregnate ourselves with it that we rely upon that "workshop of the spiritual art" which is our monastery.

Let us often reread Chapter 4 of our Rule, therefore. The more we become acquainted with it, the more we shall admire it. And ever more confident in that mercy of God of which we must never despair, to the best of our ability we shall employ as our Statutes tell us "the tools of the spiritual craft" which are indicated to us.

CHAPTER 5
On Obedience

January 22—May 23—September 22

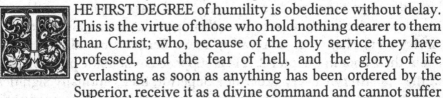HE FIRST DEGREE of humility is obedience without delay. This is the virtue of those who hold nothing dearer to them than Christ; who, because of the holy service they have professed, and the fear of hell, and the glory of life everlasting, as soon as anything has been ordered by the Superior, receive it as a divine command and cannot suffer any delay in executing it. Of these the Lord says, "As soon as he heard, he obeyed Me" (*Psalm* 17:45). And again to teachers He says, "He who bears you, hears Me" (*Luke* 10:16).

Such as these, therefore, immediately leaving their own affairs and forsaking their own will, dropping the work they were engaged on and leaving it unfinished, with the ready step of obedience follow up with their deeds the voice of him who commands. And so as it were at the same moment the master's command is given and the disciple's work is completed, the two things being speedily accomplished together in the swiftness of the fear of God by those who are moved with the desire of attaining life everlasting. That desire is their motive for choosing the narrow way, of which the Lord says, "Narrow is the way that leads to life" (*Matthew* 7:14), so that, not living according to their own choice nor obeying their own desires and pleasures but walking by another's judgment and command, they dwell in monasteries and desire to have an Abbot over them. Assuredly such as these are living up to that maxim of the Lord in which He says, "I have come not to do My own will, but the will of Him who sent Me" (*John* 6:38).

COMMENTARY

St. Benedict has already spoken to us several times about obedience. His Rule is addressed to those who desire to go to God "by the labor of obedience" and wish to take in hand "the strong, bright weapons" of obedience "to do battle under the Lord Christ." That is why he is going to devote a full chapter to the subject.

"Obedience without delay," he tells us, "is the first degree of humility." In Chapter 7, devoted to the degrees of humility, St. Benedict will make a different classification. But here the concern is not really with classification. Our holy Father simply wants to tell us that the most complete expression of humility is perfect obedience.

St. Benedict calls this obedience *obedientia sine mora*, obedience without delay. These three words are worth defining. The concern here is not with a resigned submission, still less with an unwilling submission, but with a joyous and ready compliance. And that compliance will be such because it will come from a soul wholly impregnated with faith and seeing Christ everywhere. Let us recall what St. Benedict has already told us about the Abbot in Chapter 2: "He is supposed to hold the place of Christ in the monastery." Every order of a Superior, then, normally signifies a wish of Christ, and it is truly Christ whom one obeys in the person of that Superior.

After this recall to the spirit of faith, St. Benedict indicates to us the motives of obedience. The first and principal one is the love of Christ. Is it not He ultimately who speaks and who ordains? How could obedience be other than fitting "to those who hold nothing dearer to them than Christ"?

The second motive is the profession which one has vowed. One has engaged oneself to fulfil a "sacred service," the service of the Lord. How realize one's promise if one refuses to serve, if one does not obey?

The third motive is the fear of hell. St. Benedict has already told us the place of that fear in the spiritual life. Is not hell the lot of the disobedient? For in reality every sin is disobedience, and every disobedience partakes more or less of the nature of sin.

Finally the last motive is "the desire of life everlasting." That happy life can be reserved only for those who by a constant obedience adhere unceasingly to the wishes of Him who is the Master of Eternity.

Now that we are persuaded of the necessity of obeying, St. Benedict is going to show us how we must obey. This is the commentary of the *sine mora*. To this end he piles up examples: one abandons on the spot what one had in hand; one leaves unfinished the work begun; and the act follows the voice which commands *vicino obedientiae pede*, word for word "with the close foot of obedience," an expression difficult to render in the vernacular, but which shows in a concise way how the perfectly obedient person hastens to put himself in motion as soon as the order is given. Order and execution follow with "that rapidity, that promptness" which the true fear of God, never apart from love, inspires in the heart.

In theory this ready and loving obedience is something very attractive. But St. Benedict knows that in practice it is sometimes very hard. A person will obey with a "novice fervor" for some months, perhaps for some years, then a time will come when he no longer feels anything but a sort of lassitude. Our holy Father is anxious to warn us of this. The way of obedience is the narrow way. The Lord Himself had forewarned us, "Narrow is the way that leads to life" (*Matthew* 7:14). The fact is that the spirit of obedience is in contradiction with what St. Paul called the "old man, the man of sin"; with our own will, which wants "to live according to its own choice"; with our natural tendencies; with the appeals of pleasure. It is hard to submit not only to the command but "to the judgment of others." And by this last phrase St. Benedict shows us again that obedience is not an exterior virtue, but a most interior and heartfelt compliance. He even wants his disciples to have the desire of obedience: "They wish for nothing else than to subject themselves to an Abbot."

The better to draw them on to this desire, the holy Patriarch shows them the great figure of Christ, who, although He was God, willed to make Himself obedient unto death, and who said, "I am not come to do My will, but the will of Him who sent Me" (*John* 6:38).

APPLICATION

To grasp well the full import of the virtue of obedience, let us recall what we have repeated several times already: God is our end. He is the end of every creature. The essential good of every being is to fulfil what the Lord wants it to be. The whole of creation, inanimate or living, obeys the will of its Creator. But it obeys without understanding. The privilege of man is to obey freely, to be conscious of his obedience, to be able to walk in light and in joy towards the end for which he was created, that is to say, towards God Himself.

There is as it were a mysterious attraction which draws creatures to the pursuit of the divine plan. The attraction which draws man is love, but a love which is given consciously, which is given uniquely, and which goes towards its end imperturbably even at the price of pain and sacrifice. The great and profound motive of obedience St. Benedict recalls to us when he writes, "It is fitting to those who esteem nothing dearer than Christ."

Thus our holy Father does not establish the duty of obedience upon natural reasons, drawn from social physiology, solidarity or the rights of man; but, although he does not exclude in principle all the reasons drawn from the natural order, he wants us to be animated before everything else with the spirit of faith. It is in a supernatural light that he makes us look upon obedience. And the latter, by that very fact, appears to us in all its importance. In so far as it responds to what we owe to God, obedience is attached to the virtue of justice; but it is also in close contact with the theological virtues: with faith, because ultimately it is God, discovered by faith, whom we obey; with hope, since it tends to attain what God has promised us; with charity, since it identifies the divine will and ours, and this is the most perfect expression of love.

But the practice of obedience presents itself to us under concrete forms, namely the legitimate, orders of our superiors, spiritual and temporal, of whatever sort they be. When one reflects on this, one sees that it is difficult indeed to escape some duty of obedience, be it only for half a day. At almost every moment we find it face to face with us.

As children of the Church we are submitted to her hierarchy through our Baptism; through our Confirmation we are soldiers, that is to say, obedient. Those of us who are priests promised obedience to our Bishop on the day of our ordination; and the general lines of our daily life are regulated by diocesan statutes, a veritable rule which we must follow in conscience.

The pastor in the parish, the parents in the family, the employers in the workshop, masters with regard to their servants, etc., hold the place of God in various degrees. These affirmations may appear shocking in this age of independence, of rationalism, of class war; they are, however, the most authentic doctrine of Christianity. Everything is hierarchy in what God has instituted, and where there is hierarchy there is obedience.

We as Oblates surely would not be responding to the desires of our holy Father if we did not force ourselves to put as much perfection as possible into our obedience. He wants us even to desire it. Yet, however frequent be our occasions for obeying, as Christians, citizens, members of a household, workers, servants, etc., there still remains a certain part of our life which may be found, in fact, to escape obedience.

If we wish to be truly Benedictine, we must put even that part under the protection of this virtue.

For that purpose our Rule is offered us. Adapted to our diverse situations, with the advice of our directors, it comes, in fact, to fix under the form of a particular regulation the whole economy of our days, the hours of our rising and retiring, of our daily work, of prayer and the Work of God, of spiritual reading, and so forth. By holding ourselves docilely to what has been prescribed for us instead of yielding to our caprices like those "who live according to their own choice," because such is the Lord's will, we make ourselves truly obedient; and this obedience is, without a doubt, the best sign of love we could give to Jesus Christ.

Everything St. Benedict says about the promptness of obedience, therefore, we can take literally, and imitate as well as we can the "sacred service" of our brethren of the cloister.

We have, then, our by-laws of life. These by-laws will be for us somewhat like the particular Constitutions which determine for the monks the application of the Holy Rule. We shall take care to submit them to our directors, accepting docilely the counsels of their experience. This is a very important point. Without direction we should be exposed "to building ourselves a whole spirituality upon pride, when it is not simply upon foolishness."[1] We should be equally exposed to continually modifying these by-laws to suit our ease and our caprices, like those Sarabaites reproved by St. Benedict, who, having for law only "the satisfaction of their desires," "declare holy that which pleases them and illicit that which they do not want." Let us recall from another source that St. Benedict wants us to have a director from whom we are to hide nothing and whom we are to obey (Chapter 7). It is under such conditions that a serious rule of life will be established. And once this schedule is approved we must adhere to it. It becomes the expression of the divine will. And it is by this means that we shall fulfil the promises of our profession.

Later on we shall take notice of the fact that the word "obedience" is not found in the formula of profession of the Oblates, although it comes into the formula of profession of the monks. How little Christ-like it would be to conclude from that that we are more or less dispensed from the duty of obeying! The suppression is simply meant to indicate that for us obedience is not the object of a vow and that this is one of the points which distinguish us from the monks. But it remains none the less included in the promise of the "reformation of life." Is not the reformation in reality, as St. Benedict told us in the Prologue, "the return by the labor of obedience to Him from whom the sloth of disobedience had separated us"?

Let us take up, therefore, after our holy Father, the "strong, bright weapons of obedience" and, advancing by the narrow and hard way, let

---

[1]   Abbé Gaucheron, Obl.O.S.B., "Une Retraite Bénédictine," in *Bulletin de S. Martin et de S. Benoît*, 1928, p. 601.

us do battle with a joyous docility under Christ our true Lord and our true King.

January 23—May 24—September 23

But this very obedience will be acceptable to God and pleasing to men only if what is commanded is done without hesitation, delay, lukewarmness, grumbling, or objection. For the obedience given to Superiors is given to God, since He Himself has said, "He who hears you, hears Me" (*Luke* 10:16). And the disciples should offer their obedience with a good will, for "God loves a cheerful giver" (*2 Corinthians* 9:7). For if the disciple obeys with an ill will and murmurs, not necessarily with his lips but simply in his heart, then even though he fulfil the command yet his work will not be acceptable to God, who sees that his heart is murmuring. And, far from gaining a reward for such work as this, he will incur the punishment due to murmurers, unless he amend and make satisfaction.

COMMENTARY

Throughout the latter part of this chapter St. Benedict insists on the interior qualities of obedience, qualities which render it "acceptable to God and pleasing to men."

God penetrates to the very depth of consciences: He knows the last recess of them. If a Superior can be satisfied, for the maintenance of discipline, that his subordinates give proof of outward obedience, it is not the same with God. It is with all that we are, body and soul, that we must respond to His wishes. There is no other means of rendering our obedience "acceptable" in His eyes. Moreover, coming from the inmost soul, the obedience will have for others nothing forced, nothing ill-natured—and the one who obeys will experience a certain satisfaction, full of sweetness. Dom Delatte observes in this respect that St. Benedict's spirituality is here "far removed from some modern conceptions, where, on pretext of seeing only God and referring all to Him, it is alleged that pleasure should not intervene in questions of duty, and that we degrade our obedience if we seek in it a personal joy, and a fortiori doubtless if we seek the pleasure of others."[2] Is not the end of all life happiness? And why should it be forbidden to try to please those whom we obey, when this facilitates their heavy task?

St. Benedict indicates, with a perfect gradation, what obedience ought

---

[2] *Commentary*, p. 89.

not to be, if we want it to be "acceptable to God and pleasing to men." We must obey, he says, *non trepide*, that is to say, without hesitation or fear; non tar do, without any delay; *non tepide*, without lukewarmness; *aut cum murmure*, without murmur; by a much stronger reason, without protest, vel *cum responsione nolentis*.

Among these different forms of imperfect obedience, our holy Father censures murmuring above all, undoubtedly because it constitutes a more frequent temptation. Murmuring is like the pin-prick which expels instantaneously the air that was inflating a balloon. Murmuring, says St. Benedict, destroys all the merit of obedience, and he obtains no grace who lets himself be led into it. And hence murmuring is more serious in itself than the more or less disagreeable things, whatever they be, that have provoked it. Moreover, if the murmuring is done openly, the guilty one incurs "the penalty of murmurers" unless he make amends by a "satisfaction." The penalty of murmurers is explained to us in Chapter 23; it is first a secret admonition, then admonition by the elders, then public censure, and finally excommunication or corporal punishment, as the case may be. But the monk who catches himself murmuring can avoid all that by imposing on himself one of those voluntary "satisfactions" provided in the monastic code.

But St. Benedict does not content himself with telling us what obedience considered in the depths of the soul ought not to be. He indicates also its essential quality: joy. "God loves a cheerful giver," he says with St. Paul. This joy will be facilitated by that view of faith on which our holy Father does not tire of insisting: "The obedience which one renders to Superiors is being shown to God." And God is not satisfied with gestures and attitudes. He "looks on the heart of him who murmurs" and the heart "of him who gives joyfully." And to the joy of him who gives responds that of Him who receives; for if there is joy in heaven over a sinner who returns to obedience, there is joy also for him who by a continual renouncement makes of his whole self a sacrifice more meritorious than any other gift.

APPLICATION

We shall profit from meditating these lines of St. Benedict. Every word here is important, and marks for us our line of conduct. Here again we should take everything literally.

It is thus that we shall show our separation from the world in its most profound aspect. The fact is that the world, especially the world of today, is thirsty for liberty: liberty to think anything at all, liberty to act according to one's fancy, liberty to make one's own law for oneself. Each individual becomes his own end and thinks that he has no other goal here below than to "express himself," that is to say, to satisfy all his desires, all his aspirations, good or bad, all his instincts, even the basest.

As for the Christian (and a fortiori the monk and the Oblate), the baptized Christian knows that he is created not for himself but for God. He grasps the whole worth of his *Pater: Fiat voluntas tua*—Your will be done! He does not seek himself, he does not admire himself, he does not adore himself; he renounces himself. When, in the depths of his soul, he has detached himself from all the fleeting things of earth, those *mundanas varietates* mentioned in one of the Collects,[3] he knows that a heavy task still remains for him, to become detached from himself. Enlightened by faith, his gaze is fixed as it were on the "deifying light" mentioned in the Prologue, that light which so to speak penetrates all things. He grasps the whole of God, and he lives from then on with only one desire: to do the divine will, to obey.

And after all it is he, the obedient one, it is he, the loving slave of the Lord, who is really free. The other, by seeking the satisfaction of all his passions, is forging strong chains which will drag him down and will not make him happy. And if he some day wishes to disengage himself, this will not be done without painful efforts. But he who has freed himself from every created thing and from himself can truly say: Nothing holds me, nothing detains me; I belong to God. No one is freer than a Saint. May we, by our docility to the counsels of our holy Father, approach more and more that perfect state in which one no longer has any other desire than to do the will of the Beloved, in whatever way that will may manifest itself.

---

[3] Mass of the 4th Sunday after Easter.

CHAPTER 6
On the Spirit of Silence

January 24—May 25—September 24

 ET US do what the Prophet says: "I said, 'I will guard my ways, that I may not sin with my tongue. I have set a guard to my mouth.' I was mute and was humbled, and kept silence even from good things" (*Psalm* 38:2-3). Here the Prophet shows that if the spirit of silence ought to lead us at times to refrain even from good speech, so much the more ought the punishment for sin make us avoid evil words.

Therefore, since the spirit of silence is so important, permission to speak should rarely be granted even to perfect disciples, even though it be for good, holy, edifying conversation; for it is written, "In much speaking you will not escape sin" (*Proverbs* 10:19), and in another place, "Death and life are in the power of the tongue" (*Proverbs* 18:21).

For speaking and teaching belong to the master; the disciple's part is to be silent and to listen. And for that reason if anything has to be asked of the Superior, it should be asked with all the humility and submission inspired by reverence.

But as for coarse jests and idle words or words that move to laughter, these we condemn everywhere with a perpetual ban, and for such conversation we do not permit a disciple to open his mouth.

COMMENTARY

The word *taciturnitas*, which occurs in the Latin title and text of this chapter and indicates the subject of it, has been diversely rendered, since it is not equivalent to the modern word "taciturnity." Many commentators, notably the Cistercians, translate it simply by "silence." In point of fact *taciturnitas* signifies not so much silence itself as a certain reserve or discretion in speech resulting from the love of silence. Thus Dom L'Huillier translates "On the Habit of Silence" (*De l'habitude du silence*) and Dom Delatte, "On the Spirit of Silence" (*De l'esprit de silence*). The Farnborough translators, literal-minded, kept the word "taciturnity" (*taciturnite*), even though it has an unfavorable connotation; but they took care to explain the meaning of it.

St. Benedict begins his lesson on the spirit of silence according to his custom by invoking a text from Scripture, in which is described the reserved attitude of the just man under oppression; but he gives it a general import: "I said, 'I will observe my ways, that I may not sin with my tongue. I have set a guard to my mouth.' I became dumb; I humbled myself and kept silence, even upon good things."

Does St. Benedict want his disciples to take this text literally and become "dumb" by the practice of a perpetual silence? The Holy Rule itself seems to answer in the negative. It foresees good and useful conversations, suitable and- unsuitable hours, times when silence is imposed more than at other times. More than once it forbids "buffoonery," which it would not have to do if the monks were condemned to a perpetual silence.

The monastic tradition may have varied concerning the length and the frequency of conversations among the monks. It seems certain that the tradition always admitted them.[1] Even at Cîteaux, where a rigorous silence was observed, provision was made from time to time for spiritual colloquies which had somewhat the character of a recreation.[2] In the 17th century the reformed Cistercians did not exclude recreations, and the Abbé de Rancé was the only one to forbid them absolutely. The numerous texts which he cites in his book On the Sanctity and the Duties of the Monastic Life[3] and in his commentary on the Holy Rule[4] do not seem to prove his point except by being detached from their contexts; for the passages of the Fathers from which they are borrowed were addressed to a hearer who was not vowed to a silence as rigorous as that desired by the austere reformer. He himself tells us with regard to St. Bernard and the first Cistercians "that they had such great zeal for this so holy regularity and judged it so important that they instituted signs in order to be able to express the necessary things and to deny themselves speech entirely."[5] If the use of signs seemed indispensable to replace speech, can it be admitted that absolute silence could have been observed throughout so many centuries without the use of signs? Is it true that traces of the use of signs are found in St. Pachomius, but that is only by way of exception,[6] and they

---

[1] Dom Jean Martial Besse, *Les Moines d'*Orient, pp. 489-495.

[2] Dom Paul Delatte, *Commentary*, p. 93.

[3] *De la Sainteté et des Devoirs de la Vie Monastique* (Paris, 1683), Tome 2, pp. 122ff.

[4] *La Règle de S. Benoist Nouvellement Traduite et Expliquee* selon Son Veritable Esprit (Paris, 1703), Tome 1, p. 432.

[5] *De la Sainteté* etc., pp. 133-134.

[6] Dom Jean Martial Besse, *Les Moines d'Orient*, p. 494.

were unknown elsewhere. It must have been, therefore, that the measure of speech was certainly more extended than the Abbé de Rancé would have it.

What appears certain is that at the time of St. Benedict and for long centuries after him there were no recreation periods properly so called. But the monks at that time, devoted for the most part to agricultural labors, found themselves less isolated than the monks since then consecrated to study; and hence the necessity of "spacements" (*spaciements*), as the Carthusians say, made itself much less felt.

In what circumstances and in what measure could one break the silence at the time of the holy Patriarch? It would not be easy to determine that. "I like to picture our holy Father," says a commentator,[7] "on certain days surrounded with his children and conversing familiarly with them. Could recreation periods of that sort, taken in common around the Abbot, be contrary to the mind of the holy Lawmaker? The soul relies on them in order to operate better, the silence on this account is only the more faithfully observed the rest of the time, and the monastic duties better fulfilled. It is thus that our very relaxations can and should converge towards God."

St. Benedict recommends vigilance over oneself "in order to abstain from bad speech," which will be chastised by God, as will every sin. But that is not enough. He desires that one go still further and that, according to the word of the Psalmist which he has just cited, one even forbid oneself sometimes (interdum) good discourses.

That very one who would permit himself nothing but edifying discourse, listening only to his own incessant need of talking, would certainly be exposing himself to great dangers. "In abundance of speech," says the Scripture, "you will not escape danger." The danger here is a certain inner dissipation inseparable from babbling, whatever be the object of it. It is also, and above all, vanity and pride. "For those," says Dom Laure, "who talk easily and much about the things of God, there exists a tendency to believe themselves virtuous and holy."[8]

The Abbé de Rancé said on this subject, with a great deal of truth, "Even pious people often treat the affairs of God in a manner entirely

---

[7] Dom Bernard Laure, *Règle du Patriarche Saint Benoît, Texte, Traduction, Commentaire* (Chambéry: Librairie Dardel, 1925), pp. 100-101.

[8] Ibid. p. 98.

human; they begin well enough by the movement of the Holy Spirit, but they continue and finish by the movements of nature. They seek themselves in these divine matters: they want to be listened to, they want to be applauded, they want their own opinions to prevail; and there is nothing more commonplace than to see pious colloquies become contests or degenerate into useless, vain and curious conversations."[9]

And so St. Benedict desires that these pious colloquies be rare: *Rara loquendi concedatur licentia.*

The concern here is evidently with somewhat prolonged colloquies. Thus has the monastic tradition always understood it. Dom L'Huillier reports in this regard that at Cluny the spiritual colloquies took place in small parlors adjoining the cloister, and that St. Bernard was edified by the conferences he had there with various religious.[10] The juniors would listen to the elders, who had a long experience of the things of God. "To be silent and to listen becomes the disciple," declares St. Benedict. But it would sometimes be necessary for them to ask questions. They would address themselves to their Superior (*priore*, taken here in a broad meaning) with "all the humility and submission of respect."

There is one excess which St. Benedict forbids absolutely, not only in the spiritual conferences but in every place: "buffooneries and idle words and words leading to laughter." On this point our holy Father is categorical. "We condemn them forever," he says, "and in every place, and we do not permit the disciple to open his mouth for discourses of that kind." The word "disciple" could indicate here, as above, that the concern is with spiritual colloquies; but the expressions "in every place" and "forever," word for word "with an eternal cloture," show well that the prohibition has a general import. It is in this last sense that St. Benedict had already spoken of the ban in the 54th and 55th instruments of good works.

But the presence of these expressions also lets us infer that outside of the colloquies mentioned there were other circumstances in which one might be exposed to yielding to this caprice, and consequently other circumstances in which one might speak. What good would it do to aim

---

[9] *De la Sainteté* etc.. Tome 2, p. 126. The passage is reproduced almost literally in the *Règle de S. Benoist Nouvellement Traduile el Expliquée*, Tome 1, p. 435.

[10] *Explication Ascetique et Historique*, Tome 1, p. 490.

at cases which were not going to a rise? The necessities of work and of the communal life made certain conversations indispensable. St. Benedict did not want those occasions of talking to give rise to dissipation.

The monastic Constitutions have regulated diversely the conditions of the silence. Today in the French Congregation, outside of the recreation periods twice a day, five minutes are allowed for the exchange of useful information, and an absolute silence is prescribed in Church and refectory, even outside the time of the conventual exercises. Besides, the "great silence" is to reign from Compline to the end of the Office of Prime. But in the spiritual conversations as in the others, "the spirit of silence" ought not to be absent. It is this spirit which prevents the soul from dissipating itself and maintains it in that interior peace which is an essential condition of the spiritual life.

APPLICATION

The principles which inspired in St. Benedict the chapter *De Taciturnitate* are of a general order and are of value for every Christian who, like the Oblate, aspires to perfection. The Holy Scripture long ago reminded us of the mischief of the tongue. "Death and life," say the Proverbs, "are in the power of the tongue." The good deeds and the misdeeds of speech have become a commonplace.

The rule of the ancient monastic congregation of Grandmont characterized perfectly the kind of taciturnity which is imposed on us. "There is a kind of silence," it says, "which consists in keeping still about what is useless and saying what is necessary."[11]

We need not dwell on the necessity of "abstaining from bad speech." That is quite evident.

But it might be profitable to dwell on the subject of vain and useless speech. There are Christians who spend a great part of their time in distractions, notably in purely mundane visits in which, if their neighbor is not hurt (which is very rare), they at least become worked up over an incalculable number of futilities. They are anxious to keep in the current of the latest news, of the latest fashion, of the latest opinion. How much poor food is crammed into the minds of certain self-styled pious people, and sometimes even of certain clergymen!

For our part, let us not forget that we have broken with the spirit of the

---

[11] Chapter 67, quoted by Dom Martène *De Antiquis Monachorum Ritibus*, col. 894.

world, and let us disencumber our life of so many things which dissipate it. That is difficult? But who forced us, then, to undertake those engagements which we would now consider ourselves unable to keep? We must belong to Jesus Christ or to the world. The Lord Himself admits no partition.

Besides, the supposition of frivolous conversations in which charity is not frequently injured is purely hypothetical. "Alas," says Dom Delatte, "how little remains of certain habitual conversations when all unkind criticism has been subtracted!"[12]

In that which concerns "scurrilities" and "buffoonery" we should evidently follow to the letter the prescription of our holy Father. A certain gaiety is quite natural among Christians. "There is wisdom," says Dom Delatte, "in avoiding the prudery which is shocked and scandalized by everything.... Still it remains true that there are certain subjects, a certain coarseness, a certain worldly tone, which should never enter our conversation. . . . There are matters which one should not touch, which it is wholesome to avoid. Our own delicacy of feeling and the thought of Our Lord will save us from all imprudence."[13]

Shall we fall back on pious conversations? It is natural that people who have the same tastes, the same ideal, the same love of God and of souls, should visit one another for their mutual encouragement and edification. Being outside of the cloister, they need to be reminded of their strength in numbers, to feel supported, to console and edify one another.

It was with this purpose, for example, that the Ecclesiastical Conferences were instituted and propagated, especially in the country districts of Normandy, by that admirable priest who was also to be one day a son of St. Benedict, Dom Dominique George, Abbot of Val-Richer. It is with this purpose that pious persons like to meet with one another.

But here again, let us not exaggerate. Let us not deceive ourselves. Let not the need of talking furnish a pretext for conversations which have only the appearance of piety. The danger of vanity lies in wait for us. God is perhaps on the lips, but perhaps He is also far from the heart.

What do we talk about mostly? In reality is it not too often ourselves, our own experiences, our own profound thoughts, our own advancement in prayer, our own progress in sanctity, and so forth—things which should

---

[12] *Commentary, p. 95.*

[13] *Ibid.*, p. 97.

ordinarily be reserved for conferences with the director of conscience? In all that showing off, what becomes of true love for the Lord? The Pharisees of the Gospel made show of an ostentatious zeal for the Law, but Mary listened in silence at the feet of Christ.

Let us make no mistake: *taciturnitas* is as necessary for us as for our brethren of the cloister. Outside of the necessities of our situation, then, let us love retirement. We wish to seek God; there only shall we find Him.

The love of silence ought to follow us even into necessary conversations. This it is that will give us authority over our tongue, stop in time a too hasty suggestion, a word inspired by the need to make ourselves prevail, and so forth. It will furnish us the occasion of mortifications which will bring merit and of which God will be the only witness.

Dom Delatte observes with respect to this chapter that if "the silence of words" has its importance, there exists another kind more important still: interior silence. The first, moreover, is valuable only by the fact that it assures the second.

"Some souls," he says, "do not care for external noise, nor take to endless conversations, and yet they are never in a state of silence. For behind the dumb lips there is a continuous hubbub of interior talk, in exact proportion to their unmortified passions. When Our Lord wished to declare the happiness and simplicity of contemplation, He said to Martha: 'Martha, Martha, thou art anxious and troubled about many things.' Is not this the reproach that He most often has need to address to us? Have we ever tried to review rapidly the infinite variety of objects and pictures which have just occupied the field of our interior vision? Memories, grudges, projects, regrets, vain quests, angry emotions, vexations, scruples—how many winds and waves buffet this world of our secret life!. . . Our soul becomes an entrance hall, a cinematograph, a phonograph, a kaleidoscope."[14]

And how much food this interior babble can find around us, if we are not on guard! There are the newspapers, the magazines, the novels, the radio, and so on. Sometimes a very strong resolution is necessary to close one's soul to all those ways of dissipation and maintain in it a silence in which God will speak.

Let us be well reminded that the Lord does not come in the tumult and

---

[14] *Ibid.*, pp. 98-99.

the flood of words, and nevertheless that our life must truly belong to Him.

"One never finds God in the trouble and the tumult of the world," said the Spiritual Exercises[15] in use by the Congregation of Saint-Maur; "He is alone; one must be alone to find Him. If a wise man is obliged by necessity to attend to external affairs, he does not go out of himself for that purpose; his soul is in an interior retreat, as in its center, where he conserves peace and tranquillity in the midst of the tumult." But to this tumult he does not resign himself except through necessity, and he hastens to return to his silence.

If we are anxious, therefore, to prove ourselves true disciples of St. Benedict, let us know how to renounce by the spirit of silence many useless and distracting things, many habits which are nothing but worldly, and finally many vanities. Without that renouncement we shall never advance.

---

[15] *Exercices Spirituels Tirés de la Règle de S. Benoist pour en Faciliter la Pratique à Ceux Qui Désirent Vivre selon d'Esprit de Cette Même Règle* (Paris: Vincent, 1755), p. 328.

CHAPTER 7

On Humility

January 25—May 26—September 25

OLY SCRIPTURE, brethren, cries out to us, saying, "Everyone who exalts himself shall be humbled, and he who humbles himself shall be exalted" (*Luke* 14:11). In saying this it shows us that all exaltation is a kind of pride, against which the Prophet proves himself to be on guard when he says, "Lord, my heart is not exalted, nor are mine eyes lifted up; neither have I walked in great matters, nor in wonders above me." But how has he acted? "Rather have I been of humble mind than exalting myself; as a weaned child on its mother's breast, so You solace my soul" (*Psalm* 130:1-2).

Hence, brethren, if we wish to reach the very highest point of humility and to arrive speedily at that heavenly exaltation to which ascent is made through the humility of this present life, we must by our ascending actions erect the ladder Jacob saw in his dream, on which Angels appeared to him descending and ascending. By that descent and ascent we must surely understand nothing else than this, that we descend by self-exaltation and ascend by humility. And the ladder thus set up is our life in the world, which the Lord raises up to heaven if our heart is humbled. For we call our body and soul the sides of the ladder, and into these sides our divine vocation has inserted the different steps of humility and discipline we must climb.

COMMENTARY

The resemblance of this introduction with certain parts of the Prologue has long since been noticed. In this place as in the other the tone is grave and solemn. We feel that our holy Father is going to speak to us of something particularly important. The Scriptural saying of which the whole chapter will be the commentary is introduced by a formula more expressive than those ordinarily employed: "Holy Scripture cries out to us, brethren. ... And this cry is the word of Jesus: Whoever exalts himself shall be humbled, and he who humbles himself shall be exalted!

In a few words St. Benedict explains the sacred text: Our Lord opposes the words "to exalt oneself" and "to humble oneself"; every "exaltation," therefore, is opposed to humility: "every exaltation is a kind of pride."

Here we are to understand the word "pride" in its broadest acceptation: exaltation of thoughts, of desires, of words and of acts. In support of this acceptation St. Benedict invokes Psalm 130, verse 1. "Lord," says the Psalmist, "my heart is not exalted"; that applies to the thoughts, for the Hebrews consider thoughts as coming from the heart. "Mine eyes are not lifted up"; that applies to the desires. "I have not walked in great things, nor in wonders above me"; that applies to the acts. And the quotation which follows[1] shows us the punishment of the proud one, of him "who is not humbly minded but exalts his soul." As long as he was humble and had the simplicity of a little child, did not God look upon him as a mother looks on her child? Did He not nourish him with the milk of His favors? But here he is, exalting himself, attributing merits to himself, where he should be ascribing all to the "maternal" goodness of his God. And God rejects him from His bosom. He abandons him to his misery, "as a child weaned from his mother."

According to the teaching of the Psalmist, therefore, completed by our Savior, we must practice humility. And here it is not a question of just any sort of humility, tempered by self-concern. No, it is a question of "reaching the summit of the highest humility." In the practice of bodily mortifications our holy Father will show the greatest discretion. We have seen this and we shall see it again. But in the practice of interior detachment he admits of no mitigation, no attenuation. He wants us to "aspire to the highest." And when we have set this ideal for ourselves, it will be no longer a question of dragging ourselves toward it, as do certain souls who are eager to envision sublime goals for themselves but who, after the first enthusiasm, let down in their efforts to attain the goals. The end being decided, we must "arrive at it promptly." And St. Benedict is going to indicate the course for us to follow.

This course consists in climbing the different steps or degrees of humility. Our holy Father enters into the matter by means of a parable, for which he borrows the figure from the Book of Genesis (28:12). Jacob during his sleep saw a mysterious ladder, resting on earth and reaching up

---

[1] Translator's note: The commentary to the end of the paragraph is based on a literal understanding of the Vulgate of Psalm 130:2, "If I have not been humbly-minded but have lifted up my soul; as a child that is weaned upon its mother's breast, so let my reward be in my soul." The translation given above in the daily reading, on the other hand, considers the *si non* as a hebraism which is not to be translated literally, and compares the soul to a child already weaned and content.

to heaven; on its steps Angels ascended and descended. No doubt in the mind of the inspired author the Angels are the messengers of Providence, who transmit God's gifts to us and carry back our prayers and our merits to Him. St. Benedict certainly understood it thus; but the parallel between the "steps of the ladder" and the "steps of humility" prompted him to take the different elements of the vision in an accommodated sense and to apply them to his subject. The Angels who mount from earth towards God symbolize the humble, for whom humility is the point of departure of a "heavenly exaltation"; the Angels who descend from heaven to here below are the symbol of the proud whose exaltation makes them abandon God and fall back into their baseness. And the figure is truly beautiful. Dom Maréchaux observes:[2] "He whose eyes would be open to the spectacle of the world of souls would see there a continual movement of elevation or descent which involves all the souls in opposite ways, without any of them being able to escape it: either to be lifted up through humility or to descend through pride, such is the ineluctable necessity of this life of trial."

The ground on which the ladder rests, continues St. Benedict, is "our life in the world." And, he notes, it is the Lord Himself who raises it towards heaven. Is not the Lord with His grace at the origin of every good work? Does not that grace precede and sustain us during our journey?

"The two sides of the ladder," says St. Benedict again, "are our body and our soul." In what follows, our holy Father will show us how the body and the soul, giving each other mutual aid, contribute to the progress of humility. As to the steps, they of course are the very steps of humility. And it is the divine call which invites us to climb them.

The figure of the ladder to symbolize the progressive development of perfection is classic with the ancients. It is found in the Passion of Saints Perpetua and Felicity, in a homily of St. Basil on Psalm 1, in Cassiodorus and others. Who does not know at least by name the Holy Ladder of St. John Climacus? Here St. Benedict appears to have borrowed his comparison from St. Jerome. It is remarkable that Cassian, whose chapter on humility visibly inspired St. Benedict, was not acquainted with it.[3]

On the ladder of humility St. Benedict will count twelve steps. Why

---

[2] *S. Benoît, Sa Vie, Sa Règle, Sa Doctrine Spirituelle*, p. 144.

[3] Dom Cuthbert Butler, *Sancti Benedicli Regula Monasteriorum*, 3rd ed. (Fribourg: Herder and Co., 1935), pp. 29-41.

twelve? Many commentators have striven to demonstrate the propriety of this number. It is more likely that it was chosen because it is a sacred number, that of the Apostles and that of the articles of the Creed. To discourse on its legitimacy would certainly be futile. St. Benedict held to it only as a means of aiding the memory; and, as Dom Mège remarked, after St. Bernard, "the idea is rather to climb the degrees of humility than to count them."

Did St. Benedict arrange his degrees in the manner to be followed as successive steps in the progress toward perfection? That is hardly probable. We shall see that there is indeed a certain logical connection among the degrees, but their succession is not comparable, for example, to that of the different mansions of St. Teresa's Interior Castle. We would not have to think, therefore, that according to our holy Father it is necessary to have passed one of the steps in order to get to the following one. We shall try all together, or at least several at a time, and the progress in each of them will vary with the variety of souls.

APPLICATION

"The present chapter of the Rule," says Dom L'Huillier, "has always been held in particular esteem in our Order, and it is easy to see at the first glance that the holy Patriarch himself attaches a very special importance to it." Dom Delatte says that it "is justly regarded as the finished expression of monastic spirituality."[4] And those who have written for the Oblates have always recommended particularly the meditation of this chapter.

What our holy Father desires is that his children be detached from the world and from themselves; and it is only when we have taken cognizance of the All of God and of our own nothingness that we grasp the logic of humility. St. Bernard defined it as "the virtue by which a man, knowing himself in all truth, becomes vile in his own eyes." Humility is truth, just as pride is illusion. But would not the feeling of our nothingness be vain indeed if it had not the effect of throwing us into the arms of God, to abandon ourselves to Him with the trust of a little child? The childlike spirit so much recommended by the Gospel and recalled in our days by St. Thérèse of the Child Jesus, this childlike spirit is inseparable from humility. Our holy Father reminds us of it by showing us, with the

---

[4] Commentary, p. 104.

Psalmist, that the punishment of the proud one is to be put away from the bosom of his God "like the child weaned from its mother."

As may have been noticed, St. Benedict makes humility a condition of salvation. He "brings back to humility the whole development of the interior life; in it all the virtues take constancy and vigor; if they are not steeped in humility, they wither and die."[5] It is by "it alone that we shall arrive at the heavenly exaltation" which is nothing else but the eternal possession of God.

Dom Bernard Maréchaux, in his excellent book on St. Benedict, treating especially of the degrees of humility, explains that with some distinctions St. Benedict's ladder can be proposed to all Christians. "All," he says, "will find very sure and admirably sketched landmarks for their ascent to God in St. Benedict's degrees of humility."[6] He had previously said, "There are Christians in the world who realize this ideal and who join the most exemplary religious at the summit of the perfect life: the tailor of Alexandria was as good as St. Anthony."

If that is true for all Christians, so much the more should it be so for the Oblate who has taken his place among the children and disciples of St. Benedict. It is up to us, therefore, to strive, following our holy Father and so many Saints of our Order, to arrive "promptly... at the very highest point of humility." In fact, is not this what we undertook in promising "the reformation of our life"? How could we accomplish that reformation without humility? And consequently, how could we save ourselves without it?

January 26—May 27—September 26
The first degree of humility, then, is that a person keep the fear of God before his eyes and beware of ever forgetting it. Let him be ever mindful of all that God has commanded; let his thoughts constantly recur to the hell-fire which will burn for their sins those who despise God, and to the life everlasting which is prepared for those who fear Him. Let him keep himself at every moment from sins and vices, whether of the mind, the tongue, the hands, the feet, or the self-will, and check also the desires of the flesh.

---

[5] Dom Bernard Maréchaux, S. Benoît, Sa Vie, Sa Règle , Sa Doctrine Spirituelle, p. 204.

[6] Ibid., p. 201.

COMMENTARY

The first degree of humility consists "in fleeing forgetfulness entirely." We know in theory the great truths of the faith. We know that God is our Creator and that He has created us only for Himself. We know that we are saved by the sufferings and death of Christ and regenerated by Baptism. We know that God watches over us, promises us heaven if we are good, and hell if we are sinful. We know all that—but do we really live by it?

St. Benedict wants his disciple not to yield to the lying illusions of the world, but to place himself resolutely in face of the sole reality: God. And let it be noted well, it will not suffice to divide up one's life in distinct compartments and feel intermittently, under the prompting of certain sentimental manifestations, the impression of the presence of God, His grandeur or His bounty. The concern is truly with our whole life, and it is really hour by hour that it must go on in an atmosphere of truth.

God is, and we live in Him; God invites us or threatens us; God draws us to Himself and loves us; that is what we must never forget. St. Benedict had already told us this in his Prologue. In fact, for him it is a thing so essential that he does not tire of coming back to it. Had not he himself, after all, experienced that perpetual presence and its beneficial effects in the cave of Subiaco when "alone with himself, he dwelt under the eyes of Him who sees us always"?

We will live, therefore, under the eyes of God. We will recall continually and with our whole spirit of faith that we are at His service and that He has placed us here below only to execute His wishes. And this contemplation of an infinite God unceasingly present will logically inspire us with fear. We walk, alas, in the midst of so many dangers! Do not temptations arise from everywhere? Sins "of the thoughts, of the tongue, of the hands, of the feet, of one's own will, desires of the flesh." Here are the multiple obstacles which will surely be encountered at every moment on our path. To think "at every hour" that God is there, that He detests those sins, that He judges them severely at the very moment when we are committing them and that He punishes them with eternal hell-fire, that if we are courageous we shall enter into happiness without end—such should be our ordinary attitude of soul. Is there anything, in fact, better suited to maintain us in humility?

APPLICATION

It is hardly necessary in most of these pages to dwell on the application; it imposes itself.

St. Benedict, then, puts the fear of God at the basis of humility, and humility at the basis of all spiritual life. But to be real and efficacious, this fear must depend upon a feeling of the divine presence as continual as the weakness of our spirit may allow. The Saints lived in this beneficent thought. *Vivit Dominus in cujus conspectu sto.*[7] And thus they established themselves in full reality. The worldly people who think but rarely of God live, on the contrary, in illusion.

But because the realities of faith are invisible and the illusions of this world fall under our senses, an effort is necessary, especially in the beginning, to get the right focus. And for us who are obliged most of the time to remain in the milieu of the world, that effort must sometimes be considerable. But it is absolutely necessary. Otherwise we are letting ourselves be distracted from the work of God and we are no longer in our vocation as Oblates.

Let us bear in mind that our life, to be really what St. Benedict wants, must be a life of true separation from the world. If we frequent the world, if we willingly take part in its feasts and its pleasures, it will be hard for us indeed not to leave it a portion of our heart. And how, under that condition, could we try to climb even the first step of humility?

Let us see things, then, as they are. God is there. He wants to be our one Master. He wants to be our All. His presence in no way depends on our thought. It is. *In quo vidimus, movemur et sumus.*[8] Let us rather ask without cease for the increase of this faith. *Credo, Domine, adjuva incredulitatem meam.*[9] Let us break resolutely with the world which can inspire us only with pride and exaltation of mind. God wants it thus. We have no right to resist Him. Let us tell ourselves truly that pleasures here below are always accompanied with bitterness and regret because they are vain and ephemeral while God alone is great and eternal. It is only the fear of God that can fill us with a sweet confidence, because in making us feel our weakness it shows us at the same time that weakness lovingly sustained by the infinitely Strong One.

January 27—May 28—September 27

---

[7] "The Lord lives, in whose sight I stand."

[8] "In whom we live and move and have our being."

[9] "I believe, Lord; help my unbelief."

Let a man consider that God is always looking at him from heaven, that his actions are everywhere visible to the divine eyes and are constantly being reported to God by the Angels. This is what the Prophet shows us when he represents God as ever present within our thoughts, in the words "Searcher of minds and hearts is God" (*Psalm* 7:10) and again in the words "The Lord knows the thoughts of men" (*Psalm* 93:11). Again he says, "You have read my thoughts from afar" (*Psalm* 138:3) and "The thoughts of men will confess to You" (*Psalm* 75:11).

In order that he may be careful about his wrongful thoughts, therefore, let the faithful brother say constantly in his heart, "Then shall I be spotless before Him, if I have kept myself from my iniquity" (*Psalm* 17:24).

COMMENTARY

The received text of the Holy Rule begins here with these words: "Let a man consider that God sees him from the heights of heaven continually and at every hour." Certain manuscripts have a different punctuation, and begin this sentence with the last words of the preceding one, which they read a little differently: "And in the desires of the flesh let a man consider etc.," so that the thought of God's presence would be particularly recommended to us in the temptations arising from those desires. The truth is, as Dom Delatte points out, that the word "flesh" is to be understood here in a broad meaning; it signifies "man in continual conflict with that Spirit which realizes our divine sonship by its influence and its presence."[10] So that the change in punctuation does not greatly modify the general meaning of the sentence.

God is therefore present to us. But this God is not an impersonal being and a sort of unconscious mirror in which would be reflected all that is. Nor again is He the God who evolves and makes Himself, so fashionable among certain modern philosophers. He is a personal God, and His presence is an active presence. He is looking at us. He is looking at us every hour and in every place, and not one of our acts escapes Him.

He looks at us, says St. Benedict, *de caelis*, from heaven. Heaven is where He manifests His glory to His Angels and Saints. He does not leave His heaven in order to penetrate into each soul. In Him all is infinite. He is everywhere, He sees everywhere, He acts everywhere. "He is the place of souls," said Bossuet, "as space is the place of bodies." Thus does His

---

[10] *Commentary*, p. 107.

light penetrate even to the most secret recesses of our heart. We are never alone. He is the perpetual witness.

And not only does God see us, but His Angels see us also. And they report our actions to Him at every hour. The blessed Spirits are God's friends and our protectors. They see us at the very time when they are contemplating God. Our virtues make them joyful and our sins displease them. And that joy and that reprobation correspond, in the intimate and profound communion of heaven, to the divine joy and reprobation. God sees as it were a reflection of our virtues and our weaknesses in the faces of His Angels. He acts in concert with them; He associates them to His Providence; and there are mysterious goings and comings by them between Him and His children of earth. It seems certain that in writing these words our holy Father turned his thoughts anew to Jacob's vision, but this time to understand it in its obvious sense.

The Holy Writ is full of this thought of the divine presence. Thus St. Benedict had no trouble in gathering some particularly expressive texts: "God searches minds and hearts. . . . The Lord knows the thoughts of men," etc. But does not such an active and perpetual presence imply a consequence for us? That consequence is watchfulness. Watchfulness over our deeds, to be sure, but above all, over that inmost source of our deeds which our thoughts are. St. Benedict always leads us back within ourselves, to the place where desires, resolutions, passions of every sort are born. It is there especially, it seems, that the eye of God penetrates, it is there "that He sees thoughts begin in the secret agitation of the heart, even before they are formed."[11] We know too well, alas, what a depth of wretchedness exists in us. How we ought to keep ourselves on guard!

In speaking of vigilance St. Benedict, according to the received text, designates his disciple under the name of *frater humilis*, the humble brother. It has been noted that all the manuscripts and the most ancient commentaries read *frater utilis*, the "useful brother." The Farnborough translators[12] explain that the "useful brother" is not here a brother who "renders services"; "he is a brother whose ascetic efforts serve for something, that is to say, they bring himself spiritual profit and advantages." The useful brother will say always in his heart, "I shall be

---

[11] Dom Bernard Maréchaux, *S. Benoît, Sa Vie, Sa Règle, Sa Doctrine Spirituelle*, p. 148.

[12] *La Règle de S. Benoît*, p. 243.

without spot before God if I keep myself from my iniquity." He expresses thus the consequence of a faith living in the divine presence; to keep ourselves "without spot."

APPLICATION

We will live, then, as much as we can, in the presence of God. What St. Benedict recommends in order for us to attain this end is what he himself first practiced: an assiduous exercise of that divine presence. To think of it only on occasion would be ineffective indeed. We must train ourselves to this continuity of thought so that it becomes habitual to us. "The memory and the habitual practice of the presence of God," says a commentator,[13] "by impregnating the soul with a filial fear, contributes very effectively to the valuable result of an immaculate life. That is why, in treating of the ways which lead to sanctity, the ascetical authors recommend particularly this salutary practice."

In fact, it will be the more salutary in the measure in which we represent to ourselves our heavenly Father in a more concrete and living fashion, with His justice and His love, with the kind attentions of His grace and the pursuits of His mercy. To be sure, we know that all evil will be punished and that our thoughts, those poor vagabond thoughts which escape our memory so quickly, remain forever like witnesses for the prosecution in the divine memory, to be one day expiated according to their malice. And that is something capable indeed of filling us with confusion. But we know also that God is the infinite Love who envelops us so to speak with His paternal tenderness, and that this Love is called the Father and that it is also the incarnate Son, and the life-giving Spirit; and there is something equally capable of filling us with another confusion. The whole spiritual life, according to St. Benedict, ought to move in this fear, which has no servility in it and which blossoms in love, in the love which knows that its divine object is present, and that it seeks this object because it has already found it.

Dom Marmion[14] describes thus the progress of the soul when the practice of the presence of God has created a habit in it: "This habit of the presence of God disposes the soul for the divine visits. It may happen, and to certain souls it happens frequently, that they find a real difficulty in

---

[13] Dom Étienne Salasc, *La Règle de S. Benoît Traduite et Commentée*, p. 243.

[14] *Christ, the Ideal of the Monk*, p. 368.

making their prayer at the hour assigned; weariness, sleepiness, a state of ill health, distractions, hinder, in appearance, all efforts to attain prayer: this is spiritual dryness. Let the soul, however, remain faithful and do what it can to stay near the Lord, even if it is without sensible fervor: *Ut jumentum factus sum apud te, et ego semper tecum.*[15] God will draw near to it at another moment. It can be said of these visits of the Lord what the Scripture declares of His coming at the close of our earthly life: 'You know not at what hour your Lord will come.'[16] If everywhere, in the cell, in the cloister, in the garden, in the refectory, we live recollected in the Divine Presence, Our Lord will come, the Trinity will come, with hands full of light and glory which will possess us to our very depths and have sometimes a considerable repercussion upon our inner life."

The fact is that our God is a very good Father. He loves the humble, and when He sees us in this attitude He attaches Himself to us with more love: *respexit humilitatem.* He speaks to us, He strengthens us, He exalts us even up to Himself: *et exaltavit humiles.*

January 28—May 29—September 28

As for self-will, we are forbidden to do our own will by the Scripture, which says to us, "Turn away from your own will" (*Ecclesiasticus* 18:30), and likewise by the prayer in which we ask God that His will be done in us. And rightly are we taught not to do our own will when we take heed to the warning of Scripture: "There are ways which to men seem right, but the ends of them plunge into the depths of hell" (*Proverbs* 16:25); and also when we tremble at what is said of the careless: "They are corrupt and have become abominable in their wills" (*Psalm* 13:1).

And as for the desires of the flesh, let us believe with the Prophet that God is ever present to us, when he says to the Lord, "Every desire of mine is before You" (*Psalm* 37:10).

COMMENTARY

Our interior activity is composed not only of thoughts, but also of acts of will. Now God is also the witness of our acts of will. We can never tell ourselves often enough that He has created us for Himself, that He is our end, and that with all our strength we ought to tend towards Him. There

---

[15] *Psalm* 72:13: "I have become as a beast of burden before You, but I am ever with You."

[16] *Matthew* 24:42.

should be complete harmony, therefore, between our will and His. It is for that reason that He has made us say the *Fiat voluntas tua,* "Thy will be done." When the harmony does not exist, then we can say that "our thoughts are not God's thoughts" and that the acts of will which they beget are indeed ours and are unhappily wicked. They are that "self- will" which St. Benedict sees and detests, and of which the Scripture has said, "Turn away from your own will."

Each time, therefore, that we conceive a desire, a wish, a resolve, we should control them with the help of all that represents to us the divine will: the Scriptures, our Rule, the duties of our state, the advice of our Superiors and spiritual directors. Failing that, we shall be running many risks.

We say that we will the good; it is possible that we are deceiving ourselves; it is possible that at the source of our projects there are passions hardly conscious: pride, self-love, desire of vainglory, and still others. Perhaps, indeed, we sometimes have a qualm, a doubt; but we try to reassure ourselves with reasonings too prejudiced, with words from the Scriptures whose meaning we force, or with examples from the Saints which we apply badly. On this subject St. Benedict quotes a sentence from the Proverbs that makes us tremble: "There are ways which to men seem right, but the ends of them plunge to the depths of hell." We can delude ourselves, we can fool others. One does not deceive God, who condemns everything that is not in conformity with His holy will.

Besides the proud man, slave of his own will, there is the negligent one who, to be sure, does not seek to deceive himself, but abandons himself to all his caprices, without giving any care for what the Lord wills. It is for him the Scripture speaks when it says, "They are corrupt and have become abominable in their pleasures."[17] "Pleasures" here has the sense of evil desires in general. It seems, nevertheless, to call to St. Benedict's mind a more precise thought and to lead to what follows.

Among our desires are some which are more instinctive and consequently more dangerous, the "desires of the flesh." Is it not in satisfying them that the proud and the negligent often end up? The latter

---

[17] The received text says *voluntatibus suis,* "in their wills." We must read *voluptatibus suis,* "in their pleasures." [Translator's note: According to Dom Benno Linderbauer, however, the meaning of *voluptatibus* here is the same as *voluntatibus.* See his *S. Benedicti Regula Monasteriorum* (Bonn: Peter Hanstein, 1928), p. 28, 1. 46.]

come to this end because they do not resist, and the former because God abandons them. There comes a moment, indeed, when the proud finally recognize that they are in an evil way, but in their opinion it is too late to swim against the stream, they cannot become resigned to reversing themselves, and there they are, like the negligent, adrift.

But St. Benedict is here considering the "desires of the flesh" not only as to these particular cases, but again in a general way. Are they not the temptations of all men? Ah, if those desires, at the very time when they are still no more than temptations, could appear to the eyes of other men, how ashamed we should be of them! And yet "this concupiscence which makes us blush, of which we hide the results, rises from the corrupted soil of our being in the sunlight of the presence of God. Ah, if we thought about that manifestation, how promptly should we repress every evil desire!"[18] Let us think of it indeed by repeating often to God the words of the Prophet, "Every desire of mine is before You."

APPLICATION

The doctrine of St. Benedict has a perfect unity. We find again in connection with humility and at the basis of it what we have found thus far in every chapter: a struggle against "the man of sin" who is in us. In this struggle we must look to the heart, that is to say, to the true source of all activity, to the will. Our holy Father puts us on guard against the illusions of the will.

Let us be well reminded of what we want: to belong to God, and consequently to renounce ourselves. To belong to God is to do God's will. That will manifests itself to us in various ways, of which we have spoken in the chapter on obedience. Let us be docile, therefore, to what God wills. It is in being docile that we become truly strong.

Above all let us beware of pride, sometimes so subtle. Let us ponder what has happened and what still happens to people who pretend to be zealous. They bustle about and are extraordinarily restless. But under all this movement, under all this agitation, under all these very singularities, there is such an enlargement of the ego, of the ego which looks to itself and admires itself, that there no longer remains any place at all for God. Let us recall the frightening quotation invoked by St. Benedict.

In our projects, our resolutions, our ministry, our works of zeal, our

---

[18] Dom Bernard Maréchaux, *S. Benoît, Sa Vie, Sa Règle , Sa Doctrine Spirituelle*, p. 149.

very manner of applying our Rule, let us consult those who have authority to guide us, and whose views we know to be truly supernatural. If they hesitate, let us mistrust ourselves; if they censure us, let us stop; and above all let us keep, in a general way, from going in search of some other counselor, less supernatural and more agreeable, who we know will not dare contradict us. That would be clearly to seek our own will, and to halt even before the first step in the way of humility.

January 29—May 30—September 29

We must be on our guard, therefore, against evil desires, for death lies close by the gate of pleasure. Hence the Scripture gives this command: "Go not after your concupiscences" (*Ecclesiasticus* 18:30).

So therefore, since the eyes of the Lord observe the good and the evil (*Proverbs* 15:3) and the Lord is always looking down from heaven on the children of men "to see if there be anyone who understands and seeks God" (*Psalm* 13:2), and since our deeds are daily, day and night, reported to the Lord by the Angels assigned to us, we must constantly beware, brethren, as the Prophet says in the Psalm, lest at any time God see us falling into evil ways and becoming unprofitable (*Psalm* 13:8); and lest, having spared us for the present because in His kindness He awaits our reformation, He say to us in the future, "These things you did, and I held My peace" (*Psalm-* 49:21).

COMMENTARY

St. Benedict insists on the resistance to the "desires of the flesh." To strengthen us in that resistance he reminds us of two truths. The one we know, since it forms the object of the whole first degree of humility: the presence of God. St. Benedict neglects nothing to inculcate in us the faith in that presence, so possessive and active does he want it to be, especially in moments of struggle. God, the living and loving God, must really become the beneficent obsession of our life.

The second truth is the danger of mortal sin resulting from the instinctive desires of the flesh that torment every human creature. In the measure in which the desire is consented to, fully, knowingly and deliberately, it produces a sort of delight to which a person abandons himself, at first as if in spite of himself, and then without resistance. And with this delight it is death which penetrates, "for death lies close by the gate of delight."

And now St. Benedict is going to sum up, in the form of exhortation, his whole teaching on the first degree of humility. Since the Lord is present and looking at us, since the Holy Angels are also witnesses of us and present our merits and demerits to God, "we must always be on the watch." Watchfulness is the contrary of that forgetfulness against which St. Benedict wished to forewarn us in the beginning.

If we are not on the watch, there are too many chances for us to succumb, and that under the angry eyes of God. God, quite present and quite offended as He may be, will not strike us, to be sure, in the act of sinning. He is so good and He desires so much that we come back to Him! How beneficent is that silent expectance of God for the sinful soul, to which it gives time to lift itself up again! But how terrible it is also for the hardened sinner, who abuses the divine delays to commit worse still! For those delays will be only for a time. God is patient "only until the day on which He has resolved to blaze forth His anger and to reproach (the guilty) in the sight of the universe for the contempt in which they have held all His graces."[19] "These things you did, and I was silent!"

APPLICATION

In terminating these admirable pages consecrated by St. Benedict to the first degree of humility, it may be not without profit to review briefly the whole teaching. Our holy Father has not defined humility. What he thinks of it will issue from the whole of Chapter 7. But he has set down as a principle the words of Jesus Christ, that one must humble oneself if one wishes some day to be exalted.

There is no evasion, therefore. We must be humble. To make us conceive this so necessary humility, St. Benedict has only to put us fully in contact with the realities of faith. The greatest of these realities, the one that dominates and sustains all the rest, is God: God the Creator and Conserve!', the God who lives, the God who sees, the God who acts, the God who threatens and promises. And the other reality is ourselves, finite, fragile creatures, exposed to temptations and to falls. Humility, a former Benedictine author explained,[20] is based "on two points. . which are like the two poles without which it cannot exist. The first is the recognition of

---

[19] Abbé de Rancé, *La Règle de S. Benoist Nouvellement Traduite et Expliquée*, Tome 1, p. 511.

[20] *Pratique de la Règle de S. Benoist*, p. 257.

God and of His greatness, the other is the recognition of ourselves and of our nothingness."

When that nothingness is put face to face with the infinity of God, how would it not tremble? How would it not fear to offend that divine majesty whose eyes do not leave it but penetrate to the very depths of its being? Thus the fear of God produces the fear of sin, and the one and the other maintain the soul in a humble attitude. We are so small before God and so weak against sin when we find ourselves abandoned to our own forces!

Dom L'Huillier makes a comparison between the first degree of humility and the first degree of perfection, which the ascetical authors call the purgative life: "What is the picture drawn by St. Benedict, therefore, in his first degree? Nothing else than the portrait of the purgative life. The Christian who keeps himself always under God's eye, facing the obligations which the Commandments impose on him, facing the formidable sanctions which should help him eliminate sin from his life, facing the eternal rewards which quicken and warm his heart—how shall we define that Christian? We shall say that he is a man conscious of the obligations imposed on him by his condition as creature, and sinful creature, with respect to God, who is his Creator. Now that is the definition of humility, a definition which the holy Patriarch did not formulate, but which formulates itself on the lips of anyone who reads attentively Chapter 7 of the Rule and especially the first degree."

If we wish to keep well in mind that, being Oblates, we have undertaken to seek perfection, of which the purgative life is only the beginning, should we not conclude that we must apply ourselves with our whole heart to the practice of that which our holy Father has just explained to us?

January 30—May 31—September 30

The second degree of humility is that a person love not his own will nor take pleasure in satisfying his desires, but model his actions on the saying of the Lord, "I have come not to do My own will, but the will of Him who sent me" (*John* 6:38). It is written also, "Self-will has its punishment, but constraint wins a crown."

COMMENTARY

Certain commentators have observed that apparently this degree of humility does not seem to be "distinguished much from the preceding one";[21] and in Cassian, who also treats of the degrees of humility, the two are combined. A little application to the study of the text, however, will show that there is really progress in the second degree as compared to the first.

In the first degree St. Benedict put us face to face with God, who sees every disturbance in our soul; and he passed in review all that God may find there to condemn: evil thoughts, self-will, the desires of the flesh. It was the fear of the divine vengeance especially which was to make us expel from ourselves all those things which displease Him, whatever attractions they may have for us. We were somewhat in the relation to Him of a child who withholds his action because his parents are looking at him.

But let the soul progress: then that self-will which it used to love instinctively it no longer loves; it no longer looks on it as a forbidden good, but as an evil. "One no longer takes pleasure in fulfilling one's desires." Only one thing affects us: the divine will, which alone is supremely lovable. Thus "nature is reduced to nothing and daily immolated."[22] One dies to oneself in order to follow Jesus and be joined to Him. Besides, St. Benedict reminds us, it is thus that Jesus, our model, did. Did He not tell us, in fact, "I am come not to do My will, but the will of Him who sent Me"?

To this Gospel text St. Benedict adds another which he gives as being drawn from the Scriptures. *Item dicit Scriptura*: "Self-will incurs punishment and constraint wins a crown," *Voluntas habet paenam et necessitas parit coronam*. The manuscripts differ on the letter of this text, and the most authentic read *voluptas*, "pleasure," instead of *voluntas*, "will."[23] This reading, which the most ancient commentators knew, is adopted by Dom Butler and the Farnborough translators.

But the greatest difficulty is not on that point. This text is not found at all in the Scriptures. Numerous hypotheses have been proposed to justify the word *Scriptura*. St. Benedict is supposed to have quoted Scripture from memory, giving the sense of it but not the letter; and Luke 8:14 and 2

---

[21] Abbé de Rancé, *La Règle de S. Benoist Nouvellemeni Traduite et Expliquée*, Tome 1, p. 512.

[22] Dom Bernard Maréchaux, *S. Benoît, Sa Vie, Sa Règle , Sa Doctrine Spirituelle*, p. 151.

[23] Dom Paul Delatte, *Commentary*, p. 113.

Timothy 2:5 are proposed to us. But the analogy is far from evident.—Or he may have quoted a passage now lost; a somewhat desperate hypothesis.—Or again he might have given the word Scriptura a broad meaning, as he will do in the eleventh degree of humility, where he introduces by the words *scriptum est*, "it is written," a quotation not Scriptural; a somewhat forced comparison, for *Scriptura* is more precise than *scriptum est*.—Or indeed his memory might have betrayed him, and he might have given as Scriptural a proverbial formula, a trace of which may perhaps be found in certain ancient fragments inserted in the Acts of Saints Chrysogonus and Anastasia, and in St. Optatus of Milevis.[24]

Whatever the case may be, the meaning of the formula interests us more than its origin. "Self-will," says St. Benedict, "incurs punishment." We know that the ordinary chastisement of self-will, as of pleasure, is to engender nothing but disgust, regrets and finally eternal punishment. Such is not the case, continues St. Benedict, with constraint. But of what constraint is there question? The context seems to indicate that the concern is not with that constraint which a person submits to regretfully, as it were, because he finds himself dragged into it "by the necessity of precept," but with that constraint in which the divine love puts us when it draws us on by its sweetness and establishes us in a moral impossibility of willing anything else but what God wills. This necessity of obeying, says an old commentator,[25] "is inspired in us by the law of charity, which does not permit anyone who loves God to violate His Commandments. ... It is through this necessity of love that Jesus Christ Himself, whose example St. Benedict has proposed, obeyed His Father, unable to do otherwise because of the love He bore Him; for Jesus Christ could not want to love anything else than His Father Himself."

APPLICATION

"The religious," says Dom Maréchaux, "and even in general the Christian who is penetrated to the depths with the fear of God, comes thus to renounce his own will. He understands the danger that he courts in giving himself up to his own will; and then he ceases to love that will which he used to love so much; according to the Lord's word he even

---

[24] *Traduction et Explication Littérale*, p. 163; and especially Dom Paul Delatte, Commentary, pp. 113-114.

[25] *Traduction et Explication Littérale*, p. 163.

comes to hate it, for he sees in it a treacherous enemy; he no longer delights in fulfilling his heart's desires, for those desires would lead him blindly to occasions of sin and to lapses."[26]

But he does not rest content with this rather negative attitude; he turns with love toward everything that represents for him the divine will. He dies to himself in order to live in Jesus, who is at once his model and his companion in battle. Let us recall to what extent Jesus loved His Father's will. Let us recall the *Christus non sibi placuit* of St. Paul.[27] Let us recall especially the sorrowful but generous *Fiat* of Gethsemani.

Dom L'Huillier observes that when the soul attains the second degree of humility, it "decidedly" leaves the purgative way to enter on the illuminative way. We see from this how perfect our holy Father wants us to be.

To arrive at this complete renouncement of self we must, as St. Benedict urges, meditate a great deal on the example of Jesus. Let us see how He renounced Himself! "We shall never have to pronounce a Fiat as sorrowful as that which went forth from His lips and from His heart for our salvation on the night of the Agony."[28] The contemplation of such a model is necessary for the religious soul, for the Christian soul. It is thus that one succeeds in assimilating the dispositions of the Savior and in becoming one with Him, as St. Paul says: Vivo jam non ego ... "I live, but not I; it is Christ who lives in me."

St. Bernard wrote in his third Sermon on the Resurrection: "What is it that God punishes if not self-will? Hate your own will and there is no more hell." There remains nothing indeed but the divine will, to which the faithful soul adheres with all its strength.

January 31—June 1—October 1

The third degree of humility is that a person for love of God submit himself to his Superior in all obedience, imitating the Lord, of whom the Apostle says, "He became obedient even unto death" (Philippians 2:8).

COMMENTARY

---

[26] S. *Benoît, Sa Vie, Sa Règle , Sa Doctrine Spirituelle*, p. 150.

[27] *Romans* 15:3. "Christ did not seek His own gratification" is the translation by the Very Rev. Francis Aloysius Spencer, O.P., in *The New Testament* (New York: The Macmillan Co., 1940), p. 440.

[28] Dom Bernard Laure, *Commentaire*, p. 120.

In the second degree of humility there was question, in a general way, of the necessary conformity of our will to God's. But the divine will may manifest itself in various ways, not only through the Commandments of God and of the Church, but also through the rules of ecclesiastical discipline, through the duties of our state, through our rules and our particular regulations. It may manifest itself also through the positive orders of Superiors. It is in this last case that it often requires the most abnegation on the part of our human nature. The fact is that even if faith shows us Christ in the person of the Superior, a certain latent naturalism murmurs to us that after all, this Superior is only an equal, and that perhaps—at least we are tempted to think so—he understands things less well than we and is inferior to us in virtue.

Now perfection, according to the third degree of humility, consists in listening only to faith and in submitting ourselves totally, omni obedientia, to this form of authority. This is what the monk does by his vow of obedience. In obeying his Abbot totally, he will follow Christ totally. To be sure, the Superior is fallible; but as for the subject, he knows that he makes no mistake in obeying, unless, of course, in the case envisioned elsewhere by St. Benedict in which the order given would be contrary to the law of God, to justice or to charity, something which can only be very exceptional.

But to be such as our holy Father desires, this obedience must not be purely exterior. It must come from the inmost soul, it must be inspired by love of the Lord, pro Dei amore. And to that love one should arouse oneself by considering Christ, who was truly "obedient unto death." "His entire life," says Dom Laure,[29] "was indeed a continual act of obedience : obedience to His Heavenly Father. ..; obedience to Mary, His Mother; obedience in the most humble labors to His foster father St. Joseph. Being Creator, He obeyed His creatures." And in His Passion? When He said the "loving and sorrowful Fiat," obedience led Him to death. "He remains immobile under the buffetings and the stripes; He has accepted the crown of thorns; He stretches Himself out on the Cross to be nailed there; He is there until death follows. It is thus that Christ made Himself obedient unto death and to the death of the Cross."[30]

---

[29] *Commentaire*, p. 122.

[30] Dom Bernard Maréchaux, *S. Benoît, Sa Vie, Sa Regle, Sa Doctrine Spirituelle*, p. 154.

APPLICATION

The commentators observe that the complete practice of this degree can be realized only by the religious, who in virtue of his vow "abdicates his will without reserve into the hands of the Superior."

The question, then, is to know what we Oblates can instil into our lives of the practice of this degree.

If the vow of obedience is not the portion of every Christian, on the other hand the virtue of obedience, which the vow has the purpose of safeguarding and strengthening, is imposed on all. "There is for every Christian," says Dom Maréchaux,[31] "a way of making his will give way before God's: to observe the Commandments to their full extent and to obey the voice of the Church." More than that, by the fact of living in society, the Christian finds himself concerned first with natural superiors. "The child must obey its parents; the wife, her husband; the man himself must obey the lawful authorities; and from this there results the compulsory fulfilment of the duties of one's state."[32] Let us add that in the Christian family, by virtue of the Sacrament of Matrimony[33] on which it is founded, and in virtue also of the fact that each member of the family is a baptized person, authority and subordination take on a character which is necessarily supernatural.

A step higher, there are the spiritual Superiors. The Christian must "submit to the heads of the Church in all that is in the domain of conscience.... This subjection," says Dom Maréchaux,[34] "is indispensable for every Christian in order to accomplish God's will."

And yet "there still remains some play to the very will so meritoriously subjected."[35]

The Oblate who wishes to approach monastic perfection as nearly as possible should ask himself, therefore, if there is still room to restrain what freedom is left him.

For the priest Oblate, that restriction goes without saying. By the

---

[31] *Ibid.*, p. 152.

[32] *Ibid.*, p. 199.

[33] The Sacrament of Matrimony establishes the Christian family on a supernatural plane and makes it a spiritual community. This is perhaps one of the most important and most neglected points of the Catholic doctrine on the family.

[34] *Benoît, Sa Vie, Sa Regle, Sa Doctrine Spirituelle, p. 199.*

[35] *Ibid.*, p. 152.

practice of continence he has entered, like the monk, into the way of the counsels. Moreover, he has promised obedience to his Bishop; and the authority which the Bishop possesses over him, much more personal and more precise than the authority the Bishop has over the rest of the faithful, brings serious limits to that freedom which remains to him.

But what is he to do for that remaining part? And what shall the lay Oblate do? We have already spoken of this in the explanation of the chapter on obedience. Let him have first of all the cult of obedience, but of obedience enlightened by the spirit of faith; let him have the desire to obey, demanded by our holy Father when he says of his children: *abbatem sibi praeesse desiderant.*[36] And then let him apply this spirit in the practice of his Rule as approved by his directors. There are so many decisions that we can put into the hands of those who direct us, not only as to the economy of our days, but as to our works of zeal, our practices of mortification, our intellectual labors, and so forth.

Finally, let the Oblate not forget that he cannot be a perfect son of St. Benedict without being a perfect parishioner. The role of the Oblates, wrote the Right Reverend Abbot of Solesmes, is "in the framework of their respective parishes to be models of Christian life by zeal for their churches and by participation in parochial activities."[37] From the fact that he does not actually dwell in the monastery, the Oblate finds himself a member of a parochial community. There again he will have to do a work of obedience, sometimes with a great deal of abnegation.

What the Oblate will remember above all in this manifold practice of obedience are those two short formulas of St. Benedict which give the whole meaning to the third degree of humility: *Pro Dei amore!* For love of God! *Imitans Dominum!* In imitation of Jesus Christ!

February 1—June 2—October 2

The fourth degree of humility is that he hold fast to patience with a silent mind when in this obedience he meets with difficulties and contradictions and even any kind of injustice, enduring all without growing weary or running away. For the Scripture says, "He who perseveres to the end, he it is who shall be saved" (*Matthew* 10:22); and again, "Let your heart take courage, and wait for the Lord!" (*Psalm* 26:14).

And to show how those who are faithful ought to endure all things,

---

[36] "They desire that an Abbot be over them" (Chapter 5).

[37] *Bulletin de S. Martin et de S. Benoît*, March, 1929, p. 90.

however contrary, for the Lord, the Scripture says in the person of the suffering, "For Your sake we are put to death all the day long; we are considered as sheep marked for slaughter" (*Psalm* 43:22; *Romans* 8:36). Then, secure in their hope of a divine recompense, they go on with joy to declare, "But in all these trials we conquer, through Him who has granted us His love" (*Romans* 8:37). Again, in another place the Scripture says, "You have tested us, O God; You have tried us as silver is tried, by fire; You have brought us into a snare; You have laid afflictions on our back" (*Psalm* 65:10-11). And to show that we ought to be under a Superior, it goes on to say, "You have set men over our heads" (*Psalm* 65:12).

Moreover, by their patience those faithful ones fulfil the Lord's command in adversities and injuries: when struck on one cheek, they offer the other; when deprived of their tunic, they surrender also their cloak; when forced to go to a mile, they go two (*Matthew* 5:39-41); with the Apostle Paul they bear with false brethren (2 *Corinthians* 11:26) and bless those who curse them (1 *Corinthians* 4:12).

COMMENTARY

The third degree of humility considered monastic obedience in general "with those difficulties which are inherent to it in the communal life,"[38] but also with those compensations which render it "acceptable to God and pleasing to men."[39] St. Benedict now considers cases in which obedience becomes particularly hard and even painful. Sometimes the things commanded are so contrary as to appear impossible, or they seem hardly proportioned to our strength.[40] At other times the difficulty is due to the one who commands: a difficult character, an erratic disposition, a personal antipathy — who knows? Human weakness, alas, permits us to envisage all the possibilities. Let us add to this the state of mind of the one who receives the order, who perhaps imagines things and creates difficulties for himself.

All those circumstances united, or some of them alone, make obedience at a given moment appear unbearable. It is a heavy cross, before which a person is tempted to say, and perhaps says, with the Savior, "If it be possible, let this chalice pass from me." What should we do in such a situation? What Christ Himself did. Not murmur, not recriminate,

---

[38] Dom L'Huillier, *Explication Ascétique et Historique*, Tome 1, p. 22 4.

[39] *Rule*, Chapter 5.

[40] St. Benedict will come back to this point in Chapter 68.

"undergo injuries in silence," "embrace patience," "endure all without tiring or running away," *sustinens, non lacescat vel discedat.* It is St. Paul's "With Christ I am nailed to the Cross," an embrace in which one expends in grasping the Cross vigorously all the energies that were threatening to break into revolt.

Are not the Scriptures there, the word of God, to encourage us? Do they not show us heaven as the reward of him who will have persevered? Do they not show us also the Lord Himself laying on our shoulders this part of His Cross? *Sustine Dominum.* "Endure the Lord."[41] "True words," says Dom Delatte, "because your trial comes from His Providence, He helps you to endure, and the trial has no other end than to lead you to Him."[42]

On this thought St. Benedict is going to insist, supporting himself always by Scripture. This doctrine is of such importance that he is anxious to multiply the quotations. It is the just man himself who speaks. The burden of his trial is so heavy that it seems like an endless agony. But he sees the relation between what he suffers and the divine will: "It is for You, Lord, that we are put to death all day long, and that we are considered as sheep marked for slaughter." And he finds in the cross itself a motive for hope and an ineffable joy; for He who strikes is really a God of love, and His blows can be only beneficent: "In all these things we carry off the victory, because of Him who has loved us." The fact is that suffering has a salutary effect; it purifies, it sanctifies, it raises to God: "You have proved us,O God, You have made us pass through the fire, as silver is tested in the crucible. .Happy the soul that understands thus the sufferings of obedience! The charity which sustains that soul will soon make it notice that there is something more perfect still than to carry one's cross in silence, and that is to love it, to reply to wrongs by a calm and smiling face, to ask not to be spared. Such is the sense of the well known Gospel metaphors which St. Benedict recalls.

Our holy Father has spoken thus far of persecutions met with in the exercise of obedience. Enlarging his thought somewhat, he has a word for the persecutions which come from "false brethren." What he thus designates are "suspicions, tales, erroneous reports, ill-meaning

---

[41] Dom Guéranger translates "Know how to wait for the Lord" (*Sache attendre le Seigneur*). We prefer the Farnborough translation: "Endure the Lord" (*Supporte le Seigneur*).

[42] Commentary, p. 116.

interpretations, uncivil or offensive conduct.... All that," says Dom L'Huillier, "may be encountered." The attitude will be the same as above. We must endeavor, following St. Paul, to endure these false brethren and to "bless those who curse us."

APPLICATION

Although the concern in this passage is especially with monastic obedience, it can have its application wherever obedience is in question. Is it not certain that one is even much more exposed to meeting this kind of trial outside of the cloister than within? The true Christian ought to remember then that he must obey even so, according to the word of the divine Master. This is what Dom Maréchaux observes:[43] "This subjection is indispensable to every Christian in order to accomplish God's will; and he must not fall back before the difficulties and the trials which he meets in this way of submission; just as the monk, he is to keep patience in all things, and unite himself by this patience to Jesus Crucified."

So much the more will the Oblate apply himself to the practice of this patience, so strongly recommended by our holy Father. Occasions of trial will not be lacking. Outside of the very rare case in which these would be the deed of religious authorities, they will come to him generally from "false brethren," equal or inferior, for whom his profession, his habits of life, his practices of piety will be objects of coldness, mockeries and insults. Not to refuse obedience in face of an unjust order, coming generally from an authority which has no religious character;[44] to repress the inward revolt in face of brutalities, hate, disdain; to force ourselves to obey when our strength seems to abandon us; to do all this without pose, peacefully, silently, looking fixedly on the Savior who held His peace in the midst of persecutions—what an ideal of heroic humility St. Benedict proposes to us! Our holy Father, so filled with discretion and scruple when the concern is with bodily mortifications, has no fear of going too far in the way of interior mortifications. These are the *dura et aspera per quae itur ad Deum*. But how illuminated by the divine Love are these "hard and bitter" heights!

---

[43] S. Benoît, Sa Vie, Sa Règle, Sa Doctrine Spirituelle, p. 199.

[44] The concern here is evidently only with private life. Legitimate resistance to unjust laws, for example, depends on the religious authorities who, as the case may be, direct it or authorize it. Nor could there be question of the cases in which someone would want to oblige us to commit an injustice.

February 2—June 3—October 3

The fifth degree of humility is that he hide from his Abbot none of the evil thoughts that enter his heart or the sins committee! in secret, but that he humbly confess them. The Scripture urges us to this when it says, "Reveal your way to the Lord and hope in Him" (*Psalm* 36:5), and again, "Confess to the Lord, for He is good, for His mercy endures forever" (*Psalm* 105:1). And the Prophet likewise says, "My offense I have made known to You, and my iniquities I have not covered up. I said, 'I will declare against myself my iniquities to the Lord,' and You forgave the wickedness of my heart" (*Psalm* 31:5).

COMMENTARY

"With the first four degrees," says Dom Delatte, "the theory of humility is complete."[45] The concern now is to apply that theory to certain circumstances of the spiritual life.

We have a tendency, which is nothing but pride, to make ourselves pass for better than we are, and to want "to be called holy before being so" (Chapter 4, No. 61). What strengthens that tendency and encourages it is that our interior acts are invisible to our neighbor, that they are known only to ourselves and to God. There are "evil thoughts that enter the heart" and "secret sins that one has committed," the divulging of which would be very painful for us.

Now St. Benedict wants us to push humility even to that divulgence, which, however, will not be made to just anybody, but to the Abbot.

What we are concerned with here, evidently, is not vague impressions, images which flash through the mind like lightning, but veritable hauntings, thoughts which presuppose tendencies, piercing desires of which one wonders anxiously whether they will go on to an act of consent.

We must make, says St. Benedict, "a humble confession" of them. The great majority of the commentators, Dom Hugh Mènard, Dom Martène, Dom Mege, Dom Calmet, Dom L'Huillier, Dom Delatte and others, observe that the concern here is not with sacramental Confession, since at that epoch most of the Abbots were not priests, "as it appears from the life of St. Maur, of St. Cyran and of countless others."[46] In general, St.

---

[45] *Commentary*, p. 120.

[46] Traduction et Explication Litterale, p. 169. St. Cyran (Sigirannus) was the first Abbot of Lonrey, in Berry.

Benedict does not speak of the divine and ecclesiastical laws, which he supposes are known and observed. The concern, notes Dom Delatte, is with "a quite private affair, unofficial, a voluntary confiding of our wretchedness, what we know nowadays as 'manifestation'."[47] This overture made to the Superior was in the monastic tradition. The Abbé de Rancé does not fail to recall on this subject "how St. Serapion was delivered from a temptation to which he had long succumbed, as soon as he disclosed it to his Abbot." The ascetics of all times have always taught the efficacy of this practice in temptations.

St. Benedict supports his affirmation by various texts from Scripture. We are surprised, at first glance, to notice that in these texts there is not literally a question of disclosing oneself to the Superior. We read there actually these words: "Reveal to the Lord.... Confess to the Lord...." But this is an occasion for recalling St. Benedict's great principle: The Lord and the Abbot are identified with each other. "The Abbot holds the place of God in the monastery. St. Benedict never separates him from God; on the contrary, he sees God in him, and so he believes that the most secret sins disclosed to him are disclosed to God Himself, as the Scripture orders. For to want to treat immediately with God concerning one's conscience, without taking any arbiter or mediator, and without wanting him whom God has given us for a father and a master and whom He has, as it were, interposed between Himself and us, to know about the matter, would not be a mark of humility, but an effect of our presumption and our pride."[48]

APPLICATION

The fifth degree of humility is of universal application. We have need of a guide in the ways of God, and this guide cannot very well conduct us except in so far as he knows us. Our humility, therefore, will have here a twofold result: it will enlighten this guide, and it will deliver us.

Practically, the director and the confessor are combined, but not necessarily. There are cases in which distance or certain expediencies oblige us to choose the only confessor whom we may approach as often as we need him, without feeling inclined to disclose ourselves to him. In

---

[47] Commentary, p. 120.

[48] Traduction et Explication Litterale, p. 169.

that case we must make a choice elsewhere of the guide who suits us; but in that choice let us be on guard against motives that are too human.

St. Benedict desires that the guide be the Abbot. Dom Mège and Dom Calmet think that one might supplement the text and add "or someone of the elders." Would that we Oblates might thus open our hearts to our Abbot or to the one who holds his place! But the thing is not always easy. Let us at least choose someone who is capable of guiding us in accordance with the spirituality of which we make profession.

And with this director let us be perfectly sincere. The idea is not to impress him, to edify him at the expense of truth and make him believe we are saints. We have to make ourselves known just as we are, in all sincerity. And just that, sometimes, is one of the most meritorious acts of humility; for, as Joseph de Maistre said, there are in the conscience of an honest man some things which make one shudder. And that is why this degree of humility is so rarely attained in the world. We give alms willingly; we do not shrink from austerities, which sometimes have their dangers of vainglory; we tire ourselves out with good works—all that is excellent. But how much more difficult it is to make known to a director, with full deliberation, the depth of evil inclinations in ourselves, when that declaration takes on no obligatory character. If we wish to progress, however, we must not fear to go even that far.

February 3—June 4—October 4

The sixth degree of humility is that a monk be content with the poorest and worst of everything, and that in every occupation assigned him he consider himself a bad and worthless workman, saying with the Prophet, "I am brought to nothing and I am without understanding; I have become as a beast of burden before You, and I am always with You" (*Psalm* 72:22-23).

COMMENTARY

"The sixth degree of humility," says Dom Delatte, "consists in accepting interiorly all the conditions of the monastic life and never being particular."[49]

The monastery may be poor, the habits much worn, the food less than mediocre; the faithful monk accepts all that. Moreover, he may be put in the last place, given the most repulsive labors; he accepts them as well.

---

[49] *Commentary*, p. 122.

But in this acceptance it is the depth of the heart that interests St. Benedict. He wants it to be inspired by a true humility. Humility always puts us face to face with our weakness and our wretchedness. Thus the one who is sincerely humble judges all that happens to him and everything difficult or lowly that is enjoined on him in relation to the mediocrity of his merits. He is even satisfied with it, *contentus est.* And this attitude is very sincere with him. Thus does this degree already suppose an heroic virtue. It is only the Saints who really despise themselves. Such was the thought of the Psalmist when he said, "I am brought to nothing. ... I am like a beast of burden before You, but I am always with You."

"How happy is the humble soul!" says Dom Maréchaux.[50] "It considers itself sincerely the scum of the earth; it accepts all abasements and all affronts as a due; but it is always with the Lord. The Lord, with His Angels, keeps it company."

It is in order that souls may be well penetrated with this degree of humility that it is always the custom in monasteries to make the religious pass through the lowest offices and those most humiliating in the eyes of the world. One may read in the Constitutions of the Congregation of Saint-Maur, regarding what was called "the office of humility," these truly touching lines: "This office is the best portion of all, because it has for its exercise and for its title the most precious of all the virtues, which at another time was so rare and so hidden from men that it was only the Son of God who could reveal it to the world. He it was indeed who gave the first lessons in humility by His words and His examples, having descended from heaven to cover Himself with the sackcloth of our wretched state, and having lowered Himself so far as to will to die on an infamous tree to efface men's sins." And in consideration of the abasements of Jesus Christ, it was decided that all the religious would pass through this office, because it "is not reasonable that one alone should carry off all the merit of it."[51]

APPLICATION

It is difficult to reach this degree of humility at once. We must begin, as Dom Maréchaux remarks, by "turning away from distinctions and

---

[50] *S. Benoît, Sa Vie, Sa Règle , Sa Doctrine Spirituelle,* p. 160.

[51] *Règle s Communes et Particulieres de la Congregation de Saint-Maur* (1687), p. 261.

honors, or at least not seeking them avidly, and accepting them only in view of a praiseworthy end." Is it enough to stop there? St. Benedict asks something more of us. We must take our portion of everything unpleasant that comes to us. Is it not Providence which rules us? Does not Providence know what we deserve? Humiliations, poverty, lowly employments, an inferior social situation—do they not represent at a given time a disposition or a permission of that Providence? Are they not even what is best for us at that time?

The truly humble soul, which meditates on its spiritual misery, on its infidelities, on its past and present sins, arrives at the conviction that it deserves nothing better. It blesses its humiliations. It even comes to desire them. "The soul triumphs over natural repugnances to the point of taking its delight in those very repugnances."[52] "To suffer and to be despised," said St. John of the Cross to one who asked him what he wished for.

These principles which impose themselves on the soul that desires humility, vary necessarily in their application. It is understandable that the head of a family may legitimately desire a temporal advancement, that he exert himself, moreover, to win it, for the greatest good of his children. It is only required of him not to seek vainglory in this, and to submit to what Providence dictates for him, whether that corresponds to his desires or not. For the priest, on the contrary, as for the monk, the word "advancement" does not have much meaning. The place given us, be it the last, is always the best, since it is that in which God wants us to be. Besides, we must be well persuaded that every charge, every function in Christ's Church, however lowly it may be in the eyes of the world, is always infinitely above our unworthiness.

It would not be right, however, to confuse the love of humiliations with a deliberate grossness of manners, language or habit. The Christian soul which has regard for its nobility and for the honor due the Christ who lives in it, always knows how to preserve a certain dignity, even amid "every abasement and extremity." Having become "as a beast of burden" in the service of the Lord, it takes care not to forget that He is there, that it can say to Him, "I am always with You," and that there is a respect for the divine presence which ought to be expressed in the whole attitude of the humble Christian.

---

[52] Dom Étienne Salasc, *La Règle de S. Benoît Traduite et Commentée*, p. 264.

February 4—June 5—October 5

The seventh degree of humility is that he consider himself lower and of less account than anyone else, and this not only in verbal protestation but also with the most heartfelt inner conviction, humbling himself and saying with the Prophet, "But I am a worm and no man, the scorn of men and the outcast of the people" (*Psalm* 21:7). "After being exalted, I have been humbled and covered with confusion" (*Psalm* 87:16). And again, "It is good for me that You have humbled me, that I may learn Your commandments" (*Psalm* 118:71).

COMMENTARY

In the preceding degree St. Benedict made us find humility in a comparison between our own worth and our outward situation. The virtue was already heroic, and yet St. Benedict demands still more. We must descend further and, comparing ourself with other men, esteem ourself sincerely "lower and of less account than all others."

It is not, to be sure, very difficult to make eloquent verbal protestations to that effect. The habit of reading and repeating certain rather exaggerated formulas, found in certain manuals, might carry us in that direction. A person might even succeed in deluding himself and imagining that because he never stops declaring himself lower than all others, he has that same sentiment definitely established in the bottom of his heart;[53] an illusion which will not stand up in face of an unforeseen contradiction, an unusual reproach, a slight adversity.

St. Benedict asks something else of us. It is not only "with the mouth" that one must proclaim oneself the vilest of all. One must believe it "in the inmost feeling of one's heart."

A superficial examination might let us think that this is an exaggeration and that St. Benedict is asking us to deceive ourselves. But the fact is that all the Saints arrived at St. Benedict's precept, even without having known it. They all considered themselves the greatest of sinners and the outcasts of humanity. In this they were doing nothing more than communicating in the humility of the Savior Himself, who fulfilled on the Cross the words of the Prophet: "As for me, I am a worm and no man; I am the reproach of men and the outcast of the people."

How could they come to this view?

There was evidently on their part a work of comparison, indicated by

---

[53] Dom L'Huillier, *Explication Ascetique et Historique*, Tome 1, p. 231.

St. Benedict. One cannot judge oneself lower than all others without comparing oneself with all others. But at the bottom of that comparison there is this fact, most significant, that we know ourselves well and that we cannot judge others.

The point is that what we see in others, even in the greatest sinners, are the exterior acts, which may be grave and deplorable materially; but there is an element, important for judging them well, which escapes us: the psychological element; that which more or less attenuates their responsibility; above all, the quantity and the nature of the graces granted them. There is no one but God who can judge them well, and certainly God's thoughts are not men's.

On the other hand, we know ourselves, or at least we can know ourselves. The more we meditate, under the eyes of God, the more we recognize the multitude of the graces He has showered on us and the numberless mercies with which He has surrounded us. And we have made so little progress! We are always so faithless, always so ungrateful! We never stop sinning, at the very time when, with so many supernatural aids, with so much love on God's part, we ought to be saints! We never stop sinning, and we feel that if God did not come to our assistance, we should easily go on to the gravest sins.

"It is certain," says a commentator,[54] "that a man plainly guilty is to be esteemed lower than another of whose crime we are not certain." Such indeed is our situation. We cannot judge of the responsibility of our brethren, but we are only too certain of our own abuses of grace and our own ungratefulness. That is what should help put us in our true place.

We shall not reach it, to be sure, at the first try. That is why St. Benedict did not commence with this degree. With the Saints, the knowledge of self is disengaged from illusions of self-love and vanity by the intensity of the knowledge of God.

"The most perfect," says the Abbé de Rancé, "are those who more nearly approach God; who, being more closely united to Him than the others by the greatness of their charity, receive more light from Him. As they look at themselves more penetratingly, they notice and discern the least faults, the least blemishes in themselves; in the measure in which they are raised up, their lights are increased, their knowledge becomes more profound; they see and perceive everything; nothing escapes them;

---

[54] Traduction et Explication Littérale, p. 172.

they are sensible to the slightest evils and imperfections; they are even affected by those which they do not commit, because they know that they are always close to falling into those evils if ever the hand of God should cease to sustain them and prevent them; and as they have ever before their eyes that source of cupidities and concupiscences which can in a moment flood the field of their heart, they are only too ready to put themselves below those whose wretchedness they know not, and to say without fear of exaggerating or being insincere that they are the last of men."

And if that only gives us an imperfect notion of how the Saints "in proclaiming themselves, from the heart, to be the greatest sinners, kept to the plain truth. . .let us agree. .. that in their humility there is a mystery; without a most powerful impulse and a wholly peculiar support of the Holy Spirit, man could not humiliate himself so low, could not descend to the bottom of such an abyss."[55]

APPLICATION

The seventh degree of humility finds its complete application only in sainthood. It is indeed true that at certain moments, during prayer, the thought of God and His bounty, of our sins and ingratitude, puts our finger as it were on our wretchedness and our nothingness. But that, unfortunately, is only a passing thing. What St. Benedict would wish is for us to establish ourselves in that sentiment in a permanent way. We must, therefore, work for it; for all of us, whoever we are, are called to sainthood.

Let us see, then, what God has done for us in particular. Has He not treated us as privileged persons? If we are Oblates, that is because He has managed circumstances, because He has made us glimpse a grand ideal of perfection. How many others have not been so favored! That sinner whom we are tempted to despise, has he had the same graces, the same lights as we? The Pharisees looked from the heights of their false justice on Magdalen prostrate at the feet of Jesus and on the crucified thief. At the very time when they were despising them, grace was at work in those poor people, and they were beginning to respond to it, and they were already better than those who condemned them. ' Thus every unfavorable judgment on our neighbor risks being a gross error. Let us get into the habit of reflecting sincerely on what we truly are in the sight of God. The

---

[55] Dom Bernard Maréchaux, S. Benoît, Sa Vie, Sa Règle , Sa Doctrine Spirituelle, p. 162.

wretchedness and weakness that we shall find in ourselves will excuse us from judging others.

Besides, the great Teacher of humility is God. It is He who, when we respond to His grace and when we open our eyes "to the deifying light," makes us see what we are worth. And this humiliation is itself a mark of His love. That is why St. Benedict makes us say with the Psalmist, *Bonum niihi quod humiliasti me*, "It is good for me that You have humbled me!" And our holy Father continues the quotation, making us see what are the spiritual profits of humility: ut *discam mandata tua*. He who is really humble understands better the rights of God over His creature and the importance of His commandments. Humility renders him more teachable. And that is why God reveals Himself by preference to the humble. Their heart is wholly disposed to listen to Him, to be penetrated with His will, and to follow Christ wherever He wants to lead them.

Let us recall these conditions if by the practice of humility we desire, as is our duty and the divine will, to reach sainthood.

February 5—June 6—October 6

The eighth degree of humility is that a monk do nothing except what is commended by the common Rule of the monastery and the example of the elders.

COMMENTARY

Up to now St. Benedict has occupied himself with the interior. In this he agrees with St. Francis de Sales. "I could never approve," said the latter, "of the method of those who, to reform a man, begin with his exterior, such as his gestures, his dress, or his hair. On the contrary, it seems to me that we ought to begin with his interior. . .for whoever has Jesus Christ in his heart will quickly reveal Him in all his exterior actions."[56]

Is it to be said that it is necessary to have climbed the seventh degree in order to pass to the eighth? Not so. The steps of St. Benedict's ladder, as we have already observed, do not necessarily succeed one another in practice. St. Benedict wants to indicate to us only that our exterior attitude and our ways of acting are but the expression of our interior attitude and our ways of thinking. Let us guard against supposing, however, that the exterior has no influence on the interior. On the contrary, it has an

---

[56] *Introduction to a Devout Life*, translated from the French by John K. Ryan (New York: Harper & Bros., 1950), Part 3, Chapter 23, p. 131.

influence and a very real one, but one which will be truly effective only after the reformation of the interior has already been undertaken.

St. Benedict prescribes to his disciple, then, to do nothing "outside of the common Rule of the monastery and the example of the elders."

The fact is that, especially with those prompted by "a novice fervor," there is a tendency for a person to believe that he is going to do better than the others, that the Rule does not ordain enough, that the elders live too much in routine, and so forth. It is then that a person assumes a pose, that he looks for an effect, that he presents himself as someone who has his own manner of acting and his own particular conceptions, a manner of acting and conceptions more perfect than those of the rest. Unfortunately, this fault is found not only in the young. There is always at the bottom of our nature a certain self-love which would make us desire only to put ourself forward, to make ourself distinguished.

He who is truly humble should look to his Rule in everything; it is the Rule which is his authentic guide, and not the fancies of a blind zeal and a vain imagination. He lets himself be formed by the Rule, and, when that does not speak clearly enough, by "the example of the elders."

But what is meant here by the word "elders" (*majores*)? The obvious sense seems to require that the aged monks are designated thereby, those who have a long practice of the monastic life and have guarded its ancient traditions. It has been objected that the aged monks, often being dispensed from certain observances on account of their age, could not have been proposed as models. According to the Abbé de Rancé, the majores would be "the first Fathers and the Founders, whom it pleased God to use for instruction in monastic orders and observances." For others—and this is the opinion of the Farnborough translators—the word would designate the "Superiors," whoever they be. It seems to us rather, with Dom Chauvin,[57] that the true meaning is the one signified by the word itself. The elders are the old monks, those who have long practiced and have conserved the traditions of the good observances. What does it matter that they have certain dispensations because of their age? What must be considered is their teaching: teaching by example and teaching by word. These venerable monks, who regret that they must have dispensations, will never think of prescribing dispensations for the young. It is they to whom one must listen docilely; it is in face of their example that one must

---

[57] Bulletin de S. Martin el de S. Benoît, September, 1925, p. 25i9.

restrain all the proud sallies of the ego, inspired by self-love under color of zeal.

But the ego which cannot or dares not flount itself in too showy manifestations, will perhaps have its turn in lesser things. These will be, says Dom Delatte, "a small point of pronunciation, a personal peculiarity in the common ceremonial, exceptions in the refectory. And this degenerates into a passion, whether open or concealed, and sometimes into revolt."[58]

How contrary is all that to the practice of the Saints and to their teachings, summed up by the author of the Imitation: *Ama nesciri et pro nihilo reputari*, "Love to be ignored and accounted as nothing!"

APPLICATION

The cases envisioned by our holy Father can be a danger for the Oblate just as well as for the monk. It is the danger of anyone who undertakes his "conversion." Because the Oblature puts us somewhat apart, we might have a tendency to singularize ourselves by certain attitudes, certain ways of acting, certain whims. These are true manifestations of vanity, which may not appear serious at first glance, but which it is important to watch and to restrain if we want to be truly humble. "The Christian," says Dom Maréchaux,[59] "should love in all things the simplicity which excludes every pretense, every affectation whatever it be."

Evidently we are not to bring into this case the mere practice of certain observances which are only the putting to work of our Holy Rule. What must be avoided is making a show of those practices. Let us do what our directors shall prescribe in the way of monastic observances.

The only thing in which it is permitted us to distinguish ourselves is the effort towards perfection; but of that distinction we shall be almost unconscious if the effort is sincere, for one thing alone ought to preoccupy us: to serve God as best we can in humility and in the abnegation of ourselves. "If the manifestations of daily activity," says Dom Chauvin,[60] "make the disciple of St. Benedict resemble the crowd which surrounds him, it does not follow that his soul itself must be lowered to the pitch of the surrounding mediocrities. Nothing distinguishes him in men's eyes;

---

[58] Commentary, p. 124.

[59] S. Benoît, Sa Vie, Sa Règle , Sa Doctrine Spirituelle, p. 200.

[60] *Bulletin de S. Martin et de S. Benoît*, September, 1925, p. 260.

but the interior dispositions, the intentions, the supernatural tenor, the union with God, in a word all that constitutes the true worth of acts for more perceiving eyes, will be truly select and divine.... Eternity will put its stamp on that truth."

February 6—June 7—October 7

The ninth degree of humility is that a monk restrain his tongue and keep silence, not speaking until he is questioned. For the Scripture shows that "in much speaking there is no escape from sin" (*Proverbs* 10:19) and that "the talkative man is not stable on the earth" (*Psalm* 139:12).

COMMENTARY

St. Benedict had already devoted Chapter 6 to the spirit of silence. He comes back to it here because he wants to be complete on the subject of humility, and generally the want of this spirit of silence is a mark of vanity or pride. What does the babbler seek, in reality, if not to attract attention, to make conspicuous his person, his merits, his mind?

"The desire to talk," say the Spiritual Exercises in use with the Congregation of Saint-Maur,[61] "comes only from pride, for one speaks only to instruct others and to appear learned and clever. A person persuades himself easily that he knows many things, and he gives them out willingly with the idea of making a reputation for himself.... He who does not know how to put a bridle on his tongue will not know how to acquire the gift of prayer and peace of mind, and he who knows how to discourse on others' faults rarely corrects his own. A person does not censure others and belittle them unless to exalt himself."

Thus Dom Maréchaux writes correctly, "One may say that venial sin multiplies on the tongue even when mortal sin does not break out there."

The humble monk, therefore, will have the cult of silence; not only will he not speak at the wrong time, but he will know how to wait until someone asks him a question, and even in recreation to repress his urge to talk.

APPLICATION

The true Christian, writes Dom Maréchaux,[62] ought to be restrained "in

---

[61] *Exercices Spirituels*, p. 353.

[62] S. Benoît, Sa Vie, Set Règle , Sa Doctrine Spirituelle, p. 200.

his speech, modest in his conversations; to lend an ear willingly, not to open his mouth except to edify his neighbor," without, however, let us add, posing at every turn as a preacher, something which would be another manifestation of pride. So much the more should the Oblate, like the monk, cultivate the spirit of silence.

Even when the conversation has its rights, it is good to restrain, for love of the Lord, a witticism, a smart bit of repartee, a word which would have no other result than to assume an attitude and to satisfy our vanity. In many circumstances is there not occasion to wait until someone questions us? In others, when a conversation is in progress, can we not wait, before speaking, for "the tacit question which results from every dialog," and keep from interrupting our companion and cutting short his words?[63]

We have already remarked, in commenting on Chapter 6, what opposition there is between vain babbling and that silence of the soul in which God is pleased. When anyone takes care to keep interior silence the better to listen to God's voice and to live more intimately with Him, he does not indulge wilfully in idle or foolish talk. Even in recreation he keeps a certain attention to the presence of God, to which he frequently returns; and the respect for that divine presence makes him sacrifice in useful conversations that which could come only from pride.

February 7 June 8-October 8
The tenth degree of humility is that he be not ready and quick to laugh, for it is written, "The fool lifts up his voice in laughter" (*Ecclesiasticus* 21:23).

COMMENTARY

St. Benedict had already put us on guard against "much and violent laughter." He comes back to it here, since this kind of laughter is contrary to humility. The Abbé de Rancé appears to exaggerate the thought of our holy Father in this passage, affirming that he forbids every kind of laughter, because laughter "cannot befit a man who is obliged to live in tears." In reality, the case is the same with laughter as with speech. What St. Benedict forbids is a certain tendency to laughter which makes it "ready and prompt" and which denotes giddiness and conceit.

---

[63] Dom L'Huillier, Explication AscStiqueet Historique, Tome 1, p. 238.

"Laughter," says a Cistercian commentator,[64] "is a need of nature, which depends a great deal on the diversity of temperaments more or less sensitive to the causes which excite it. It would be absurd to want to prohibit it entirely. Such is not the condition intended for humanity, nor the mind of our Father St. Benedict." More than that, laughter "is a relaxation sometimes necessary."[65] By a stronger reason, St. Benedict does not forbid the smile, which is the index of interior peace and the expression of goodwill and charity.

But the tendency to laugh at everything and at every excuse, a tendency too often expressed by "scurrilities" and pleasantries which are sometimes neither charitable nor seemly, that tendency is not compatible with what Bossuet calls "the inexpressible seriousness of the Christian life." How can a person live with the thought of eternity, with the memory of past sins and the fear of sins to come, above all with the thought of God's presence, and abandon himself without cease to witticisms, pleasantries and buffooneries? Does he not feel that there is a sort of opposition between the one and the other? To the thinking person continual laughter appears as a mark of giddiness, lack of reflection and foolishness. "The fool," says the Scripture, "lifts up his voice when he laughs."

APPLICATION

Moderation in laughter is a consequence of the thoughts which should be habitual to every Christian. Now in becoming Oblates we have made profession of more perfect Christian life. We should live, therefore, as our holy Father wishes: in the habitual thought of God. When a person strives to practice interior humility as it is described in the first degrees, he feels himself to be in the attitude of a servant whose eyes are always on his master's face. To be sure, the service of God puts an ineffable joy into the heart, but that joy always has of necessity something grave about it. The reason is that the divine Master is of infinite majesty, that everything which displeases Him will be severely judged, that our soul is the price of His Son's blood, that He detests all that self-love and all that vanity of which habitual laughter is a manifestation. Do not all the thoughts on

---

[64] Dom Étienne Salasc, *La Règle de S. Benoît Traduite el Commentée*, pp. 271-272.

[65] Dom Bernard Mareehaux, *S. Benoît, Sa Vie, Sa Règle, Sa Doctrine Spirituelle*, p. 167.

which the Christian soul ought to nourish itself exclude of themselves that regrettable tendency against which St. Benedict is putting us on guard? Let us strive, therefore, to comprehend and to feel profoundly "the inexpressible seriousness of the Christian life," and we shall be led quite naturally to practice the tenth degree of humility.

February 8—June 9—October 9

The eleventh degree of humility is that when a monk speaks he do so gently and without laughter, humbly and seriously, in few and sensible words, and that he be not noisy in his speech. It is written, "A wise man is known by the fewness of his words."

COMMENTARY

The monk will bear witness to his humility by silence, but he will bear witness to it also by his speech when he is permitted to speak. In a few words, therefore, St. Benedict is going to indicate what the monk's conversation ought to be. He ought to speak gently. Calmness in language is the index of interior peace. Violence in speech is in general the mark of some disorder. He will speak "without laughter," that is to say, without manifesting at every excuse that giddiness and self-satisfaction which was treated of in the preceding degree. His language will be humble, and quite the opposite of that peremptory or arrogant tone taken by the proud and the vain. It will be serious, as the language of a man for whom life is something serious, since it prepares for eternity. He will avoid vain babbling, pretentious phrases, posing; but will express himself readily "in few words," as someone who knows the value of silence. He will watch over his words, that they may always be the expression not of passion or of levity but of reason. He will avoid the loudness which so little befits true humility.

In support of his affirmation our holy Father, as is his habit, cites a text: *sicut scriptum est,* "as it is written. ..." But, although the formula seems rather to introduce a Scriptural quotation, the text invoked by St. Benedict is from a Greek Stoic or Pythagorean philosopher of the first century after Christ, named Sextus. That is what Dom Hugh Menard had already observed. Rufinus had translated into Latin the work of this philosopher entitled Enchiridion and had attributed it to St. Sixtus, Pope and martyr. St. Jerome denounced the mistake several times. But it is possible that Rufinus was not the first to be responsible for it; and for a certain time, despite St. Jerome, the Enchiridion continued to be attributed to this Christian martyr. However that may be, the sentence of Sextus, "A wise man is known by the fewness of his words," has its equivalent in the Holy Writ, notably in *Ecclesiastes* 10:14 and *Proverbs* 17:27.

APPLICATION

It has been remarked that the prescriptions given by St. Benedict in the eleventh degree of humility correspond to the prescriptions of manners and politeness among "genteel" people. That results, no doubt, from the fact that the rules of good manners were born in a milieu wholly impregnated with Christianity. And if too often, in the world, they are no longer anything but a front, that results from the fact that Christian forms have survived the paganization of souls.

It is in the monk, in the Oblate, in the perfect Christian that politness in speech and the most refined sense of manners are manifested most naturally, because they are the fruit of interior humility and charity. And it may be said that in souls profoundly virtuous politeness has a quite special charm which is like a radiation of grace.

"It belongs to the monk, ostensibly enrolled in the militia of Christ," wrote Dom Étienne Salasc (and we shall add: it belongs to the Oblate, who is attached to the same militia) to imitate Jesus Christ "in His language full of gentleness, free from unbecoming laughter, always humble and serious, sober, reasonable, never noisy, ever seasoned with the salt of wisdom. In face of this model of a correctness so perfect and so attractive, the desire of imitation imposes itself with more charm the more one recognizes in these good effects of humility the marks of a refined courtesy and of a finished education. The case with humility is as with true piety: it is useful for everything, with its promises for the present life and for the future life. The perfect Christian yields in nothing to the perfect gentleman."

February 9—June 10—October 10

The twelfth degree of humility is that a monk not only have humility in his heart but also by his very appearance make it always manifest to those who see him. That is to say that whether he is at the Work of God, in the oratory, in the monastery, in the garden, on the road, in the fields or anywhere else, and whether sitting, walking or standing, he should always have his head bowed and his eyes toward the ground. Feeling the guilt of his sins at every moment, he should consider himself already present at the dread Judgment and constantly say in his heart what the publican in the Gospel said with his eyes fixed on the earth: Lord, I am a sinner and not worthy to lift up my eyes to heaven (Luke 18:13, cf. *Matthew* 8:8); and again with the Prophet: "I am bowed down and humbled everywhere" (*Psalms* 37:7,9; 118:107).

Having climbed all these steps of humility, therefore, the monk will presently come to that perfect love of God which casts out fear (1 *John* 4:18). And all those precepts which formerly he had not observed without fear, he will now begin to keep by reason of that love, without any effort, as though naturally and by habit. No longer will his motive be the fear of hell, but rather the love of Christ, good habit and delight in the virtues which the Lord will deign to show forth by the Holy Spirit in His servant now cleansed from vice and sin.

COMMENTARY

Profound sentiments, love, sorrow or joy, always express themselves outwardly. They give each individual a characteristic appearance. Thus should it be with humility. The twelfth degree is realized when this virtue which is "in the heart" shows itself also in the body. The concern here, let us note well, is not with a pose, a forced attitude, but with the natural attitude which answers to humility really lived. The proud person walks with head up, looks down from above, takes on arrogant and domineering airs. The humble one, he who feels the eyes of God on him, readily turns his face and his eyes towards the earth. Not that he is, as it were, crushed under that divine gaze, but because it is impossible to hold another attitude when he truly believes in the reality of that presence and in the reality of our wretchedness. He cannot but bow down like the Prophet or strike his breast like the publican, saying, "Lord, I am not worthy, sinner that I am, to raise my eyes to heaven." And this truly humble attitude should be kept in every circumstance and at every moment. It should be manifested "at the Work of God, in the oratory, in the monastery, in the garden, on the road, in the fields, whether one be sitting, walking or standing."

It would not be right to suppose, however, that in this humble attitude there is nothing voluntary, and that it is purely instinctive. St. Benedict knows that if the moral acts on the physical, the physical also is not without influence on the moral. There are gestures and manners which awaken sentiments or predispose to them, accentuate them or support them. Thus it is of set purpose that the monk is to keep "his eyes fixed on the earth and his head bowed." At the same time he must not be preoccupied with producing an effect. But the attitude will quickly become natural to him if only he takes care to avoid everything in his ways of acting which could savor of immodesty, arrogance or conceit. What would be an hypocrisy if he had no humility in him becomes, on the contrary, a help if he has already begun to walk in this way of perfection. The ideal is that the harmony be total between the interior and the exterior. That is the sign that the monk has attained a very high degree of humility.

Thus are achieved, in the integral harmony of the whole being, the degrees of humility. They have not necessarily been climbed in the order in which our holy Father has placed them. Their development has varied with temperaments and circumstances. There may even have been recoils and renewals of energy. But, quickly or slowly, all have been climbed. And the final result is "that love of God which, being perfect, casts out fear."

Such is St. Benedict's conclusion, a conclusion of extreme importance for anyone who wants to understand the nature of Benedictine spirituality. What indeed is perfect charity if not perfection in its full bloom, at least as far as it can be attained here below? It follows that for St. Benedict humility is a method of perfection. Others may have recommended other methods, may have shown that the ladder of perfection is composed of the various degrees of patience or charity, or again that its steps are climbed with the help of the different graces of prayer: discursive prayer, prayer of simplicity, passive prayer.

St. Benedict excludes nothing of all that, but he considers the soul's forward march first of all and above all "under the aspect of humility."[66] And this is very personal to him. It may have been noticed that in Chapter 7 St. Benedict has borrowed much from Cassian,[67] and in particular almost the whole of the last paragraph. But in comparing the two texts one easily establishes that in assimilating Cassian the Patriarch of the monks has remade him to his own image. He has improved, "by retouching them, amplifying them and attaching them to words of Jesus and of the Scriptures," the degrees of humility set forth in the book of the Institutes; and "the twelve degrees form (in him) a remarkably penetrating and harmonious whole, indicating what a combination of fear and trust, obedience and energy, recollection and charity, makes up the attitude of

---

[66] Dom Idesbald Ryelandt, *Essai sur la Physionomie Morale de Saint Benoît* (Lille: Desclee de Brouwer & Cie., 1924), pp. 9-10.

[67] *Institutes*, Book 4, Chapter 39; in C.S.E.L., Vol. 17, pp. 75-76; translated by Edgar C. S. Gibson in Nicene and Post-Nicene Fathers, 2nd series, Vol. 11, p. 232.

the monk who progresses in the spiritual life."[68]

"Perfect charity," the goal of humility, is represented to us by St. Benedict as casting out fear. The concern here is evidently with the servile fear which terrorizes the sinner at certain moments of his conversion by showing him God provoked and hell open for just chastisements. That fear is little by little transformed in contact with trust and love and in the measure in which God is better known.

But there is a fear which remains in eternity and is not incompatible with love. It arises from our situation as a weak, small creature face to face with Him who is the All-Powerful, the Infinitely Just and the Infinitely Great. We dread hell less than we fear to offend our God because He deserves only affection. That fear cannot but arouse energies of love in the soul. It allows us to measure the distance spanned by the divine Goodness when it lowers itself to us and invites us to love it.

Perfect love renders everything easy. It puts sweetness into suffering. It penetrates the soul which has reached it in such a way as to make virtue as it were natural to it. And that soul can say with St. Paul: *Quis me separabit a caritate Christi?* "Who then, will separate me from the charity of Christ?"

APPLICATION

Since the twelfth degree of humility is nothing but the reflection of humility lived and progressing to perfect charity, it follows that, like the monk, the Oblate should apply himself to realizing it. "Should not his outward countenance, his walk, his way of dressing be inspired by the humility of his heart?"[69] As our holy Father prescribes, therefore, we shall watch over the modesty of our bearing.

"There is no question here," says Dom L'Huillier, "of made-up attitudes in which, under the pretext of religious bearing, simplicity would be lost, to be replaced perhaps by a pious vanity, the most tenacious of all vanities." But there is a good simplicity which is found in all really pious persons, a simplicity made of mildness and gravity, a simplicity which all the contortions of an affected piety will never simulate. This simplicity makes one readily lower the eyes, that is to say, "look on no one from

---

[68] Dom Idesbald Ryelandt, *Essai sur la Physionomie Morale de Saint Benoît* p. 11.

[69] Dom Bernard Maréchaux, *S. Benoît, Sa Vie, Sa Règle, Sa Doctrine Spirituelle*, p. 200.

above, but esteem oneself smaller beyond comparison than all whom one sees."[70] It is the stamp and the charm of a soul truly humble.

As we have seen, St. Benedict with his twelve degrees of humility presents to us a method of perfection. Since by profession we are his disciples and his children, this will be for us, therefore, the most normal and the surest way to "seek God." Consequently we shall have to meditate often this so essential chapter of the Holy Rule.

We need not return to what we have said above on this subject. Let us add to it simply an observation which will elucidate still more what our holy Father desires.

There are methods of spirituality which may present a certain danger. They are those which make of personal perfection—"self-improvement" as Father Faber called it, without approving of it—the first goal of our effort. Man considers himself first. His asceticism has the end of reforming him, modeling him, completing him, as an artist does with a statue which he would make a masterpiece. And in practice God finds Himself relegated to the background. Asceticism, says Father Faber, is then no more than "a systematizing and a glorifying of self-will."[71] Regret for sin is nothing more than "the bitterness of endless piecemeal failure," and perhaps, if the sin has had witnesses, the pique at having let others get an impression other than that which one wished to give them. Thus the method ends in pride.

St. Benedict, on the contrary, invites us to look at God. He wants us to seek God truly: *si vere Deum quaerit.* He wants us to follow in Christ's footsteps, *pergamus itinera* Christi, and to have our eyes wide open to the "deifying light." The gaze fixed on God, whom we know to be present, is at the first step of humility and at the base of perfection. It is because this God who sees us detests sin that we avoid committing it. It is to make room for God that we renounce our own will. Obedience is nothing but a complete docility to all the divine desires. It is for God, to be more united to the Crucified, that we accept humiliation and suffering. It is for Him that we renounce ourselves. If our sins trouble us, it is not because they "mar the symmetry of our character,"[72] but because they grieve the Holy

---

[70] Dom L'Huillier, *Explication Ascetique et Historique*, Tome 1, p. 241.

[71] Rev. Frederick William Faber, D.D., *Growth in Holiness; or, The Progress of the Spiritual Life*, 10th American ed. (Baltimore: Murphy & Co.), Chapter 20, p. 380.

[72] *Ibid.*, p. 381.

Spirit. Thus is the soul quieted and confident, even in the face of its faults. And because it is looking on the supreme Beauty, it forgets itself, it immolates itself and it mounts in Love. It understands that its whole existence should be like a divine praise. It expands in joy: the joy of knowing its God, the joy of loving Him, the joy of possessing Him already and of counting on the eternal possession of Him.

The more we study the Holy Rule the more we understand that for St. Benedict life is nothing but a "search for God," an ardent and joyous search, thanks to which we reach that end from which egoism had turned us away and which is none other than perfect love.

CHAPTER 8
On the Divine Office During the Night

N WINTER TIME, that is from the Calends of November until Easter, the brethren shall rise at what is calculated to be the eighth hour of the night, so that they may sleep somewhat longer than half the night and rise with their rest completed. And the time that remains after the Night Office should be spent in study by those brethren who need a better knowledge of the Psalter or the lessons.

From Easter to the aforesaid Calends of November, the hour of rising should be so arranged that the Morning Office, which is to be said at daybreak, will follow the Night Office after a very short interval, during which the brethren may go out for the necessities of nature.

COMMENTARY

We have just seen that our whole life ought to be an unceasing praise of the Creator. This praise is not peculiar to us. It is realized generally in the universal obedience of created beings to the Infinite Being who is their source and their end; unconscious obedience in beings without reason, but conscious in the Angels and in men. But this praise cannot remain vague. It befits our nature that it have its precise expression in certain words, gestures and rites, and, since man lives in society, that words and gestures have a collective, social character. The skies and the earth, the mountains and the rivers, the plants and the animals sing in their own way a magnificent hymn to the One who made them; that is what is recalled to us by the admirable canticle of the Three Young Men: *Benedicite omnia opera Domini Domino.* ...But something would be lacking to that immense song of glory if there were not a creature in whom it was conscious and who, so to speak, summed up in his praise the thousand voices of earth and sky and quickened them with his intelligence and his love. And there is the role of man.

But the man regenerated by Baptism, sanctified by the blood of Christ, forms but one with that Christ. He forms a part of the mystical body of Jesus. Each man is a living stone of the spiritual city. And just as Christ, God and Man, eternally praises His Father, to whom He is substantially united in that living, infinite Love which is called the Holy Spirit, so also it is necessary that we express our adherence to Him who is our "Head" and our life by uniting ourselves to His praise.

Such is the role of the Church, Society of Christians, society of the divine praise. Every Christian ought to praise God privately; but his unity with his brethren in Christ should also be manifested in a communal prayer which will be no longer the prayer of an individual but the universal prayer, the social prayer, the prayer of the whole Church. Admirable prayer, from which disappear the too personal preoccupations and that selfishness and those earthly cares which infect too many individual prayers! Admirable prayer, unceasingly the same for centuries, whose praises are always those which God loves and whose aspirations are in harmony with His eternal plans!

The center of this praise is the sacrifice of the Mass and, converging towards it, the different parts of the Divine Office. And just as man is delegated by the Creator to praise Him in the name of every creature, so in the Church, although no Christian is dispensed from the public office of praise, there are privileged ones whose principal function is this office: the clergy and the religious.

Formerly, that is to say in the first Christian centuries, all the faithful took part in the Divine Office, which was always solemn. Later, with the weakening of fervor and under the pressure of circumstances, the solemn Office became little by little the function of the clergy and the monks. Then the necessities of the apostolate, which separated the priests from the cathedral chapter to establish them in isolated churches, made it necessary to reduce the solemnity. All the same, in many rural churches themselves, the celebration of the Office, though it was assured only by one priest and one cleric, persevered until the 14th century, and even here and there until the 15th.

The private recitation of the Office is today a fait accompli for the parochial clergy, with the exception of chapters. But even in the private recitation the clergyman and also the monk when he is separated from his monastery or cannot attend choir ought to unite themselves in spirit to the whole Church, and especially to the particular church of which they form a part. It is for that reason that certain formulas are rigorously maintained which would presuppose choral recitation, such as the *Dominus vobiscum*.

The Church has always regarded the recitation of the Divine Office as of capital importance. That is why she has made of it a grave obligation for her priests. Consequently, it is easy to see why our holy Father, so penetrated with devotion toward the Church and so desirous of making his children perfect Christians, wanted to give a large place in his Rule to what was for him the work par excellence, the Work of God, the opus Dei. He will devote 13 chapters to it.

St. Benedict occupies himself first with "the Divine Offices during the night." These Offices are two in number: the *Vigiliae* or Vigils, which we today call Matins; and the *Matutinae* or Matins, which we call Lauds.

For a good understanding of Chapter 8 it must be remembered that the Romans divided the day of 24 hours into two portions, bounded by the rising and the setting of the sun. The day, which began with the rising and ended with the setting, counted 12 hours, just as did the night, which went from the setting to the rising. But as the days and the nights so measured were longer or shorter according to the seasons, it followed that the length of the hours varied with that of the day and of the night. It is on those variations that St. Benedict's schedule is based.

The holy Patriarch distinguishes two liturgical seasons, winter and summer. The first extends from the Calends of November until Easter; the second, from Easter until the Calends of November.

What must be understood by Calends of November? Is it the day on which they fall, that is to say the 1st of November, or the day on which they begin to be counted, that is to say the 16th of October? The opinions on this point are very much divided. Hildemar, referring to the custom of the Roman church, followed by Dom Calmet, thinks that the date concerned is the 1st of November. Defending the contrary opinion, the author of the Translation and Explanation[1] wrote, speaking of St. Benedict: "He does not understand by this term Calends the first day of the month of which they are called the Calends, but all the days counted by the Calends; that is to say, with regard to the month of November, from the 16th of October; for it is thus that St. Benedict is accustomed to take the Calends of the month: that is why we shall see afterwards (Chapter 48) that he gives the order to change the regulation of the hours which the fast is to follow on the Calends of October, although he has noted in another place (Chapter 41) that the fast is to be commenced on the Ides of September, which immediately precedes the day on which one

---

[1] *Traduction et Explication Littérale*, p. 183.

began to count the Calends of October: this makes it evident that by the term Calends of October he understood the 14th of September, when the days began to be counted by the Calends of October, and this seems clear by the mere reading of this passage in Chapter 48."

The Abbé de Rancé is of the same opinion, but he adds wisely: "It makes no difference what opinion a person follows in this matter." Today, indeed, when the hours are counted otherwise, the question no longer has any but a retrospective interest.

Whatever the case may be, the hour of rising varied continually with the length of the night hours. St. Benedict wants his monks during winter to rise after having rested a little more than half the night, namely at the eighth hour. He does not say whether this is at the beginning or at the end of the said hour, and consequently whether he means 2 o'clock or 3 o'clock in the morning. He has fixed this hour in order that the monks "may rise with the process of digestion completed." The word "digestion" should not be taken here in too strict a sense. "It seems," say the Famborough translators, "that for the ancients the profoundness of sleep and the heaviness of digestion were two states strictly associated, so much so that the end of the former supposed the achievement of the latter." In short, St. Benedict wants his monks to be rested and disposed the better to praise the Lord.

The nights of winter are long. When the Office is ended, it is still too soon to begin Lauds, which are the prayer of dawn. There will be, then, an interval. How will it be filled? "As to the time that remains after the Vigils," writes the holy Lawgiver, "it will be employed in the study of the Psalter or of the lessons by those of the brethren who need it." But what will the others do? St. Benedict does not say. Undoubtedly, notes Dom Hugh Menard, they will apply themselves to individual prayer or to holy readings. In any case, it does not seem that they are to return to bed, as was the custom introduced later in certain congregations.

But let us come back to the former monks. St. Benedict tells us concerning the interval: meditationi inserviatur. The term meditatio has sometimes been understood in the sense of a meditation which would be prescribed to a part of the monks while waiting for Lauds. In reality the concern is with quite another thing. To meditate, remarks the Abbé de Rancé, is to employ oneself "not in a simple reading, but in a serious, applied and attentive reading. . .with the de- sign of learning what one reads." And Dom Calmet specifies that "in low Latin meditari often has the meaning of to study, to learn by heart, to think over." In the age of St. Benedict, when not all the monks were lettered, when Psalms and lessons had to be chanted by the feeble light of oil lamps, from manuscripts more or less soiled with use, on which the ink had paled and in which the abbreviations were numerous, a certain knowledge of the liturgical texts was necessary both for reading well and for making oneself well understood by one's listeners, who, in view of the rarity of manuscripts, had no text before their eyes.

In summer the hour of rising will not be the eighth hour; but the time necessary for reciting Matins before dawn will be calculated, with care to allow a short interval for the necessities of nature. There will be not any study of Psalms then, this study being moved to another time.

APPLICATION

In the last days of his life Dom Guéranger wrote the following words for the benefit of the priests "affiliated to the monastic Order," who were in reality the first Oblates of the French Congregation: "The priest attached to the monastic Order should... more than any other, understand the importance of the Divine Office; and if he is deprived of its solemn celebration, which, however, was at another time the function of the clergy as well as of the monks, he will nonetheless strive in so far as he is able to keep the hours proper to each Office, because God Himself seems to have indicated them. When several of our priests find themselves together, they will be glad to say their Breviary together, not doubting that there is a special grace attached to that communal recitation and that they are thus entering more into the desires of their Holy Mother Church." "The Breviary" adds Dom Guéranger, "in the eyes of the priest who loves the divine praise, will not be a heavy yoke to which he is subjected by severe penalties, nor a duty of which he acquits himself dryly, more through fear than through love. Happy in the thought that the Church has chosen him to express to her divine Spouse the homage of her love and her prayer, he will regard it as one of his first obligations to enter by study and meditation into the sentiments of which he has the honor of being the interpreter."[2]

For the lay Oblates Dom Guéranger wrote also: "After the Holy Sacrifice of the Mass they will esteem nothing so highly as the Divine

---

[2]   "Le Prêtre et l'Ordre de Saint-Benoît," in L'Église ou la Société de la Louange Divine, pp. 34-35.

Offices in which the Church renders her continual homage to God through the canonical Hours. On Sundays and feastdays, they will be eager to assist at Vespers and Compline, and they will arrange as far as possible to unite themselves with the Holy Church in the singing of the Psalms and the hymns. If God gives them the grace of a taste for the Psalter, they will have a particular knowledge of it for Him, remembering that in the ages of faith it was always through the Psalms that God communicated with souls. They will prefer the churches in which the Divine Office is celebrated according to the ecclesiastical rule.... In their particular devotions they will love to make use of the Church's prayers as the expression of their own sentiments."[3]

The Statutes of the Oblates specify for our lay Oblate brethren these recommendations of the venerable Abbot of Solesmes. "It is very commendable for Oblates," they say, "to pray the Divine Office, if this be reasonably possible," or "the Little Office of our Lady," which constitutes the choir Office in many communities of women. "By so doing," continue the Statutes, "they will offer most acceptable prayers to God in the name of the Church, in thanksgiving for favors already received and in petition for new ones."[4]

In fact, a certain number of Oblates, men and women, like to unite themselves thus with the Church's prayer, which is the essential occupation of their Order. The others, those who could not reasonably do this, are invited to recite only one part of the Breviary, whether the day Hours, or Prime and Compline, as do the Oblates Régulières Servantes des Pauvres, or an abridged Office, like the one published at the end of *L'Eglise ou la Société de la Louange Divine*, or again by Dom Laure at the end of his *Commentaire;*[5] or, according to the opinion of the director of the Oblates, the Rosary or other approved prayers. The essential point is that they unite themselves to the Church's prayer, the ideal remaining always the recitation of the canonical Hours.

In the chapter on which we are commenting, our holy Father treats of the schedule of the night Offices. The very text of these Offices, as also their origin, demands indeed that they be celebrated at the proper hours.

---

[3] *L'Eglise ou la Société de la Louange Divine*, pp. 24-25.

[4] *Manual for Oblates*, p. 46, §24.

[5] Or one of the Offices in the Manual for Oblates; or A Short Breviary, published by The Liturgical Press, Collegeville, Minn.

We have seen what Dom Guéranger says about this. As to Lauds, there can be no difficulty: they are the prayer of dawn and their normal place is at daybreak. As for Matins, which cannot be celebrated in the night, some have put them back to the preceding evening, and others say them very early in the morning before Lauds. We know that in many Abbeys of Benedictine nuns Matins are said in the evening, as they are with the Carmelites. For the monks they are always in the morning.[6] The Oblates will choose according to their opportunities. In the sketch devoted by Dom Leonce Crenier to Dona Eugenia da Camara, secular Benedictine Oblate, we learn that she "always ended her Matins at midnight, recited Lauds before the morning Mass and Prime after it."[7] One may follow that example. Others, perhaps more numerous, will prefer the morning. A certain number of formulas of Matins suppose the time of rising. And then, in the morning the mind is calmer, better predisposed to recollection, and above all one is more rarely exposed to being disturbed. In the evenings, on the contrary, after days of work or of fatiguing ministry, it is difficult to escape sleepiness, distractions and disturbances.

In his admirable little Treatise on the Ecclesiastical Ministry, Pere Emmanuel, who was at the same time a monk and a parish priest, wrote a penetrating passage on this subject, from which some extracts will naturally find their place here. [8]

"That the canonical Hours should be said at the canonical hours, that is something which is not generally known.

"And yet what do these words of the Breviary mean: *ad Matutinum, ad Primam, ad Tertiam, ad Sextam, ad Nonam, ad Vesperas, ad Completorium?*

"It will be said, 'Yes, at another time it was so.' Assuredly, but why and how has it come about that it is no longer so?

"Today we say Matins in the evening, that is to say, we make of the night and the morning prayer an evening prayer, or rather a prayer for any time.

"And why, if not because we have found it easier to rise late than early?

"We say, 'It is in order to have time for meditation.' But were not our fathers acquainted with meditation? Did they give it no time? Are we,

---

[6] This does not apply to all the Congregations.

[7] *Une Ame Réparatrice* (Paris: Giraudon, 1928).

[8] *Traite du Ministere Ecclésiastique*, p. 45.

then, more meditative people than our fathers?

"Alas, one fact is certain: we meditate less than our fathers, and we have a dose of laziness and lack of mortification which our fathers certainly did not know!"

Dom Bernard Maréchaux, in presenting Dom Emmanuel's little work, makes this observation:[9] "Thirty years ago this conception of the priest's life would have appeared strange, unrealizable. Today we are led to it by the liturgical renewal heeding the voice of Rome. Let us hope even that a time will come—may it be near!—when people will be astonished that priests were able, with so much uniformity and thinking that they were doing an excellent work, to transform the morning Office into an evening Office and to group in a bundle the Hours meant to be distributed according to the phases of the day, so as not to hinder their exercises of piety, as if the Divine Office were not the priest's essential function, and as if his labors did not require to be vivified by an unceasing recall to prayer."

In truth it is for us, Benedictine Oblates, to give the example. Let us remember the priests and laypeople of the ages of faith who rose early in the morning to sing the praises of God. Does not the author of the Song of Roland repeat to us constantly, regarding Charlemagne:

> Li empereres est par matin levet,
> Messe et Matines ad li reis escultet. ..
> In the early morning the emperor arose,
> He heard Mass and Matins...

Let us be persuaded above all that the sweetest, the most luminous hours of our spiritual life will be those in which, despite the night, despite the cold, facing Jesus in His tabernacle, united to the distant choirs of monks, we shall offer the Lord the prayer He prefers. There the Psalms, the hymns, the versicles will take on their full meaning, and we shall be able to put our whole soul into them.

With his usual discretion our holy Father St. Benedict wishes the hour of rising to be fixed *juxta considerationem rationis*, that is to say according to a reasonable appraisal.

And we have seen that for the summer he leaves to the Abbot the care of determining the time necessary to finish Matins at dawn.

---

[9]   Preface, p. 9.

For most Oblates the time which may serve as a basis for a reasonable appraisal will be the hour set for Holy Mass. Each one can regulate his rising in such a way as to be able to recite sedately the Offices of Matins and Lauds before Mass, taking care to allow for a few minutes of reflection, or, if you will, of meditation, the better to recollect the fruits of the Office just completed and to prepare for the Holy Sacrifice which, as has been said above, forms the center of the opus Dei.

What we say here about Matins and Lauds can also be applied to the Office of Prime for the lay Oblates who say only certain Hours, especially if their work takes them away very early.

CHAPTER 9
How Many Psalms Are to Be Said at the Night Office

February 11—June 12—October 12

I N WINTER TIME as defined above, there is first this verse to be said three times: "O Lord, open my lips, and my mouth shall declare Your praise." To it is added Psalm 3 and the "Glory be to the Father," and after that Psalm 94 to be chanted with an antiphon or even chanted simply. Let the Ambrosian hymn follow next, and then six Psalms with antiphons. When these are finished and the verse said, let the Abbot give a blessing; then, all being seated on the benches, let three lessons be read from the book on the lectern by the brethren in their turns, and after each lesson let a responsory be chanted. Two of the responsories are to be said without a "Glory be to the Father"; but after the third lesson let the chanter say the "Glory be to the Father," and as soon as he begins it let all rise from their seats out of honor and reverence to the Holy Trinity.

The books to be read at the Night Office shall be those of divine authorship, of both the Old and the New Testament, and also the explanations of them which have been made by well known and orthodox Catholic Fathers.

After these three lessons with their responsories let the remaining six Psalms follow, to be chanted with "Alleluia." After these shall follow the lesson from the Apostle, to be recited by heart, the verse and the petition of the litany, that is "Lord, have mercy on us." And so let the Night Office come to an end.

COMMENTARY

St. Benedict has set the hour of rising according to the two sections of the year, winter and summer. He is now going to regulate the arrangement of the Office of Vigils or Matins, beginning with the winter period.

The Office in general is composed of preparatory prayers, the nocturns which form the body of it, and a conclusion. The Office in question here will be that of the ferias.

According to the "received text" of the Holy Rule, the Office begins with the invocation dear to the monks of Egypt: *Deus in adjutorium* etc. The ancient manuscripts make no mention of this, and the passage seems to be an interpolation designed to codify a usage introduced after St. Benedict's time.

One began, then, with the triple invocation: Domine, labia mea aperies. The monk asks the Holy Trinity for the grace to fulfil worthily his work of praise. There follows Psalm 3: *Domine, quid multiplicati sunt.* Its use in this place is undoubtedly due above all to the verse *Ego dormivi et soporatus sum.*[1] But the fact is that the whole of the Psalm harmonizes with this beginning of the Office, with this morning hour when the shades are not yet banished. It is in the night that the demons are astir, that impious works are multiplied; the soul experiences a sort of terror in face of these numerous enemies which threaten it, and it turns trustingly towards God, who will be its Savior and its glory and who will exalt His servant. The Psalm is ended with the Gloria.

Psalm 94 is then intoned. It is the Invitatory. It is always chanted and generally antiphonated, that is to say that between verses one of the choirs will repeat one of the verses, always the same, which will form a refrain.

It is perhaps unnecessary to dwell on the beauty of this prayer, which, as its name indicates, is an urgent invitation joyously to praise the Most High in psalmody. "He is the great God and the great King... the whole earth is in His hands.... The sea is His, it is He who made it. ... Let us cast ourselves at His feet, let us cry before the Lord who made us, for He is the Lord our God, we are His people and the sheep of His flock."

This Psalm, executed slowly, permitted the tardy ones to be in choir before the beginning of the first nocturn.

The series of preparatory prayers ended with the Ambrosianum, namely a hymn borrowed from the Milanese liturgy. We know that St. Ambrose, himself the author of several hymns, had introduced them into this liturgy, while the Roman liturgy at first had no knowledge of measured poetry.

We arrive now at the body of the Office. For the ferias of winter there will be two nocturns, which St. Benedict presents to us successively.

The first nocturn is composed in the first place of six "antiphonated" Psalms. The antiphon at St. Benedict's time was not, as it is today, a verse repeated only at the end of the Psalm, but, as at the Invitatory, a formula repeated in the manner of a refrain between verses. These six Psalms, thus

---

[1] "I have slept and have taken my rest."

lengthened, were recited standing. One may imagine the fatigue of those monks of heroic times, who had not as we have today the help of the *misericordia.*

When the Psalms were finished, a versicle with its responsory was chanted, as it is now. Then the reader went to the lectern, on which a manuscript was placed. He asked the Abbot's blessing, undoubtedly a single blessing for the three lessons to follow. The blessing given, all seated themselves on the benches; then the reader, standing, chanted one lesson. This lesson, like the ones that followed, was taken either from the Old or the New Testament or from the commentaries of the Fathers. Sometimes the Abbot would choose the passage to be read; at other times, no doubt, a general tradition determined these passages.

The lesson was followed by a responsory without Gloria. Another monk then went to the lectern and chanted the second lesson, which was likewise followed by a responsory without Gloria.

Finally the third lesson, chanted by a third monk, was followed by a responsory with Gloria. As soon as this word Gloria was intoned, all were to rise from their seats "because of the honor and reverence due the Holy Trinity."

The lessons were sometimes very long. Dom Calmet, who cites examples of them, recalls in particular that at Cluny the whole of Genesis was read in the week of Septuagesima, and the whole of Isaias in six ferial days.

With the third responsory the first nocturn was completed.

The second nocturn was likewise composed of six Psalms, but with Alleluia as antiphon. It is probable, notes Dom Delatte, that this Alleluia was repeated in the course of the Psalms. Following these there was only one lesson, taken from St. Paul, and quite short, so that it could be learned by heart.

We have now arrived at the final formulas. They are composed of a versicle, then the supplicatio litaniae, namely a Kyrie repeated several times and a series of invocations including, no doubt, the Pater recited silently, and likely the collect.[2]

Thus were ended the Vigils in winter time.

---

[2] On the *Litaniae* see Dom Baumer, "*Litaniae et Missae,*" in Studien und Mittheilungen (1886), pp. 287 ff., and Dom Fernand Cabrol, article "Litanies" in the *Didionnaire d'Archeologie Chrétienne et de Lilurgie,* Tome 9, part 2 (Paris: Librairie Letouzey et And, 1930), cols. 1540-1571.

APPLICATION

The Monastic Breviary has conserved the whole arrangement organized by St. Benedict. The Roman Breviary, on the other hand, does not have Vigils of two nocturns either for ferias or for feasts. Its ferial Vigils have only one nocturn. There is divergence likewise in the distribution of the Psalter. For the rest, we find the same elements in both: *Domine, labia* and *Deus in adjutorium*, but in reverse order; Invitatory; hymn, unfortunately revised in the 16th century for the Roman Office; Psalms; blessings; threefold lesson with responsories, the last being accompanied by the Gloria.

Which Breviary will the Oblates use?

The lay Oblates who live near a monastery and can actually unite themselves to the choirs of the monks will naturally choose the Monastic Breviary. The others, no doubt, will choose freely.

As for the priests, save during their stay at a monastery, where an indult permits them to use the Monastic Breviary, they will use the Roman Breviary. This indeed is the Breviary of the particular church to which they are attached. "A secular priest," says the liturgist Piller, "especially if he is beneficed or attached to some church in a diocese, even if he is a Tertiary of St. Francis or the like, cannot without a special privilege recite the Breviary of his Order. Moreover, a regular promoted to the Episcopate must leave the Breviary of his Order and recite the Office according to the rite of his diocese. Likewise, a regular attached as pastor or vicar to a diocesan church, while being held to the Office of his Order, should nevertheless ... celebrate all the public parochial Offices according to the diocesan calendar."[3]

However, the Sacred Congregation of Rites appears to have been less strict for some time now. A decree of April 15, 1904, in favor of the Franciscan Tertiaries, declares that : "The priest Tertiaries who are not bound to choir and who are attached to the service of some church, whatever it be, even parochial, may recite the Office in conformity with the Roman-Seraphic Ordo of their obedience. But they may not celebrate the Mass corresponding to that Office except in private oratories and in the churches and oratories of one of the three Orders of St. Francis. When a priest Tertiary has adopted the use of the Office and the Mass according to the Seraphic Ordo, he is not free to change at will and use sometimes

---

[3] *Manuale Rituum* (1884), p. 26.

the Seraphic Ordo and sometimes the Ordo of his diocese."[4]

We know that from the canonical point of view the Oblates and the Tertiaries are similar, as both living *"sub moderatione alicujus ordinis."*[5] Is it to be said that the Oblates may apply to themselves the privileges accorded the Tertiaries of St. Francis? Evidently not. The thing to do, then, until a new order is given, is to abide by the former decrees.

Let us note, however, that even in the recitation of the Roman Breviary the priest Oblates are authorized, in virtue of a decree of the Sacred Congregation of Rites dated February 28,1927, to add in the *Confiteor* the words *beato Patri nostro Benedicto* and *beatum Patrem nostrum Benedictum.*[6]

Let us add that it is lawful for them on the principal feast days of their Order to add to the daily Office some part of the Monastic Office, in order to associate themselves more closely with their brethren of the cloister, while still safeguarding the integrity of the Roman Office to which they are obliged.

Besides, whatever the Office be, it is always the prayer of the Church. We shall see further on that our holy Father did not insist particularly on the form he had adopted, and that the essential thing in his opinion, and the thing that he asked of his children, was to fulfil as best they could the opus Dei. It is by the care which we bring to the Office, therefore, that we shall show ourselves truly worthy of him.

Another problem, which confronts not the priest Oblate but many lay Oblates, whether they choose the one or the other Breviary or even the Office of the Blessed Virgin, is the use of the Latin. When one does not know that language, how is one to perform the Divine Office with attention and piety? Let us note that the problem is the same for a certain number of Sisters who do not know Latin.

As we have seen in reading Chapter 9, St. Benedict wants the Office to be at the same time a praise to God and a nourishment for the soul. That is why the lessons follow the Psalms and hymns in it. It is always true that in order to draw profit from those readings, one must know their meaning at least broadly.

---

[4] Manuel du Tiers-Ordre de la Pénitence..., by a Friar Minor of the Province of Saint-Denis, 2nd ed. (Rennes: Librairie Saint-Yves), p. 175,

[5] *Codex Juris Canonici,* Canon 702, 51.

[6] "Statutes of the Oblates," in *Manual for Oblates,* pp. 49-50, §38.

Dom L'Huillier has treated this question in an appendix of his commentary on the Holy Rule,[7] and here are the solutions he proposes:

"1. It would be necessary before all and to satisfy the first duty of monastic piety, to work at acquiring a certain knowledge of the language, sufficient at least for keeping the soul attuned to the Office in its general progress.

"2. If one has not the means for this study, whether through want of a teacher, or by reason of urgent occupations, or finally as a result of natural inaptitude or difficulties created by age, then there are the translations: translations of the Psalter in great number, and one may easily grasp more of the general idea of a Psalm in them, in order to conform one's intention to it during the psalmody;[8] translations of the entire Breviary, which will give the meaning of the lessons.[9]... Thus one will keep oneself in union with the mind of the Church, and one will draw much greater profit for one's own self from the graces of the Divine Office. It is not important to understand everything. The formulas are always holy ones, and we are addressing to God nothing but praises and prayers pleasing to His ears; the Church is our warrant for that, and her intention is imputed to us as long as we seek to conform ours to it.

"3. Are these measures themselves impracticable? That is regrettable, and it is urgent that one seek all means of remedying so serious a lack, far from regarding the Divine Office as a useless charge because one does not understand it." And Dom L'Huillier advises a person to "look for some considerations which help him draw near to the meaning of the Office and enter into its current." Let him think about the divine attributes, mercy, justice and the rest, the praise of which fills the Psalms, or about the benefits of the Redemption which the Psalms announce. Let him meditate on the feast of the day during the lessons, the hymns and the collects. Here and there some word whose meaning he recognizes will conjure up

---

[7] Tome 2, pp. 380 ff.

[8] "The more easily because the most frequently used Psalms are few in number" (Dom L'Huillier's note).

[9] *Roman Breviary in English* (New York: Benziger Brothers, 1950). There is no complete English translation of the Monastic Breviary. Most of the lessons, however, are translated in The Lessons of the Temporal Cycle and the Principal Feasts of the Sanctoral Cycle According to the Monastic Breviary (St. Meinrad, Ind.: St. Meinrad's Abbey Press, 1940). The Day Hours are translated in the Monastic Diurnal (Mechlin : Dessain, 1950).

thoughts proper to those divine objects. He will be sure of "thinking with the Church."

"Moreover," concludes Dom L'Huillier, "even if a person understood nothing of the letter of the Office, it would be a mistake to think that he draws no fruit from it. The Church benefits from it, because it is not a material and mechanical exercise on our part, but an act accomplished in virtue of an obligation of supernatural order, and by force of will. Hence there is at the same time as the Church's prayer a merit for the one who serves the Church by lending her his voice and his will. Merit again because the sentiments which the lips express are those of the Church, which attributes them to us in imposing on us the obligation of repeating them to God (or at least, for the Oblates, in inviting us to do this). Finally a quite special blessing, because they are holy rites, inspired words, and because in their passing through our lips and our organs of speech, as long as our will applies them to ourself, even without lights of understanding, a blessing remains attached to the channels thus traversed by the Word of the Divinity."

CHAPTER 10
How the Night Office Is to Be Said in Summer Time

February 12—June 13—October 13

rom Easter until the Calends of November let the same number of Psalms be kept as prescribed above; but no lessons are to be read from the book, on account of the shortness of the nights. Instead of those three lessons let one lesson from the Old Testament be said by heart and followed by a short responsory. But all the rest should be done as has been said; that is to say that never fewer than twelve Psalms should be said at the Night Office, not counting Psalm 3 and Psalm 94.

COMMENTARY

It remained to determine the organization of the Vigils during the summer season, namely from Easter to the Calends of November. We know that the nights are shorter then, and consequently there is less time at disposal before dawn if the monks are to have the necessary amount of rest.

Still, nothing will be changed in the Psalms. There will always be twelve of them. The commentators have long since observed that this number of twelve, according to Cassian,[1] was supposed to have been revealed by an Angel. It will be kept, therefore. Even in the Office of the feasts which have three nocturns, the third nocturn will be composed not of Psalms but of canticles. The abridgment, consequently, will not bear on the psalmody but on the lessons and the responsories. In place of three lessons there will be only one, and so short that it will not be necessary to have a manuscript before one's eyes in order to recite it. It will be said from memory. The lesson will be followed by a short responsory. The rest of the Office will be identical with that of winter.

Obviously, neither the preparatory Psalm *Domine, quid multiplicati sunt* nor the Invitatory will be counted in the twelve required Psalms.

APPLICATION

---

[1] *Institutes*, Book 2, Chapter 5; in C.S.E.L., Vol. 17, pp. 20-22; in *Nicene and Post-Nicene Fathers*, 2nd series, Vol. 11, pp. 206-207.

This little chapter hardly lends itself to ascetical or mystical applications. The former authors of meditations on the Holy Rule have nevertheless found in it themes for reflection, from which we can always draw profit. Dom Philippe Francois in his Considerations remarks "the discretion" of St. Benedict, who in disposing the "divine service, arranges it in such a way that it accommodates itself to the quality of the seasons and condescends to the weakness of the religious." He concludes from this that, following the holy Father's example, in the service of God and in all our actions we must use "a holy discretion" and "have regard for the time and for the extent of our strength."[2]

Dom Robert Morel[3] draws from the same chapter this consideration: "the fact that the shortness of the nights or some other reason makes us curtail our service" should be compensated for "by a redoubling of fervor," for the "good servants" neglect nothing of what may render "their service agreeable to their Master."

Aside from such considerations, Chapter 10 has always its literal application in the Monastic Breviary. The Roman Breviary makes no distinction between winter and summer as to length of Office.

---

[2] *Considerations en Forme de Mèditations sur la Règle de S. Benoît* (1664), p. 224.

[3] *Meditations*, p. 214.

CHAPTER 11
How the Night Office Is to Be Said on Sundays

February 13—June 14—October 14

N SUNDAY the hour of rising for the Night Office should be earlier. In that Office let the measure already prescribed be kept, namely the singing of six Psalms and a verse. Then let all be seated on the benches in their proper order while the lessons and their responsories are read from the book, as we said above. These shall be four in number, with the chanter saying the "Glory be to the Father" in the fourth responsory only, and all rising reverently as soon as he begins it.

After these lessons let six more Psalms with antiphons follow in order, as before, and a verse; and then let four more lessons be read with their responsories in the same way as the former.

After these let there be three canticles from the book of the Prophets, as the Abbot shall appoint, and let these canticles be chanted with "Alleluia." Then when the verse has been said and the Abbot has given the blessing, let four more lessons be read, from the New Testament, in the manner prescribed above.

After the fourth responsory let the Abbot begin the hymn "We praise You, O God." When this is finished the Abbot shall read the lesson from the book of the Gospels, while all stand in reverence and awe. At the end let all answer "Amen," and let the Abbot proceed at once to the hymn "To You be praise." After the blessing has been given, let them begin the Morning Office.

This order for the Night Office on Sunday shall be observed the year around, both summer and winter; unless it should happen (which God forbid) that the brethren be late in rising, in which case the lessons or the reponsories will have to be shortened somewhat. Let every precaution be taken, however, against such an occurrence; but if it does happen, then the one through whose neglect it has come about should make due satisfaction to God in the oratory.

COMMENTARY

Sunday is the Lord's day. Thus it should be marked by a redoubling of piety and fervor. The Office of Vigils, therefore, will be longer than on ferial days; and since it is to end in time for Lauds, the hour of rising will be earlier.

St. Benedict does not consider it necessary to go over the preparatory parts of the Office again. For the Psalms, he says, the "measure" previously indicated will be followed, that is to say, there will be six of them at each of the first two nocturns, and these six Psalms will be chanted. After the versicle of the first nocturn, the reader will go to the lectern as usual, and he will read from the manuscript not three but four lessons. Each lesson will be followed by a responsory, and the fourth responsory will be accompanied by the *Gloria*.

During the lessons the monks will be seated *disposite et per ordinem*, that is to say in the order assigned by their time of profession or by the will of the Abbot. The point was that they did not assist at the Office in confusion and take the first place at hand, but observed an order established in advance. At the Gloria all will rise immediately with reverence.

The second nocturn likewise will include six Psalms with antiphons. It will have four lessons and four responsories. Its structure will be like that of the first in everything.

With the two nocturns we have completed the traditional cycle of twelve Psalms. We have seen that St. Benedict, following Cassian, holds to that number. And yet there will be a third nocturn; but the Psalms will be replaced in it by canticles, and there will be only three of them. The text says *tria cantica de Prophetarum*, which must be translated word for word, "three canticles taken from the *Prophetarum*," just as *lectionem de Evangelia*, below, would be "the lesson from the *Evangelia*." *Prophetarum* (*liber* understood) and *Evangelia* were the names of the manuscripts in use, so designated from the first word of their title.

St. Benedict did not invent the liturgical use of the canticles. It was already found in the churches of the East, of Rome and of Milan. He merely specifies that it is the Abbot who will choose them. The canticles will have Alleluia as antiphon.

After the versicle of the third nocturn and the Abbot's blessing, four lessons from the New Testament will be chanted. The New Testament here can mean only the Acts of the Apostles and the Epistles, since the Gospels are reserved for the final part of the Office. Responsories will be alternated with the lessons as above.

After the fourth responsory the Abbot will intone the Te Deum. This is the wonderful song of thanksgiving in which the Church on earth unites her accents with the ineffable harmonies of the Angels and of the Saints. And still this is not yet the culminating point of the Office. The *Te*

Deum completed, all remain standing "'with reverence and fear," and the Abbot reads a passage from the Gospel, probably that of the day's Mass. "Thus St. Benedict wants us to pass through an admirable order from the instructions of the Prophets to those of the Apostles, thence to be raised to the word of Jesus Christ, which is a more vivid image of eternal life, in order that we may rest in that divine word as in the end to which we aspire."[1] At the end of the reading all answer Amen, and the Abbot intones the very short chant of the *Te decet laus.*

St. Benedict tells us that the *Te decet* is to be followed by the *benedictio,* "blessing." Probably this word is the equivalent of the *litaniae.* We have seen that the ferial Vigils were ended thus. In Chapter 17, regarding Compline, St. Benedict will tell us that it is completed with *Kyrie eleison* and *benedictio.* The presence of a *Benedicamus Domino* by itself or more or less developed at the end of the litany may have served to give the litany also the name of blessing. Thus St. Benedict would be taking the part to designate the whole.

"Matins," that is to say Lauds, can then be commenced, not without allowing the short interval spoken of previously.

The solemnity of the Sunday is something so important that it will be alike in every season. St. Benedict seems to be considering the fact that its length may cause displeasure in winter time. That is the period when rising takes more effort and also when, given the rather rudimentary means of knowing the hour, one is exposed to the error of beginning somewhat tardily. St. Benedict does not like to consider this possibility, however. But the fact remains that the case can present itself. Then nothing is to be changed in the number of the Psalms. But in order that the monks may be ready for Lauds, the lessons, which as we have seen were sometimes quite long, will be abridged. As for the negligent bell-ringer, he is to "make due satisfaction to God in the oratory." "By this satisfaction," says an old commentator,[2] "St. Benedict means that he is to prostrate himself before everybody... to suffer himself to be reprimanded or even to have some greater punishment added thereto if the fault demands it."

APPLICATION

[1]   *Traduction et Explication Littérale,* p. 201.

[2]   Ibid,., p. 203.

It is quite natural that the Office of the Lord's day be longer and more solemn than that of the other days. It is the day of the Lord!

In the Roman Office as in the Monastic Office there will be three nocturns and the solemn singing of the Te Deum. This is the rite for festivities, and the Sunday celebrates the great mystery of the Resurrection.

We shall strive, therefore, on this day to belong more to the Lord than on the other days. The Lord's day is profaned by a considerable number of Christians. How is it kept holy by many of those who think they are still good people? How completely they imagine they have paid their debt to God by having assisted at a morning Mass, where they even went to Communion! And yet it is not a half hour, it is not an hour that the Lord claims, it is the whole day. If we are not giving it to Him, we are stealing it.

We shall keep holy, therefore, the whole day of the Lord. Now to keep this day holy is not only to give oneself to private prayer; it is to serve God as He wants to be served, namely by assistance at all the Offices, therefore at the parochial or community High Mass, at Vespers, at Compline. An Oblate has by no means the Benedictine spirit if he stays away willingly from Vespers and from Compline. He who says Benedictine says man of the divine praise, of the liturgical praise. The mania for making oneself a little religion apart must be left to certain devotees. St. Benedict has taught us in the eighth degree of humility the necessity of being pliable to the "common Rule." For us who live away from the monastery the "common Rule" is to identify ourselves with the parochial community of which we are members, to give it the example, to be towards the lukewarm the ardent apostles of the liturgical life.

Let the priest Oblates among us not be of those who, for reasons often trivial, suppress the only public Offices which, outside of the Mass, unite the faithful to the prayer of the Church. Let us not replace them by ceremonies of our own fancy, often in doubtful taste and of questionable efficacy. Let us explain the liturgical Offices, give commentaries on them, cause them to be carried out with dignity and piety, make them appreciated and loved.

Let those of us who are lay Oblates be unfailingly faithful to the liturgical prayer, even if we have to make ourselves noticed by the tenacious character of our devotion to it. Let us recall that we are "the monks of the outside," those who separate themselves from the lazy and the negligent to belong wholly to the Work of God.

CHAPTER 12
How the Morning Office Is to Be Said

February 14—June 15—October 15

THE MORNING OFFICE on Sunday shall begin with Psalm 66 recited straight through without an antiphon. After that let Psalm 50 be said with "Alleluia," then Psalms 117 and 62, the Canticle of Blessing and the Psalms of praise; then a lesson from the Apocalypse to be recited by heart, the responsory, the Ambrosian hymn, the verse, the canticle from the Gospel book, the litany and so the end.

COMMENTARY

In spite of the title, which lacks precision, the concern in this chapter is only with Sunday Matins. Let us recall that for St. Benedict Matins or the Morning Office corresponds to what we call Lauds. This is an Office the institution of which antedated St. Benedict by several centuries. This hour when the night is dispelled and gives place to the first radiations of the day symbolized for the Christians the coming of Jesus Christ the Savior and His victory over the powers of darkness.

It has been asked whether this Office began with *the Deus in adjutorium* for St. Benedict makes no mention of it. Dom Hugh Menard, Dom Haeften, the author of the Translation and Explanation and others hold for the negative. Dom Delatte does not presume to take sides. Dom L'Huillier declares for the affirmative; for, he says, there are many other details of rubrics which St. Benedict passes over in silence and which existed none the less. If the text in its present state were not doubtful, one could even offer in proof of this opinion the passage in Chapter 18 where it is said that the *Deus in adjutorium* is to be said at the day Hours, among which St. Benedict includes Lauds.

The Office will be begun with the slow recitation of Psalm 66, *Deus, misereatur nostri,* in order to give the tardy ones time to arrive, as at Vigils. This Psalm will have no antiphon. Following this the *Miserere* will be chanted with Alleluia as antiphon. This chanting of the *Miserere* is found in the Roman Office in the Lauds of Advent and of Lent. The idea is to purify our soul by the tears of compunction before saluting the mystical coming of the Savior.

160

There follows Psalm 117, *Confitemini Domino, quoniam bonus.* This Psalm is a cry of confidence, of a joyous and resolute confidence in God, "whose mercy is eternal" and who never abandons those who have the joy of belonging to Him. Is not this trustful prayer most fitting for the beginning of the day, at the time when we must again take up the daily struggle? It is at the same time the Psalm of the Resurrection, which every Sunday commemorates and which took place at the hour of Lauds. Do we not read there that *Haec dies quam fecit* Dominus which will come back so often in the solemnity of the "holy Pasch"? In the Roman Office the *Confitemini* is found only on the Sundays of Advent and of Lent. On the other Sundays it is carried over to Prime.

The Deus, Deus mens which comes next is plainly indicated for the Office of dawn. It has been kept in the Sunday and feastday liturgy of the Roman Office, and St. Benedict had found it almost generally used in the Morning Office.

The "blessings" of which our holy Father speaks designate the canticle *Benedicite.* All creatures, awakened from their sleep, are invited to sing to their Creator. The last Psalms are the "Lauds," namely three Psalms of praise beginning with the words *Laudate* and *Cantate.* The use of the *Benedicite* and of one of the Psalms of praise has likewise been kept in the Sunday and feastday liturgy of the Roman Office.

After the last Psalm comes a short lesson or little chapter, taken from the Apocalypse and chanted from memory, then a responsory, a hymn and a versicle.

The versicle is followed by the canticle from the Gospel, namely the Benedictus, chosen especially because of the passage *Visitavit nos oriens ex alto,* in which the Savior is compared to the rising sun. Finally comes the litany, that is to say the *Kyrie,* terminated likely by a collect, although St. Benedict does not say so; and the Office is finished.

APPLICATION

The Office of Lauds, especially on Sundays and ferias, is one of real beauty, but that beauty is not truly sensed unless the Office is recited at the time of day for which it was composed, namely at daybreak. Then the light is appearing little by little in nature; objects are being colored with a very soft tint; life seems to be taking hold again and thrilling, as it were, in all creatures; in the church the windows are taking on a coloring and shadings which they will no longer have when the sunlight is brighter. It is then that we understand and feel more profoundly the comparisons in the hymns and the Psalms greeting Christ, light and splendor. In this supernatural light our soul, scarcely come forth from the night's repose, opens itself more easily to the thoughts of eternity. The visible things and the invisible which have become luminous unite and combine to touch our soul profoundly, to inspire in it a loving, joyous praise for Him from whom it awaits all strength, all life, all salvation:

Jesu, labantes respice
Et nos videndo corrige. . .
Tu, lux, refulge sensibus
Mentisque somnum discute:
Te nostra vox primum sonet....
"Look on us, Jesu, when we fall,
And with Thy look our souls recall...
Shed through our hearts Thy piercing ray.
Our souls' dull slumber drive away:
Thy Name be first on every tongue ..."[1]

Would there not be a real loss in performing this Office at an hour which would be unsuited to it and when most of these prayers and hymns would lose part of their application? The Church, and St. Benedict with her, wanted Lauds to be an Office of dawn. If we have the sweet obligation of the Divine Office or if as lay Oblates we have the opportunity of reciting it, let us follow the Church's directives and put ourselves in the school of our holy Father.

---

[1] Translation by W. J. Copeland as quoted in Rev. Matthew Britt, O.S.B., *The Hymns of the Breviary and Missal* (New York: Benziger Brothers, Inc., 1948), p. 21.

CHAPTER 13
How the Morning Office Is to Be Said on Weekdays

February 15—June 16—October 16

N WEEKDAYS the Morning Office shall be celebrated as follows. Let Psalm 66 be said without an antiphon and somewhat slowly, as on Sunday, in order that all may be in time for Psalm 50, which is to be said with an antiphon. After that let two other Psalms be said according to custom, namely: on Monday Psalms 5 and 35, on Tuesday Psalms 42 and 56, on Wednesday Psalms 63 and 64, on Thursday Psalms 87 and 89, on Friday Psalms 75 and 91, and on Saturday Psalm 142 and the canticle from Deuteronomy, which is to be divided into two sections each terminated by a "Glory be to the Father." But on the other days let there be a canticle from the Prophets, each on its own day as chanted by the Roman Church. Next follow the Psalms of praise, then a lesson of the Apostle to be recited from memory, the responsory, the Ambrosian hymn, the verse, the canticle from the Gospel book, the litany, and so the end.

COMMENTARY

The "Matins" of ordinary days will begin, like those of Sunday, with the preparatory Psalm *Deus misereatur*, which will be said with a little prolongation "in order that all may assemble in time for Psalm 50." This condescension of St. Benedict shows his great kindness. "There is nothing," remarks the author of the Translation and Explanation, "in which St. Benedict does not take care to accommodate himself to all his children, and it is wonderful to see the kindness he has for them."

As on Sunday, the Psalm *Miserere* begins the Office properly speaking. It is accompanied by an antiphon. There follow two Psalms which change every day. St. Benedict adds "according to custom." What custom is meant: the one followed in Italy or, as Dom Mège would have it, the one followed at Monte Cassino? And then, do these words refer to the use of two Psalms or to the determination of those two Psalms? Dom Delatte declares for the latter opinion; and Dom Calmet, who likewise adopts it, believes that the choice of these Psalms arises from the fact that they "speak of the morning light and refer to the Resurrection." In the present Roman Office one of the two Psalms used from Monday to Thursday is still the same, namely: Monday, Psalm 5, *Verba mea*; Tuesday, Psalm 42,

Judica; Wednesday, Psalm 64, *Te decet*; Thursday, Psalm 89, *Domine, refugium*. For Friday and Saturday there is an inversion: Psalm 91, *Bonum est*, found on Saturday in the Roman Office, is read on Friday in the monastic rite; and Psalm 142, *Domine, exaudi*, set for Saturday in the Monastic Office, occurs on Friday in the Roman.

The two Psalms are followed by a canticle which varies every day "as chanted by the Roman Church." Although at Sunday Vigils the Abbot chose canticles for the third nocturn because the Roman Church, which uses Psalms there, could not serve as model, the case is quite otherwise for Lauds. Thus these canticles remained identical in the two rites for ferial days.

There follow the Psalms of praise, the short lesson taken from St. Paul, the short responsory, the Ambrosian hymn, the versicle, the Gospel canticle or Benedictus and the litany. The Office is thus ended.

APPLICATION

There is no need to dwell on the application of this chapter, which speaks for itself. Let us content ourselves with reproducing this pious consideration which Dom Philippe Francois adds to it in his Spiritual Exercises on the Rule of St. Benedict: "Consider that the servants of earthly princes and kings sometimes have vacations and intermissions in their service; they are not always in court. But the servants of God have no respite. They must serve this great King of heaven and earth without cease and without any intermission, and always with the same affection and devotion. That is why St. Benedict did not content himself with arranging the Office of the holy days—Sundays and feasts— but arranged also that of the work days, in order to make his religious see that in the service of God there is no pause nor intermission."

Since we, like the monks, are the men of the divine praise, let us therefore rejoice in returning each morning to God with our tribute of praises "ever old and ever new." We may well experience some weariness at times, but on reflection we shall be obliged indeed to avow that our lot is really the best.

February 16—June 17—October 17

The Morning and Evening Offices should never be allowed to pass without the Superior saying the Lord's Prayer in its place at the end so that all may hear it, on account of the thorns of scandal which are apt to spring up. Thus those who hear it, being warned by the covenant which they make in that prayer when they say, "Forgive us as we forgive," may cleanse themselves of faults against that covenant.

But at the other Offices let the last part only of that prayer be said aloud, so that all may answer, "But deliver us from evil."

COMMENTARY

The litany which terminates the Offices includes the recitation of the Pater. St. Benedict wants this recitation to have something more solemn about it at Lauds and at Vespers. The Superior himself is to recite it aloud, all being attentive to his words. Why this chant more solemn at Lauds and at Vespers than at the other Offices? Undoubtedly because the one marks the beginning and the other the end of the day and because thus chanted it takes on the character of an exhortation.

At these times there is one part of the Pater which should especially hold the attention of the monks: "Forgive us our trespasses, as we forgive...Is not this a sort of treaty entered into with God, in virtue of which mutual pardon is the condition of the divine pardon? When the Evening Office is ended should not the monk, after having examined himself on the faults of the day, make sure that the sun does not set on antipathies and hates? These indeed are "thorns of scandal," of which it behooves him to rid himself. God does not like them, for He is the God of peace and of charity, and He wills absolutely that the one and the other reign in souls. And in the morning, is it not useful to take all the precautions possible that the day may pass without any fault of this kind?

At the end of the other Hours the Pater will also be recited, for the Lord's prayer ought to be found in all the Offices; but it will be said silently except for the final "And lead us not into temptation," to which all will answer, "But deliver us from evil."

The solemn chant of the Pater morning and evening is not peculiar to St. Bendeict. It was decreed by the Council of Girone in 517. But our holy Father adopts it and gives us the reason for it.

APPLICATION

In the Roman Breviary the chant of the Pater at Lauds and at Vespers takes place only on the ferias of Advent and Lent and in the Offices of Vigils and of Ember Days.[1] With this Office, or that of the Blessed Virgin, how shall we respond to the formal intention of our holy Father, which is

---

[1]   This rubric is of monastic origin.

above all to take advantage of the recitation of the Pater for our renewal in charity? Easily enough, if we really want to. If it is not lawful for us, indeed, to insert into the Office what has not been put there by the rubrics, it always remains possible to attach a special intention to one or another part of that Office. Now the Pater is always recited, though silently, after the *Fidelium animae* of Lauds and of Vespers.

Is this not the occasion for remembering St. Benedict's prescription and examining ourselves well on the precept of the forgiving of trespasses?

"One of the principal effects of the Lord's Prayer," says Dom Morel in this regard,[2] "is to contribute to the remission of our sins and to the cure of the maladies of our soul. It is, says St. Augustine, like a daily Baptism in which we are washed and purified of our stains ... but for its effects to be felt it must be said with holy dispositions and in a spirit of peace and charity. He who says it with hate and vengeance in his heart, far from finding in it a Baptism which purifies him ... meets in it only a rock on which he perishes and a poison which brings death to him. ...Oh, how important it is to have an indulgent and charitable heart! We cannot dispense ourselves from saying the Lord's Prayer every day, and we could not say it with a vindictive heart without condemning our own selves."

If the Lord's Prayer, come forth from the divine heart and lips, is the most beautiful one there is, and also the most complete, and like a summary of the Gospel, it is likewise the most serious in its consequences. It saves us or condemns us according to the dispositions of our heart. Cassian[3] recounts that certain Christians who entertained animosities in their heart dared not pronounce it entirely, and were silent at the words "as we forgive." How many others there are today who recite it mechanically, without thinking of the seriousness of their words! Let us recite it, therefore, always with attention and with faith, pondering the advice of St. Benedict, who, "as a good Father, feared nothing so much as to see the sun set on the anger of his children."[4]

---

[2] *Méditations*, p. 222.

[3] *Conference* 9, Chapter 22; in C.S.E.L., Vol. 13, p. 271; in Nicene and Post-Nicene Fathers, 2nd series, Vol. 11, p. 395.

[4] Traduction el Explication Litérale, p. 210.

CHAPTER 14

How the Night Office Is to Be Said on the Feasts of the Saints

February 17—June 18—October 18

 N THE FEASTS of Saints and on all festivals let the Office be performed as we have prescribed for Sundays, except that the Psalms, the antiphons and the lessons belonging to the particular day are to be said. Their number, however, shall remain as we have specified above.

COMMENTARY

Although the title of this chapter speaks only of the Vigils, the text seems to refer to the whole of the Offices for the feasts in honor of the Saints. To the mention of these feasts St. Benedict adds that of "all the solemnities," By these last words must evidently be understood the great feasts consecrated to the mysteries, like Christmas, Epiphany and so forth.

All these feasts will be celebrated like Sundays, that is to say that they will have three nocturns and twelve lessons. On this point there is no difficulty, but where the text becomes obscure is when St. Benedict adds, "except that the Psalms, the antiphons and the lessons belonging to the particular day are to be said." What is meant by the expression "belonging to the particular day"? Does St. Benedict mean "belonging to the feria" or "belonging to the feast"?

In favor of the first opinion we find the translators of the text of the Holy Rule for the use of the Congregation of Saint-Maur, in a note which appears to be by Dom Simon Bougis;[1] the author of the *Translation and Explanation*; Dom Calmet and others. The reason which these authors allege is that if the existence of Psalms proper to the feast were admitted, the integral recitation of the Psalter as St. Benedict himself required would no longer be observed, since perforce certain Psalms would be left aside, to be replaced by others more appropriate to the occasion. One may object, it is true, that as St. Benedict puts "Psalms, antiphons and lessons" on the same footing, and as the ferias have only two nocturns and three lessons, or even one lesson only, in summer, and antiphons only for the first nocturn, one would lack some elements necessary for fulfilling what

---

[1] *La Règle de S. Benoist,* pg. 34, following the *Exercices Spirituels.*

has just been prescribed, namely to celebrate the Office as on Sundays. Dom Calmet replies that one could take twelve lessons from the source from which one had taken three, and that one could have a choice of antiphons for this particular case. The explanation is rather laborious, for it would give the term "belonging to the day" two different acceptations, one for the Psalms and another for the antiphons and the lessons. In the former case they would mean "belonging to the feria," and in the latter "belonging to the feast." If St. Benedict had wanted to tell us that, he would certainly have avoided the ambiguity and would have been more explicit.

Dom Mège, the Abbé de Rancé, Dom Étienne Salasc, Dom Delatte, Dom Laure and others admit the second solution. "One may suppose," says the Abbé de Rancé, "that this word 'day' is not to be understood of the feria, but that it is determined by the lessons, which could only be those of the feast or of the solemnity; thus the Psalms were peculiar to the feast, as were the antiphons and the lessons." The objection made by Dom Calmet and the rest on the integrity of the Psalter, which would not be respected, is certainly negligible. At that epoch the feasts of the Saints were few in number. They constituted only exceptions, and consequently the great principle of the weekly recitation of the Psalter could be considered safe. Let us add that the feasts of the Saints had proper Offices well before St. Benedict's time, and that it is probable that the holy Lawgiver, who borrowed from the ancient churches the essentials of the festive and sanctoral calendar, likewise borrowed from them the content of the Offices.

APPLICATION

In devoting a chapter to the feasts of the Saints, St. Benedict was not exactly making an innovation. At least, notes Dom Delatte, he was assuring their cult a place of honor and a regular place in the properly monastic liturgy. We know that our holy Father had a great devotion for the Angels and for the Saints. He has already spoken to us several times of the providential rôle of the former (Chapter 7), and he will speak of it again (Chapter 19). St. Gregory informs us that at Monte Cassino St. Benedict erected oratories to St. John the Baptist and to St. Martin. We shall see later that he wants the profession to be made before the relics, and consequently that these occupy a place of honor in the oratory.

The sanctoral cycle, having become more full today than in the sixth century, has at least the advantage of placing before us the virtues of the Saints, arousing us by their example and calling down upon us the power of their intercession. Apostles, martyrs, confessors, virgins, holy women, they surround the throne of the Lamb, but they are always our brethren. They draw us into their paths by showing us the reward of their trials and their struggles. *Quod isti et istae fecerunt, cur non ego?* "Why cannot I do what these men and women have done?" It is good for us to apply ourselves to honoring them well, uniting ourselves to the intentions of the Church. That is what our Statutes recommend to us: "They should cultivate a tender devotion to the Immaculate Mother of God, and pay all due honor to the Angels and Saints, in particular to Saint Joseph and to our glorious Father Benedict, and to all the Saints of the Benedictine Order."[2] Among so many blessed souls who have arrived in the fatherland, are not the Holy Monks in particular our brethren and our models, since by the Oblature we have entered into the monastic family?

---

[2] *Manual for Oblates*, p. 46, §26.

CHAPTER 15

At What Times "Alleluia" Is to Be Said

February 18—June 19—October 19

rom holy Easter until Pentecost without interruption let "Alleluia" be said both in the Psalms and in the responsories. From Pentecost to the beginning of Lent let it be said every night with the last six Psalms of the Night Office only. On every Sunday, however, outside of Lent, the canticles, the Morning Office, Prime, Terce, Sext and None shall be said with "Alleluia," but Vespers with antiphons.

The responsories are never to be said with "Alleluia" except from Easter to Pentecost.

COMMENTARY

The Alleluia is an acclamation which marks the supernatural joy of certain periods and of certain Offices. Now there is one liturgical period joyful above all: Paschal Time. Thus our holy Father desires that during this time, namely "from holy Easter until Pentecost," Alleluia be chanted "without interruption both in the Psalms and in the responsories." In other words, the Psalms will be antiphonated with Alleluia, and it will be added to the responsories.

From Pentecost until the beginning of Lent, outside of Sundays, it will be said at the Vigils with the last six Psalms. As for the Sundays, since they are a renewal of Easter, the Alleluia will be found there in the canticles of the third nocturn of Vigils, at Matins, at Prime, at Terce, at Sext and at None. On the other hand, it will not be said at Vespers, which have their own antiphons. St. Benedict does not speak of Compline, for its Psalms are always recited *in directum*, that is to say without antiphon.

St. Benedict was not acquainted with Septuagesima.

During Lent, a time of penance, there will never be an *Alleluia*.

It will not be used in the responsories either, at any time outside of Paschal Time.

APPLICATION

By devoting a chapter to the Alleluia, St. Benedict shows us how dear to him is the liturgical life. The Church through her wonderful cycle of seasons and of feasts guides our soul in the meditation of the mysteries, teaches it joy and compunction, makes it penetrate deeply into supernatural realities and makes it participate in the graces which flow therefrom. There is a life of the Church, a piety of the Church, a prayer of the Church in which all the faithful, members of the Mystical Body, ought to be found; a wonderful communion, which is quite the opposite of certain individualistic pieties living alongside the riches of the liturgy without profiting from them. St. Benedict lives the life of the Church fully. With her he will weep for the sins of men during Lent; with her he will rejoice with a true joy at that time of the Holy Pasch which one cannot approach without the thrill "of spiritual longing" (Chapter 49).

So should it be with his children. "The heedlessness of liturgical forms," says Dom Guéranger, "which is the most palpable index of the weakening of the faith in Christianity, and which reigns so universally around us, is the reason why many Christians, even those who frequent the Church and the Sacraments, see each year, without being moved by it, this suppression of the *Alleluia*. Hardly any of them give it even a fleeting and distracted attention, preoccupied as they are with a piety wholly private and outside of the Church's thought. ...We exhort them to reflect on the sovereign authority and the profound wisdom of our common Mother, who regards the suspension of the Alleluia as one of the gravest and most solemn incidents of the liturgical year. ... The piety of our fathers, at the age when the Christian faith was still the supreme law of individuals as of societies, was very sensitive to the interruption of that heavenly cry."

CHAPTER 16
How the Work of God Is to Be Performed During the Day

February 19—June 20—October 20

EVEN times in the day," says the Prophet, "I have rendered praise to You" (*Psalm* 118:164). Now that sacred number of seven will be fulfilled by us if we perform the Offices of our service at the time of the Morning Office, of Prime, of Terce, of Sext, of None, of Vespers and of Compline, since it was of these day Hours that he said, "Seven times in the day I have rendered praise to You." For as to the Night Office the same Prophet says, "In the middle of the night I arose to glorify You" (*Psalm* 118:62).

Let us therefore bring our tribute of praise to our Creator "for the judgments of His justice" (*Psalm* 118:164) at these times: the Morning Office, Prime, Terce, Sext, None, Vespers and Compline; and in the night let us arise to glorify Him.

COMMENTARY

Thus far St. Benedict has spoken especially of the Offices of the night. He has included Lauds in them, because that Office follows Matins almost immediately. We shall see, however, that as Lauds are celebrated at daybreak, our holy Father does not hesitate to count them as an Office of the day in order to complete a mystic number. This indeed is the principle he states, that there ought to be seven Offices of the day, and he supports the principle by the Psalmist's declaration, "Seven times in the day I have said Your praise." It is certain that in the language of the Scriptures "seven times" means "often." But St. Benedict takes the sacred text literally. We are to praise God, therefore, seven times a day, and "we shall fulfil the sacred number by the Offices of Matins, Prime, Terce, Sext, None, Vespers, and Compline."

The most ancient and most solemn Offices are Lauds and Vespers, which were celebrated daily from the first half of the fourth century. Vespers used to begin at the hour when Vesper, the evening star, appeared. They were also called Laicernarium, for the lamps of the church were lighted at that time. Perhaps these Offices had their origin in Jewish customs.

Some suppose that it is the same with the three little Hours of Terce,

172

Sext and None, although it appears more probable that they were originally "Offices peculiar to monks."[1]

The Office of Prime is certainly monastic, and Cassian tells us its origin. It had come about in a monastery at Bethlehem, not that of St. Jerome, that certain monks coming from Lauds and waiting for Terce would go to bed instead of reading or meditating. A reaction necessarily followed, and the elders decided that there would be "another Matins," altera matutina, which would begin at sunrise. It was at the same time a morning prayer and a preparation for work. Such today is the meaning of the Office of Prime.

It has sometimes been supposed that Compline was instituted by St. Benedict. In reality it existed before him. The Abbé de Rancé had already demonstrated that St. Basil made mention of it, and Pere Pargoire has since then repeated the demonstration more fully.[2] But perhaps it was St. Benedict who gave it the name of *Completorium*. Perhaps also it was the introduction of this Office into the Benedictine *cursus* that brought about its diffusion. Cassian had no knowledge of it. It is an evening prayer more appropriate than Vespers for the hour at which it is recited.

It is thus, says St. Benedict, that "we fulfil the duties of our service," *nostrae servitutis officia persolvamus.* Here the *officium servitutis* offers nothing difficult; it is not a pen- sum, still less a drudgery; it is a service joyfully offered to a beloved Master who is also a most loving Father.

St. Benedict, who wished to justify by the Scriptures the number of the day Offices, feels also the need to justify the very existence of the Night Office. He has recourse to the same Psalm. "In the middle of the night," says the Psalmist, "I would arise to praise You." And so it is that the monk sanctifies by his divine praise both the days and the nights.

APPLICATION

We too, if we want to show ourselves true sons of St. Benedict, must render to the Lord the *officium servitutis*. Our Office, our Breviary, must frame our life, so to speak, must furnish it the spiritual nourishment necessary for the rest of the hours and lead it back without cease towards Him whom we ought never to leave.

---

[1] Dom J. Baudot, *The Breviary*, translated from the French by the Benedictines of Stanbrook (St. Louis: B. Herder Book Company, 1929), p. 12.

[2] "Prime et Complies," in *Revue d' Histoire et de Littérature Religieuses, 1898, pp. 281-288.*

Dom Maréchaux, in presenting the little Treatise on the Ecclesiastical Ministry, sketches what would be the priest's day if he consented, as St. Benedict desires, to perform the Divine Office at the proper hours: "Lauds would richly nourish his meditation. Prime would again become his morning prayer, Terce would enter into his preparation for Holy Mass, Sext would prevent him from neglecting his particular examen, None would sound the renewal of the life of prayer after the noonday rest, Vespers would constitute an excellent invitation to the visit to the Blessed Sacrament and to the Rosary, Compline would take on again its authentic role of evening prayer."[3]

Thus would the "Work of God" be accomplished. But to fulfil it better, it is important to understand it well, to grasp its character as Office of praises due to God by His creature, as official prayer made in communion with the Church, and to devote oneself to it joyfully because to praise God, and praise Him as He wants to be praised, constitutes our most precious portion, and because in reality it is the most genuine happiness that a creature can experience.

Certain Benedictines of the Middle Ages were so conscious of the happiness and the beauty of this role that they established the *laus perennis* or perpetual praise, fulfilled by groups of monks succeeding one another without interruption before God. Although the intention was admirable, perhaps they were passing beyond that discretion often recommended by our holy Father. 'The generous," says Dom Delatte,[4] "must have the opportunity of doing something spontaneously and quite willingly. However, there is a form of Laus perennis which does not require an army of monks, which is open to each individual to realize: it is secret prayer, attention to God and the things of God, the attitude of submission and love, a certain constant contact with Beauty ever present. Thus, not only the monastery, but the soul of each monk" (and we shall add: of each Oblate), "and the united chorus of all, may sing to God an unceasing song."

---

[3]   See also the *Specimen vitae clericalis* given by Msgr. Harscouet, Obl.O.S.B., Bishop of Chartres, at the end of the *Notes sur les Messes du Careme.*

[4]   Commentary, p. 173.

CHAPTER 17
How Many Psalms Are to Be Said at These Hours

E HAVE already arranged the order of the psalmody for the Night and Morning Offices; let us now provide for the remaining Hours.

At Prime let three Psalms be said, separately and not under one "Glory be to the Father." The hymn of that Hour is to follow the verse "Incline unto my aid, O God," before the Psalms begin. Upon completion of the three Psalms let one lesson be recited, then a verse, the "Lord, have mercy on us" and the concluding prayers.

The Offices of Terce, Sext and None are to be celebrated in the same order, that is: the "Incline unto my aid, O God," the hymn proper to each Hour, three Psalms, lesson and verse, "Lord, have mercy on us" and concluding prayers.

If the community is a large one, let the Psalms be sung with antiphons; but if small, let them be sung straight through.

Let the Psalms of the Vesper Office be limited to four, with antiphons. After these Psalms the lesson is to be recited, then the responsory, the Ambrosian hymn, the verse, the canticle from the Gospel book, the litany, the Lord's Prayer and the concluding prayers.

Let Compline be limited to the saying of three Psalms, which are to be said straight through without antiphon, and after them the hymn of that Hour, one lesson, a verse, the "Lord, have mercy on us," the blessing and the concluding prayers.

COMMENTARY

St. Benedict has regulated the order of the psalmody for Matins and Lauds; he is now going to treat of the other Hours.

Prime will begin with the versicle *Deus, in adjutorium*, which will be followed by the Ambrosian hymn, then by three Psalms, each with its *Gloria*, after which will be said a lesson, the versicle, the *Kyrie eleison* and, concludes St. Benedict, *missae sint*. This little phrase has been translated in very diverse ways. Dom Philippe Frangois translates: "and it will be at an end" (*et on cessera*); the Maurists: "and thus it will be finished" (*et on finira de la sorte*); the Abbé de Rancé: "they will be finished" (*on les finira*); the author of the Translation and Explanation: "after which they retire"

175

(*après quoi on se retire*); Dom Guéranger: "then the dismissal" (*puis le renvoi*); Dom L'Huillier: "and the final prayers" (*et les oraisons finales*); the Benedictines of Farnborough: "and the dismissals" (*et les renvois*).[1] The fact is that the translations depend upon the interpretations of the word *missae*, and these are numerous.

Dom L'Huillier, who treats at length of this term, referring to Cassian and completing the explanations of Dom Martène and Dom Calmet, thinks that the "term *missae* in the Benedictine Rule comprises. .. the secret, mental prayer made at the end of each Office with the collects said aloud by the one who was charged with reciting them." The whole forms what he calls the "final prayers." Dom Delatte does not exclude this acceptation, but he thinks that *missa* has a much more extended meaning. Originally, it is the dismissal given the assembly, it is the farewell; but by extension it is also the formula of dismissal, the whole body of prayers which completes a liturgical function, the canonical Office itself, then the Office par excellence, the Mass.[2] In any case it cannot designate the prayers which today terminate Prime (reading of the martyrology, prayers for work, reading of the Holy Rule, recommendation of the souls of the deceased members and benefactors of the Order), prayers which are indeed of monastic origin, but which date only from the eighth or ninth century.

Terce, Sext and None are constructed exactly like Prime. When the community is numerous, the Psalms of the four little Hours are said with antiphons. The concern here is with that sort of alternated refrain of which there was question above. If the community is not numerous, they are said *in directum*. The former commentators thought that the presence of the antiphon, which they understood in its present sense, indicated that the Psalms were to be sung, while the Psalms *in directum* were only to be recited. Actually, singing is not in question here; both the antiphonated

---

[1] Translator's note: The English versions show different interpretations also. Dom Oswald Hunter-Blair translates: "the Collect"; Dom Justin McCann: "concluding prayers"; the Rev. Boniface Verheyen, O.S.B.: "the collects."

[2] Commentary, p. 156. At the epoch when the Holy Rule was composed, notes Dom Fernand Cabrol (*Saint Benedict,* translated from the French by C. M. Antony; London: Burns Oates & Washbourne, 1934, p. 74), *Missa* was "a generic term for the conclusion of an Office; a conclusion which usually comprised the *Kyrie eleison* and the Pater, a prayer and a blessing, and also sometimes versicles or Litanies." Dom Calmet certainly goes too far in including in it the secret prayer which followed the Office.

Psalms and those without antiphons could be sung.

Vespers, which are called ""evening synaxis," are composed of four antiphonated Psalms followed by a lesson, a responsory, the Ambrosian, the versicle, the canticle from the Gospel, namely the Magnificat, the litany and the Lord's Prayer. Their structure resembles that of Lauds.

Compline will have three Psalms not antiphonated, followed by the hymn, a lesson or little chapter, the versicle, the *Kyrie* and the blessing. The other Offices, except Vigils, did not include this blessing. That of Compline has always had a special importance in the monastic customs: ""No one should be absent at that moment; it is an act of communion with brethren and Abbot; and the blessing should be carried to those in the monastery who cannot be present to receive it."[3]

It may be asked why St. Benedict, who speaks at such length about the Office, says nothing about the Mass. It has long since been remarked that he generally leaves aside points of common ecclesiastical discipline, on which there was nothing to decide. Besides, St. Benedict speaks in passing of the Mass (Chapters 35, 38, 63); this took place only on Sundays and feast days. But since everyone was authorized to carry the Sacred Species with him, the monks could communicate outside of the days of Mass.[4] Moreover, the custom of the daily conventual Mass spread very quickly. Dom Martène even cites an example of it at the beginning of the fifth century.[5]

APPLICATION

The arrangement of the day Hours in the Monastic Office is also in its general lines that of the Roman Office. The monastic prayers of Prime even passed intact into the latter. The Monastic Breviary, however, adds to them the "commemoration of all our brethren, of all the members of our Order, and of all our benefactors," This is a prayer in which we Oblates also have a part. And as it is very simple, being composed of the Psalm *De profundis*, some familiar versicles and the oration *Deus veniae largitor*, we might profitably adopt it, even if we are held to the Roman Office, since it follows Prime and in no way harms the integrity of that Hour. It is

---

[3] Dom Paul Delatte, *Commentary*, p. 176.

[4] Dom Jean Martial Besse, *Les Moines d'Orient*, pp. 351-354; *Les Moines de VAncienne France*, pp. 445-448.

[5] *De Antiquis Monachorum Ritibus*, II, Chapters 4-8. See also Dom Augustin Calmet, Commentaire, Chapter 35.

found also in the Little Office of the Oblates.[6]

In the Roman Office the final litany of the little Hours is said only on the ferias of Advent and of Lent, on the Ember Days of September and on vigils. On the other hand, these Hours have a responsory which is not found in the Monastic Breviary. In the latter, however, two of these responsories are found, at Lauds and at Vespers, where the Roman Breviary does not have any. Also, the Roman Vespers have one more Psalm than the monastic, and no litany. Finally, although the Monastic Breviary at Compline has neither antiphons nor responsory nor canticle, the Roman Breviary has them, and the responsory is the beautiful *In manus tuas*.

Prime is the monk's true morning prayer, and Compline is his true evening prayer. Such should they be for the Oblates, priests or lay persons. This is the opinion of all those who have written of the liturgical life of the Oblates. Let us content ourselves with quoting one of the most recent manuals:[7]

"What will be the Oblate's morning prayer? We would not know anything more appropriate to advise him than to recite the Office of Prime; he thus unites himself to his monastic family and to the official prayer of the entire Church; he pronounces the incomparable praise of the Psalms whose accents the Holy Spirit dictated, and addresses to God that beautiful oration, *Domine Deus omnipotens*, so strong, so concise that no prayer of our manuals of piety could be compared to it."

Let us add that, in conformity with the monastic custom, the reading of the section of the Holy Rule marked for each day could follow the recitation of Prime.

Likewise, the Oblate's evening prayer "is the Office of Compline, essentially Benedictine, since it took birth in our monasteries" (we should say more exactly that it was propagated there) "under the impulse of St. Benedict. ... When the Oblate pronounces the last formula which terminates this Hour, he will be able to picture our glorious Patriarch St. Benedict soliciting God's blessing for all the members of his Order, both regular and secular, and saying: 'May the almighty and merciful Lord, the Father, the Son, and the Holy Ghost, bless and protect you. Amen.'"

---

[6] Manual for Oblates, pp. 148-150. This practice is also recommended by Msgr. Harscouet, *Notes sur les Messes du Careme*, p. 310.

[7] Les Oblats de S. Benoît. Leur Esprit, les Prieres dLeur Usage (Paris: Monastery of the Benedictines of Saint-Louis-du-Temple, 1918), p. 31.

CHAPTER 18
In What Order the Psalms Are to Be Said

February 21—June 22—October 22

irst let this verse be said: "Incline unto my aid, O God; O Lord, make haste to help me," and the "Glory be to the Father"; then the hymn proper to each Hour.

Then at Prime on Sunday four sections of Psalm 118 are to be said; and at each of the remaining Hours, that is Terce, Sext and None, three sections of the same Psalm 118.

At Prime on Monday let three Psalms be said, namely Psalms 1, 2 and 6. And so each day at Prime until Sunday let three Psalms be said in numerical order, to Psalm 19, but with Psalms 9 and 17 each divided into two parts. Thus it comes about that the Night Office on Sunday always begins with Psalm 20.

COMMENTARY

We now know the arrangement of each Hour. The concern here is to distribute the Psalms according to that arrangement.

The text begins by recalling that each Hour of the day is to start with the *Deus, in adjutorium.* In the received text we read actually: "at the day Hours let this verse always be said." The most ancient manuscripts do not have "at the day Hours," and it is probable that these words were interpolated. Lauds are a day Hour, and it is not certain that they began originally with the *Deus, in adjutorium.* And besides, what follows applies only to the little Hours, which have the hymn after the versicle. The original text was likely: "let this verse always be said."

St. Benedict commences with Prime for Sunday. It is the first day of the week, and the principal one. After the hymn of Prime, Psalm 118 will be taken up. This is an alphabetical Psalm; that is to say, in the Hebrew it is composed of 22 groups of eight verses, or octonaries, and each of the eight verses of each group begins with the same one of the 22 letters of the alphabet. For that reason it is the longest Psalm in the Psalter. The first four octonaries will be taken for Sunday Prime, each octonary being followed by the *Gloria.* At Terce the three following octonaries will be

179

said, and similarly at Sext and at None. Thus 13 octonaries are used on Sunday. The other nine will serve at Terce, Sext and None for Monday.

For the rest of the week, with regard to the Office of Prime, St. Benedict takes the Psalter at its beginning and portions it out, starting from Monday Prime, on the plan of three Psalms to the Hour. Psalm 3, said at the beginning of Vigils, will be passed by, as wall Psalm 4, reserved for Compline, and Psalm 5, reserved for Monday Lauds. Psalms 9 and 17, which are very long, will be divided into two *Glorias*. Thus the first 19 Psalms will be distributed, and Sunday Vigils can begin with Psalm 20.

APPLICATION

This passage of the Holy Rule carries its own application. Perhaps it will be appropriate, however, to say a word about Psalm 118. We see that St. Benedict gives it a privileged place. This cannot be without reason. The commentaries of Origen, St. Hilary, St. Ambrose, St. Augustine and others on this Psalm show that they considered it "as the richest in doctrine and the most profound: they saw in it an incomparable program of the Christian life."[1]

"This Psalm," says the Abbé de Rancé, "speaks only of the happiness which the souls enjoy who belong to God, who attach themselves to His ways, who prefer the privilege of obeying Him to all other things, who seek Him with the whole expanse of their heart, and who know neither well-being, nor rest, nor glory here below except that of being in submission to Him and in dependence on Him in every circumstance. You see in it everywhere the mercies of God, His bounties. His truths, His judgments, His justices, His ordinances. Finally, everything in it enlightens, everything elevates, everything inflames, everything inspires, everything leads, everything directs; and it would suffice by itself to excite in hearts a holy passion, to kindle in them the sacred fire of a wholly divine charity, and to render useless all that the demons could do in their efforts to extinguish and destroy that charity."

The author of the Translation and Explanation thinks that our holy Father wanted to place this Psalm on the first day of the week in order to put before our eyes at the start 'The duties of the Christian life" and "in order that everyone may turn his eyes upward to the model on which he

---

[1] Dom Paul Delatte, *Commentary*, p. 178.

is to regulate himself." It is from the same motive, no doubt, that the Roman Breviary likewise chants this same Psalm 118 at Prime and the little Hours for Sunday.

It is certain that our holy Father was pleased to meditate it often. We shall imitate him, therefore, by making it one of our preferred readings, aside from its recitation in the Divine Office. Its pages are among those which we cannot read without experiencing a great peace and a profound sentiment of joy in belonging to God. Why must it be that too often the variety of new prayers and devotions has caused to be neglected the treasures of spirituality and of grace which are found in those inspired songs in which the great contemplatives of the past took their delight? As children of St. Benedict we shall hold to that spirituality of past centuries which went to seek its nourishment in the divine word and which, according to the words of St. Bernard, delighted in the *ruminatio Psalmorum*, the "chewing" of the Psalms.

February 22—June 23—October 23

At Terce, Sext and None on Monday let the nine remaining sections of Psalm 118 be said, three at each of these Hours. Psalm 118 having been completed, therefore, on two days, Sunday and Monday, let the nine Psalms from Psalm 119 to Psalm 127 be said at Terce, Sext and None, three at each Hour, beginning with Tuesday. And let these same Psalms be repeated every day until Sunday at the same Hours, while the arrangement of hymns, lessons and verses is kept the same on all days; and thus Prime on Sunday will always begin with Psalm 118.

COMMENTARY

Psalm 118, as we have seen, was to furnish its octonaries to Prime and the other little Hours of Sunday. Thirteen thus found their place. There remained nine of them, which could not be used for Monday Prime, because that Office employed Psalms 1, 2 and 6. The nine octonaries will serve for Terce, Sext and None of that same day. Thus Psalm 118 is used up in two days.

We have seen how the Office of Prime for the other days was formed. It remains to provide for the last three little Hours. The provision will be made with nine Psalms, from the 119th to the 127th, that is to say the first nine Gradual Psalms. Thus, save for Sunday and Monday, the little Hours will be always of the same composition. On the other hand (nihilominus), there is to be no exception for the hymns, the lessons and the versicles, which will remain absolutely invariable.

APPLICATION

It has often been observed that the Psalms set for the little Hours by St. Benedict are quite short. They are suitable to religious whose life is going to be occupied with labor and who will sometimes be obliged to recite the Divine Office in woods and fields, and consequently from memory. Our holy Father thought that in view of the circumstances one could not easily do more, but also that one ought not to do less.

In the Roman Breviary the Psalms of the little Hours are not the same. Nevertheless, they are likewise brief.

The thought of Holy Church and that of St. Benedict are in agreement here, as everywhere. Would we be right in complaining that there is still too much and that the task is cumbersome for those who are charged with the ministry? Too cumbersome—the divine praise? But is not prayer the first of our duties? We were created and put into the world for prayer, before being chosen for the apostolate. And prayer itself is the first and indispensable condition of the fecundity of the apostolate. Who was it that converted the people to the faith? Who was it, amid difficulties and perils without number, that gave the most beautiful example of apostolic zeal? The monks! And those monks were bound to observances, and they would have thought themselves wanting to God and to souls if, under pretext of ministry, they had made any reduction in the divine praise which they chanted night and day. There we Oblates have our models.

What a small thing they are in reality, these little Hours of the day! And how useful for us can be this recall to the Work of God at certain times of the day! It prevents us from dissipating ourselves, from spreading ourselves out. It leads us back to the feet of Him from whom proceed all graces, those which will sanctify us as well as those which, through us, will sanctify others.

February 23—June 24—October 24

Vespers are to be sung with four Psalms every day. These shall begin with Psalm 109 and go on to Psalm 147, omitting those which are set apart for other Hours; that is to say that with the exception of Psalms 117 to 127 and Psalms 133 and 142, all the rest of these are to be said at Vespers. And since there are three Psalms too few, let the longer ones of the above number be divided, namely Psalms 138, 143 and 144. But let Psalm 116 because of its brevity be joined to Psalm 115.

The order of the Vesper Psalms being thus settled, let the rest of the Hour—lesson, responsory, hymn, verse and canticle—be carried out as we prescribed above.

At Compline the same Psalms are to be repeated everyday, namely Psalms 4, 90 and 133.

COMMENTARY

For Vespers, which have four Psalms (we have seen that the Roman Office has five), 28 Psalms will be needed. They will be counted starting, as in the Roman Office, with Psalm 109, Dixit Dominus, and going to Psalm 147. We know that in this series several Psalms have been or will be preempted for other Offices, such as the first nine Graduals Psalms, assinged to the little Hours, Psalm 117, designated for Lauds on Sunday, and Psalm 142, for that Hour on Saturday. Psalm 133 will occur in Compline. Among those that remain, one, Psalm 116, is so short that it will be joined to Psalm 115 under a single Gloria. But then there remain to us only 25, and we need 28. To attain this latter number we shall divide into two *Glorias* Psalms 138, 143 and 144, which are the longest.

Compline will have three Psalms, which are to be repeated each day, Psalms 4, 90 and 133. It is the same in the Roman Office for Sundays and for first and second class feasts. For the weekdays different Psalms are assigned to each day, since the reform of Pius X.

APPLICATION

The choice of the Vesper Psalms evidently was not determined by any special relation between their meaning and the Hour at which they were chanted. Nevertheless, the Office of Vespers is, along with Lauds, one of the most solemn of the Work of God. It is also the most popular. Vespers are, in fact, the part of the liturgical praise in which the faithful most commonly take part.

Today, praiseworthy efforts are in evidence almost everywhere towards bringing people back to the total sanctification of the Sunday by assistance at Vespers, towards making them understand this Office better, towards getting them actually to take part in it. But alas, how much still remains to be done! Is not the role of the Oblates, priests and laity, to give themselves with their whole heart to this movement? We cannot imagine that a priest Oblate in charge of a parish would suppress the Office of

Vespers or seldom hold it, contrary to the statutes of his diocese. But could we any more allow that a lay Oblate, member of an Order whose principal occupation is the divine praise, should stay away from Vespers for trivial reasons?

As was said above, the Office of Compline, which ordinarily accompanies Vespers in the parochial liturgy, is an admirable evening prayer. The Psalms for Sunday in particular express a boundless confidence in the divine aid, which we shall need perhaps more urgently at the hour of darkness. They invite us to take our rest under the wings of the Most High. They remind us that the Angels are watching over us, to remove from our sleep the enemy's ambushes. How regrettable it would be for prayers of such beauty and such efficacy to disappear from the customs of the faithful! We shall love Compline, therefore, not only recited privately, but chanted in the church with the parochial community; we shall become penetrated with its spirit; we shall try to make it understood and loved by those around us.

February 24 in leap years—February 23 (continued) in other
years—June 25—October 25

The order of psalmody for the day Hours being thus arranged, let all the remaining Psalms be equally distributed among the seven Night Offices by dividing the longer Psalms among them and assigning twelve Psalms to each night.

We strongly recommend, however, that if this distribution of the Psalms is displeasing to anyone, he should arrange them otherwise, in whatever way he considers better, but taking care in any case that the Psalter with its full number of 150 Psalms be chanted every week and begun again every Sunday at the Night Office. For those monks show themselves too lazy in the service to which they are vowed, who chant less than the Psalter with the customary canticles in the course of a week, whereas we read that our holy Fathers strenuously fulfilled that task in a single day. May we, lukewarm that we are, perform it at least in a whole week!

COMMENTARY

The psalmody for the day Hours is now regulated. There remain to us for the Vigils 75 Psalms. These go from Psalm 20 to Psalm 108, allowing for those in this portion which have been preempted for the Invitatory (Psalm 94), for Compline (Psalm 90) and for Lauds. But as each Vigil requires twelve Psalms, we would need 84. There is a deficit of nine Psalms, therefore. This will be made up by dividing the nine longest Psalms into two Glorias.

The apportioning of the Psalms throughout the whole week is completed. In his humility St. Benedict does not flatter himself that he has found the best distribution possible. He even thinks that it may not be agreeable to some, and he sees nothing improper in a Superior's proposing another distribution which he would consider more perfect. And this proves well enough that at that time, aside from the traditional use of certain Psalms, the Bishops and the Abbots enjoyed a great freedom in the organization of the liturgical Office.

But there is one point to which St. Benedict holds absolutely, and which must be safeguarded in every apportionment: the entire Psalter is to be sung or recited during the week. To do less is "laziness," especially for monks "vowed to the service" of God. The Psalter recited in a week is still very little; and we are really lukewarm in comparison with those monks of the heroic ages, the desert Fathers, who fulfilled bravely in one day what we fulfil in seven.

We know that sometimes certain congregations, pricked by St. Benedict's *nos tepidi,* "lukewarm that we are," added to the prescriptions of the Rule. So was it done in the ancient monasteries of Cluny. But, notes Dom Calmet, "the excessive prolixity of Offices has met with the disapproval of several very judicious persons," and the historians have observed that this prolixity had not been profitable on the whole to the piety in the order of Cluny.

APPLICATION

In requiring the recitation of the Psalter during the week, St. Benedict has agreed, as always, with the mind of the Church, who has also demanded this of her clergy. We know that the reform of the Psalter by the Sovereign Pontiff Pius X had no other end than to safeguard that principle. The point is, observes Dom Delatte,[2] that the Psalter was created by God Himself to be "forever the authentic formulary of prayer. With its thoughts and in its language God has willed to be praised and honored. The Psalms express the deepest, most varied, and most delicate sentiments

---

[2] *Commentary,* p. 183.

of the human heart, and answer all its needs. They served the Saints of the Old Testament; they have served the Apostles and the Saints of all ages. And their words have been uttered by other and more august lips: for they were said and said again by Our Lady and Our Lord. In the pilgrimages to Jerusalem Our Lord and His Mother and St. Joseph chanted the Gradual Psalms. Some authors have thought that Our Lord used to recite the Psalter every day, and that He was only continuing His prayer when in His Passion, raised aloft on the Cross, He said: *Deus mens, Deus mens, ut quid dereliquisti me?*,[3] and again: *In manus tuas commendo spiritum meum.*"[4]

In his *Religious and Monastic Life Explained*,[5] Dom Guéranger addressed to novices these recommendations, which we can also apply to ourselves: "Once convinced that its familiar use will constitute a long step on the way to contemplation, we shall learn to appreciate the sacred psalmody which has been, as it were, the daily bread of the Saints of our holy Order. Let us, therefore, ask this grace of God and also that of understanding and relishing the other parts of the Divine Office." He said likewise of his Oblates: "If God gives them the grace of a taste for the Psalter, they will have a particular knowledge of it for Him, remembering that in the ages of faith it was always through the Psalms that God communicated with souls."[6]

Since by vocation we are called to praise the Lord *in hymnis et canticis*, let us not neglect so efficacious a means of nourishing our spiritual life.

---

[3] "My God, My God, why hast Thou forsaken Me?"

[4] "Into Thy hands I commend My spirit."

[5] Translated from the French by the Rev. Jerome Veth, O.S.B. (St. Louis: B. Herder, 1908), pp. 9-10.

[6] L'Église ou la Société de la Louange Divine, p. 24.

CHAPTER 19
On the Manner of Saying the Divine Office

February 24 (25)—June 26—October 26

E BELIEVE that the divine presence is everywhere and that "the eyes of the Lord are looking on the good and the evil in every place" (*Proverbs* 15:3). But we should believe this especially without any doubt when we are assisting at the Work of God. To that end let us be mindful always of the Prophet's words, "Serve the Lord in fear" (*Psalm* 2:11) and again "Sing praises wisely" (*Psalm* 46:8) and "In the sight of the Angels I will sing praise to You" (*Psalm* 137:1). Let us therefore consider how we ought to conduct ourselves in the sight of the Godhead and of His Angels, and let us take part in the psalmody in such a way that our mind may be in harmony with our voice.

COMMENTARY

St. Benedict has finished organizing the various elements of the Offices for night and day. He will concern himself now with the interior dispositions for performing the divine praise well.

Let us recall that in the first degree of humility our holy Father put us in the presence of God. He wanted us to be permeated with that presence and to make it as habitual as possible. We know that in fact God does not leave us: "we believe that the divine presence is everywhere." His look is not a glance from afar; it is a penetrating and attentive look, which extends to good and bad actions alike.

But there are places and circumstances in which the divine presence manifests itself in a more particular and more efficacious way. To be sure, He is everywhere by His nature, and the theologians teach us that in Him operation cannot be separated from presence. Nevertheless, said St. Bernard, "He is in heaven in such a way that by comparison He does not seem to be on earth at all."[1] And St. Fulgentius teaches us that if God is everywhere by His power, He is not everywhere by His grace: *Ubique enim adest per potentiam, non ubique per gratiam.*[2] And St. Ambrose: "He

---

[1] 1st Sermon on Psalm 90, *Qui habitat*; in PL., Tome 183, col. 188. 225

[2] *Ad Trasimundum*, Book 2, Chapter 8; in P.L., Tome 65, col. 255.

is always and everywhere present, but... He is more present to those who love Him, and He absents Himself from those who neglect Him." *Ubique semper praesens est, sed ... est praesentior diligentibus, negligentibus abest.*[3] So that we may say that God is more present wherever He pours out His graces more abundantly. And where will these be most abundant if not wherever several are united to pray in the Lord's name, where the divine work par excellence is being accomplished, where He gives to His own "a solemn audience"?[4]

Whoever comes to the Divine Office, forgetting every created thing to see and praise God alone, we may say that such a one plunges himself into the invisible Presence. He is as it were enveloped by an outpouring of graces. St. Benedict wants us to have a deep faith in this radiating and sanctifying presence. He insists on it: "Above all, let us believe this without any doubt."

The texts from Scripture which our holy Father quotes specify the attitude of soul which the lively sentiment of God's presence should provoke: fear, for our God is infinitely great and holy; wisdom, which prevents us from wandering, to keep us preoccupied with Him who is the only necessary One. Fear and wisdom are inseparable. The one is the beginning of the other: *Initium sapientiae timor Domini.*

The presence of God, as we have seen, is an active presence. When we sing His praises, there is something of heaven in our souls and around us. Our exercise is that of the Angels. There is no void in the material world; no more is there in the spiritual world. Thousands and thousands of blessed Spirits people the divine immensity. God, as Bossuet said, is the place of the spirits, just as space is the place of bodies. If we strive to perform the divine praise well, then we are putting our voices in unison with the Angels' voices. We are fulfilling the sublime prayer of the Preface: *Cum Angelis et Archangelis.* ... With the Angels and the Archangels, with the Thrones and the Dominations, with the whole militia of the heavenly army, we take our part in the unceasing concert which sings the glory of the Most High.

APPLICATION

The first condition for fulfilling our Office as St. Benedict wishes is to

---

[3] Homily for Friday of the second week in Lent.

[4] Dom Paul Delatte, *Commentary*, p. 186.

live a life profoundly supernatural and turned always towards God. If we are detached from the world, as we have undertaken to be, then not only shall we have no trouble in "losing ourselves in God" at the hour of prayer, but we shall see that hour come with a feeling of eagerness, even at those times when weariness is at the soul's surface.

Obviously, that will not prevent distractions from assailing us. We cannot avoid being sometimes taken up more or less by certain preoccupations, intellectual or otherwise, which ask nothing more than to make a little noise in us, despite the audience with God.

It is to withstand those assaults and give us time to recollect ourselves that the monastic Constitutions have provided a few minutes of "station" in the cloister before each Office. During those few minutes the monk puts himself resolutely before God and His Angels and summons his energy to banish distractions. We have only to do the same. These brief moments in which we "accord" our soul for the divine praise are of real importance. Let us not neglect them.

A practice no less useful: let us prepare our Office. Let us study it a little beforehand for a better grasp of its outline and a better penetration of its spirit.

And then, we know what is the influence of the physical on the moral. Let us always take a respectful attitude. Many priests, especially in the country, live near their church. Would it not be the normal thing to follow the example of the monks and perform there, face to face with the Lord, all or a considerable part of the Divine Office: Matins, Lauds, Compline?[5] And why should we not assume, as do a certain number of Oblates, the different positions of the choir, which, moreover, St. Benedict requires in another chapter of those who recite the Office in isolation? We shall assure "attention and the dignity of the Office," says the Abbé Gaucheron, "first of all by chanting slowly and regularly, even when we are alone, full of divine fear and on bended knees, as it is said of the brethren on a journey (Chapter 50), a directive which invites us to observe the ceremonies of the choir as far as possible in private recitation."[6]

---

[5] Abbé Gelle, "*Aux Pretres Isolds*," in *Bulletin de S. Martin et de S. Benoît*, October, 1923, p. 274. This is the place to recall the plenary indulgence granted by His Holiness Pius XI to clerics who recite all the Hours of the Breviary before the Most Blessed Sacrament.

[6] "Une Retraite Benedictine," *in Bulletin de S. Martin et de S. Benoît*, April, 1928, p. 472.

And why not also sing or chant one or another part of the Office as determined by our particular schedule, where such a thing is possible? The desert Fathers chanted the Psalms and canticles even at the Hours when they were not together. "Perhaps it would not be too scandalizing a singularity," says the Abbé Gelle, "that we might be surprised while singing alone some part of the Office."[7] Besides, in our rural churches the solitude will hardly be disturbed at the hour when we may be saying Matins or Compline.

"If the church is not easy to get to," says the Abbé Gelle, "one may go into an oratory, which it is easy to install in a presbytery."[8] The Church herself invites us to celebrate our Office thus by granting 100 days indulgence to anyone, priest or layman, who "himself chants in public or in private" an Office "in a public or private chapel," each time he chants it. Is it not thus that the Carthusians in their cell, where a stall is always found, carry out the parts of the Office which are not recited in common?

The preceding was written especially for priest Oblates. The ideal would be that lay Oblates, where the pastor is himself an Oblate, might join him at certain Hours for the recitation or the singing of the Office. But what remains generally possible for most of them is the recitation either before the Blessed Sacrament or in an oratory or in a solitary corner of their dwelling place, where they may avoid distractions and unite themselves even by their outward attitudes to the prayer of their brethren in the cloister.

All these precautions and practices will help them fulfil the so often admired maxim of our holy Father: *Mens nostra concordet voci nostrae*. "Let our mind be in accord with our voice." Indeed our Office must be above all a prayer which maintains the life of our soul: it ought to be the principal food of our prayers and provide the matter for our meditations. "The psalmody," said Dom Calmet, "should be for us the source of light, graces and blessings." Dom Guéranger wrote in other terms, addressing priest Oblates: "Prayer can never have a more supernatural and more fruitful source than when it flows directly from this sacred center (the Divine Office); and our priest will hold to the honor of using the word of God and the prayers of Holy Church for his prayer, rather than the human word.. .. Having experienced, as it were, a certain sweet preoccupation

---

[7] *"Aux Pretres Isolds,"* in *Bulletin de S. Martin et de S. Benoît*, October, 1923, p. 275.

[8] *Ibid.*, p. 274.

with divine things in this attentive recitation, he will maintain it in himself by habitual recollection amid his various occupations."[9]

---

[9] L'Eglise ou la Societe de la Louange Divine, p. 35. See also Dom Symphorien, La Règle de S. Benoît MeditSe, p. 571, who affirms in speaking of the Office that "It is in this monastic devotion more than in our private devotions that we shall grasp the spirit of our Fathers and that we shall find God."

CHAPTER 20
On Reverence in Prayer

February 25 (26)—June 27—October 27

HEN WE WISH to suggest our wants to men of high station, we do not presume to do so except with humility and reverence. How much the more, then, are complete humility and pure devotion necessary in supplication of the Lord who is God of the universe! And let us be assured that it is not in saying a great deal that we shall be heard (*Matthew* 6:7), but in purity of heart and in tears of compunction. Our prayer, therefore, ought to be short and pure, unless it happens to be prolonged by an inspiration of divine grace. In community, however, let prayer be very short, and when the Superior gives the signal let all rise together.

COMMENTARY

In Chapter 19, St. Benedict was concerned with conventual prayer; in this chapter the concern will be with private prayer.

Conventual prayer is regulated by a ceremonial which puts the body in a dignified attitude, symbol and manifestation and aid of the interior attitude.

Private prayer has no outward ceremonial, yet it should be inspired by the same dispositions as conventual prayer. We are speaking to God, "to the Lord of the universe." How could we fail to show Him due respect, when we speak only with "humility and reverence" to the great men of the earth to whom we have some request to present?

According to St. Benedict our prayer ought to have three principal qualities: 1) humility, 2) purity of devotion, 3) compunction of tears.

Humility is the necessary consequence of what we know about God. Our God, even when He presents Himself to us in the humiliation of the Eucharist, even when He appears to us covered with the opprobrium of His Passion, is no less the All-Powerful. And our love, ardent as it may be, cannot forget the infinity of its object. When the Spouse calls Him her Beloved, when she cries with the Canticle: *Osculetur me osculo oris sui ...*" Let Him kiss me with the kiss of His mouth! ... she yet does not forget her littleness and the fact that the divine Spouse comes to her only through an astonishing condescendance. Our prayer is not a summons, a requisition;

192

it is a trusting petition whose object itself ought to be worthy of God. "One of the most certain marks of delusion," says Dom Delatte, "is to treat God as an equal, as one who has made a bargain with us and with whom we are doing business."[1]

Purity of devotion is a feeling of belonging to God (*devotio*), a belonging which suffers no division, but separates us from all created affection (*puritas*). God is our all, and we must belong to Him. Nothing in us should displease Him, nothing should give Him offense when we address ourselves to Him in prayer; on the contrary, He must find us animated with a sincere and unique desire to do His will and to seek His kingdom both in ourselves and around us. *Adveniat regnum tuum, fiat voluntas tua.*

Compunction is a sort of interior softening produced by the vision of our sins when we contemplate them in the light of faith. And this softening sometimes goes as far as tears. Let us not forget, however, that the gift of tears is a grace from God, and here again let us avoid delusion. The concern here is not with "tears. .. forced by a more or less nervous excitement, as harmful to the body as to the soul," but with tears that are clam "and mild, whose sole source is humility."[2] The former come from a more or less conscious vanity; the latter, which are not sought, have the merit "of not leading to pride and also of leaving no room for distractions."[3]

Moreover, private prayer ought to avoid two faults: wordiness and excessive length.

The Gospel has already taught us that true prayer does not consist in abundance of words.[4] Prayer is not an exercise of eloquence; no more is it an exercise of vocabulary. If words are not without use to us when we pray, often to make more precise what we think and what we will, we should remember nevertheless that God looks to the depths of the heart; it is the intentions, the desires, the love that interest Him. And we know that prayer at a certain degree finds no more words, but becomes a silent contemplation in which the heart alone adores, sings and loves.

St. Benedict does not like prayer which is too long. Save in cases which he foresees, prolonged prayer runs the risk of degenerating "into fatigue,

---

[1] *Commentary*, p. 190.

[2] Dom L'Huillier, *Explication Ascétique et Historique*, Tome 1, pp. 869-370.

[3] Dom Paul Delatte, *Commentary*, p. 191.

[4] *Matthew* 6:7.

torpor and decay." We have only to look at what too often happens in our half hour of daily meditation. "A moment may find all said, and then the mind is off elsewhere. Sometimes we may recall it, but it is off again, no matter in what direction. Sometimes we do not even think of recalling it, and the time is spent in mental wanderings, so that we reach the end of our half hour and wonder what part God has taken."[5]

What must we conclude from that? Not that the half hour ought to be shortened. On the contrary, we must hold to it; but aside from that, it is better to put ourself in contact with God often during the day by those rapid and multiple prayers called ejaculations. Such was the practice of the desert Fathers and of the ancient monks of Egypt in particular. This practice led them back unceasingly before God and maintained their soul in "that immovable tranquillity and perpetual purity" extolled by the monk Isaac, Abbot of Scete, in the ninth *Conference* of Cassian.[6] It assures a certain orientation of heart and mind which is also in its own way a prayer. "When we cherish uninterrupted desire," wrote St. Augustine, "along with the exercise of faith and hope and charity, we 'pray always.' "*In ipsa fide, spe et caritate, continuato desiderio semper oramus.*[7]

But there are times when prayer can legitimately be prolonged: when divine grace prompts an interior movement of devotion. There is nothing to do then but give way to the solicitation of God.

However, no one is permitted to prolong the moment of silent prayer following each Office. As soon as the Superior has given the signal, all must rise at the same time to go out of the oratory.

APPLICATION

The application of this chapter presents no difficulty. If we really have the spirit of faith, if we live under the eyes of God, if we love Him sincerely, we shall often experience the need of turning to Him. And even when we experience no sensible attraction, our love will inspire us to tell Him that despite our apparent dryness we belong to Him indeed and do not want to be separated from Him. The ejaculatory prayers which we shall say will express that love and support it.

---

[5] Dom Paul Delatte, *Commentary*, p. 192.

[6] Chapter 2; in C.S.E.L., Vol. 13, p. 250; in *Nicene and Post-Nicene* Fathers, 2nd series, Vol. 11, p. 387.

[7] *Epistle* 130, Chapter 9; in C.S.E.L., Vol. 44, p. 60; translated by J. G. Cunningham in *Nicene and Post-Nicene Fathers*, 1st series, Vol. 1, p. 465.

In recommending "short and pure" prayer, does the Rule of St. Benedict exclude the half hour of meditation customary today not only in all religious communities but also among fervent Christians? Evidently not. To be sure, St. Benedict was not familiar with prayer conceived as an exercise apart, submitted to a rigorous method, with a preamble, a composition of place, three points, resolutions and a spiritual bouquet. But he regarded as the monk's normal occupation, outside of the Office and manual labor, those long periods devoted to the "divine reading," *lectio divina*, and to the study of spiritual things; periods when the reading provokes reflections, when the mind and the heart contemplate, when prayer arises naturally; for one cannot think about God, His mysteries, His perfections, His Providence, His Saints, and so on, without admiring Him, praising Him, confiding in Him.

Whichever it be, whether our prayer be along the lines of methodic prayer or whether it be sustained by the *lectio divina*, prayer at a fixed hour, what we might call "prayer by Rule," is absolutely necessary for us. Like the Office, it is a sort of halt in the midst of our diverse occupations, and these in general should yield before it, as before the Divine Office. We must reserve, therefore, a half hour in our daily schedule in which we may gather the fruits of our liturgical prayer or of our Mass, meditate on the mysteries celebrated by the Church or on some passage of Scripture which has impressed us, implore the graces indicated to us in the collects, lay before the Lord our soul's needs, and so forth.

Happy shall we be if this exercise brings us an increase of humility, of compunction, of charity! Happy shall we be if we feel ourselves prompted to prolong it, and if it permeates like a perfume all the acts of our day!

CHAPTER 21
On the Deans of the Monastery

F THE COMMUNITY is a large one, let there be chosen out of it brethren of good repute and holy life, and let them be appointed deans. These shall take charge of their deaneries in all things, observing the commandments of God and the instructions of their Abbot.

Let men of such character be chosen deans that the Abbot may with confidence share his burdens among them. Let them be chosen not by rank but according to their worthiness of life and the wisdom of their doctrine.

If any of these deans should become inflated with pride and found deserving of censure, let him be corrected once, and again, and a third time. If he will not amend, then let him be deposed and another be put in his place who is worthy of it.

And we order the same to be done in the case of the Prior.

COMMENTARY

With Chapter 21 begins a series of prescriptions concerning the interior regime of the monastery.

The Abbot, especially in large communities, needs assistance. He can be assisted by the Prior or *praepositus*, to whom a special chapter will be devoted later on. He can be assisted also by the deans.

It has been observed that the term "dean," *decanus* or *decurio*, passed from the camps into the monasteries well before St. Benedict's time. Cassian repeatedly speaks of deans. There is nothing surprising about this borrowed term. Are not the monks the soldiers of Christ the King, doing battle under His command?

For sufficiently large communities, then, deans are to be chosen. As "deans" are spoken of in the plural, it seems correct to suppose that there are to be at least two of them.

Consequently, the community will begin to be large when it numbers at least 20 monks, the dean himself being counted in the deanery, according to St. Jerome.

Who is to choose the deans? Likely the Abbot. St. Benedict will not want the Prior to be chosen by anyone but the Abbot. For the same reasons, he must have taken the same measure with regard to the choice of the deans. Otherwise how would the Abbot have had them well in hand, as our holy Father wishes, if they had held their authority from anyone else than him?

Who can be a dean? It will not necessarily be the longest professed nor the most aged monks. One does not become a dean "according to rank," that is to say by the privilege of the time of profession. The Abbot is to choose among the brethren "of good repute and of holy life," "according to their worthiness of life and the wisdom of their doctrine." The deans, therefore, will be monks who have acquired the esteem of their brethren by the holiness of their conduct and their lights on the religious life.

What will be their role? They are to be the collaborators of the Abbot as far as their deanery is concerned. The objects of their solicitude are not determined; it is for the Abbot to specify them, their function being to "share his burden."

It might happen that the deans, like anyone who possesses some portion of authority, would become proud and make themselves liable to censure. The Abbot is to warn the guilty dean three times. If he will not amend his conduct, the Abbot is to depose him and replace him. The same will be done also with the Prior.

Today this chapter of the Holy Rule has been modified by the various Constitutions. The "deans" no longer have deaneries; they are merely the advisors of the Abbot. Some are chosen by the Abbot and the rest, a majority, by the community. Elected by the Abbot or by the monks, the deans always help the Abbot bear "his burden." With respect to the community, says Dom Delatte, their office is a function of "kindly supervision ... they have to set a good example."[1]

"Practically," continues Dom Delatte, "in a peaceful community, there is no difference between the case where the counselors are chosen by the Abbot, according to the text of the Rule, and that where the majority are elected by the monks: for all are, by the same title, counselors of the Abbot and of the community. The Abbot chooses counselors, and counselors are chosen for him; they are not to be either opponents or partisans."[2]

---

[1] *Commentary*, p. 195.

[2] *Ibid.*, p. 196.

APPLICATION

From this chapter we shall retain especially the conditions demanded by St. Benedict of those who have to fulfil, under the direction of Superiors, some charge having to do with the government of souls. They should know that they are not doing their task in the best possible way unless they have "worthiness of life," a worthiness which is established, evident, and of which one may bear "witness." The point is that teaching bears little fruit without example. Holiness by itself is one of the most effective of teachings. We do good far more by what we are than by what we say. "Without good example," says Pere Emmanuel,[3] "the priest can neither act nor speak usefully for souls. He must do good in order to deserve to be the man of God with respect to souls; he must do good in order to have the right to teach the good to others."

But "wisdom of doctrine" is also necessary; that is to say, not only doctrine, even theological science, but the experience, the tact, the sense of the things of God which allows one to apply the doctrine with wisdom.

And that is still not enough. One who directs souls is not their absolute master. He may act only "according to the commandments of God" and the precepts of his Superiors. He must understand that with relation to his Superiors he is only a modest collaborator, who receives his part of the burden. Let him guard, therefore, against the pride which would make him unworthy of the charge entrusted to him.

These principles which guided our holy Father in this whole chapter on the deans will find application quite often both in the priestly life and in that of all persons who are engaged in good works.

---

[3] *Traite du Ministere Ecclésiastique*, p. 73.

CHAPTER 22
How the Monks Are to Sleep

February 27 (28)—June 29—October 29

ET EACH ONE sleep in a separate bed. Let them receive bedding suitable to their manner of life, according to the Abbot's directions. If possible let all sleep in one place; but if the number does not allow this, let them take their rest by tens or twenties with the seniors who have charge of them.

A candle shall be kept burning in the room until morning.

Let the monks sleep clothed and girded with belts or cords—but not with their knives at their sides, lest they cut themselves in their sleep—and thus be always ready to rise without delay when the signal is given and hasten to be before one another at the Work of God, yet with all gravity and decorum.

The younger brethren shall not have beds next to one another, but among those of the older ones.

When they rise for the Work of God let them gently encourage one another, that the drowsy may have no excuse.

COMMENTARY

After having spoken about the deans in general, St. Benedict is going to concern himself with an important circumstance in which they will have to exercise their charge. The concern is with the monks' sleep, a subject closely related to the Night Office of which there was question previously.

First there is the bedding. Each monk is to have his own bed with its bedclothes. Beds and bedclothes will be, says St. Benedict, *pro modo conversationis*, that is to say "suitable to the poverty and austerity of his way of life," the monastic life.[1] As to the number and the quality of the covers, they will depend upon the Abbot, who will take account of the climate, the season and the monk's health. Later on, St. Benedict will enumerate the different pieces of bedding.

The beds are to be arranged in a dormitory, or in several if the community is large. The deans will watch solicitously over the groups of 10 or 20 monks composing each dormitory. The deans are here called

---

[1] Dom Paul Delatte, *Commentary,* p. 200.

senior es, the elders, the seniors, but the words *deni* and *viceni* as well as the function assigned these *seniores* prove that it is indeed the deans who are meant.

Each "cell" is to be illuminated until morning by a light. This light, says Dom Calmet, was furnished by "wax, tallow, oil, wood, rush, or reed, but principally by torches of pine or fir."

Today, save among the reformed Cistercians, who have preserved the custom of the common dormitory, partitioned, however, in closed alcoves, the use of separate cells has been definitely adopted. Certain transformations in the conditions of monastic life have made this necessary. With the institution of the *fratres conversi* and the accession of a great number of monks to the priesthood, the original *scriptorium* no longer sufficed. The monk needed a certain privacy for his theological studies, a privacy hardly to be found in a common hall open to an endless coming and going. Further, since the practice of prayer as transformed into a private exercise demanded solitude, there was one more reason for preferring the cell to the dormitory. Finally, it must be admitted, certain abuses tended in the same direction. The monastic posts endowed with particular incomes having ended by being considered as the lifetime property of the incumbent, each beneficiary was allowed to have the right to a special lodging; and since in the 15th and 16th centuries, when decadence made vocations fewer, there were almost as many beneficiaries as there were monks, each one found himself living in a separate room. At the time of the great reforms in the 17th century, it was agreed among the Black Benedictines that if there were just reasons for condemning the possession of benefices separate from the conventual income, there were reasons equally just for keeping the use of cells. They were adopted, therefore; but, to safeguard the spirit of the Holy Rule, each door was provided with a movable shutter, and a lighted lamp was kept in the gallery commanding the cells, which gallery preserved the name of *dormitorium.*

The monks are to sleep clothed; they will have a night garb composed of a tunic and a cowl. But in place of the large belt or bracile worn during the day, they will wear any belt whatsoever of leather or cord. They will not keep the scapular, which is a garment for work; they will probably have stockings or light shoes (*pedules*). They will take great care, for fear of wounding themselves or their neighbors during sleep, to remove the large knives which hung from their belt during the day and served them for all sorts of work.

Why does St. Benedict want the monks to sleep clothed?

The commentators give different reasons, all true, no doubt, but only one of which is indicated by our holy Father. It is first of all out of motives of decency and of poverty. It is also from devotion to the monastic habit, considered as a safeguard against diabolical inroads. It is finally, as St. Benedict says, "that the monks be always ready, and that when the signal is given they may rise without delay and hasten to be before one another at the Work of God."

St. Benedict is especially anxious about the regularity of this rising, which, like every action prescribed by obedience, is to be accomplished *absque mora*, "without delay." He will even come to the aid of the lazy or the young, by inviting the monks to "be before one another," to exhort one another, guarding gravity and decorum, however.

St. Benedict does not want the young and the old to be separated in the dormitory. They are to be mixed with one another, no doubt to avoid temptations of playfulness for the young, some of whom are children, and also to facilitate the common rising. We know, however, that the novices had their "cell" for sleeping. But there were children among the professed.

APPLICATION

We have much to take for ourselves in this chapter. St. Benedict wants the beds to be *pro modo conversationis*, that is, in keeping with the profession. We shall remember, therefore, that we have promised to cling to the Cross of Christ, and that we ought to avoid in all things that which caters to sensuality and that which savors of softness. Do not our Statutes remind us of the necessity of despising pomp and practicing penance with a particular zeal?[2]

The Declarations of the French Congregation on this chapter prescribe as follows: *Lectulus is esse debet ad quem somni necessitas compellat, non mollities alliciat.* The bed ought to be such as to answer to the need of sleep, yet without favoring softness. We shall come back later to the makeup of the bedding (Chapter 55). There is nothing unseemly in the possibility that our bed may be a little hard. For us Oblates as for the monks "it is merely a camp-bed whereon we stretch ourselves for a few

---

[2] *Manual for Oblates,* p. 43, §§12, 13.

hours."[3] Monks and Oblates are soldiers and, as St. Benedict will soon say, they ought to be ready to arise at the first signal to conduct each day's good fight.

St. Benedict wants his monks to sleep clothed in their monastic habit. It is "a safeguard against the attacks of the devil."[4] For the same reason the Oblates can keep a scapular on during their sleep.

But what St. Benedict demands of us above all is punctuality in rising. *Et facto signo sine mora surgentes.* "We must not rise piecemeal, bit by bit," says Dom Delatte,[5] "but immediately and as it were mechanically: it is easiest in the end. The Divine Office, both the work and our disposition towards it, will suffer from the unhappy self-indulgence and petty calculation which gives us an additional 20 minutes of sleep every morning.... And even though punctual rising imply some weariness and mortification, let us face it resolutely. It is by such courage in details that we come to be morally stronger, more fully masters of our body, and lords over our passions. Moreover, the most wholesome mortifications are those which enter into the tissue of everyday life and are with difficulty perceived

Let us conclude with this remark of Dom Delatte which, he tells us, is related to the general matter of the chapter:[6] "Some people, before they go to sleep, review the intellectual work of the day so as to fix and assimilate the results; which is a good practice, if it be brief. St. Teresa tells us that she never went to sleep without thinking of the Garden of Olives, of that dreadful night and of the agony of Our Lord: which is a far better practice. The last thought of our day is of very great importance, for it influences our sleep and influences the morrow. It is quite possible for us to consecrate to God even the unconscious moments of slumber. Our last thought is like a seed entrusted silently to the earth: *Terra ultro fructificat* (The earth gives fruit of itself); while it fades away, its blessed influence sinks slowly into our souls, impregnates them and permeates the whole."

---

[3] Dom Paul Delatte, *Commentary*, p. 200.

[4] *Ibid.*, p. 202.

[5] *Ibid.*, p. 203.

[6] Ibid., p. 204.

CHAPTER 23
On Excommunication for Faults

February 28 (29)—June 30—October 30

IF A BROTHER is found to be obstinate, or disobedient, or proud, or murmuring, or habitually transgressing the Holy Rule in any point and contemptuous of the orders of his seniors, the latter shall admonish him secretly a first and a second time, as Our Lord commands (*Matthew* 18:15). If he fails to amend, let him be given a public rebuke in front of the whole community. But if even then he does not reform, let him be placed under excommunication, provided that he understands the seriousness of that penalty; if he is perverse, however, let him undergo corporal punishment.

COMMENTARY

The present chapter and those which follow it, up to Chapter 30, form what may be called the monastic Penal Code or Penitential. Dom Herwegen has conjectured that these eight chapters had formed a whole, separated for the use of the Superiors, and that they were later brought into the final editing of the Rule.[1] The hypothesis seems far from being proved. All the monastic rules envisaged the possible breaches of their precepts; they had to reckon with human weakness. Prescriptions and punishments alike resulted from the state of morals, the customs, the social state of the time in which they were promulgated. They depended also on the lawgiver's character. The austerity of St. Columban, with his repeated scourgings, differs from the austerity of St. Benedict.[2]

Our holy Father does not define excommunication here. The meaning of that word was known. He indicates the principal breaches which can justify its use. The concern evidently cannot be with interior sins, which are amenable to the tribunal of Penance, but with misdeeds contrary to monastic observance. All these misdeeds have their common seat in the rebellious will. They are: open resistance to the rules or to orders given;

---

[1] *Gesckichte der Benedikiinisehen* Profess formed, p. 23.

[2] Dom Paul Chauvin, "*Le Penitentiel Bénédictin*," in Bulletin de S. Martin et de S. Benoît, April, 1926, p. 97.

grave disobedience; manifest pride; murmuring, against which St. Benedict has already spoken out; or contempt, when the guilty monk adds this to the breaches of the Rule or the resistance to the orders of the elders. It is evident that St. Benedict does not mean just any breach in these matters, but a notable breach, the gravity of which is left to the estimation of the Abbot or of the elders.

The evil must be remedied, then. Our holy Father wants to be an affectionate father before being an austere master. Inspired by the evangelical meekness, he is not going to punish the guilty one at once. There will be first a secret admonition, made by the elders. If this produces no effect, it will be repeated. Then, in face of the ineffectiveness of so mild a measure, the next procedure will be public censure in the presence of all the brethren. And it is only when the guilty one has shown himself impervious to all the procedures of mercy that the Superiors will resort to excommunication.

It is supposed ordinarily that the guilty one is intelligent, capable of understanding those who come to speak to his heart and his reason. It is supposed that excommunication, a penalty which is above all moral, is of a nature to affect him, to make him reflect and to lead him back. It was possible, however, especially in St. Benedict's time, to find coarse natures, hardly amenable to reasonings, natures too uncouth or sometimes perverse. It is probable that St. Benedict prescribed preliminary rebukes with regard to them also. But such natures could not be very sensitive to excommunication, which is therefore to be replaced by corporal punishments. The commentators have not failed to indicate here the whole series of these chastisements, of which the principal one was the rod. It hardly needs be added that this last procedure has long since gone out of usage in the monasteries and that, if there is corporal punishment, it is the monk who inflicts it on himself, under the form of the "discipline."

APPLICATION

This little chapter underlines the vices which our holy Father particularly detests: pride, which makes us regard as far below us any submission, not only to our Rule but to the orders, directives and counsels of our Superiors; formal disobedience; resistance, hidden or open; murmuring; contempt. Serious obstinacy in such vices can separate us morally from our monastic family, whose spirit is wholly pervaded with the contrary virtues; and if we should persist in those vices we would indeed be lying to God by our scapular and our affiliation.

Horror of those vices and fear of their consequences ought to inspire in us the resolution to cling more and more to the opposite virtues, to humility, obedience, loving and fervent submission. What good would it do us to be Oblates if we had nothing but the name? Let us maintain ourselves, therefore, in perfect communion of thought and action with all those who, yesterday and today, in the cloister and in the world, have sanctified and do sanctify themselves under the Rule of St. Benedict.

On the other hand, we may happen to find in others pernicious examples of these faults condemned by St. Benedict; and there are cases in which it is part of the duty of our state in life to bring a remedy to this evil. Let us consider the very paternal conduct of our holy Father. He does not inveigh against the rebellious souls or strike them pitilessly at first, but he tries to move them by speaking heart to heart with them. He does not fear to make a new attempt in case of failure. Even in the publicizing he shows himself a father, and he comes to punishment only when he cannot do otherwise. And this punishment itself is proportioned not only to the misdeed but to the guilty one's mentality; it is moral or corporal as the case may require, but more often moral than corporal. A simple-minded person or a child is not corrected like a reasonable person. And under its twofold aspect the punishment is still as much a mark of bounty as of justice. "Who loves well chastises well," says the Proverb; and we know that the most loving parents, masters, superiors or friends are not those who do not dare act against vices and who leave them without censure or punishment.

CHAPTER 24
What the Measure of Excommunication Should Be

March 1—July 1—October 31

THE MEASURE of excommunication or of chastisement should correspond to the degree of fault, which degree is estimated by the Abbot's judgment.

If a brother is found guilty of lighter faults, let him be excluded from the common table. Now the program for one deprived of the fellowship of the table shall be as follows: In the oratory he shall intone neither Psalm nor antiphon nor shall he recite a lesson until he has made satisfaction; in the refectory he shall take his food alone after the community meal, so that if the brethren eat at the sixth hour, for instance, that brother shall eat at the ninth, while if they eat at the ninth hour he shall eat in the evening, until by a suitable satisfaction he obtains pardon.

COMMENTARY

Not all faults are equally serious either in their nature or in their consequences. Thus there ought to be a proportion between the punishment and the gravity of the offense. The judge in this matter is to be the Abbot. It is he who will pronounce the excommunication.

St. Benedict considers two kinds of excommunication: excommunication from table for slight offenses, total ex- communication for serious offenses. The concern here will be only with the first.

Before we pass on, it may be of interest to inquire whether the monastic excommunication was of the same nature as the ecclesiastical, which is itself distinguished into minor and major excommunication.

The great majority of the commentators favor the affirmative. "The excommunication of which St. Benedict speaks in this chapter," says the Abbé de Rancé, "is that of the Church. This opinion is not only my own; it is that of a great part of the commentators, such as Boherius, Turrecremata, Guido Juvenalis, Perez, Craesberk, Alardus, Gazaeus, Theophilus Renaudus, Aphtenus, Père Ménard, the Congregation of Saint-Maur, etc." At the same time, Rancé made a distinction between major excommunication and minor excommunication, which latter according to him is not canonical but monastic. Dom Calmet, followed by Dom Delatte,

208

pronounces likewise for ecclesiastical excommunication. And this is undoubtedly right.

As Dom Gréa explains in his book *On the Church and Her Divine Constitution*,[1] two kinds of churches were distinguished at that time, secular churches and monastic churches. It was by his belonging to one of these churches that the Christian was part of the universal Church. Every church had the right to excommunicate any one of its members who so deserved, and the member thus cut off received no letter from his ecclesiastical Superior, whether Bishop or Abbot, permitting him to enter into communion with the other churches. In that way he found himself excluded from the universal Church.

In connection with this chapter a curious passage of St. Gregory's *Dialogs*[2] has often been recalled, in which St. Benedict is shown threatening with excommunication and then excommunicating "two religious women of distinguished origin who lived not far from his monastery." To these religious, who by their unseasonable language incensed the good man who looked after their material needs, St. Benedict speaks as having authority over them: "Curb your tongues; if you do not, I shall excommunicate, you." Yet these religious did not communicate at the monastic church, but in a secular church. Should we not say that we have to do here with some sort of Oblates, living at some distance from the monastery but under the direction of St. Benedict and joined by certain ties to the monastic church? For how could St. Benedict have excommunicated them if they had not by some title been in communion with him and his brethren?

The monastic church, then, could extend its communion outside of the group of monks over certain pious persons living under their direction and in fraternity with them. Among these fervent Christians joined to the monastery by titles which it is difficult to determine, could we not cite also the brother of the monk Valentinian,[3] who came every year to the monastery "to commend himself to the prayer of the man of God"? St. Benedict is truly this good Christian's spiritual father, with such right that "even when away" he acted "under the eyes of Benedict"; and St. Gregory

---

[1] *De L'Eglise et de Sa Divine Constitution* (Paris: Palme, 1885), p. 360.

[2] Book 2, Chapter 23; in P.L., Tome 66, cols. 178, 180; in *Life and Miracles of St. Benedict*, pp. 52-54.

[3] St. Gregory, *Dialogs*, Book 2, Chapter 13; in P.L., Tome 66, cols. 158, 160; in Life and Miracles of St. Benedict, pp. 32-34.

tells us how the holy Patriarch reproaches him because he has not come fasting to the monastery according to the custom sanctioned, no doubt, by St. Benedict.

For slight offenses the guilty monk, after the three warnings of the Rule, was barred from table. After the oratory, the refectory is the place where the unity of the family is best affirmed. Still, as there is an offense against God, the guilty one, though not deprived of participation in prayer, will take a less active part in its external celebration. He is to intone neither Psalm nor antiphon nor is he to recite a lesson until he has made satisfaction.

In the refectory he is to eat alone, after the brethren's meal. The received text tells us also that his portion is to be diminished "in the measure and at the hour which the Abbot shall consider suitable for him," but the most authoritative manuscripts do not carry these words, which are an interpolation from the following chapter.

APPLICATION

St. Benedict desires that every breach, even a slight one, be repaired by a suitable satisfaction. It is in virtue of this same spirit that in all the Benedictine Congregations the "satisfactions" have been instituted, designed to repair even slight breaches. Some are imposed by the Abbot; others are due to the initiative of the delinquent himself. The cases are specified, moreover, in the Customaries. In his article "The Benedictine Penitential,"[4] Dom Paul Chauvin notes how well founded are these satisfactions: "It is by reiterated and sincere satisfactions that the soul acquires the art of fruitful examinations of conscience and that of delicacy in the fulfilment of a thousand daily duties. Generally the lightness of the punishments which one inflicts on oneself or which the Abbot imposes would be such as to make a person smile; in reality, despite the frequent repetition, they remain an effective impulse to humility and detachment. They progressively increase purity of heart and attract God's graces. Hardly are the offenses committed, even material offenses, all the way down to mere awkwardness, when they become the object of an expiation which goes beyond them in moral import and in supernatural worth. This is a beautiful spectacle for the Angels and an edification for men."

Perhaps we Oblates also would gain by making use of "satisfactions"

---

[4] "Le Pénitentiel Bénédictin," in *Bulletin de S. Martin et de S. Benoît*, April, 1926, p. 100.

the better to put into practice our duties and our daily schedule. Prostration during the recitation of the Office, or even in the midst of some other occupation when we are alone, short prayer and on occasion the "discipline"—all these means can help us fulfil with ever more perfection the service of the Lord, by putting us on guard against negligences and by making reparation for them in the measure in which they are committed.

CHAPTER 25
On Weightier Faults

March 2—July 2—November 1

ET THE BROTHER who is guilty of a weightier fault be excluded both from the table and from the oratory. Let none of the brethren join him either for company or for conversation. Let him be alone at the work assigned him, abiding in penitential sorrow and pondering that terrible sentence of the Apostle where he says that a man of that kind is handed over for the destruction of the flesh, that the spirit may be saved in the day of the Lord *(1 Corinthians* 5:5). Let him take his meals alone in the measure and at the hour which the Abbot shall consider suitable for him. He shall not be blessed by those who pass by, nor shall the food that is given him be blessed.

COMMENTARY

"Grave faults," says Dom Étienne,[1] "were supposed to be forever banished from the harbor of sanctity." But human frailty must be reckoned with; and however rare ought to be the occasions for severity, prudence demands that they be foreseen. St. Benedict had encountered some of these grave offenses in his first monastery.

For the very guilty, therefore, there will be an excommunication more complete than that described in the preceding chapter. Let us note well, however, that this excommunication is not a final rupture. The guilty one is excluded from the communal life, but he is not excluded from the monastery. The point is that the punishment has a medicinal character and that the prodigal's repentance is counted on.

The one excommunicated for grave fault is excluded from both table and oratory. He does not assist at the liturgical prayer, which is the highest expression of the communion of souls. He does not eat with his brethren, and the Abbot may reduce the quantity of food allotted him. Between him and his brethren there is a moral separation: no one will associate with him; no one will speak to him; no one will bless him in passing; even his portion of food will not be blessed. At manual labor he will be alone. He is the plague-stricken one, the excommunicated one.

---

[1] *La Règle de S. Benoît Traduite et Commentée*, p. 370.

212

Thus "the blessed current of divine influence," the circulation of spiritual life, which may be said to constitute the atmosphere of the monastic family, are as it were intercepted for him.[2] And outside of that life there is no longer anything but the influence of Satan. By the fact of his exclusion he finds himself more particularly exposed to the suggestion and the action of the evil spirit. But the purpose is by no means that he abandon himself to the evil one; rather that he sense the danger and dread it, and that "his spirit be saved in the day of the Lord." Should not the painful sense of his sad loneliness prompt him to regret his offense? Should not the sufferings of soul and body bring about his "abiding in penitential sorrow"? Then, no doubt, he will find himself ready to give satisfaction; and St. Benedict will soon tell us how.

APPLICATION

By his profession the Oblate has entered into fraternal communion with his monastery. On the day he became a member of the monastic Order, his Abbot or the one who took the Abbot's place said to him, "We receive you into society and fraternity with us," and reminded him that henceforth he was entering into the current of spiritual life of a new family: "We give you a share in all the good works done, with the aid of the Holy Spirit, in this monastery."[3]

It is evident that for good reasons the Abbot may take back what he has given, and consequently that he may exclude an Oblate temporarily or permanently.

But the point on which it is well to insist is the necessity of keeping fully alive in ourselves the thought of the obligations assumed in our "communion" with our brethren, the monks. In reality, through our efforts towards perfection we must not feel too inferior to those who have welcomed us. If we weaken, if we go back to our old ways, is it not evident that we render less perfect that fraternal communion? And if, which God forbid, we were to fall into mortal sin and persist in attachment to it, would we not in truth be excommunicating ourselves, despite our nominal

---

[2] Dom Paul Delatte, *Commentary*, p. 216.

[3] Translator's note: The above formula differs somewhat from that used in the American-Cassinese Congregation as given in the *Manual for Oblates*, pp. 239-240: "And I, as God's representative, accept your Oblation and admit you into union and affiliation with our monastery as an Oblate and adopted son of our holy Father Benedict, and give you the privilege of sharing in our spiritual goods..."

affiliation? We could not help feeling unworthy to be members of a family whose fervor and charity we no longer shared. We should be as strangers in the house. May God keep us from experiencing such an "excommunication"; may He give us the grace to persevere in the joy of belonging with our whole heart to our monastic family and of living the same spiritual life as our brethren of the cloister.

Dom Laure adds another consideration to this chapter. It was certainly in spite of himself, he remarks, that St. Benedict had to bring himself to promulgate such unpleasant prescriptions. But his experience told him that it would have been a cruel shame to leave the guilty unpunished. His example can be of use to those who have the weighty charge of guiding others. "Who loves well chastises well," says the Proverb. It sometimes requires a real effort to punish those we love, but there are cases in which we would not be really loving them if we left them unpunished.

CHAPTER 26
On Those Who Without an Order Associate With the Excommunicated

IF ANY brother presumes without an order from the Abbot to associate in any way with an excommunicated brother, or to speak with him, or to send him a message, let him incur a similar punishment of excommunication.

COMMENTARY

The purpose of excommunication is to isolate the guilty one, to establish around him a solitude which may become salutary to him. No one can be permitted, therefore, to break that solitude by speaking to him or addressing a message to him without the order of the Abbot, who alone is judge in the question. He who would allow himself to consort with the excommunicated one would participate by the very deed in the excommunication.

Is it to be said that one ought not to be interested in him? Far from it. St. Benedict will tell us later on how the charity of all ought to come to his aid. But the remedy of the punishment must be allowed to act on Him. Who knows whether an untimely sympathy might not produce in his spirit an effect contrary to the one intended?

APPLICATION

Numerous commentators have drawn from this chapter practical considerations on the influence of bad example. "Consider," says Dom Philippe Francois, "that sin is something so contagious that, if one draws near it even a little, it is very difficult not to be infected by it."

"Consider," says Dom Morel, "that we ought to look with a kind of horror on all those whose conduct and life are obstacles to our salvation; to shun as excommunicated and plague-stricken those whose morals may corrupt us; to renounce the friendships and the company of those who lead us into evil and turn us away from our duty."

No doubt this concern was not foreign to our holy Father. But other commentators come nearer, it seems, to his chief concern in putting us on guard against certain indiscreet compassions. St. Benedict certainly had in mind a passage from Cassian on the same subject.[1] This kind of consolation, said Cassian, "gives him grounds for still greater arrogance" and "will make his heart still harder."

Dom Étienne quotes in this regard a text from St. Teresa of Avila: "A Sister will think she is doing an act of charity in coming to say (to a guilty one): 'I do not understand how you can endure such an affront; I pray God to give you patience ...; a Saint could suffer no more.' O my dear daughters, I hope none of you will let herself be carried away to that indiscreet charity, for that would be to imitate the friends and the wife of holy Job."

Similar cases may present themselves to us. Unless the duties of our state put on us the obligation of intervening in the case of a culprit who is undergoing his punishment, let us be very discreet, very prudent in our speech; and let us make it a practice to intervene only after taking counsel with the one who imposed the punishment. Otherwise we shall be likely to do the guilty one much more harm than good.

---

[1] *Institutes*, Book 2, Chapter 16; in C.S.E.L., Vol. 17, p. 31; in *Nicene and Post-Nicene Fathers*, 2nd series, Vol. 11, pp. 211-212.

CHAPTER 27
How Solicitous the Abbot Should Be for the Excommunicated

March 4—July 4.—November 3

ET THE ABBOT be most solicitous in his concern for delinquent brethren, for "it is not the healthy but the sick who need a physician" (*Matthew* 9:12). And therefore he ought to use every means that a wise physician would use. Let him send "*senpectae*," that is brethren of mature years and wisdom, who may as it were secretly console the wavering brother and induce him to make humble satisfaction; comforting him that he may not "be overwhelmed by excessive grief," but that, as the Apostle says, charity may be strengthened in him (*2 Corinthians* 2:7,8). And let everyone pray for him.

For the Abbot must have the utmost solicitude and exercise all prudence and diligence lest he lose any of the sheep entrusted to him. Let him know that what he has undertaken is the care of weak souls and not a tyranny over strong ones; and let him fear the Prophet's warning through which God says, "What you saw to be fat you took to yourselves, and what was feeble you cast away" (*Ezechiel* 34:3,4). Let him rather imitate the loving example of the Good Shepherd who left the ninety-nine sheep in the mountains and went to look for the one sheep that had gone astray, on whose weakness He had such compassion that He deigned to place it on His own sacred shoulders and thus carry it back to the flock (*Luke* 15:4-5).

COMMENTARY

In the preceding chapters we have seen St. Benedict using severity, as duty required, against those who become guilty of grave faults. We knew that his intention was to lead them to repentance. In the present chapter his very paternal soul will have its day. The Penitential Code will end on a note of mercy and of bounty.

The prodigal child is always a child; one does not abandon him to his misery, however deserved. Did not Christ come for the sick? The Abbot, who holds Christ's place, is to surround his suffering child with "all his solicitude." That solicitude is not weakness, or it would not attain its end. It is an attention which is tender, yet calm and patient, and which, like that of a "wise physician," resolved at any cost to heal his sick client, will use all possible remedies.

The Abbot will not act directly on the guilty one. He will send *senpectae* to him.

This word *senpecta* has long exercised the critical mind of the commentators, and there is still no agreement on its etymology. The most natural opinion is that which traces it to the Greek *sympaiktes,* coming from *syn* and *paizo,*[1] "one who behaves like a child with," "one who plays with," whence the meaning of "playmate."

The etymological sense, taken too strictly, has sometimes caused a certain consternation, which we no longer share. "The brethren do not play in the monasteries," gravely declares the Abbé de Rancé. And the author of the *Translation and Explanation* explains no less gravely that St. Benedict cannot have used a Greek word because he was not learned enough for that: "For one thing, we do not find that it was customary to use purely Greek words and write them with Latin letters; and for another, it may be doubted whether St. Benedict knew Greek well. It seems most likely that he was not very expert in Greek, since he left his studies before having completed them. ...It is true that the word *sympaiktes* was used often enough in the Greek; but we do not find it having passed into use among the Latins and having been common enough there for St. Benedict alone in his day to have made use of it without understanding the Greek tongue." Thus the opponents of the Greek etymology have gone so far as to correct the word and suggest the reading *senipetas,* namely men tending to old age, elders.

Aside from the fact that this word *senipetas* is little known elsewhere, although there exist examples of nouns compounded with *-petas,* we do not see why St. Benedict could not have retained from his studies, cut short though they were, the recollection of a very expressive Greek word and one which may have been used among young students with an acceptation larger than the purely etymological sense.

Thus the majority of the moderns declare in favor of the Greek origin. Dom L'Huillier likens this word to the French *compere,* and Dom Delatte explains: "There are in the community amiable and earnest brethren, in whom the excommunicated brother has confidence. They are monks of mature years and solid virtue, upon whom the complaints, or even the

---

[1] συμπαίκτης, συν-παίζω.

violent recriminations of the condemned man, will have no harmful effect; they are also skillful and diplomatic. So the Abbot makes them parties to his game of mercy and accomplices of his charity. They shall go secretly to, find the excommunicated brother, as though of their own accord and not as formal ambassadors; and their action will appear to him as though merely sanctioned by the Abbot."[2]

To send the *senpectae* the Abbot has chosen his moment, he has observed the guilty one closely. The latter is no longer in his original stubborn frame of mind; he is tormented, buffeted by contrary feelings; the first fever is gone. He appears to be absorbed in a deep sadness. It is now that exhortations to humility and repentance, marked by affection, have the best chance of producing a favorable effect. The unhappy one must not be allowed to fall into a despair which would not save him. His punishment has no other end than to heal him. And while the *senpectae* are helping him with their consolations and their counsels, the community will pray for him, for the community has never lost interest in the outcast, and it knows all the strength there is in prayer.

In the preceding lines our holy Father has occupied himself especially with the offender. His tender, fatherly soul, which must have suffered from a punitive measure he could not avoid, has spied on the poor prodigal, so as to seize the favorable moment for his return home. And now he turns again to the Abbot, to remind him that his solicitude for the guilty is not something optional, a mere affair of sentiment, but a question of duty and of justice. He must know that he was not set up to command healthy souls whose holiness will bring them to obedience, but rather more to guide, sustain and restore feeble or sick souls. He must tax his ingenuity and "exercise all prudence and diligence so that he may not lose any of the sheep entrusted to him." He has not the right to lose interest in the sinners and abandon them to their erring ways. Let him remember the Good Shepherd whose place he holds. And here it seems that the love of Christ and His fatherly kindness deeply move the heart of our holy Father. How many times must he have meditated this passage of the Gospel! He himself is penetrated by the Lord's compassion. *In tantum compassus est.* He had such compassion! And the chapter ends on some lines which recall the most personal and the most moving passages of the Prologue.

---

[2] *Commentary*, p. 222.

APPLICATION

Our holy Father was an admirable shepherd of souls. We have already had occasion to remark, especially with regard to the chapter on the Abbot, that the Holy Rule furnishes us all the elements of a pastoral treatise. The chapters of the Benedictine Penitential are also to be meditated from this point of view. Whoever has charge over souls, by any title whatsoever, will find in them a sure line of conduct with regard to sinners or those who have gone astray. Here are the principal points:

1) Never to lose interest in the sinners, even when one must make a void around them to prevent the contagion of the evil.

2) To watch for the propitious moment for their conversion; for an incautious attempt, made at the wrong time, may have very bad results. Let us not forget that the question for us is not at all the vanity of having carried off a difficult triumph, but a soul which is being lost, a soul which must be loved and must be saved.

To pray and to have prayers said, for we can do nothing without grace.

To be permeated with the spirit of Jesus, whom no difficulty stops when He must go through the mountains in search of the lost sheep. Sin is hateful, to be sure, but the sinner is our brother, and his soul is worth the blood of Christ. And then, what are we? Who of us can believe himself perfect before God? Who, from time to time, is not weak and lax in the divine eyes? And God puts up with us despite our wretchedness. Let us become permeated with His compassion for the infirmities of our brethren, however repulsive they may sometimes appear. We want to live with Christ's life! How can we fail to love those whom He never stops loving, and how can we forget that He labors with us when we search the trail of the lost sheep?

CHAPTER 28
On Those Who Will Not Amend After Repeated Corrections

March 5—July 5—November 4

F A BROTHER who has been frequently corrected for some fault, and even excommunicated, does not amend, let a harsher correction be applied, that is, let the punishment of the rod be administered to him.

But if he still does not reform or perhaps (which God forbid) even rises up in pride and wants to defend his conduct, then let the Abbot do what a wise physician would do. Having used applications, the ointments of exhortation, the medicines of the Holy Scriptures, finally the cautery of excommunication and of the strokes of the rod, if he sees that his efforts are of no avail, let him apply a still greater remedy, his own prayers and those of all the brethren, that the Lord, who can do all things, may restore health to the sick brother.

But if he is not healed even in this way, then let the Abbot use the knife of amputation, according to the Apostle's words, "Expel the evil one from your midst" (*1 Corinthians* 5:13), and again, "If the faithless one departs, let him depart" (*Ibid.* 7:15), lest one diseased sheep contaminate the whole flock.

COMMENTARY

Let us recall everything St. Benedict has prescribed thus far to lead back the errant monk: private warning, public admonition, excommunication for some, corporal punishment for others, the sending of *senpectae*, individual prayers of the brethren. Despite all the measures taken, no result has been obtained. The offender persists in his pride. A person cannot see what more he could say to persuade him.

A last means will be tried, however. Word are useless; the soul is intractable; all the remedies which St. Benedict obligingly lists have been unable to affect it. The body will be acted on: recourse will be had to the penalty of the rod. This had already been prescribed, it is true, for those whose minds were unable to appreciate excommunication. It is to be more rigorous this time; and it is normal that it be employed likewise for the excommunicate, since experience has shown that he too was unable to understand.

But one is not to content oneself with this material means. There is a remedy of incomparable efficacy: prayer. True, it has already been used,

221

but individually. This time it is to be communal prayer. We know how much the Lord recommended communal prayer. The monks are going to gather, therefore, to prevent a family tragedy, the loss of a brother. Without any doubt the Lord will be touched. Perhaps even "from a human point of view, the culprit kneeling outside near the door" will feel himself moved "by the spectacle of all his brethren busied with him before God in the sanctuary."[1]

The Lord will be touched. May the soul of the obstinate one not shut itself, like that of Judas, to God's secret appeals! For Christ is ever knocking at the door of the heart, even of the most hardened sinners, and it is indeed of their own will that they do not open.

The last graces have been rejected. The offender has indeed voluntarily excommunicated himself, in the literal sense of the word. It is quite evident that the least thread no longer binds him to the community. On the contrary, he becomes a danger for it; and charity demands that the whole family be not contaminated for the sake of a member whose cure is despaired of. There is nothing more to do but use the knife to cut off this gangrenous member, that is, to expel him from the monastery.

"Who dares," says Dom L'Huillier, "with a look to sound the depths towards which the soul descends which has broken with the most sacred duties, trampled underfoot the most choice graces? The promise of a hundredfold even in this world made by the Savior to those who follow Him is turned back on those who abandon Him; the poor wretches ordinarily find nothing in this world but a hundredfold of miseries."

APPLICATION

Is there any need to be reminded that the extreme measure prescribed by St. Benedict against the great offenders, namely expulsion, could be applied, *mutatis mutandis*, to Oblates? How could the Abbot maintain in affiliation with his monastery a scandalous sinner or even a sinner who is simply unedifying?

But there are other applications, more widely practical, to be drawn from this chapter.

There are certain sinners who have fallen into such a degree of corruption that it behooves us never to consort with them, even under the pretext of bringing them back. How many times has it not happened that

---

[1] Dom L'Huillier, *Explication Ascétique et Historique*, Tome 1.

the imprudent reformer has himself been perverted? There are environments which we should not frequent and people whom we ought absolutely to erase from our relations. If we retain some affection for them, there remains for us in witness of it the means *par excellence*: prayer.

This chapter of the Holy Rule contains, in fact, an admirable teaching on the efficacy of prayer. According to St. Benedict prayer is more powerful for the conversion of sinners than the most urgent warnings, the most terrible threats, the most eloquent exhortations. It is the supreme recourse, *quod majus est.*

An apostle who does not pray is quite likely to have only rare successes! At the basis of every apostolate, therefore, we shall put prayer; and, if possible, prayer in common, in the family, in a gathering, at church, and so forth. And this practice will accustom us to placing our trust in God, to counting on Him more than on ourselves, and to not attributing to ourselves what can only have been a triumph of grace.

In particular, we should not let ourselves be rebuffed by a first failure. St. Benedict had already prescribed prayer, before coming back to it for a supreme assault. And if he orders the obstinate sinner cut off from the monastery, nowhere does he prescribe that he is no longer to be prayed for. The works of God are mysterious. He often leaves us ignorant of the results of our supplications; and many who have persevered in prayer for a sinner and apparently gone unheard, will undoubtedly see in the light of eternity that the grace implored so insistently has really been granted at the last minute, when it was no longer humanly possible to ascertain its effects.

CHAPTER 29
Whether Brethren Who Leave the Monastery Should Be Received Again

March 6—July 6—November 5

F A BROTHER who through his own fault leaves the monastery should wish to return, let him first promise full reparation for his having gone away; and then let him be received in the lowest place, as a test of his humility. And if he should leave again, let him be taken back again, and so a third time; but he should understand that after this all way of return is denied him.

COMMENTARY

In the received text this chapter begins with these words: "If any brother through his own fault departs from the monastery or is cast out of it." Thus two causes for leaving are supposed: voluntary abandonment and expulsion. According to Dom Butler, Dom Chapman, the Farnborough translators and others, the original text is supposed to have read only "the brother who through his own fault departs from the monastery." The words "or is cast out of it" would be an interpolation. St. Benedict would have had in mind only the departure by deliberate intent, under the impulse of some vicious motive. But "the most ancient manuscripts," observes Dom Delatte, are in accord with the received text.[1] It is not certain, then, that there was any interpolation; and, on the supposition that there really was, it could only have been introduced by the fact that from the very beginning, even from St. Benedict's time, the same policy had been observed with regard to those expelled and those who fled.

Again in this little chapter we find the most paternal soul of our holy Father. St. Basil wanted never again to see the monk who had been expelled, even under title of guest and for a few hours. St. Benedict, on the other hand, cannot help feeling that he was the father, and does not refuse to welcome the prodigal son. "Mercy is not asleep; let him knock, and it will be opened to him,"

A re-entry of the sinner into the monastery supposes nevertheless "a

---

[1] *Commentary*, p. 228, note 1.

total amendment of the vice for which he left,"[2] for it would be futile to take him back with the certainty of putting him out again. He must be a new man; and to mark this renewal outwardly he will take the last place, as if the whole past had been wiped out. This measure will have the further advantage of testing his humility. Humility is the touchstone of the sincerity of a conversion. "It is certain," says a commentator,[3] "that there is nothing more salutary to the welfare of penitents than humility, which by itself includes all the other penances, and which is incomparably more useful than austerities; for they can deceive us, while humility never deceives."

But there are souls so weak, so unstable that one may think of a second departure. Shall this one be final? We feel that all St. Benedict's tenderness cannot resign itself to a loss without return. He will put it off as long as possible. "The mercy will make itself greater than the error; and if the brother comes back, he will be received again."[4]

And he will be thus taken back not one time, but even up to three times. The majority of the commentators think that the words *usque tertio*, "until the third time," do not include the first reception before any voluntary or forced departure, but that it is really a question of a third reintegration, "including the first one that followed the excommunication and the expulsion."[5] We know that the customs of Cluny extended indefinitely the possibilities of reintegration. To St. Bernard's reproaches on this point, Peter the Venerable replied that according to the Holy Rule the fugitive had no right to be reintegrated more than three times, but that the Abbot had the right to take him back as many times as he would deem necessary. It must be admitted that the true interpretation of the Rule was on St. Bernard's side.

APPLICATION

We shall not dwell on this literal interpretation of this chapter, which like the preceding ones could be applied to Oblates of the monastery in certain cases if the Abbot deemed it advisable. To him alone belongs the

---

[2] Translator's note: This is a translation of the received text, which adds the word *vitii* after *emendationem*.

[3] *Traduction et Explication Littérale*, p. 267.

[4] Dom L'Huillier, *Explication Ascétique et Historique*, Tome 1, p. 429.

[5] *Ibid.*

right to welcoming them, cutting them off and receiving them again.

Dom Philippe François[6] and Dom Robert Morel[7] have given this chapter a moral application worth meditating. "Consider," says Dom Morel, "that we must not think that what St. Benedict says of the apostates does not pertain to us because by God's mercy we have neither put off our habit nor abandoned our profession; for there is more than one kind of apostate. There are some in body; there are some at heart.... It is the heart that God looks at principally, and it is by the heart that we are truly what we are. ... Not to live in conformity with what one has promised..., to relax one's first fervor, one's original faithfulness ..., to have a worldly heart ..., loving what the world loves, fearing what it fears, being grieved and gladdened by that which gladdens and grieves the world, this is what the Saints call apostasy of the heart, and who among us has no cause to reproach himself on that score?"

"Consider," continues Dom Morel, "that after three new falls, an apostate in body is not received for re-entry, but that it is not the same with an apostate of the heart.

Mercy's door is always open to him, unless he closes it himself by his impenitence. God never rejects a true penitent... Oh, how dangerous it is not to listen to God's voice! How much we should fear lest He despise us in His turn! ... There is a measure of sins and a measure of graces.. ... Let us never despair of pardon, but also let us never abuse grace, because that despair and that abuse would be equally fatal to us. Let us fear always, let us hope always; and may that fear and that hope keep us ever in the path of duty or lead us back to it."

---

[6] *Exercices Spirituels*, p. 268.

[7] *Méditations*, pp. 287-289.

CHAPTER 30
How Boys Are to Be Corrected

VERY AGE and degree of understanding should have its proper measure of discipline. With regard to boys and adolescents, therefore, or those who cannot understand the seriousness of the penalty of excommunication, whenever such as these are delinquent let them be subjected to severe fasts or brought to terms by harsh beatings, that they may be cured.

COMMENTARY

"Every age and degree of understanding," says St. Benedict, "demands a particular rule of conduct." That is why there must be a gradation of punishments not only according to the faults but also according to age, intelligence and education.

Our holy Father distinguishes three classes of religious whom it is not expedient to submit to excommunication, because they could not understand it and consequently would draw no benefit from it: boys, adolescents, and the simple-minded already mentioned in Chapter 23.

According to Chapter 70, childhood ceased after 14 years completed, that is to say at the age when Roman children generally discarded the *toga praetexta*. We do not know exactly to what age adolescence went.

These three classes are much more easily reached through the senses than through reasoning. The child fears that punishment which deprives him of something or makes him suffer. The adolescent winces in face of the humiliation of bodily chastisements. The simple-minded is never anything but an overgrown child.

In these three cases recourse will be had either to severe fasts or to harsh floggings. It is evident that the severity of the fast or the harshness of the flogging are something very relative. St. Benedict desires that a person take account of the weakness of the culprits and treat them "according to their measure." The idea is to bring them back to health, and the punishment which permits the attainment of that end is sufficient.

APPLICATION

St. Benedict has already appeared to us as an educator full of tact and discretion. He does not propose an inflexible line of conduct which is supposed to be applied to all without distinction. The formation of souls implies the knowledge and discernment of spirits, and consequently an adaptation of each one's capacities. "Every age and degree of understanding should have its proper measure."

The child, notes Dom Delatte, is "a being, doubtless, rich with future promise, but for the present scarce revealing any phenomena but those of the animal life."[1] Reasoning with him is often wasted effort when there is no sanction to support the reasoning. Thus in the family, as in the monastery, a person should not fear to use corporal punishments on occasion. In spite of the prejudice which has caused them to be all but abandoned in the present day, it must really be admitted that in former days they proved their worth by fashioning strong, well-tempered souls.

"He who spares the rod," say the *Proverbs* (13:24), "hates his son." And further on: "If you strike him with the rod, he shall not die" (23:13). That is why a person charged with the formation of children's characters must not fear to employ in their regard certain sanctions which instil a certain fear in them, without destroying their trust and affection. The child generally understands that he ought to be punished when he does wrong, and not to dare punish him is not truly to love him, St. Benedict was an affectionate father. He tenderly loved the young Maurus, the little Placidus and the other boys who had been entrusted to him; and he was loved by them. That did not prevent him from prescribing for their benefit "severe fasts" and the rod. His love had nothing weak about it, and it knew how to do violence to itself in order to assure their perfection and their salvation.

After having commented on this chapter, Dom Étienne adds that fasting and the "discipline" can be useful to others than children, to heal their wounds. *Ut sanentur.* Has not Our Lord recommended fasting to us, and does not St. Paul inform us that he "chastised his body"? Thus, he continues, "fasting and the discipline are two afflictive penances which virtuous souls from St. Paul down to our day have used to chastise the body and bring it into servitude, to assure the triumph of the soul over the senses, and to obtain the remission of sins. ... And this in union with Calvary's Victim, the Lord Jesus, who subjected Himself to a fast of 40 days and endured the fiercest, bloodiest scourging ever undergone at the pillar of the pretorium."

---

[1] *Commentary*, p. 231.

CHAPTER 31
What Kind of Man the Cellarer of the Monastery Should Be

S CELLARER of the monastery let there be chosen from the community one who is wise, of mature character, sober, not a great eater, not haughty, not excitable, not offensive, not slow, not wasteful, but a God-fearing man who may be like a father to the whole community.

Let him have charge of everything. He shall do nothing without the Abbot's orders, but keep to his instructions. Let him not vex the brethren. If any brother happens to make some unreasonable demand of him, instead of vexing the brother with a contemptuous refusal he should humbly give the reason for denying the improper request.

Let him keep guard over his own soul, mindful always of the Apostle's saying that "he who has ministered well acquires for himself a good standing" (*1 Timothy* 3:13).

Let him take the greatest care of the sick, of children, of guests and of the poor, knowing without doubt that he will have to render an account for all these on the Day of Judgment.

Let him regard all the utensils of the monastery and its whole property as if they were the sacred vessels of the altar. Let him not think that he may neglect anything. He should be neither a miser nor a prodigal and squanderer of the monastery's substance, but should do all things with measure and in accordance with the Abbot's instructions.

COMMENTARY

The cellarer, called the "steward" (*oeconomus*) in Cassian, is the monk charged by the Abbot with the whole administration of temporal things. In the long chapter devoted to him, there will be less question of the cellarer's prerogatives than of the supernatural qualities with which he should discharge them.

The cellarer is evidently chosen by the Abbot. He ought to be "wise, of mature character, not a great eater, nor haughty, nor turbulent, nor offensive, nor slow, nor prodigal, but God-fearing," These qualities will have a twofold effect: they will prevent him from abusing certain opportunities which his charge presents to him, and at the same time they will assure the good administration of the monastery's goods and the satisfaction of all.

There should be in him something of the paternal character of the Abbot. In the Christian family the father must supply his children at the same time with food for the soul and food for the body. In the monastery the Abbot assumes especially the first obligation; and although he does not lose interest in the second, still he entrusts its care almost entirely to the cellarer. The latter is to watch over "everything." On him will depend all the material services of the community, but he will remain nonetheless always dependent on the Abbot: "Let him do nothing without the Abbot's order. What is commanded, let him observe."

The cellarer's commission is difficult on various grounds. It obliges the one who holds it to give to material things a time which he would rather devote to meditation, study and the like. It charges him with responsibilities; sometimes with worries, when the monastery is poor. And yet our holy Father does not permit him to let this appear outwardly in his disposition or his attitude. He must show himself of amiable access. "Let him not vex the brethren." And there again is one of the difficulties of his task. The characters in a community are varied: there may be difficult ones, exacting, cross, nay even unreasonable. The cellarer must welcome all alike with a perpetual goodwill. Not that he is to accede, to all demands, but he must know how to refuse without grieving. "If any brother makes an unreasonable demand of him, let him not vex him with a contemptuous denial, but reasonably refuse what is asked of him out of turn."

For the realization of so many virtues, our holy Father asks the cellarer to "keep guard over his own soul," that is, to protect it by a strong interior life against all dissipation and all bitterness. The habitual thought of the presence of God, living in his soul, will help him not to spread himself out, but to guard that peace and that calm which will allow him to remain always even-tempered, always benevolent.

The cellarer will have to concern himself with all his brethren, but there are certain categories which require more delicate and more attentive cares, and which St. Benedict recommends to him particularly: "the sick, children, guests, the poor." For them he ought to show the greatest solicitude. St. Benedict reminds him, as he had previously reminded the Abbot, that of his conduct "with regard to all these he will have to render an account on the Day of Judgment."

After the persons come the things. The goods of the monastery are

God's goods. The cellarer will watch over them and will hold nothing as negligible. They will be as sacred for him as "the vessels of the altar."

In the administration of the funds he will avoid at the same time avarice and prodigality, and he will know how to practice discretion. It is not proper either to hoard or to dissipate. The idea is to assure the brethren "just measure." As we can see, the cellarer's functions, of little interest in themselves, demand on his part a considerable sum of qualifications, virtues and sacrifices.

APPLICATION

The monastery is *par excellence* the house of God. That is why, according to Cassian, the religious look on everything that enters there as a holy thing, consecrated to God, which must be neither abused nor misused.[1]

To a lesser degree, yet very really, the goods entrusted to all Christians by Providence should be regarded as God's goods. The one who possesses is the steward and, to use the monastic expression, the cellarer of God. If he is the head of a family, he should know that he has no right to squander goods which are more the property of his dependents, whose well-being they assure, than they are his own. According to the Church's traditional doctrine, the individual exists much less for himself than for the family of which he is constituted the head, the guardian and the protector. And he is also God's steward with respect to the orphans, the poor, the sick. He must not fail to come to their aid according to his means. He who performs no charity fails in his religious duties.

Thus the Christian, and *a fortiori* the Oblate, should administer the goods at his disposal in such a way as on the one hand to avoid a guilty prodigality, and on the other hand to stint neither his family nor the poor. The spirit of faith, reflection, a charitable attention to the needs of others, a certain self-abnegation will show him where the just measure is found. We shall have to come back to certain details of this subject in speaking of poverty.

But there is a certain category of Oblates whom, on the one hand, the Lord has not willed as a general rule to charge with the care of a family, and to whom, on the other hand, are entrusted the "sacred vessels of the altar." These are the priest Oblates. They have to administer the goods of

---

[1]   *Institutes*, Book 4, Chapter 20; in C.S.E.L., Vol. 17, p. 61; in *Nicene and Post-Nicene Fathers*, 2nd series, Vol. 11, p. 225.

their church, the funds of various works of zeal or charity, to watch over the parish movables: statues, vestments, sacred vessels and so forth. How useful for them can be the meditation of everything our holy Father recommends to the cellarer! Indeed it is here above all that we must "hold nothing as negligible," we must avoid the avarice which would deprive God's house of what becomes it as well as the prodigality which would exhaust in foolish, useless expenditures that property which does not belong to us.

All, moreover, will benefit by examining themselves on the qualities which St. Benedict requires of a cellarer, and in particular on that thing so delicate among all: not to vex one's brethren. What a spirit of faith, what supernatural delicacy is sometimes necessary in order to know how to refuse one who asks for something unreasonably or inopportunely!

"He may be asked," says Dom Delatte,[2] "for what is unreasonable. Let him learn to refuse it reasonably—that is, explaining the refusal, simply, humbly, sweetly, without insult or taunt; so that the brother who prefers the unreasonable request may not be able to charge him with impatience or prejudice, whether in the substance or the manner of his refusal. There is a manner of giving which enhances the gift; so, too, there is a manner of refusing which softens the refusal: spiritual tact will find this manner."

"Never despise him who makes supplication of you," says St. Augustine.[3] "If you cannot give a person what he asks for, do not despise him. If you can give, give; if you cannot, at least show yourself courteous."

March 9—July 9—November 8

Above all things let him have humility; and if he has nothing else to give let him give a good word in answer, for it is written, "A good word is above the best gift" (*Ecclesiasticus* 18:17).

Let him have under his care all that the Abbot has assigned to him, but not presume to deal with that he has forbidden him.

Let him give the brethren their appointed allowance of food without any arrogance or delay, that they may not be scandalized, mindful of the Word of God as to what he deserves "who shall scandalize one of the little ones" (*Matthew* 18:6).

If the community is a large one, let helpers be given him, that by their assistance he may fulfil with a quiet mind the office committed to

---

[2] *Commentary*, p. 236.

[3] *Enarratio Prima in Psalmum CIII*, v. 19; in P.L., Tome 37, col. 1351.

him. The proper times should be observed in giving the things that have to be given and asking for the things that have to be asked for, that no one may be troubled or vexed in the house of God.

COMMENTARY

Humility is the capital virtue of the Benedictine monk; to it St. Benedict traces the other virtues, as we have seen in Chapter 7. The cellarer, therefore, whose office might occasion some temptations of vanity, should apply himself to humility "before everything." This virtue will show itself particularly in his manner of refusing what he cannot give. Above, there was question of a refusal opposed to an unreasonable demand. The concern here is rather with a thing that the cellarer does not have. To the one who asks he is to reply with goodwill as previously. "If you must disappoint," notes Dom Delatte,[4] "you need not do it tauntingly. How excellent is kindness, and how little it costs! Just a word of regret, some small compensation, a promise, an affable air, a friendly smile. If the money or object which is asked for cannot be given, then 'let him give at least a kind answer.'" A good word is worth more than the best of gifts, says *Ecclesiasticus*.

The cellarer's humility will be shown also in his submission to the Abbot's orders. He will be careful to do well what has been prescribed for him, and he will not meddle in the things with which he has been forbidden to concern himself.

Finally, his humility will also be noticed in the manner in which he distributes the assigned portion to the brethren. He will avoid arrogance. The text reads: *sine aliquo typo*. The word *typum*, model, figure, image, does not make sense here. The Abbé de Rancé and the author of the Translation and Explanation already proposed the reading *typho*, "as it is in several books," remarks the latter. Dom Delatte also regards this reading as the better. *Typhum* corresponds to the Greek word *typhos*, smoke of pride, arrogance. *Sine typho* is therefore the equivalent of *cum humilitate*. He who feels that all have need of him is so likely, if he has not a true virtue, to exaggerate his own importance! The cellarer should not make others wait for him, either. If through pride or through negligence he lets the brethren suffer, there will be murmurings, discords, petty scandals. All of that is contrary to the calm and the peace which should reign in the monastery.

---

[4] *Commentary*, p. 240.

There could be an involuntary delay, however, if the cellarer were overwhelmed with excessive cares. St. Benedict has provided for that. If the community is large, the cellarer will receive helpers. Overwork is not favorable to the soul's peace and to the life in God. Thanks to his helpers the cellarer will be able to fulfil his office "with a more tranquil mind."

The peace and equanimity which he needs must not be disturbed, either, by the demands of this one and that one at all hours. There will be fixed times for asking and for giving. The different Constitutions specify these times and determine their duration. Thus the virtues of the cellarer and the charity and discretion of the brethren conspire to realize our holy Father's desire: "Let no one be troubled or vexed in the house of God."

APPLICATION

The final wish of our holy Father should have a general import. Among Christians it is good that "no one be troubled or vexed." Do not all form an immense family? And in those various homes of which the great family is composed, whether it be a question of natural families or of spiritual families like the parish, should not the. case be the same? The humility which inspires kindness and bounty, the humility which opposes brutal refusals and arrogant attitudes, finally the humility which keeps each one in his place and prevents him from meddling in what does not concern him, that humility will always be the best condition for any peace.

This virtue, to be sure, has its distinctions. It does not always manifest itself in the same way in the master and in the servant, in the father and in the child, in the pastor and in the parishioner; but when it is drawn from its true source, the very humility of the Savior, it inspires in each one the tact and the discretion proper to his situation. It realizes that harmony in mutual kindnesses (Chapter 72) which prevents "trouble and vexation in the house of God."

Regarding the words "When he cannot give what is asked of him, etc." the Abbé de Rancé observes that the concern here is not merely with the brethren but also with people outside, especially the poor. And he adds this reflection, from which we can always take profit: "He must regard himself as the salt and as the light of those with whom he deals; thus all his manners must be irreproachable. As far as the poor are concerned, he must know them, assist them, console them, relieve them, and not do like those who give to them only grudgingly and to get rid of their importunity, a thing which hurts them more than to be refused with evidences of the charity one has for them and the compassion one has for their miseries. The man who begs is ashamed enough of his own condition and of the necessity which makes him a burden on others, without having anyone add to his confusion by treating him rudely."

CHAPTER 32
On the Tools and Property of the Monastery

March 10—July 10—November 9

F OR THE CARE of the monastery's property in tools, clothing and other articles let the Abbot appoint brethren on whose manner of life and character he can rely; and let him, as he shall judge to be expedient, consign the various articles to them, to be looked after and to be collected again. The Abbot shall keep a list of these articles, so that as the brethren succeed one another in their assignments he may know what he gives and what he receives back.

If anyone treats the monastery's property in a slovenly or careless way, let him be corrected. If he fails to amend, let him undergo the discipline of the Rule.

COMMENTARY

In the preceding chapter there was question of the helpers to be given the cellarer. Dom L'Huillier, Dom Laure and others think that it is with these helpers that we are here concerned. But as the helpers in question were contemplated only in case the community would be large, and as there seems to be question in this passage of stewards to be established in any case, that opinion seems hardly probable.

The monastery's substance in tools, clothing or any other objects will be entrusted, therefore, to certain brethren, most likely chosen by the Abbot. One, for example, will have charge of the instruments of work, another of the clothing supply, another of the library. These brethren should be of an exemplary life. Thus there will be assurance that they will watch over everything entrusted to them most conscientiously. Moreover, the Abbot, who always holds a supervisory hand over everything, will keep an inventory of the objects given out by him as well as of those returned to him.

St. Benedict foresees a certain succession in the offices, but he does not specify its conditions. It seems just as gratuitous to affirm with Dom Martène, on the basis of Chapter 53, that the office-holders were always named for one year, as to assume with Dom L'Huillier that they changed every week, on the grounds that this was the custom with St. Pachomius.

237

If anyone, steward or not, treats the monastery's goods carelessly, he will be warned and, if he does not amend, subjected to the regular "discipline."

APPLICATION

If our holy Father demands that the objects belonging to the monastery be treated with care, this is certainly because, as was said above (Chapter 31), these objects belong to the Lord, who is the true Master of the house. Here again we find the principles taught in the chapter on the cellarer, with the same practical applications.

It is not impossible that St. Benedict thought of the fact of experience that there is often a certain relation between exterior carelessness and dirtiness on the one hand and a kind of carelessness and indolence in the interior life on the other hand. "From the outward decorum of religious," says Dom Philippe Frangois,[1] "one may draw... some probable conjecture about the purity of their souls." In the respect for the things entrusted to us, as well as in our outward bearing, there is indeed something like an index of a certain delicacy of soul, which has nothing in common, however, with the quest for well-being or vanity. One may wear old clothes in a very dignified way without lacking respect for oneself and for good bearing. On the other hand, bad appearance in our clothing or in what belongs to us is often a mark of laziness. Let us add that this carelessness can sometimes be very distressing to those who live with us, and that it then bears witness to a certain lack of charity. From every point of view, therefore, it is to be avoided.

The commentators on this chapter have not failed to imply from St. Benedict's concern for the care of exterior things an a fortiori as to the things of the soul. "Think," writes Dom Philippe François,[2] "that if neatness must be guarded in these exterior things, which in themselves are of so little value, much more care must be taken of interior things; we must be more careful to keep neat the tools of the soul, which are its powers and its faculties, to preserve them from all dirt, from vice and from imperfection, cleansing and scouring them as often as by human weakness they are however little soiled." And the Abbé de Rancé writes: "If we ought to take particular care to conserve the exterior property in furniture

---

[1] *Considérations*, p. 269.

[2] *Ibid.*

and in all things for the use of the monastery, what diligence should we not have to procure the purity of souls, to keep them without spot, to banish from them everything that could tarnish that beauty which God demands of them and could prevent their acquiring the perfection to which He has destined them."

CHAPTER 33
Whether Monks Ought to Have Anything of Their Own

March 11—July 11—November 10

HIS VICE especially is to be cut out of the monastery by the roots. Let no one presume to give or receive anything without the Abbot's leave, or to have anything as his own— anything whatever, whether book or tablets or pen or whatever it may be—since they are not permitted to have even their bodies or wills at their own disposal; but for all their necessities let them look to the Father of the monastery. And let it be unlawful to have anything which the Abbot has not given or allowed. Let all things be common to all, as it is written (*Acts* 4:32), and let no one say or assume that anything is his own.

But if anyone is caught indulging in this most wicked vice, let him be admonished once and a second time. If he fails to amend, let him undergo punishment.

COMMENTARY

The religious life is the seeking of God alone, and consequently the detachment from all that is not God. St. Benedict has already provided for that detachment by obedience, which condemns self-will. Here he demands of his disciple that he be effectively detached from earthly goods.

In the Gospel Our Lord prescribed detachment in spirit: *Beati pauperes spiritu*. The better to safeguard that detachment, St. Benedict, like the previous Masters of the monastic life, prohibits private property itself. This point lies so close to his heart that he puts an unaccustomed vigor into his reprobation: "Let great care be taken to cut this vice out of the monastery." No one must either give or receive or keep "absolutely anything...in a word, anything at all." And the holy Patriarch enumerates the usual objects which the monk might be tempted to regard as his property on the pretext that they are of little value and that they are indispensable to him: a book, a tablet, a pen.

How could the monks possess anything? They fulfil none of the conditions necessary to possession. A person cannot posses without willing, and they are not masters of their wills. A person cannot possess without occupying and appropriating the object bodily to his own use, and they are not masters of their bodies. Hence they must look to the Father of the monastery for everything. Anything not given or permitted by him is illicit.

This total renunciation will appear even in speech. One will not say "my cell, my breviary, my scapular,' but "our cell, our breviary, our scapular." "And if the worldlings are astonished at this language," remarks Dom L'Huillier, "let us not care about that: they have long failed to understand the delicate reason for such a custom; that is not sufficient cause for abandoning the custom, for words have more influence on the course of ideas than is ordinarily supposed." If any monk "is caught indulging in this detestable vice," he will receive two warnings; and if he persists, he will be subjected to the regular "discipline."

APPLICATION

Our Lord numbered poverty among the beatitudes. But the Gospel text specifies clearly that the concern is first of all with a poverty in spirit, a detachment of the heart. A monk who regretted what he had given up or who willingly indulged the desire for possession would not really be a poor man; while a rich man whose heart was not attached to the goods entrusted to him by Providence would have every right to that title. "It is by the heart," wrote Dom Morel,[3] "that we are poor or greedy in God's sight. It is there that the passion for wealth dwells, and it is that passion which is the root of all evils. If we will be truly poor, let us dig out that evil root as far as lies in our power, and substitute in its place a sincere love of poverty and a burning desire for eternal wealth."

"Riches, in themselves," observes Dom Delatte,[4] "are neither good nor bad; nor is poverty itself good, save when it permits us to enjoy the Sovereign Good in all completeness." The great advantage of the vow of poverty is that it facilitates and protects the virtue of poverty. But its absolute practice is hardly possible except in the monastery. It behooves us Oblates, therefore, finding the fulfilment of the vow impossible, to strive to practice the virtue as best we can.

The Oblate has taken God for his portion. If he is a priest, his Oblation only underlines the obligation to practice the poverty inherent in the clerical state. "The ecclesiastical state ... requires an entire detachment

---

[3] 1 *Méditations*, p. 301.

[4] *Commentary*, p. 249.

from the goods of earth."[5] In conferring the tonsure on us and in making us put away "the ignominy of the secular habit," the Church "separates us from creatures and the solicitudes of life for the sole end that we may adhere to God alone. She desires us to be men of another world, men of a new generation, continually occupied in pleasing God and procuring His glory."[6] It is for a similar end that we have been invested with the Benedictine scapular. Is it not the "vestment which the Fathers of old wished to be worn by those who renounced the world,"[7] that is, the love of the things of this world?

True detachment requires at least four conditions:

1) not to seek the goods we do not have; 2) not to be attached to the goods we do possess, and to be ready to give them lip without regret when the service of the Lord demands it; 3) not to regret the loss of those we no longer have;[8] 4) not to be attached to superfluities1 and, as St. Benedict says, "not to seek delights."

The better to realize those conditions, we must put ourselves into a certain frame of mind with respect to the goods from which we really cannot separate ourselves. Let us consider them not as belonging to us, but as belonging to God. How could we dare dissipate in superfluities,[9] in luxury, in objects designed to satisfy our sensuality, that which we recognize as coming from God and of which, as we have seen, we are only the stewards? We must be able to say with St. Basil, "If you rob me of what I possess, you will injure the poor more than you will myself."[10]

Here are some principles set forth by Pere Cotel in his Catechism of the Vows, which has become a classic. These principles, it seems, can be

---

[5] Rev. Pierre Chaignon, S.J., *Meditations for the Use of the Secular Clergy*, translated from the French by the Right Rev. L. de Goesbriand, revised ed. (New York: Benziger Brothers, 1907), Vol. 1, p. 389.

[6] *Ibid.*, p. 390.

[7] "Investiture of Oblate Novices," in *Manual for Oblates*, p. 226.

[8] 6 Rev. Pierre Chaignon, S.J., *Meditations for the Use of the Secular Clergy*, Vol. 1, p. 390.

[9] Rev. Peter Cotel, S.J., *A Catechism of the Vows*, translated from the French (London: Burns Oates & Washbourne Ltd., 1930), p. 57.

[10] Quoted by the Rev. Pierre Chaignon, S.J., *Meditations for the Use of the Secular Clergy*, Vol. 1, p. 395.

proposed to Oblates, especially to the priests.[11]

I. For the exterior practice of poverty:

1) To be satisfied with what is necessary, to remove all irregular affection, as well as all that is superfluous for our support (this is the obligatory matter of the virtue).

2) To be inclined to what is least...and to be content that it be our part for habitation, garments, etc.

3) To love sometimes to want what is necessary; with discretion, however, and without prejudice to health; and to rejoice when Jesus Christ Our Lord gives us a part of His poverty.

II. For the interior practice:

A person will practice detachment: 1) "through a principle of mortification and penance, in expiation for his sins"; 2) "through contempt of earthly goods, and to secure for himself those of heaven"; 3) "through love for Jesus Christ ... and through the desire of resembling Him in His poverty, and in order that all his affections may be undividedly given to his Lord."

In a retreat preached in 1928 to lay Oblates, the Abbé Gaucheron specified the different aspects under which the practice of poverty may present itself for an Oblate living in the world:[12]

"As for those whom Providence itself has endowed with the enviable privilege of no more than moderate means or even of a certain penury, how happy they ought to consider themselves, and how careful they should be to do nothing which lessens the merit of their involuntary privations! As for those who have in appearance received more than others, those on whom a certain obligation not to distinguish themselves too much from their environment imposes the necessity of living outwardly like the rich, how they must apply themselves to discovering, in the midst of the enjoyments to which their situation condemns them, occasions of depriving themselves!

"Could they sincerely call themselves poor in spirit if they never really divest themselves of the use of any of their riches? Would they dare pretend faithfulness to the rule of 'never seeking delights' if, being

---

[11] Pp. 63-64. We start with Pere Cotel's second principle, the first being the effective abandonment of temporal goods.

[12] "Une Retraite Bénédictine," in *Bulletin de S. Martin et de S. Benoît*, May, 1928, pp. 502 ff.

constantly solicited by delights, they did not know how sometimes to refuse them? Would they be faithful to their monastic profession if they did not sometimes force themselves to liken their daily routine to that of a well regulated community? And if it sometimes happens that they find themselves alone at table, on an outing, on a trip, what will prevent them then from taking advantage of the occasion to eat, sleep, travel, serve themselves, as a religious would do?

"We have things for our strictly personal use with which we serve ourselves, and always without witnesses; in these objects of real necessity, where luxury has no legitimate motive for displaying itself, why should not the Oblates offer poverty an asylum everywhere else denied to it?... The voluntary privation which the Oblate will be able to impose on himself from time to time will remind him of his incorporation in that great monastic line of which penance is one of the most certain and most glorious traditions."

"Without being bound by vows," says the Abbé Gaucheron farther on,[13] "without having officially divested himself of the goods he possesses nor of the right to acquire others, without even seeking in everything—since his duty would not always permit him to do so—the greatest privation or even the greatest simplicity, joyfully accepting the one when it presents itself and tending to the other every time a higher obligation does not forbid it," the Oblate "will never regard himself as the absolute master of what he possesses; and, having reserved for the present and future needs of himself and his loved ones a modest living, variable according to his station, he will consecrate the rest wholeheartedly to the glory of God, that is to say, to the service of the divine worship, of the poor and of good works.

"Certain ones of these great needs, which are those of Christ Himself, will even appear so sacred to him that he will know how to put them ahead of his own and take something from what is not absolutely superfluous to satisfy them. And how he will have to tax his ingenuity so as gladly to cut down on what appeared necessary to him at first glance and to be able to increase by that much the portion he can give!

"And in consequence, the day we ourselves must feel the pinch of straitened circumstances or even of real poverty, having joyfully served the apprenticeship, we shall welcome with joy the visit of this friend of

---

[13] *Ibid.*, p. 503.

Jesus; we shall not complain of lacking in reality that of which we have already divested ourselves in spirit and at heart. We shall recognize that God is but granting our desires and taking seriously our professed renouncement; and from the bottom of our heart we shall thank Him for having acknowledged us loving enough to follow Jesus to that point and to merit reigning with Him in the possession of the sweetest of the beatitudes."

CHAPTER 34
Whether All Should Receive in Equal Measure What Is Necessary

March 12—July 12—November 11

ET US FOLLOW the Scripture, "Distribution was made to each according an anyone had need" (*Acts* 4:35). By this we do not mean that there should be respecting of persons (which God forbid), but consideration for infirmities. He who needs less should thank God and not be discontented; but he who needs more should be humbled by the thought of his infirmity rather than feeling important on account of the kindness shown him. Thus all the members will be at peace.

Above all, let not the evil of murmuring appear for any reason whatsoever in the least word or sign. If anyone is caught at it, let him be placed under very severe discipline.

COMMENTARY

This chapter continues the preceding one and completes it. All should look to the Father of the monastery for everything. It is his function, therefore, to distribute or cause distribution to be made. But according to what principles shall the distribution be made? According to the principle observed in the primitive Church. It has often been pointed out that the ideal of life of the first Christians was identical in sum to the monastic ideal. This agreement has even provided the subject of a substantial work by Dom Germain Morin.[1]

In this apportionment of the necessities of life, the Abbot will give to each one according to his needs. He will have no favorites and will make no distinction of persons. He will act according to justice, which is not the brutal equality of those Utopians who see nothing in individuals but somewhat abstract entities. Not equality but rather inequality is a law of nature. Temperaments, characters and needs differ with the individuals. The Abbot is not an administrative head nor a military leader, he is the father of a family. He considers the necessities of each of his children, and proportions his gifts to them.

But the religious for their part ought to understand how legitimate is

---

[1] *The Ideal of the Monastic Life Found in the Apostolic Age*, translated from the French by C. Gunning (New York: Benziger Brothers, 1914).

246

this conception of justice. Let him who is strong and needs little not imagine that he is harmed because little is given him. On the contrary, let him thank God. Having fewer needs, he is less tied down; it is a misfortune to have many needs. How little of the monastic spirit would that one have who would become vexed at not having for his own use as many things or things as desirable as certain others have! He would be lacking at once in poverty, charity and mortification.

Let the weak one, on the other hand, not imagine himself an object of favoritism because people are good to him, and let him not become vain on that account. "To have more needs than the rest is a weakness in which self-love could not find any foundation."[2] On the contrary, one must be humiliated at needing so many things which the rest can forego.

Let all, therefore, receive with joy what is given them, without making envious comparisons, and above all without murmuring. Our holy Father has already condemned murmuring; he comes back to it here: "Above all, let murmuring never appear, for any reason whatever, either in the least word or in any sign." If any brother was caught murmuring, he was to be subjected to "a severe correction."

APPLICATION

This chapter can receive manifold applications. We too often have the prejudice of equality, and the concupiscence which is in us impels us as if instinctively to envy him who has more than we or who seems more favored by our Superiors. We should, on the contrary, rejoice at being able to forego many things; and we should not judge badly those who have needs which we have not, and the Superiors who consider it their duty to condescend to their weakness. Rarely does any Superior, even if he forces himself to make no distinction of persons, escape the judgement of the envious. Let us who want to have the spirit of St. Benedict guard against sharing both that jealousy and those false judgments.

And if we establish that there are things which we do not believe we can forego, while others forego them willingly, let us be humiliated by our weakness and our helplessness. Above all, let us avoid murmuring. "Murmuring," writes Dom Étienne, "is a complaint manifested in words or in signs against the order of things established, willed or permitted by a superior or legitimate will. Murmuring is called by St. Bernard *grave*

---

[2] Dom L'Huillier, *Explication Ascétique et Historique*, Tome 2, p. 31.

peccatum, a grave sin. For St. John Chrysostom, murmuring approached blasphemy. St. Basil wants the murmurer expelled from the society of the brethren. *O quam pestis miser a et mortalis, o quam venenosa,*[3] cries St. Augustine. No murmurer, according to St. Gregory, will enter into the kingdom of heaven." Dom Étienne goes so far as to say that "murmuring is a species of mental atheism, a denial of God's providential ways over His creatures." He recalls that one of the glories of the martyrs, according to the liturgy, is not to have murmured:

> Non murmur resonat, non querimonia;
> Sed corde tacito mens bene conscia
> Conservat patientiam.[4]

In reality, murmuring destroys the peace among the brethren, takes away all merit from obedience, keeps the heart troubled, and it is always the index of self-love and pride. How could the murmurer really seek God at the very time when he makes such a buzzing inside of himself. We understand, then, our holy Father's aversion to "the vice of murmuring."

"Let us be humble," concludes Dom Morel,[5] "if we wish never to be discontented with our lot or envious of that of others."

---

[3] "Oh, what a miserable, deadly plague! Oh, how poisonous!"

[4] "No murmuring is heard, no complaint; but with a silent heart the soul self-possessed preserves its patience." Cf. the Rev. Matthew Britt, O.S.B., *The Hymns of the Breviary and Missal*, p. 363.

[5] *Meditations*, p. 308.

CHAPTER 35

On the Weekly Servers in the Kitchen

March 13—July 13—November 12

ET THE BRETHREN serve one another, and let no one be excused from the kitchen service except by reason of sickness or occupation in some important work. For this service brings increase of reward and of charity. But let helpers be provided for the weak ones, that they may not be distressed by this work; and indeed let everyone have help, as required by the size of the community or the circumstances of the locality. If the community is a large one, the cellarer shall be excused from the kitchen service; and so also those whose occupations are of greater utility, as we said above. Let the rest serve one another in charity.

The one who is ending his week of service shall do the cleaning on Saturday. He shall wash the towels with which the brethren wipe their hands and feet; and this server who is ending his week, aided by the one who is about to begin, shall wash the feet of all the brethren. He shall return the utensils of his office to the cellarer clean and in good condition, and the cellarer in turn shall consign them to the incoming server, in order that he may know what he gives out and what he receives back.

An hour before the meal let the weekly servers each receive a drink and some bread, over and above the appointed allowance, in order that at the meal time they may serve their brethren without murmuring and without excessive fatigue. On solemn days, however, let them wait until after Mass.

COMMENTARY

The organization of the kitchen service is extremely simple in St. Benedict's plan. The brethren will take turns at it, each one serving his week unless he be prevented, whether by sickness, for it is a tiring service, or by another occupation of essential utility.

Our holy Father knows how difficult the kitchen service may be, especially when the community is large and when the new kitchen server has no experience. He knows also that for certain monks coming from patrician families it may present the character of a humiliation, humanly speaking. As for those who would be frightened at the amount of toil or the lowliness of the work, St. Benedict, who never loses sight of the spiritual side of life, reminds them of the increase of reward and of charity they will find in it. He who keeps account of a glass of water given to a poor man will keep account also of the kitchen brother's fatigue, and will reward with abundant graces of love the charity which makes him overcome natural repugnance.

Still the holy Father, always tender and good, does not want the poor kitchen server to be overcome with the labor. The community may be large, the condition of the place unfavorable; there may be a long way to go, for example, to draw water from the well. In these cases he will be given one or more brothers to help him.

In important communities the cellarer will not take his week in the kitchen because of his weighty tasks. Nor will the Abbot, obviously, for the same reason. But the others "shall serve one another with charity." Note St. Benedict's insistence on this viewpoint of mutual charity.

At the end of the week the kitchen brother will do a general cleaning. He will wash in particular the cloths with which the hands are dried and those used for drying the feet after the weekly washing of feet. This washing of feet will take place in community. It will be done by the outgoing kitchen server and the incoming one together.

The cellarer will be witness of the going out and the coming in; it is to him that the utensils of the office will be given back that he may ascertain their condition, and it is he who will entrust them to the new kitchen server.

Our holy Father, as we have already seen, does not forget what a tiring work is the service of the table. Let us remember that there was no breakfast and that the servers had to eat after everyone else. It would be too hard for them to wait fasting until the end of the common meal which they have to serve. That is why, an hour before this meal, they are to be given "a drink" and a piece of bread. They will thus be able to serve the brethren "without murmuring and without undue hardship."

The "drink" or *biberes*, according to the commentators, comprises the contents of a little goblet, such that it may be swallowed at one draught.[1] As to the bread, it is no doubt "one of those little loaves, measured and weighed according to the sudivisions of the *pitance*, such as we know it. To each monk was given the number of them necessary to constitute the

---

[1] Dom Augustin Calmet, *Commentaire*, on this passage.

weight prescribed by the Rule. These loaves were of rather general usage at that time, as is witnessed by the present which the priest Florentius sent St. Benedict; it was an *eulogia*. .. and of limited enough weight so that the raven could take it in his beak."[2]

The commentators are not in agreement as to whether this little loaf was given in addition to the daily fare or deducted from that fare. The majority, with Dom Calmet, Dom Delatte, the Farnborough translators and others, think the words *super annonam* indicate an addition and not a subtraction. The Abbé de Rancé does not assume to say for sure, and considers the difficulty not too serious, since the morsel of bread in question is "nothing much."

"On feast days," continues St. Benedict, "they shall wait until after Mass," at which, according to the custom, they were to have received Holy Communion. The purpose of this prescription must be to prevent anyone, even if the Mass should be prolonged well into the hour before the meal, from taking a pretext either for eating first and thus missing Holy Communion or for leaving before the end of the ceremony.

APPLICATION

After noting that this chapter has mostly an historical interest, since the kitchen service is taken care of today by a kitchen brother specially assigned to it, Dom L'Huillier points out, however, that the spirit which inspired this chapter is, on the contrary, one "of all times" "It is," he continues, "the principle of brotherly love ...vivified by a more exact imitation of the Lord Jesus! 'I am in the midst of you as one who serves,' He told His Apostles; and as proof He was willing to wash their feet, a duty of hospitality which He thus sanctified, imprinting on it a special stamp of humble, active charity."

We find in this chapter also a lesson in mortification. "The function thus established by the holy Patriarch," says Dom L'Huillier again, "remained in force for at least 600 years in our Order; and the monastic kitchen service saw crowned heads pass during that time; the brethren were often served by kingly or princely hands. It must be recognized that this represents a considerable sum of mortifications of detail, besides an incalculable number of acts of charity. However rudimentary the monastic

---

[2] Dom L'Huillier, *Explication Ascétique et Historique, Tome 2, p. 38.*

cuisine may have been in the Middle Ages, still it certainly was not safe from hazards, considering the succession of cooks.

"And let us not suppose that the customs of the world at that time were such that in entering the cloister a person had no adjustment to make in order to become used to the diet. ... We can be sure that there was more of a gap in the Middle Ages than there is in our days between the table of the rich and that of the poor or of the monks. In sitting down to the latter, therefore, a good number had to begin not only with a daily sacrifice of all elegance in food, but also with a really courageous apprenticeship in that field, in proportion to their own inexperience and that of their confreres. And yet the holy Patriarch is anxious that it be so. There again is a sense of mortification which ought to stay with us.. .."

Finally, there is in this chapter a lesson in humility, in which all the commentators have seen an application of the teaching given by the Lord to His disciples: "The Son of Man is not come to be served but to serve" (*Matthew* 20:28) ... "And I am in the midst of you as one who serves" (*Luke* 22:27).

Let the Oblate also be in the midst of his brethren, in the midst of his family, "as one who serves," not fearing to humiliate himself by humble tasks. Let him substitute the refinement of charity for the false refinement of the world. And let him not fear interior mortification any more than exterior mortification, in particular with regard to meals. There is every evidence that in establishing the rotation of kitchen service, St. Benedict did not want his children to be too concerned over the nicety of the dishes. The manducate *quae apponuntur vobis*[3] can be the occasion of many small sacrifices which must not be allowed to pass.

March 14—July 14—November 13

Immediately after the Morning Office on Sunday, the incoming and outgoing servers shall prostrate themselves before all the brethren in the oratory and ask their prayers. Let the server who is ending his week say this verse: "Blessed are You, O Lord God, who have helped me and consoled me." When this has been said three times and the outgoing server has received his blessing, then let the incoming server follow and say, "Incline unto my aid, O God; O Lord, make haste to help me." Let this also be repeated three times by all, and having received his blessing let

---

[3] "Eat what is set before you."

him enter his service.

COMMENTARY

The chapter on the weekly kitchen servers concludes with the description of a liturgical ceremony. When the Morning Office on Sunday is finished, those ending their week and those beginning their week go and prostrate themselves in the middle of the oratory. This prostration is an act of reverence. Is it addressed to the Abbot and the brethren? Some say yes, for it is to them and to their prayers that the servers are going to recommend themselves. Is it addressed rather to God? We should readily suppose so, for the words recited are a cry of thanksgiving and an appeal for help to God's bounty.

The outgoing servers chant this verse: "Blessed are You, Lord God, who have helped me and comforted me." If they have indeed suffered fatigue and have sanctified it, the Lord has heaped His consolations on them and there is good reason to thank Him for them. The chant is repeated three times and probably taken up each time by the choir. Then the Abbot or the one presiding gives his blessing, and the brethren go to their places.

Those who are going in, likewise prostrated, then chant three times the *Deus, in adjutorium*. The choir takes up the invocation, as above. They need God's help in order to fulfil their humble task in a holy manner. They thereupon receive the blessing and enter into their office.

APPLICATION

St. Benedict wants the monk's whole life to be permeated with the thought of God, and he wants everything in that life to minister to sanctification and progress in charity. "A duty of a very material kind and one often grievous to nature," remarks Dom Delatte, "was consecrated by prayer. It became from that moment a religious and meritorious work, accomplished for the glory of God."[4]

There is nothing in the truly Christian life, then, that escapes the supernatural spirit. It is not a life partitioned, in which more or less large rooms are reserved for God. Everything is for God. The daily toil, whatever be its nature, becomes matter for humility, matter for sacrifices, matter for imitation of the Lord Jesus; it becomes a holy thing, it becomes

---

[4] *Commentary*, p. 257.

prayer. And in this sense it is true to say: He who works, prays.

For the sanctification of toil St. Benedict demands a direction of intention. We must offer the toil to God beforehand and ask Him to come to our aid. There is a formula which adapts itself to all our needs, and which we can often repeat at the beginning and in the midst of our occupations: the *Deus, in adjutorium* so dear to the ancient monks. The Declarations of the French Congregation, which accompany and comment on the Holy Rule, recommend it before work.

Thus sanctified, intellectual or physical labor fills the soul with consolation. It feels near at hand Him who of old worked, was tired, and fell beneath the weight of the Cross. And when this labor becomes hard, it is then especially that He upholds the soul with His grace, that He consoles it, and that it can say to Him, "Blessed are You, Lord God, who have helped me and comforted me."

St. Benedict has the invocations repeated by the choir. The idea is that we are not isolated individuals. All those who belong to Christ, especially all those who belong to the same family in Christ, ought to help one another by prayer, call on the aid of the Most High for one another, give thanks for one another. "The prayer of all," says Dom Étienne, "fuses with the prayer of each; and that of each, with that of all. Wonderful commerce of exchange in charity!"

CHAPTER 36
On the Sick Brethren

March 15—July 15—November 14

BEFORE ALL THINGS and above all things, care must be taken of the sick, so that they will be served as if they were Christ in person; for He Himself said, "I was sick, and you visited Me" (*Matthew* 25:36), and, "What you did for one of these least ones, you did for Me" (*Ibid.* 25:40). But let the sick on their part consider that they are being served for the honor of God, and let them not annoy their brethren who are serving them by their unnecessary demands. Yet they should be patiently borne with, because from such as these is gained a more abundant reward. Therefore the Abbot shall take the greatest care that they suffer no neglect.

For these sick brethren let there be assigned a special room and an attendant who is God-fearing, diligent and solicitous. Let the use of baths be afforded the sick as often as may be expedient; but to the healthy, and especially to the young, let them be granted more rarely. Moreover, let the use of meat be granted to the sick who are very weak, for the restoration of their strength; but when they are convalescent, let all abstain from meat as usual.

The Abbot shall take the greatest care that the sick be not neglected by the cellarers or the attendants; for he also is responsible for what is done wrongly by his disciples.

COMMENTARY

We have often had occasion to admire our holy Father's spirit of faith. The monk is God's workman; he seeks God, and his faith causes him to find Him. He sees Christ in his Abbot, in his brethren, in the guests. Here it is in the person of the sick that he is made to discover Him particularly. To make that discovery the monk has only to listen to the word which does not deceive, that of Christ Himself: "I was sick, and you visited Me. ... What you have done to one of these least ones, it is to Me that you have done it." Thus one must serve the sick "as one would serve Christ in person."

And this is not a mere passing consideration. It is the application of a particularly important doctrine which the holy Father wishes to inculcate in his disciple "before all things and above all things."

If the brethren ought to see Christ in the person of His suffering

255

member, the sick one on his part ought to recognize what he is for the others. He ought to "consider that it is for the honor of God" that he is being served. He should lean on this Christ who lives and suffers in him, unite himself to Him and sanctify his sufferings through Him.

From this twofold consideration there will arise in the brother who approaches the sick one a mild patience inspired by a supernatural affection, and in the sick one a special care not to "provoke by his superfluous demands" the brother who is serving him.

But St. Benedict does not leave the sick to the improvised cares of this one and that. He desires that there be a special "cell" for them, a sort of small community near the big one. Over this "cell" will preside a brother who is "Godfearing, diligent and attentive." The holy Father does not like his suffering child to be taken away from his monastic family; except in case of absolute necessity, he does not want to see him looking elsewhere, among people of the world or in health institutions, for the care which he thinks he needs. He must know how to practice poverty and self-denial; he must know how to be a monk, even when he is sick.

But with his usual discretion, St. Benedict sees to it that certain indispensable cares will be at the disposal of the sick one. There are the baths, which are less readily granted to those who are well, especially if they are young, but which will be "offered to the sick as often as may be expedient." There is the use of meat when the malady has brought on weakness. We find again in all these provisions the affectionate and attentive father, who without being weak knows how to sympathize with every suffering and every weakness, because his heart is filled with the charity of Christ.

Thus he concludes with a new and urgent recommendation to the Abbot to watch over the sick and over those who have to be particularly occupied with them: the cellarer and the infirmarian. It is the Abbot whom the Lord will hold responsible for their negligences.

APPLICATION

This chapter of our Rule can find frequent application. Here St. Benedict speaks only of sick brethren; but in his thought, his precepts provide for every sick person whom Providence may have put in the way of the monastery. Had he not without qualification listed among the instruments of good works:

To help the poor
To clothe the naked
To visit the sick
To bury the dead
To bring aid in tribulation
To comfort the afflicted.

That is why hospices were often erected quite near the cloisters. The Oblate ladies of St. Frances of Rome devoted themselves to the care of the sick. It is this thought likewise that recently inspired Dom Leduc, monk of the French Congregation, to found a new branch of the old Benedictine Order, the Oblate Ladies Servants of the Poor, consecrated to visiting and caring for the needy sick.

But the care of the sick, for the children of St. Benedict, does not come under the heading first of a philanthropic work, still less of an experimental work. The sick one is not an object of medical observation. He is the suffering member of Christ. Thus it is above all and first of all a religious work which is in question, a work of faith, a divine service. Not only in face of the pious Christian tried by suffering, but also in face of the wretch who is perhaps sicker in soul than in body, the Gospel and St. Benedict, who makes himself the echo of it, require us to overcome our apprehensions and even our repugnances. They want us with the eyes of faith to recognize in this sick person Him who suffered and bore the sins of the world. Is it not true that the patient and persevering devotion of the one who is taking care of him, especially when that devotion is sustained by supernatural forces and lights, is often also for the sick one the most efficacious of apostolates? Is it not a meritorious work of the first rank? In all these things, says St. Benedict, "is gained a more abundant reward."

But at the same time that St. Benedict shows us what we ought to do for our suffering brethren, he teaches us how we ourselves ought to practice "good suffering." He says it in a few words, but those words are worth meditating.

Every suffering is a little of the Cross of Christ. Although it is a consequence of the divine curse, it can still become a source of graces. It can be redemptive when we know how to unite it to the great suffering of Calvary. The idea, then, is for us to welcome suffering for what it is: a trial and a gift from God, who wants to sanctify us through it. The Christian, therefore, above all the one who, like the Oblate, tends to perfection, ought to ask for patience and strive to practice it, in the thought that the trial unites him more intimately to his Savior. He will not be exacting, will not demand extraordinary remedies, remembering that he is poor and detached. "He will not provoke those who serve him by his unreasonable demands."

Moreover, as Dom Morel pointed out, do not those who serve the sick also represent Jesus Christ? Does not every good which comes to us, even through the least of creatures, come from Him? "What docility would be ours, what gratitude... if this divine Savior visited us in person and served us with His own hands! Oh, how far we should be from letting ourselves fly into that impatience, those complaints, those unnecessary demands and that restlessness into which our weakness pushes us and which are a cause of distress to those who serve us and of scandal to those who see us! Everything would seem good to us, everything would content us, because it would come from Him. But does it come any the less from Him because we do not see Him?"[5] In reality, He serves us not only in the person of His servants; but while they apply themselves to relieving the sufferings of our body, does not He personally apply Himself, in the measure of our good dispositions and by using our very sufferings, to dressing the wounds of our soul?

---

[5] Meditations, p. 313.

CHAPTER 37
On Old Men and Children

March 16—July 16—November 15

LTHOUGH human nature itself is drawn to special kindness towards these times of life, that is towards old men and children, still the authority of the Rule should also provide for them. Let their weakness be always taken into account, and let them by no means be held to the rigor of the Rule with regard to food. On the contrary, let a kind consideration be shown to them, and let them eat before the regular hours.

COMMENTARY

Nature draws us instinctively to sympathy for childhood and for old age. The child charms us by his prettiness, his naivete, his trust, his purity. The old man attracts us by the wisdom which experience gives and the confidence which wisdom inspires. And so these are two weaknesses to which a good, compassionate soul will devote itself voluntarily. St. Benedict, with his so tender and paternal heart, was aware of all that. Still he wanted that natural sympathy and devotion to be transformed, raised and strengthened by supernatural motives. We are to surround the child and the old man with cares and attentions not only in order to follow the impulses of our nature, but also and above all in order to fulfil the divine will manifested through the Holy Rule.

Neither the one nor the other, therefore, is to be subjected to the rigor of the fast. Dom Haeften[1] thought that here St. Benedict was authorizing the children and the old men to take advantage of the *mixtum*, namely a light collation, like that of the servers, and with them. The opinion is quite doubtful, since the hour of the *mixtum* was too near the community meal, of which the servers did not partake.

The idea is not to give them a greater quantity of nourishment either, since in Chapter 39 we shall see that the children are to receive a smaller quantity. It is fitting rather to admit with Dom Ménard, therefore, that the exception of which our holy Father speaks is to bear rather on the quality of the food.

---

[1] *Disquisitionum Monatticaium* Libri XII, Book 10, Treatise 4, Disquisition 5.

It is to bear likewise on the schedule of the meals. "Let the regular hours be advanced for them." The children, we learn from Chapter 63, took part in the community meals. The question here is likely one of "small instalments," as Dom Delatte says,[2] similar to the *mixtum* but taken at different hours.

APPLICATION

The lesson of tender consideration which our holy Father gives us will find frequent application. There is hardly any life that does not find itself in contact sometimes with childhood, sometimes with old age. We Oblates shall remember, therefore, that in surrounding with devoted attentions the little children entrusted to us and the old people with whom we live, we are following the will of our Father St. Benedict.

Purely natural sympathies seldom last long; they proceed from caprice; they are prompted more by personal satisfaction than by a supernatural enthusiasm for devotion to souls.

Only the one who loves and devotes himself under the eyes and in the light of God, finds the strength to repress the little child, to support the old person's infirmities, never to yield to unreasonable caprices. He finds also the strength to sacrifice himself constantly, to forget himself, to expend without keeping account the treasures of his affection in order to give the one and the other those delicate attentions, spiritual and corporal, which their age or their condition may require.

---

[2] *Commentary*, p. 263.

CHAPTER 38
On the Weekly Reader

March 17—July 17—November 16

HE MEALS of the brethren should not be without reading. Nor should the reader be anyone who happens to take up the book; but there should be a reader for the whole week, entering that office on Sunday. Let this incoming reader, after Mass and Communion, ask all to pray for him that God may keep him from the spirit of pride. And let him intone the following verse, which shall be said three times by all in the oratory: "O Lord, open my lips, and my mouth shall declare Your praise." Then, having received a blessing, let him enter on the reading.

And let absolute silence be kept at table, so that no whispering may be heard nor any voice except the reader's. As to the things they need while they eat and drink, let the brethren pass them to one another so that no one need ask for anything. If anything is needed, however, let it be asked for by means of some audible sign rather than by speech. Nor shall anyone at table presume to ask questions about the reading or anything else, lest that give occasion for talking; except that the Superior may perhaps wish to say something briefly for the purpose of edification.

The brother who is reader for the week shall take a little refreshment before he begins to read, on account of the Holy Communion and lest perhaps the fast be hard for him to bear. He shall take his meal afterwards with the kitchen and table servers of the week.

The brethren are not to read or chant in order, but only those who edify their hearers.

COMMENTARY

According to Cassian[1] the custom of reading at table comes from the

---

[1] *Institutes*, Book 4, Chapter 17; in C.S.E.L., Vol. 17, p. 58; in *Nicene and Post-Nicene Fathers*, 2nd series, Vol. 11, p. 224.

monks of Cappadocia. Its purpose, he says, was to put a stop to unnecessary or frivolous conversations and to disputes which might be harmful to charity. But certainly also, in the intention of most monastic legislators, it had another, still nobler purpose: to distract souls from a too material satisfaction and keep them occupied with the things of God. This is evidently also St. Benedict's idea.

According to Dom Calmet, in the Benedictine monasteries "the Holy Scriptures were commonly read" and "what was not read in church was finished in the refectory." The same procedure was followed for the homiletic lessons which had not been completed at Matins. Further, Chapter 66 of the Holy Rule seems to insinuate that some passage of the Rule was likewise read. Today the Holy Scripture and the Holy Rule are read, but the greater part of the meal is taken up with the reading of certain historical works relating to Church history, monastic history, hagiography, and so forth.

Our holy Father requires of the reader certain aptitudes, of which the Abbot will be judge. A person does not make himself reader extempore. He will read what the Abbot has designated, and he will fill his office for a week. St. Benedict requires likewise certain dispositions of the soul, and humility in particular. Reading in public could indeed give certain natures occasion for "the spirit of pride." It is for this reason that the reader is not to enter into his office until he has implored the help of God and the prayers of his brethren. On Sunday, after Mass and Communion, he will prostrate or incline himself (St. Benedict does not specify) in the middle of the choir and chant three times: Domine, labia mea aperies.. ."Lord, open my lips, and my mouth shall announce Your praise." And the Abbot will give him the blessing, probably by chanting a collect.

The table reading has for corollary the absolute silence of the monks. To facilitate that silence, St. Benedict asks the brethren to serve one another, that is, not to be uninterested in what may be wanting to their neighbors, and to offer it to them spontaneously. If someone is obliged, however, to ask for something, he will do so with the help of some sign or a discreet sound. It will not even be permitted to ask any question on the subject of the reading. Only the Superior may, for the purpose of edification, comment occasionally but very briefly on some passage not quite clear or on an application particularly practical. In reality, as Dom Martène, Dom Calmet, Dom L'Huillier and others observe, "to edify" here has rather the broad meaning of to explain, to clarify, to underline the sense or the importance of the text.

Since the reader cannot take his meal with the community but must wait until that meal is over, he will eat with the weekly kitchen servers. But he will be permitted, before reading, to take the *mixtum.* It is probable that at St. Benedict's time the *mixtum,* as opposed to the *merum,* or pure wine, was a little wine mixed with water. One may see some developments on this point in Dom L'Huillier's commentary.[2] Later on, it consisted of a little cup of wine in which a few morsels of bread were soaked. And it is this custom, common to Cluny and Cîteaux, which has led certain commentators to suppose that *mixtum* in St. Benedict means a mixture of wine and bread.[3]

For this concession of the *mixtum* St. Benedict gives two reasons, of which the second needs no explanation, but of which the first has caused rivers of ink to flow. "The brother who is reader," he says, "shall receive the *mixtum* before beginning to read, on account of the Holy Communion and lest perhaps the fast be hard for him to bear."

What is the meaning of these words, "on account of the Holy Communion"?

According to Cardinal Turrecremata, the Abbé de Saint-Cyran, Dom Claude Lancelot, the author of the *Translation and Explanation* and more recently Dom Étienne, there would be no question here of the Eucharistic Communion, but rather of a sort of rite in virtue of which the reader, "To mark the holy union which he has with his brethren," a union of which the communal meal is the symbol, likewise took a bit of nourishment. To which the Abbé de Rancé objected that the gesture would not have had any significance unless the reader had taken the *mixtum* at the beginning of the brethren's meal. But, he observes, "there is no likelihood that the reader took this *mixtum* in the presence of the community, but rather well before he entered the refectory."

For Dom Claude de Vert, "in an advertisement which he joined to a translation of the Rule of St. Benedict which he caused to be printed in 1689 and of which he was not the author,"[4] and in "a dissertation which

---

[2] Explication Ascetique et Historique, Tome 2, pp. 59-62.

[3] Dom Du Cange, Glossarium Mediae et Infimae Latinitatis (Niort: L. Favre, 1885), Tome 5, p. 430, under the word mixtum.

[4] Dom Filipe le Cerf de la Viéville, *Bibliothèque Historique et Critique des Auteurs de la Congrégation de St. Maur* (La Haye: Pierre Gosse, 1727), pp. 271-272. The author of this version was the Abbé de Rancé.

he published in 1694," as also for the Jesuit Père Brouver, the *mixtum* was an *eulogia*, that is to say, a blessed cake which the religious had the custom of dipping in wine before the meal.[5] By taking it the reader marked his "holy communion" with his brethren. But where does one see that St. Benedict's monks originally made use of these *eulogiae*?

Dom L'Huillier admits a similar opinion, but reduces the supposed custom of "communion" to some wine which was supposed to have been distributed to all the monks before the meal.

The opinion most commonly admitted and most probable is that of Dom Mabillon, which he developed in a treatise published in 1689, an opinion recently set forth by Dom Delatte in his commentary. The concern here is indeed with Eucharistic Communion. The *mixtum* plays the rôle of ablution. As the meal probably followed very closely after the Mass, the purpose was to prevent the reader while speaking from rejecting anything of the sacramental species he had just received. One may point out in opposition that between the Mass and the meal there had been Sext, and that the chants at the end of the Mass and the psalmody of Sext would have presented the same difficulties as the reading in the refectory. Thus none of the proposed solutions satisfies the mind completely, and we do not know how to declare ourselves.

APPLICATION

This chapter and the following ones have for their subject the sanctification of the meals. In every family, monastic or natural, the meals represent not only the satisfaction of a necessity, but one of the times at which the union of the members is best realized. But it is important that this union be perfect, and that for Christians it have something of the supernatural.

We may show ourself unchristian at our meals by yielding to sensuality or to gluttony. This will be the object of the next chapters.

We may be unchristian by lacking charity, by behaving with a sort of selfishness which would cause us to pay no attention to the little necessities of those at our side. That is to hurt the "communion," the brotherly union. Our holy Father wants the brethren to look out for one another. "For the things they need as they eat and drink, let the brethren pass them to one another, so that no one shall need to ask for anything."

---

[5] Dom Filipe le Cerf de la Viéville, Bibliothèque Historique, p, 272.

A beautiful lesson in Christian courtesy, observes Dom Delatte, a lesson which the Oblates of St. Benedict will want to practice as best they can.

We may be unchristian at our meals by lacking charity in our conversations, or by indulging in vulgar, facetious and perhaps coarse talk. It was to remedy this failing that the Cappadocian monks had instituted the reading at table. That is a radical means which, while practiced in monasteries, has ceased to be practical ordinarily in the world. But where can we show our faithfulness to the spirit of St. Benedict is in knowing how to keep its truly Christian atmosphere about the table conversation. There are subjects which one avoids, hurts against which one guards; and there is a delicate way, which truly pious souls readily find, to lead the conversation back gently onto proper ground. Thus one realizes what our holy Father certainly wanted: "moderating the animal satisfaction in eating and drinking by an appeal to the things of piety and the mind."[6] Moreover, we have only to remember his saintly example. Let us imagine what must have been his conversation with his sister St. Scholastica, when they met each year and took their meal together, their minds wholly occupied with "the joys of heaven."[7]

It often happens that we take our meals alone. Here there can no longer be question of reading done while eating; if some can do it, the thing cannot be recommended as a general practice, for reasons of health. But what remains possible and profitable is to read before the meal some passages from a pious book, or preferably from the Gospel, from the Imitation, from the Holy Rule. These passages read attentively will be able to furnish our solitary thought with a spiritual food while our body is being sustained with material food.

Is there need to recommend to Oblates the recitation of the grace before and after meals? These prayers also will have the effect of giving our meal its truly religious character.[8]

---

[6] Dom Paul Delatte, *Commentary*, p. 265.

[7] St. Gregory, *Dialogs*, Book 2, Chapter 33; in P.L., Tome 66, col. 194; in *Life and Miracles of St. Benedict*, pp. 67-69.

[8] See "Prayers for Everyday Use," §§9-12, in *Manual for Oblates*, pp. 194-195.

CHAPTER 39
On the Measure of Food

March 18—July 18—November 17

E THINK it sufficient for the daily dinner, whether at the sixth or the ninth hour, that every table have two cooked dishes, on account of individual infirmities, so that he who for some reason cannot eat of the one may make his meal of the other. Therefore let two cooked dishes suffice for all the brethren; and if any fruit or fresh vegetables are available, let a third dish be added.

Let a good pound weight of bread suffice for the day, whether there be only one meal or both dinner and supper. If they are to have supper, the cellarer shall reserve a third of that pound, to be given them at supper.

But if it happens that the work was heavier, it shall lie within the Abbot's discretion and power, should it be expedient, to add something to the fare. Above all things, however, over-indulgence must be avoided and a monk must never be overtaken by indigestion; for there is nothing so opposed to the Christian character as over-indulgence, according to Our Lord's words, "See to it that your hearts be not burdened with over-indulgence" (*Luke* 21:34).

Young boys shall not receive the same amount of food as their elders, but less; and frugality shall be observed in all circumstances.

Except the sick who are very weak, let all abstain entirely from eating the flesh of four-footed animals.

COMMENTARY

St. Benedict has assured to the meal an atmosphere at once fraternal and religious. Now he is going to treat of the nourishment. The idea is to avoid two excesses: an abundance which would foster gluttony, a parsimony which would be harmful to health. Certainly St. Benedict was personally a very mortified ascetic. Walking in the footsteps of the desert Fathers, he had forced himself at Subiaco to imitate them in their mortifications. But here he is concerned with his brethren, their different constitutions and aptitudes. Thus he experiences a certain hesitation before declaring himself. "It is with some misgiving," he will say in the following chapter, "that we undertake to regulate for others the measure of nourishment."

266

"He has to find a mean," writes Dom Laure. "He thinks he has found it; and yet he gives it only with a certain apprehension which reveals to us his most fatherly charity."[1]

There will be two dishes for the daily nourishment; by this St. Benedict understands cooked foods, not including fruits or raw vegetables. Undoubtedly one dish could suffice; but the presence of two will allow those who experience a rather strong repugnance for one or the other to satisfy their appetite sufficiently. As to fruits or fresh vegetables, they will constitute a little supplement, a sort of dessert.

What was the nature of the *pulmentaria cocta* or cooked foods which made up the usual nourishment? The text of this chapter itself informs us that they excluded "the flesh of quadrupeds." Besides that, the mention of the fresh vegetables given as supplement permits cooked vegetables to enter into the *pulmentaria*; perhaps also certain pastries and undoubtedly fish, although at a certain period the practice of many monasteries excluded large fish. It has been asked whether fowl were allowed, since quadrupeds alone are mentioned. Serious authorities have been cited for and against this view. In practice the matter is almost regulated, and long since, remarks Dom Laure, fowl have disappeared from the number of foods admitted by the monastic abstinence.

Naturally, bread was at the basis of the monastic diet. St. Benedict considers it proper to allow a pound "of good weight," Unfortunately we do not know what was the value of the pound at Monte Cassino and in St. Benedict's time. Today the monks take the quantity they consider sufficient.

It seems most likely that the two dishes and the pound of bread constituted the whole nourishment of the day; and it is probable that when there was an evening meal the cellarer withheld for that meal a third of the pound of bread, and of the other foods a portion provided by custom. For the children the quantity was less; on the other hand, as we have seen, they had received an instalment before the regular hour.

At times of heavy work, in particular at harvest time, the Abbot could add something to the fare, being careful, however, to avoid all excess.

And the holy Patriarch concludes with serious, forceful admonitions on frugality in meals. In his day those warnings were certainly necessary, for uncouth natures might be encountered among the candidates for the

---

[1] *Commentaire*, p. 271.

monastic life. He invokes Scripture, that is to say the word of God, and points out that a monk would be seriously guilty if he fell into the excesses forbidden by the Lord to all Christians.

Naturally, one will have particular attentions for the sick and for those who are "quite weak,"[2] and one will not constrain them to total abstinence from meat. It is this very paternal consideration of our holy Father which justifies, in our times of weakened constitutions, the presence of meat on certain days on the monastic table.

APPLICATION

St. Benedict makes himself clear as to the spirit which has inspired him in the editing of this chapter; it is a spirit of mortification. This virtue is particularly necessary for us with respect to food; for, as the Lord says, "gluttony and drunkenness make the heart dull," and St. Benedict adds, "there is nothing whatever so opposed to the Christian's character as excess in eating."

The excess may bear on the quantity of food. It may also bear on its delicacy. It is not fitting that one who professes to renounce himself and to carry his cross in Christ's footsteps should pose as a gourmet, a lover of fine plates and, as an old monk of the 16th century said, that he should be "more expert in the rule of cuisine than in the Rule of St. Benedict." The nourishment we are obliged to take, remarks Dom Laure, is not an end but a means, which we must relate to God, according to the very advice of the Apostle: "Whether you eat or whether you drink or whatever you do, do all for the glory of God."

Let us add that the Oblate, especially if he is a priest, should not pose as a "jolly table companion" in quest of invitations and feasts. The diocesan statutes remind the priest that he should rarely take part in meals with lay people. And for Christian parents is not the preferred meal the one at which, every day, in the beloved atmosphere of the home, they unite around them those whom Providence has entrusted to their charge? There we find an intimacy, a "communion" which is blessed by God, which it is always lawful and even advisable to sanctify specially by little mortifications, so much the more meritorious as they are often repeated and as they are seen only by God.

---

[2] Translator's note: The commentary here follows the received text, which has *omnino debiles et aegrotos*. The best manuscripts, according to Dom Benno Linderbauer, omit the *et*.

CHAPTER 40
On the Measure of Drink

March 19—July 19—November 18

"EVERYONE has his own gift from God, one in this way and another in that" (*1 Corinthians* 7:7). It is therefore with some misgiving that we regulate the measure of other men's sustenance. Nevertheless, keeping in view the needs of weaker brethren, we believe that a *hemina* of wine a day is sufficient for each. But those to whom God gives the strength to abstain should know that they will receive a special reward.

If the circumstances of the place, or the work, or the heat of summer require a greater measure, the Superior shall use his judgment in the matter, taking care always that there be no occasion for surfeit or drunkenness. We read, it is true, that wine is by no means a drink for monks; but since the monks of our day cannot be persuaded of this, let us at least agree to drink sparingly and not to satiety, because "wine makes even the wise fall away" (*Ecclesiasticus* 19:2).

But where the circumstances of the place are such that not even the measure prescribed above can be supplied, but much less or none at all, let those who live there bless God and not murmur. Above all things do we give this admonition, that they abstain from murmuring.

COMMENTARY

St. Benedict affirms, as we have already observed, that he experiences some scruple in setting the measure for eating and drinking. If a certain spirit of penance should be inseparable from our meals, the idea here is not mainly to impose a mortification on the brethren but to give them what is necessary without giving occasion for abuse.

The fact is that the gifts of Providence vary with each one. By reason of differences in body, in soul and in graces, the needs are not the same with all individuals. In order not to make anyone suffer, St. Benedict prefers to take into consideration the natural infirmity of the weak. He judges, therefore, that a *hemina* of wine will be enough for each religious.

In St. Benedict's day everyone knew what the *hemina* was, as everyone knew what the pound was. The monks of Cassino, on the word of Paul the Deacon, had preserved the *hemina* in usage at St. Benedict's time; thus Theodamar, Abbot of that monastery, was able to send Charlemagne two measures, one for the morning drink and the other for the evening, whose total equaled the *hemina*.[1]

Later on, the capacity of the *hemina* was somewhat forgotten; some reduced it and others extended it, according to their tendencies. For Dom Hugh Ménard it equaled 7½ ounces. The Maurist scholar referred to St. Isidore, who confounded the Greek measures and the Latin measures. Others went up to 20 or 30 ounces, which was certainly excessive. Dom Claude Lancelot, who in 1667 published a *Dissertation on the Hemina*, re-edited in 1688, attributed to it the value of a Roman half pint, namely 10 ounces, and Rancé subscribed to that opinion "after the so scholarly and so exact dissertation," as he said, "which was made several years ago on this matter." This was the opinion most commonly accepted in the 18th century.[2] Dom L'Huillier thinks the *hemina* was equal to three fourths of a liter. According to Daremberg and Saglio,[3] followed by Dom Delatte,[4] the Roman *hemina* equaled approximately one fourth of the liter.

It is very difficult, therefore, with opinions so divergent, to say precisely what might be St. Benedict's idea of the reasonable mean. At any rate the question is of little utility, since the various Constitutions have legislated on the measure of drink in each Congregation, taking into consideration the spirit of the Holy Rule.

Evidently St. Benedict would prefer complete abstinence from wine. He is going to tell us a few lines lower, referring to a passage from the *Verba Seniorum*, that "wine is by no means a drink for monks." And so he reminds "those to whom God gives the strength for abstinence" that they will thus be doing a meritorious work and will receive "a special reward." St. Benedict allows wine, therefore, only because he cannot do otherwise. "The monks of our day," he says, "cannot be persuaded" that it would be better to forego it. He himself used it, both at Vicovaro and at Monte Cassino, undoubtedly so as not to sadden his monks by the sight of an abstinence which they were unable to practice. On the other hand, with a certain insistence he recommends that no one drink to satiety. "Wine," says the Scripture, "makes even the wise fall away."

---

[1] Paul the Deacon, *Epistola Prima*; in P.L., Tome 95, col. 1585.

[2] *Traduction et Explication Littérale*, p. 332.

[3] *Dictionnaire des Antiquités Grecques et Romaines*, under the word *Hemina*.

[4] Dom Justin McCann, in a footnote on p. 275 of his translation of Dom Delatte's *Commentary*, mentions that the Roman *sextarius*, of which the hemina was a half, is generally equated with the English pint.

There are cases, however, in which the *hemina* can legitimately be surpassed. The monastery may be situated in a rigorous climate, "in dry, warm or hot places which make it necessary to drink more."[5] Or one may have had to sustain hard toil, or again one may have been exposed to the sun's heat. In these different cases the Superior may somewhat increase the daily allowance, but taking great care not to make it excessive. Dom L'Huillier points out that our holy Father says here "the Superior," prior, a term more vague than Abbot, because in certain circumstances the whole community does not need the extra wine, and the dean or the eldest of a group may have to determine who are those of that group who, in consequence of their present occupations, need a little more sustenance.

But it may happen that the monastery makes or buys too little wine to assure each one his *hemina*, or even that it has none at all. Perfection then consists not only in being resigned, but in "blessing God." Is it not His Providence that wills this privation? It is not serious; it will be welcomed joyfully. "We should never murmur or grow sad," says Dom Delatte, "on account of such matters."[6]

APPLICATION

The lesson of this chapter is evident. St. Benedict puts us on guard against all elegance in drinking, as he had already done for eating. Let us repeat: it would not be at all in conformity with his spirit to show oneself scrupulous about the quantity and yet fussy about the quality. Let us remember that after all, abstinence remains the ideal proposed by our holy Father. St. Benedict teaches us also equanimity and even joy in forced abstinence. Here as elsewhere he forbids absolutely any sadness, ill humor, murmuring. It so often happens that we have not the courage to impose mortifications on ourself. At least we ought to give the Lord a good reception when He Himself chooses for us the matter of our penances. "If a limited or absolute privation should be the case," says Dom Étienne, "... it ought to be considered as a divine permission and to excite in faithful souls a feeling of thanksgiving instead of complaints and murmuring. And not only in this circumstance, but every time it pleases God to impose a privation. That is the meaning of the conclusion of this chapter: 'Before everything, we desire that murmuring be banished.'"

---

[5] *Traduction et Explication Littérale*, p. 333.

[6] *Commentary*, p. 277.

CHAPTER 41
At What Hours the Meals Should Be Taken

March 20—July 20—November 19

rom holy Easter until Pentecost let the brethren take dinner at the sixth hour and supper in the evening.

From Pentecost throughout the summer, unless the monks have work in the fields or the excessive heat of summer oppresses them, let them fast on Wednesdays and Fridays until the ninth hour; on the other days let them dine at the sixth hour. This dinner at the sixth hour shall be the daily schedule if they have work in the fields or the heat of summer is extreme; the Abbot's foresight shall decide on this. Thus it is that he should adapt and arrange everything in such a way that souls may be saved and that the brethren may do their work without just cause for murmuring.

From the Ides of September until the beginning of Lent let them always take their dinner at the ninth hour.

In Lent until Easter let them dine in the evening. But this evening hour shall be so determined that they will not need the light of a lamp while eating, but everything will be accomplished while it is still daylight. Indeed at all seasons let the hour, whether for supper or for dinner, be so arranged that everything will be done by daylight.

COMMENTARY

St. Benedict had previously spoken to us about the abstinence; now he is going to speak about the fast. He distinguishes four periods in the year:

1) *From Easter to Pentecost.* At noon, that is at Sext, there was a principal meal, and towards the end of the day a *coena* or lighter meal. The order was opposite to the Roman custom, which placed the principal meal at evening; but the order was justified by the fact that after the Night Office and the morning's labors the monks must have been famished.

2) *From Pentecost to September 14.* The regime was the same except Wednesdays and Fridays, when there was a fast. This double fast had formerly been the practice of all Christians. Then the one meal took place at None, namely at 3 o'clock. When the work was hard or the heat excessive, however, the meal of None could be moved up to Sext; and perhaps there was an evening collation with the remainders of the noon

meal, "so that," says Dom Delatte, "the fast was completely dropped."[1] This measure was inspired in St. Benedict by discretion and charity. His design was not to overwhelm the brethren with penances, but to assure the peace of the monastery. The desire to "save souls" keeps him on guard against excesses of nourishment; the fear of murmuring, against excesses of fasting.

3) *From September 14 until the ecclesiastical Lent.* This is what has been named the monastic Lent. There will be fasting every day except Sunday, and the one meal will be taken at the hour of None.

4) *The ecclesiastical Lent,* which lasts until Easter. The one meal then will take place after the Office of Vespers. This was also the custom of the whole Church. This meal was to be finished before nightfall, so that there was no need of lamps. Vespers had to be said, therefore, at an hour which would allow for that much daytime afterwards.

Moreover, St. Benedict lays it down as a general rule that at all seasons, whether there was a fast or not, the meal should occur in daytime. Let us recall that in winter, at the time when the days are shortest, there was likely no meal except at None or at Sext, as the case might be. Still on Sundays and feast days on which there was no fast, the supper must thereby have come quite close to the dinner if eating at night was to be avoided. The author of the *Translation and Explanation* notes in this regard that at the Abbey of Orval, where they prided themselves on following the Holy Rule to the letter, they took the second meal, at the time of the winter solstice, at about 3:30 or 4 o'clock.

Dom Calmet reminds us that St. Benedict wrote in Italy, "where the days during winter are longer than in France, Germany and the North." He adds that the evening meal was very light. It was composed, in fact, explains Dom L'Huillier, "of a piece of bread with some cooked vegetables or some fruits and a glass of wine. We shall have to admit," he adds, "that the vigorous stomachs of the sixth century could not have been embarrassed by it."

Dom Delatte justifies the principle of taking the meals in daytime by reasons of discipline. "The reader will not require a light, and the brethren, moreover, will be less tempted to distractions during the meal.

---

[1] *Commentary,* p. 279.

Conversation would have been easy in a badly lighted refectory."[2] The Abbé de Rancé thinks St. Benedict acted rather because of poverty. Dom L'Huillier prefers to attribute to him a liturgical intention: Vespers and Compline, being day Offices, should be concluded before night.

Today, in view of the spirit of discretion of the Rule and the latitude accorded the Abbot to make compromises in it, the evening collation in winter always takes place under artificial light. We know that on the other hand, throughout the Church as well as in the monasteries, Vespers are moved up before noon during Lent, to safeguard the principle that on fast days it is not desirable to eat until after this Office.

APPLICATION

The prescriptions enumerated in this chapter have been partially modified, especially as regards the hours. The practice of the one meal taken after Vespers, that is to say towards evening, which had been maintained until the 19th century among the Cistercians, was abrogated by Pope Leo XIII. On the other hand, the four great divisions of the year with regard to fasting have always been maintained.

No doubt there would be nothing wrong with certain Oblates following, if they have the gift to do so, the usage received in their monastery, with their director's permission. Whatever the case may be, let us be content to recall that fasting, justified by the practice of the Lord and the Apostles and prescribed by the Church for all Christians, ought to be held in esteem by the Oblates. Let us recall in particular what our holy Father recommended to us in the 13th instrument of good works:

> *Jejunium amare*
> To love fasting.

If, therefore, following the mind of the Church, we ought to rejoice on her feast days and especially at the time of "Holy Easter," we ought likewise to do penance spiritually and corporally at the times when she prescribes it for us. If interior mortification is superior to bodily mortification, let us remember, however, that this latter, practiced with discretion and obedience, belongs to the evangelical, ecclesiastical and monastic traditions, in particular under the form of fasting. It is only too

---

[2] *Ibid.*, p. 280.

likely that those who disdain bodily mortification as inferior will soon come to abandon interior mortification also.

The commentators have often pointed out that the fasts prescribed by St. Benedict were those in use at his time among good Christians, whether they were ordained by the Church, like that of the ecclesiastical Lent, or were only counseled, like that of the "monastic Lent," and that he thereby wanted to show us what importance we ought to attach to the mortifications established by the Church. "One who is little enlightened," says Dom Marmion,[3] "prefers his own mortifications to these; but it is beyond doubt that the expiations imposed by the Church are more pleasing to God and more salutary for our souls."

The point is that our mortifications draw their value from our union with the sufferings of Christ. And when are we more united to Christ if not when we suffer with the Church, mystical body and spouse of Christ? Our mortification is then no longer a private work; it is a participation in the mortification of the whole Church, willed specially by the Church and offered by her to the heavenly Father as a "prolongation" of Christ's Passion, with which it forms but one passion.

---

[3]   *Christ, the Ideal of the Monk*, p. 177.

CHAPTER 42
That No One Speak After Compline

March 21—July 21—November 20

ONKS ought to be zealous for silence at all times, but especially during the hours of the night. For every season, therefore, whether there be fasting or two meals, let the program be as follows:

If it be a season when there are two meals, then as soon as they have risen from supper they shall all sit together, and one of them shall read the Conferences or the Lives of the Fathers or something else that may edify the hearers; not the Heptateuch or the Books of Kings, however, because it will not be expedient for weak minds to hear those parts of Scripture at that hour; but they shall be read at other times.

If it be a day of fast, then having allowed a short interval after Vespers they shall proceed at once to the reading of the Conferences, as prescribed above; four or five pages being read, or as much as time permits, so that during the delay provided by this reading all may come together, including those who may have been occupied in some work assigned them.

When all, therefore, are gathered together, let them say Compline; and when they come out from Compline, no one shall be allowed to say anything from that time on. And if anyone should be found evading this rule of silence, let him undergo severe punishment. An exception shall be made if the need of speaking to guests should arise or if the Abbot should give someone an order. But even this should be done with the utmost gravity and the most becoming restraint.

COMMENTARY

The Latin text of the beginning of this chapter is variously punctuated. Most editors read: *Omni tempore silentio debent studere monachi, maxime tamen nocturnis horis. Et ideo omni tempore, sivejejunii sive prandii, si tempus fuerit prandii, mox ut surrexerint*, etc. And they translate: "At all times monks should be given to silence, especially during the hours of the night. Thus at every season, whether there be fasting or supper, if it is a time when there is supper, as soon as they have risen from table," etc. This punctuation is followed by the Farnborough translators, Schmidt and Wollflin, and others, with slight variations in the translation. But the sentence so construed seems to Dom Delatte[1] to offer difficulties: if the words "whether there be fasting" refer both to the fasts of the Rule and to the ecclesiastical fasts, it is not correct to say that "at every season the readings will be begun after they have risen from table," since there is no supper on the days of the regular fast. If, on the other hand, those same words refer to the ecclesiastical fast, during which the one meal takes place after Vespers, the formula omni tempore, "at every season," no longer seems appropriate, since it excludes the period of the regular fasts.

Dom Delatte, following the Abbé de Rancé, Dom Guéranger and others, proposes the following punctuation, therefore : *Omni tempore. ..., maxime tamen nocturnis horis, et ideo omni tempore, sive jejunii, sive prandii. Si tempus fuerit prandii, mox ut surrexerint*, etc. "At all times, monks should be given to silence, especially during the hours of the night, and consequently on all days, whether of fast or of supper. If it is a day of supper, as soon as they have risen," etc.

This punctuation has the disadvantage of giving a double meaning to omni tempore, translated at the beginning by "at all times" and later by "on all days." Besides, the words *sive jejunii sive prandii* hardly come naturally as an explanation of omni tempore in regard to silence. They have no *raison d'etre* except as connected with the explanations which follow. It is not right, therefore, to separate them from those explanations.

But in reality the difficulty is only apparent, and it is much more natural to accept the traditional punctuation which we indicated first. To be sure, the sentence seems ill-constructed, and the word *jejunium* can lend itself to equivocation; but we know that St. Benedict is not a stylist, and in fact the meaning is nevertheless clear. It is evident that St. Benedict presents two hypotheses: the evenings when one eats, whether there be ecclesiastical fast or no fast, rep resented by the expression *sive prandii*; and the days of regular fast, which alone are designated by the words *sive jejunii*. Below, indeed, the expression *Si autem jejunii dies fuerit* can only designate the regular fasts. Of the two paragraphs which follow, therefore, the one explains the *sive prandii*, and the other the *sive jejunii*.

St. Benedict had already spoken to us of the spirit of silence in a special chapter. Here he recalls its importance. But he insists particularly on certain hours when it is important to practice it more rigorously: these are the hours of the great silence, that great silence which commences after

---

[1] Commentary, p. 282.

Compline, not to end until after the Office of Prime the next day.

And this leads the holy Patriarch to describe for us the monastic customs concerning Compline.

After the meal which follows Vespers, or after a certain interval if there is no meal, the brethren come together and sit down. It is not probable that the gathering takes place in the refectory, even though, according to Dom Martène,[2] that is the practice in certain monasteries. The text indicates that they have risen (*surrexerint*) to go into a gathering and sit down. This double movement would not have been necessary in the refectory, where they had already been seated and gathered together. It is not said that the gathering takes place in the oratory. Dom L'Huillier points out that at that time there was no chapter room. It is almost certain, therefore, that Compline originally took place in the cloister "near the refectory where the meal had taken place."[3]

Once the brethren were gathered, one of them began a reading. This was taken either from the Scriptures or from Cassian's *Conferences*, or from the *Lives* of the desert Fathers, or from some other edifying book. The reading had a twofold purpose. First, to prepare the minds for the calm of the night by leaving a supernatural thought with them. It is for that reason that the Heptateuch, that is the Pentateuch, *Josue* and *Judges*, was omitted, also the *Books of Kings* and perhaps *Ruth*. Certain stories, at that hour of peace, might have troubled the imagination of the weak. The reading of them will be reserved for another time, probably at meals.

The other purpose of the reading was to give certain monks time to arrive for Compline. The idea was that during the reading "the servers of the kitchen and of the refectory and also the reader of the refectory were hastening their light meal; the cellarer was seeing to it that the kitchen and various places of work were put in summary order; the infirmarian was preparing for the night of his patients; the porter was closing the gate of the monastery; and so forth. And all were then arriving as soon as possible to rejoin the community."[4] Two or three pages were read, according as the hour permitted; then, the monastic family being complete, Compline was begun.

After coming out of the Office, no one was any longer to say a single

---

[2] *De Antiquis Monachorum Ritibus*, Book 1, Chapter 11.

[3] Dom Fernand Cabrol, *Saint Benedict*, p. 75.

[4] Dom L'Huillier, *Explication Ascétique et Historique*, Tome 2, p. 95.

word, under pain of a very severe punishment. There were only two exceptions: the arrival of a guest, or a necessary order given by the Abbot. But then one was to hold oneself to indispensable words and to behave "with all gravity, restraint and decorum."

APPLICATION

We have two points especially to retain in this chapter: 1) the evening reading; 2) the night silence.

The night is the hour of the "power of darkness," when one is more exposed to unwholesome dreams and to the ambushes of the devil. That is why the liturgy makes us say to God:

> *Procul recedant somnia ...*
> May evil thoughts depart
> And the phantasms of the night.
> And repulse our enemy,
> That our bodies be not polluted.

It is worth while, therefore, to put oneself on guard and to go to sleep with supernatural thoughts. In the monasteries the reading recommended by St. Benedict is always customary. Why should not we do the same? Compline is our evening prayer. Is it not natural that it be preceded by a spiritual reading which will help us repel dangerous musings before sleep?

As for the night silence, exterior silence of speech and, above all, silence of the soul, which abandons itself filially into God's hands, is it not recommended by all the ascetic authors? We must, says Dom L'Huillier, "love the night silence, guardian of the hours when all this world's business has stopped and the soul is no longer accountable except to God." What reasons there are for cherishing this religious silence!

The night is for many the hour of sin. "The evil committed on every side under its shadow is out of proportion with that of which the day is witness." Why should we not offer the Lord a compensation by going to bed in prayer, with the peace of pure hearts?

During the night "the demons are more active and powerful than ever." If we do not fill our mind with God, will there not be danger of offering the enemy those "little fissures" through which he will penetrate further ahead under the cover of half-sleep and easily reach consciousness?

The night, as long as sleep has not taken us, is often propitious for the illumination of the soul "that watches with the Lord and questions Him about His mysteries." *Nox illuminatio mea in deliciis tuis.* "Silence is then for the soul what sleep is for the body. The life of the Saints, their invariable preference for night prayer, orientates us in this subject, us who are so far from the point where they live and converse with God. They help us understand what treasures there are in the night silence; and if unfortunately nature is not disposed to let go from a necessary repose many of these holy hours, let us know how to have so much the more regard for what remains to us of them, and to contribute for our part to safeguarding the nocturnal silence. Such will be the natural bent of every soul in which the spirit of prayer reigns; such will be the exercise of the soul that wishes truly to acquire that spirit. Negligence on this point, on the contrary, would denote habitual dissipation."[5]

---

[5] *Ibid.*, pp. 93-94.

CHAPTER 43
On Those Who Come Late to the Work of God or to Table

March 22—July 22—November 21

T THE HOUR for the Divine Office, as soon as the signal is heard, let them abandon whatever they may have in hand and hasten with the greatest speed, yet with seriousness, so that there is no excuse for levity. Let nothing, therefore, be put before the Work of God.

If at the Night Office anyone arrives after the "Glory be to the Father" of Psalm 94—which Psalm for this reason we wish to be said very slowly and protractedly—let him not stand in his usual place in the choir; but let him stand last of all, or in a place set aside by the Abbot for such negligent ones in order that they may be seen by him and by all. He shall remain there until the Work of God has been completed, and then do penance by a public satisfaction. The reason why we have judged it fitting for them to stand in the last place or in a place apart is that, being seen by all, they may amend for very shame. For if they remain outside of the oratory, there will perhaps be someone who will go back to bed and sleep or at least seat himself outside and indulge in idle talk, and thus an occasion will be provided for the evil one. But let them go inside, that they may not lose the whole Office, and may amend for the future.

At the day Hours anyone who does not arrive at the Work of God until after the verse and the "Glory be to the Father" of the first Psalm following it shall stand in the last place, according to our ruling above. Nor shall he presume to join the choir in their chanting until he has made satisfaction, unless the Abbot should pardon him and give him permission; but even then the offender must make satisfaction for his fault.

COMMENTARY

This and the three following chapters form a complement to the monastic penal code. They are brought in here through the preceding regulation of the meals, since the concern here will be not only with tardiness in the oratory but with tardiness in the refectory.

As soon as they hear the signal for the Divine Office, they will hasten to gather for it. The nature of this signal has varied with the eras and the regions. In Egypt they rapped on the doors with a mallet, except at Tabennisi, where the monks were called together at the sound of a trumpet. Dom Calmet thinks that at Monte Cassino a hand bell was used, as is insinuated by the words *signum pulsaverit* of Chapter 48.

The monks' haste is to be marked with gravity, however, for fear that a running on the stairways and in the corridors might provoke disorder. It should be inspired by the esteem due the Divine Office, for it is necessary "that nothing be preferred to the Work of God." This maxim borrowed by St. Benedict from the monastic tradition shows what importance for the Benedictine that liturgical prayer should have which is truly the Work of God, the *opus Dei*. Is it not the raison d'etre of his life and the source of his whole supernatural activity?

If they should not run, still less should they allow themselves to arrive late. St. Benedict wants tardiness to have its sanction; and to establish this, he distinguishes between the Office of the night and the Offices of the day.

For the night, the holy Patriarch shows an extreme condescension. He wants sanctions only for those who arrive after the *Gloria*, not of Psalm 3, but of the Invitatory, and again he asks that the latter be said "drawn out and slowly." The tardy one is to take the last place, or even stand apart, in a determined place assigned to delinquents of this kind. This place will be in full view, in such a way that they may experience some shame at being thus under the eyes of all. At the end of the Office they are to "do penance by a public satisfaction," probably in choir or at the church door.

Our holy Father does not favor the practice of the Palestinian monks mentioned by Cassian, who left the culprit at the door of the oratory. He knows that the "evil one" is always prowling about us, and he knows what temptations may come to threaten the monk in that situation: to go back to bed or, if there are several, to gossip. In the church, on the contrary, he will be able to associate himself at heart with the prayer of his brethren, and thus "he will not lose all."

At the day Hours the penalty will apply to those who arrive after the Gloria of the first Psalm following the versicle, *Deus, in adjutorium*. St. Benedict does not mention the hymn, undoubtedly because he intends to include under the same regulation the Offices in which there is no hymn in this place, such as Lauds, Vespers and Compline. It will be recalled that for Lauds the preparatory Psalm *Deus misereatur nostri* was to be said slowly, that all might be present for Psalm 50 (Chapter 13).

The tardy ones, says St. Benedict, "shall not be permitted to join the choir of the brethren in the psalmody until they have made satisfaction."

It has been asked whether they were supposed to be completely passive, and whether by the "choir of the brethren who sing," *chorus psallentium*, was not to be understood only the *schola*, so that it would have been forbidden them only to chant alone, or with the schola in the parts reserved to the latter. Dom Delatte does not presume to declare himself, but inclines to the second hypothesis. More generally the commentators suppose that the delinquent had to remain in complete silence. Still the fact remained that the Abbot could permit him to take his usual place and join in the chant. The Abbot is judge of the excuses and attenuating circumstances. This does not prevent the offender from owing satisfaction after the Office.

APPLICATION

There is one principle which dominates this whole passage, and even the entire Holy Rule: "That nothing be preferred to the opus Dei " It is one of the maxims dear to the Benedictine Order. Thus this principle ought to guide our Oblate life. Prayer, and liturgical prayer above all, is the source of all interior life and the soul of every apostolate.[1]

"No ministry, no labors, however fruitful or necessary they be in themselves, will ever replace the preponderance of prayer, the preferential esteem to which it has a right. Let that ministry, that work, that toil infringe on the time reserved before all for the Work of God, and once more will the word of Scripture be realized: "You have sowed much and reaped little," (*Aggaeus* 1:6); for the Lord will not fail to exercise His right of reprisal. In our Order it is a fundamental truth; but what Order is there, even the most active, in which it is not true? And is it not here that we must look for the principal cause of the meager results sometimes obtained by manifold and sustained efforts, by labors which naturally speaking ought to have produced much more?"[2]

If we want our action to be truly fruitful, therefore, we must give the Office the preponderant place in our life.[3] It is through liturgical prayer

---

[1] On this subject see the excellent book of Dom J.-B. Chautard, O.C.R., Abbot of Sept-Fons, *The Soul of the Apostolate*, translated from French by the Rev. J. A. Moran, S.M. (Trappist, Ky.: Abbey of Gethsemani, 1941).

[2] Dom L'Huillier, *Explication Ascétique et Historique*, Tome 2, pp. 103-104.

[3] Let us say, in particular for the lay Oblates involved in duties of their state more or less absorbing, that the place of liturgical prayer is not necessarily "preponderant" in the time devoted to it, but in the importance attributed to it, the

that the life in God will be maintained in our souls; it is thence that we shall draw the strength and the light necessary in order to attract souls to us and to direct them. Without this basis there is only human activity, that is to say, almost nothing.

Love of the *opus Dei* implies regularity in the manner of performing it. Since prayer is what gives our life its orientation and its whole meaning, since it is what should be most dear to us and what is most necessary for us, let us apply ourselves to it as often as our schedule calls for it. "Let us never be slow," says Dom Delatte,[4] "to appear in the audience chamber of God; there is the one interest of life. Moreover, regularity is the school of abnegation. Let us be forgiven for repeating that it is the truest mortification, sounding the very depths of our wills, though it remain unnoticed by men."

The Abbé Gellé, in a work which we have already quoted, advises the adaptation to our life as Oblates of the satisfactions demanded by our holy Father. "Let us be punctual," he says, "and let us punish ourself if we come late to choir."[5]

As Dom L'Huillier points out, there may be accidental cases in which the necessities of the ministry, duties of our state, of charity, and so forth, constrain us to modify, on a particular occasion, the rule we have set ourselves for the Office. These must be exceptions, and exceptions which will be very rare if we know how to organize our life, and which consequently will change in no way its general orientation. Once more, let this orientation be truly dominated by the Benedictine maxim: "Let nothing be put before the Work of God."

March 23—July 23—November 22

Anyone who does not come to table before the verse, so that all together may say the verse and the oration and all sit down to table at the same time—anyone who through his own carelessness or bad habit does not come on time shall be corrected for this up to the second time. If then he does not amend, he shall not be allowed to share in the common table, but shall be separated from the company of all and made to eat alone, and his portion of wine shall be taken away from him, until

---

attention brought to it, and the little sacrifices which one knows how to impose on oneself at times in order to be faithful to it.

[4] *Commentary*, p. 287.

[5] "Aux Prêtres Isolés," in *Bulletin de S. Martin et de S. Benoît*, October, 1923, p. 274.

he has made satisfaction and has amended. And let him suffer a like penalty who is not present at the verse said after the meal.

And let no one presume to take any food or drink before or after the appointed time. But if anyone is offered something by the Superior and refuses to take it, then when the time comes that he desires what he formerly refused or something else, let him receive nothing whatever until he has made proper satisfaction.

COMMENTARY

The refectory is, after the church, the place in which the monastic family ordinarily is found complete. With St. Pachomius and in certain monasteries of the East, the monks went to the refectory if they wanted to, and departed from it at will. St. Benedict desires that all the brethren enter and leave at the same time. They are supposed to be present for the verse. Our holy Father designates thus the prayer before the meal. This prayer comprises not only a verse but an oration which the text does not specify. *Dicant versum et orent.* St. Benedict holds particularly to this act of devotion, as ancient as Christianity, by which we ask God to bless the meal which Providence has provided for us. After the meal there is likewise a verse.

He who arrives late by caprice or by negligence, or who goes out before the end, will receive a warning first. If he repeats the offense, he will be warned again. But at the third breach he will be excluded from the communal table, yet not from the refectory. He will eat at the same time as his brethren, but isolated in a special place, and he will be deprived of his portion of wine. The punishment will last until "satisfaction and amendment."

If it is forbidden to arrive late or to leave too soon, so much the more is it forbidden to eat outside of the communal meal. Is that not to fail at once in regularity, in poverty and in mortification?

The last part of the chapter has given some trouble to the commentators. Some have thought that he who would refuse to receive from the Superior a special dish offered him would be deprived of every meal until he made amendment. This explanation, which is that of Dom Mège, Dom Martène, Dom Calmet and others, is hardly admissible; for, supposing the offender has not been willing to correct himself, he could not be left to die of hunger, and so authority would have the worst of it.

Dom L'Huillier proposes another explanation. The "something" offered a monk by his Superior would be, in his opinion, an *eulogia*. We have already seen that it was rather customary to offer little loaves so named as a sign of communion. The refusal of the *eulogia*, therefore, is a lack of charity. To the one who has committed this rudeness, not only will the *eulogia* which he spurned be refused even if he change his mind, but also any other *eulogia* (it is in this restricted sense that *aliud omnino* must be understood), until he has given evidence of his regret and has amended his conduct.

Perhaps a more satisfactory meaning could be obtained by regarding the word "the Superior" as subject of *desideraverit*. St. Benedict has just forbidden the monk to take anything to eat or drink outside of "the appointed hour." But someone may offer him something. If anything is offered anyone by the Superior, says St. Benedict, and he refuses to accept it at the time the Superior would have desired, he is no longer to be given either what he refused at first or any other thing, etc. The question here would be of a little supplementary refreshment, outside of the regular hours, offered a monk by a Superior who judges it useful either because of his state of health or because of his labors. If the monk refuses, he may sin somewhat by false austerity, somewhat by rudeness, somewhat by want of obedience. There is an imperfection over which it will be well to watch and which it will be profitable to correct.

APPLICATION

St. Benedict wants the meals to be a manifestation of communion among brethren. It is around the family table that the father and the children feel themselves truly united. Thus it is also in every Christian family. But for the meal to be a veritable act of Christian charity, it must not be merely the satisfaction of a necessity of life. It must be sanctified, and it will be so through constant temperance, through mortification when the occasion for it presents itself, and also through mutual attentions if there are several at table.

It is to place us in this state of mind and to rouse in us sentiments of acknowledgment and of thanksgiving towards Providence, that the Church offers us short but admirable prayers, the grace before and after meals, to which the Oblates will want to be faithful. These same prayers will help them, following the practice of the Saints, to "lift up their heart from the food which perishes to that which does not perish, and to sigh after that heavenly table, that eternal supper mentioned in these prayers, and after that bread of God's kingdom which makes happy those who eat it."[6]

St. Benedict desires that his children be content with the regular meals and not eat at all hours. "It would have been unseemly for a monk," says Dom Delatte, "to eat at any time or to drink when he had opportunity, seeking a little dessert in the vineyard or the orchard."[7] Habits of that kind are indeed contrary to the spirit of mortification, and would hardly be any more in harmony with the more perfect life which the Oblates have undertaken.

---

[6] Dom Robert Morel, Méditations, p. 333.

[7] Commentary, p. 292.

CHAPTER 44

How the Excommunicated Are to Make Satisfaction

March 24—July 24—November 23

NE WHO FOR serious faults is excommunicated from oratory and table shall make satisfaction as follows. At the hour when the celebration of the Work of God is concluded in the oratory, let him lie prostrate before the door of the oratory, saying nothing, but only lying prone with his face to the ground at the feet of all as they come out of the oratory. And let him continue to do this until the Abbot judges that satisfaction has been made. Then, when he has come at the Abbot's bidding, let him cast himself first at the Abbot's feet and then at the feet of all, that they may pray for him.

And next, if the Abbot so orders, let him be received into the choir, to the place which the Abbot appoints, but with the provision that he shall not presume to intone Psalm or lesson or anything else in the oratory without a further order from the Abbot. Moreover, at every Hour, when the Work of God is ended, let him cast himself on the ground in the place where he stands. And let him continue to satisfy in this way until the Abbot again orders him finally to cease from this satisfaction.

But those who for slight faults are excommunicated only from table shall make satisfaction in the oratory until an order from the Abbot. They shall continue in it until he blesses them and says, "It is enough."

COMMENTARY

St. Benedict continues the explanation of the means of satisfying for offenses committed against the observance. The concern is first with the great excommunication, from prayer and from table. The satisfaction is not made all at once, but gradually.

First of all the excommunicate who has testified to the desire to be reconciled comes, at the hour when the Divine Office is celebrated, to prostrate himself in silence before the door of the oratory, his face in the dust.

The clause *hora qua opus Dei in oratorio celebratur* is somewhat vague. It is not probable that St. Benedict wanted the culprit to remain thus prostrated outside during the whole Office, especially during the long nights of winter. That would have been too hard, despite the covered atrium which was generally found before the entrance of the churches; and it is not in the character of our holy Father. The text indeed seems to indicate that the end of the Office is meant, and the Benedictines of Farnborough translate: "at the hour when the celebration of the Work of God is concluded" (*à l'heure où l'oeuvre de Dieu achève de se célébrer*). Besides, prostration presupposes someone before whom to prostrate. That will be the monks who are going out of the church.

It is not said that the penitent prostrates himself before each one individually; it is more likely that he would remain thus, without moving and without saying anything, while all the monks went past. After the first time, the Abbot might judge that it was enough; but he might also pass by, and the excommunicate would repeat the exercise until the Abbot made a sign to him that this kind of satisfaction could end.

That did not mean that he was wholly reconciled. At a sign from the Abbot he would go and prostrate himself at his feet, asking him to pray for him. He would do the same for all the monks. Perhaps this ceremony would take place in the atrium.

The penitent would then take his place again in choir, but not necessarily the place he had occupied before. What he did was to take whatever place the Abbot assigned him; and until a new order was given, he could "intone"[1] neither Psalm nor lesson.

Finally, after each Hour, the moment the Office is ended, he will prostrate himself at his own place and remain in that attitude, until the Abbot indicates to him that "it is enough."

The reconciliation was then an accomplished thing. Did the completely reconciled monk take his original place? St. Benedict does not say so, and it is probable that the matter was left to the Abbot's judgment.

For one excommunicated from table the expiation was much less complicated. It consisted in "satisfactions" (undoubtedly prostrations) in the oratory until the Abbot had given his blessing and pronounced the *sufficit*. These satisfactions probably took place, as above, at the end of each Hour.

"The text of the Rule," says Dom Delatte at the end of the commentary

---

[1] Of the meaning of the words "to intone a Psalm" see the commentary on Chapter 47.

on this chapter,[2] "has never been abrogated. It remains still and it may be put into force. And though occasions for the incurring or infliction of excommunication be much rarer than once they were, yet they are still possible. Given the occasion, it would be the strict duty of the Abbot to apply the penalties of the Rule, if he were forced thereto by obstinacy or by prolonged and formal contempt."

APPLICATION

St. Benedict has such a feeling for justice that he does not conceive of a single fault remaining without reparation. Satisfaction must be made to God by repairing the injury done Him, and to men by repairing the scandal given them. St. Benedict does not speak here of interior contrition, but it is presupposed by the very course of the penitent and the various attitudes to which he has to subject himself. Indeed there is a real share of spontaneity which makes him accept the different phases of the reconciliation rather than persist in his revolt.

We said above that one who shows himself unworthy of the profession he has embraced and the promises he has made to God, excommunicates himself more or less, according to the greatness of his infidelities, from the spiritual family which has deigned to adopt him. There is always more or less need for reparation in our life, therefore, to keep ourselves at the desired level of perfection. Now St. Benedict recommends as principal means of expiation humiliating courses, and consequently humility. "The first remedy for every evil," writes Dom Delatte, "is humility, and humiliation is the means to obtain humility. Moral virtues are acquired by exercise, by the accumulation and repetition of acts."[3]

"In the matter of penance and satisfaction," says also Dom Robert Morel, "everything or almost everything consists in humiliating oneself; without humiliation all the penalties are insufficient; and when it is such as it ought to be, it can make up for everything."[4]

We can satisfy God for our failures through certain exterior humiliations recommended by the spiritual writers and by the examples of the Saints, such as prostrating ourself, kissing the earth, holding the arms out as on a cross, and taking the "discipline." But the essential thing

---

[2] *Commentary*, p. 296.

[3] Ibid., p. 295.

[4] Miditations, p. 334.

is to keep ourselves meanwhile humiliated in spirit at the Lord's feet.

Dom Morel recalls in this connection the attitude of the penitent Magdalen. That attitude indeed is not unlike that of the excommunicate at the church door and on the passing of his brethren. "Let us hold ourselves," continues Dom Morel, "at the feet of Jesus, for there is the place of penitents. Let us keep ourselves even at everyone's feet by deeming ourselves lower than all others."[5] Besides, we shall only be applying the seventh degree of humility, which desires that we feel ourself from the bottom of our heart "inferior to all others and vilest of all." Every infidelity, every weakness can furnish occasion for us to put that maxim into practice.

---

[5] Ibid., p. 336.

CHAPTER 45
On Those Who Make Mistakes in the Oratory

March 25—July 25—November 214

HEN anyone has made a mistake while reciting a Psalm, a responsory, an antiphon or a lesson, if he does not humble himself there before all by making a satisfaction, let him undergo a greater punishment, because he would not correct by humility what he did wrong through carelessness.

But boys for such faults shall be whipped.

COMMENTARY

In the preceding chapter the concern was with considerable offenses; here the concern is with material faults, "at the most with offenses due to some negligence or inadvertence,"[1] There will not even be question of any faults except those committed in the oratory; the others will form the subject of the following chapter.

These slips may be "a fault in pronunciation, by which we substitute one word for another or curtail a word, or else a fault in chanting, or the intoning of a wrong versicle."[2] For all such, satisfaction must be made at once "in place, in the presence of all," in order to "repair by humility" what has been committed "through carelessness."

The "satisfaction" in St. Benedict's time undoubtedly consisted, as it does today, in kneeling or prostration. If the delinquent did not subject himself to it spontaneously, the Abbot was then supposed to subject him "to greater punishment," of the nature of which he was judge.

The children who lived in the monastery, those little Oblates who were already little monks, were still too young to comprehend the meaning of this discipline and to subject themselves by their own choice to a humiliation. They were treated as children, therefore; that is to say, they were punished for a mistake in chant or singing by a few blows with the rod.

APPLICATION

---

[1] Dom Paul Delatte, *Commentary*, p. 297.

[2] *Ibid.*

We have only to apply literally what St. Benedict asks of us.[3] "The ancients" writes Dom Delatte, "teach us not to be too easygoing" in our little infidelities. And the reason is that these little negligences, even if they do not bother anyone else, even if no one is aware of them, cheat God of something which is due Him. In our liturgical praise we owe Him everything, and it is our duty to tend to perfection in it.

"It is not a question of esthetics," continues Dom Delatte,[4] "but of religious justice. Imperfection has appeared where there should be full and continuous perfection, so that we have a real debt to pay to the majesty of God. Our religion takes its whole character from the idea we have of God, and the attitude which this idea makes us adopt before Him. Under the New Covenant, God has not loaded us with a weight of manifold ritual ordinances, because He thought that charity would suffice to regulate our attitude in the presence of His Beauty. There are attentions which we should not expect of slaves, but should be astonished not to find in sons."

There is every reason to suppose that St. Benedict, who wanted the Divine Office to be recited even in private with "genuflections and a godly fear,"[5] likewise desired that the errors committed even on such occasions be repaired at once, and therefore that there be satisfactions there as in the oratory. It seems very logical, therefore, and in conformity with the spirit as well as the letter of the Holy Rule, for us to conform to this practice in the recitation of our Office. These satisfactions should be made "spontaneously, generously, with zealous faith and love. They should be done at once, without debate or secret self-justification." Thus Dom Delatte expresses himself, and he concludes, "There is nothing better for making conscience delicate than this generous reparation for trivial faults and errors of frailty."[6]

---

[3] Of course, the concern here for Oblates is with the recitation of their Office either privately or in a group of Oblates. The idea is not to single oneself out during a parish Office. At such a time one may either put off the "satisfaction" until later or practice some kind which does not attract attention.

[4] *Commentary,* p. 297.

[5] Chapter 50.

[6] Commentary, pp. 297-298.

CHAPTER 46

On Those Who Fail in Any Other Matters

March 26—July 26—November 25

 HEN anyone is engaged in any sort of work, whether in the kitchen, in the cellar, in a shop, in the bakery, in the garden, while working at some craft, or in any other place, and he commits some fault, or breaks something, or loses something, or transgresses in any other way whatsoever, if he does not come immediately before the Abbot and the community of his own accord to make satisfaction and confess his fault, then when it becomes known through another, let him be subjected to a more severe correction.

But if the sin-sickness of the soul is a hidden one, let him reveal it only to the Abbot or to a spiritual father, who knows how to cure his own and others' wounds without exposing them and making them public.

COMMENTARY

It is not only in the oratory that the monk is at the service of God. His whole life, his every instant are consecrated to that service. And so he should everywhere and always be careful to avoid every fault. He will exercise a continual watchfulness, therefore, over the way in which he performs his labors and his observances. The anxiety to serve his divine Master well will follow him in all places, "in the kitchen, in the cellar, in a workshop, in the bakery, in the garden, in the practice of a craft or in any other place whatsoever."

Inattention, carelessness may be the cause of his damaging some object, or losing it, or causing some trouble or other. St. Benedict does not specify further. Whatever happens, the offender should come immediately and of his own will to declare to the Abbot or to the community grouped around him the misdemeanor he has committed, and to make satisfaction for it. The various Constitutions have determined the application of the Holy Rule on this point through the institution of the "chapter of faults," which takes place several times a week and at which each one accuses himself of his faults against the Rule and of damage committed. A satisfaction is imposed on him which is ordinarily made in the refectory.

If the delinquent does not accuse himself and someone comes to discover his fault, he is to be subjected to a "more severe correction."

The faults which are to be thus revealed to the Abbot and to the community are the exterior faults only. As to the secret faults, which "take place in the soul," as also the temptations and the private dispositions which may provoke them or accompany them, they are not amenable to the chapter of faults. They are to be confided to the Abbot or to those elders whom a long experience has formed to the knowledge of spiritual things.

The concern here obviously is not with sacramental Confession; often at that epoch neither the Abbot nor the elders were priests. The concern is with "direction." The Abbot, father of the monastic family, and the seniors know how to keep the secrets of the souls who confide in them; above all, they know how to enlighten and direct them. Having been able to heal their own wounds, they are able to heal those of others. Here we find again the fifth degree of humility.

APPLICATION

In concluding his commentary on this passage, Dom Bernard Laure writes:[1] "We see no need to expound the teachings of this chapter and their advantages. He who knows how to recognize his faults and humble himself for them will readily make amendment; and the advice asked from wise and prudent men, while making him avoid the dangers in wanting to direct himself, will be for the soul a source of light and energy."

Chapter 46 teaches us all of that indeed. But Dom Delatte draws from it another teaching still more precise. What St. Benedict demands of his disciple is in reality a sort of examination of conscience, "not examination at a fixed hour and for a stated time, but continuous and assiduous examination, which nothing may escape."[2] The soul which forces itself to seek and to find God everywhere, ends by impregnating itself with the sentiment of His presence and by encountering Him, so to speak, in all its actions. There is a blessed haunting, a holy obsession which brings it about that, even in the most absorbing occupations, there is always a mental reservation and a frequent recall of God. There results a certain nicety of the soul which strives to please Him even in the least things.

Despite this vigilance there will undoubtedly be infidelities of detail,

---

[1] *Commentaire*, p. 307.

[2] *Commentary*, p. 301.

weaknesses of distracted nature. We shall not be content at such times to recognize them; we shall repair them at once through an act of love or even through a satisfaction of the same kind as that of which we have spoken with regard to the Office. The examination of conscience as an exercise will be prudently and usefully maintained, to be sure; but, necessary as it may be, it will certainly be less profitable than this delicate attention to serving the Sovereign Master with perfection and this care to make up for our errors as soon as we become conscious of them.

The Benedictine mind hardly contrives a life cut up in distinct slices, where one seems to distinguish methodically between the portion of God and that of the world, and even the portion of action and that of contemplation. It tends to penetrate the action itself with contemplation; it tends to unify.

God, said St. Augustine, manifests his greatness through the smallest things. *Maximus in minimis cernitur esse Deus.* Let us force ourselves, therefore, to see Him in everything.

There is nothing small in His service. "Guard against underestimating those faults you call slight," said St. Augustine again. "Many little things make one great thing. Many drops of water form a river."[3] It is thus that the soul living in unity sees and judges. For it, God is all; it loves this All uniquely, and fears nothing so much as to displease Him and to let pass without spontaneous and generous reparation the thoughts or acts which might have diminished even slightly its charity for Him.

---

[3]   Quoted by Dom Étienne Salasc, La Règle de S. Benoît Traduite et Commentee, p. 473.

CHAPTER 47
On Giving the Signal for the Time of the Work of God

March 27—July 27—November 26

HE INDICATING of the hour for the Work of God by day and by night shall devolve upon the Abbot, either to give the signal himself or to assign this duty to such a careful brother that everything will take place at the proper hours.

Let the Psalms and the antiphons be intoned by those who are appointed for it, in their order after the Abbot. And no one shall presume to sing or read unless he can fulfil that office in such a way as to edify the hearers. Let this function be performed with humility, gravity and reverence, and by him whom the Abbot has appointed.

COMMENTARY

The Work of God being the occupation *par excellence* of the monk, and that Work being ordained for determined hours, it is important that the signal for it be given very exactly. St. Benedict deems the thing so important that he entrusts it to the Abbot. This is also the mind of the Church, which has willed to entrust the liturgical ringing of bells to ministers specially consecrated for that task.[1] At the time of the holy Patriarch, and for a long time after him, the task was so much the more delicate since the duration of the hours varied continually, as has been said above.

The signal was given in various ways: sometimes by rapping on the doors, as in Cassian; sometimes by sounding the trumpet, as in St. Pachomius; or by using clappers or those rattles whose use has been kept on Good Friday. Perhaps at the time of St. Benedict gongs or hand bells were already in use. Let us recall that the monk Romanus, who used to bring St. Benedict his meal in the grotto of Subiaco, apprised him of it with the aid of a hand bell. Besides, it is probable that the *signum* mentioned repeatedly in the Holy Rule[2] was a bell.

However, as the Abbot's occupations would not always allow him to take care of this service, he could entrust it "to such a careful brother that

---

[1] Dom L'Huillier, *Explication Ascétique et Hisiorique*, Tome 2, p. 120.

[2] Chapters 22, 43, 48.

everything will take place at the appointed hours." Thence was born the
office of regulator.

From the times for the Office St. Benedict passes to the Office itself,
and completes the prescriptions given previously. It will be recalled that
at St. Benedict's time the Psalms were chanted in turn by the monks, the
choir contenting itself with repeating the antiphons which were inserted
like refrains. "To intone a Psalm," therefore, was to chant it.

St. Benedict does not want the intonation of the Psalms left to chance.
It is the Abbot who should begin; and, after him, those whom he shall
designate. It would be presumptuous to want to chant or read without
having been invited to do so. One of the purposes of the Office, even
though it be not the principal one, is "the edification of the hearers." It is
for the Abbot alone to judge the aptitudes of each one. Most likely he did
not make a new choice every day. The rank of seniority was undoubtedly
followed.[3] But he could pronounce exclusions.

In conclusion St. Benedict indicates the qualities which ought to
characterize an Office well executed, and at the same time the impressions
which should be gained from it: "humility, gravity and reverence."

APPLICATION

If our holy Father devotes a chapter to the care of announcing the
Work of God, this is because he judges it extremely important that it be
performed *horis competentibus*, "at the proper hours." We have already
said that the different Hours do not really receive their full meaning
unless they are performed at the desired time. We shall put the greatest
exactitude, therefore, into observing the schedule prescribed by our
regulations, and we shall practice in that regard the solicitude (*sollicito
fratri*) our holy Father demands.

St. Benedict wants the liturgical Office to edify: *ut aedificentur
audientes*. This anxiety to edify contributes to the liturgy's character of
apostolate. And so in general, whether we take part in the Office by
assisting at it, or as "officers" of the choir or as celebrant, we should
contribute by our deportment to that dignity of the Work of God which
surrounds it as with an atmosphere of piety. Nothing so elevates the soul,
nothing so invites it to prayer as an Office well celebrated, in which all,
assisting and officiating, seem permeated with the grandeur of the holy

---

[3] Dom Paul Delatte, *Commentary*, p. 303.

task they are fulfilling.

But this should be not merely an attitude. St. Benedict had already said to us, "Let our mind be in harmony with our voice."[4] Here our holy Father specifies the dispositions which should assure that concordance of the exterior with the inmost soul. The first is humility, which consists in the secret sentiment of the unworthiness of one's person in face of the divine majesty; the second is a certain gravity, inspired by the awareness that one is fulfilling a divine work; and the third is religious fear in seeing oneself engaged in actions which demand a holiness and a perfection we do not have. This, moreover, is what the Church makes us ask for in the preparatory prayer: *ut digne, attente ac devote hoc officium recitare valeam*, "that I may worthily, attentively and devoutly recite this Office."

---

[4] Chapter 19.

CHAPTER 48
On the Daily Manual Labor

March 28—July 28—November 27

DLENESS is the enemy of the soul. Therefore the brethren should be occupied at certain times in manual labor, and again at fixed hours in sacred reading. To that end we think that the times for each may be prescribed as follows.

From Easter until the Calends of October, when they come out from Prime in the morning let them labor at whatever is necessary until about the fourth hour, and from the fourth hour until about the sixth let them apply themselves to reading. After the sixth hour, having left the table, let them rest on their beds in perfect silence; or if anyone may perhaps want to read to himself, let him read in such a way as not to disturb anyone else. Let None be said rather early, at the middle of the eighth hour, and let them again do what work has to be done until Vespers.

And if the circumstances of the place or their poverty should require that they themselves do the work of gathering the harvest, let them not be discontented; for then are they truly monks when they live by the labor of their hands, as did our Fathers and the Apostles. Let all things be done with moderation, however, for the sake of the faint-hearted.

COMMENTARY

Our holy Father starts from the general principle that "Idleness is the enemy of the soul" to organize the monk's life in the hours not taken up with the opus Dei. He knows what are the pernicious results of idleness. It is necessary to work, therefore. But at what labors?

Let us not forget that St. Benedict is legislating not primarily for the monk in general, for the monk as such, but for the religious whom he has under his eyes and of whom he is the Father. It is according to their aptitudes that he will organize the labor. Among them are a few nobles, a few patricians; but the majority is composed of ordinary men, of a rather restricted intellectual formation, or even next to none, such as that good Goth of whom St. Gregory speaks. From these men, therefore, St. Benedict will require a rather large amount of manual labor; but he will be desirous that all those who know how to read do a good share of *lectio divina*, the reading of the things of God. "At certain times," he says, the brethren

300

should be occupied in manual labor, and again at certain hours in sacred reading.

We do not have to narrate here the famous discussion of Mabillon and the Abbé de Rancé about monastic studies and manual labor. The story goes that after having argued eruditely, Mabillon to prove that studies had always been in honor among the monks, Rancé to establish that the preponderance of manual labor over intellectual labor was more in conformity with the letter of the Holy Rule, the two antagonists met each other after a journey which Dom Mabillon made to La Trappe. They explained themselves, embraced each other fraternally, and parted filled with an esteem for each other in which there was affection.

Today the arguments have ceased. Black Benedictines and white Benedictines, while remaining faithful to their respective traditions, would no longer deny each other the right to be called monks, as Rancé had done with the Maurists. Manual labor, in fact, has always been esteemed among .the Black Benedictines; the Maurists did not neglect it,[1] and today, even aside from the Lay Brothers, monks still seek in it an element of sanctification. On the other hand, it might not be difficult to cite Cistercian Abbeys where studies are in honor, despite the long hours devoted to working with the hands.

The *lectio divina* which shares the monk's days with manual labor is indeed in a certain sense an intellectual labor, a study, a research; but it is not a pure speculation, nor the satisfaction of curiosity, even of a legitimate curiosity. It is a search for God, to which could be applied the words of St. Augustine: *Jesum quaerens in libris,* Jesus sought in books. It is a slow, attentive reading of works fit to raise the soul to God and make it know Him better and love Him better.

We know with what kind of books the monastery's library was provided. They were the books of the Holy Writ, the works of the "Holy Catholic Fathers," the conferences of the "Fathers," their "Institutes," their "Lives," the Rule of Our Father St. Basil, and so forth.[2] With the help of the quotations and reminiscences of the very text of the Holy Rule, one might reconstruct accurately enough the library at Cassino.

The monk was to read carefully, in a spirit of prayer, those books so full of God, and through them to enter into contact with Him. The reading

---

[1] *Exercices Spirituels*, p. 326

[2] Rule, Chapter 73.

inspired desires, stirred up prayer, provoked aspirations; and the soul was absorbed at times in a fervent contemplation. The *lectio divina* was thus during several centuries the principal method of prayer for the monks.

One would be mistaken, therefore, in seeing in spiritual reading a study properly so called. Purely intellectual and speculative study did not issue out of the *lectio divina*, but was progressively substituted for manual labor as an occupation. Surely in St. Benedict's time there were some monks occupied in labors less material than working in the kitchen or on the soil. Manuscripts had to be copied, reading and chant had to be taught, the little Oblates had to be instructed. But it was when priests were no longer the exception but the great number, that manual labor lost its primary importance. Before the reform of Cîteaux there was hardly any great lack of propriety seen in this substitution. It was said that what St. Benedict had wanted to prevent was idleness, and that intellectual labor was quite as much opposed to idleness as was manual labor. In either sense the essential principle proclaimed by St. Benedict was safeguarded.

Our holy Father organizes the labor and the reading according to the great periods of the year. Here he counts three of them.

The first period extends from Easter to the Calends of October, namely to September 14. It is the summer period, when the days are long and the nights are short. The monks will go out the first thing in the morning, likely after Prime, about 6 o'clock, and work until about the fourth hour, namely about 10 o'clock. According to the proximity of the monastery, the Office of Terce had been said either in the oratory or in the fields. At that hour, in Italy, the heat becomes oppressive. It is then that they will give themselves over to reading. This will last almost two hours, that is, until the end of the sixth hour, the time when Sext is said. After Sext, on the days they do not fast, they sit down to table; and the meal is followed by the siesta customary in all the Mediterranean countries. This is a time of great silence. Still, the monk is not obliged to lie down. He may read, but silently and for himself alone (*sibi legere*), contrary to the habit of the ancients, which was to read aloud. After the siesta, and even though it be only the middle of the eighth hour, None will be said. Then they will return to the manual labor until the Hour of Vespers.

The ordinary manual labor of the monks was in the kitchen, the bakery, the mill, the garden and various crafts indispensable in a house which wants to suffice for itself. Ordinarily, farming did not enter into the occupations of the monks. It was assured, no doubt, by servants or paid workmen. But it might happen that in monasteries too poor to pay for labor or too far away to get workmen to come in numbers, the monks themselves would have to cultivate the ground. Were they to consider these labors unworthy of them? No. "Our Fathers," the monks of Egypt, and the Apostles indeed worked thus. They were none the less Apostles and monks for it. The monk remains truly a monk if he lives by the work of his hands. At the same time, discretion is to be used in this matter, and the Abbot will see to it that his children are not crushed under the burden of the labors.

APPLICATION

The application of this passage of the Holy Rule offers no difficulties. Our holy Father's maxim, "Idleness is the enemy of the soul," holds for every Christian. We should divide our life, consequently, between prayer and work.

If we are constrained by necessity and by the duties of our state to long hours of manual labor, let us remind ourselves what St. Benedict tells us of the Apostles and the Fathers. By working to the best of our ability, we can be perfect Oblates and true sons of St. Benedict, *vere monachi sunt*, on the condition that we sanctify that work by the thought of God. Many manual labors leave the soul much liberty to raise itself to Him. And then, are they not in certain cases acts of mortification or means of humility?

For others, for the priest especially, manual labor is often only an exception, and the part of intellectual labor becomes more important. There are labors required by the very nature of our ministry or of our profession. A soul filled with God knows how to find Him everywhere, and there is no science which does not in some way lead to Him.

But there are sciences which ought to be more dear to us. They are those which have for their object theology, exegesis, patristic, liturgy, Church history, monastic history, religious archeology and so forth. These sciences put us face to face with God, with His manifestations or with His activity in the world; they put us in contact with the thought of the Fathers, with the soul of the Saints, with those ancient institutions in which our forebears found peace of soul and the monuments through which they expressed their faith. Although remaining critical and scientific, research readily becomes meditation, and study allies itself to *lectio divina*.

The *lectio divina* properly so called must necessarily find its place in our life. St. Benedict imposes it on us. Let us recall that for 16 centuries it was the method of prayer of the Christians. "For 16 centuries," writes Dom Delatte,[3] "clerics, religious, and simple lay folk knew no other method of communicating with God than this free outpouring of the soul before Him, and this 'sacred reading' which nourishes prayer, implies it, and is almost one thing with it." "It was eminently," says Father Faber,[4] "the badge of the old Benedictine ascetics."

The spirit of prayer feeds on two sources: the Divine Office and the divine reading. The ancients, says Dom Delatte again,[5] "thought that the words of God, of the Saints, and of the liturgy, meditated and repeated without ceasing, had a sovereign power of withdrawing the soul from anxious self-consideration, in order to possess it wholly and introduce it into the mystery of God and His Christ. Once there, the need of beautiful considerations or of the well-constructed arguments of a keen intellect vanished; there is need for naught but contemplation and love, in all simplicity."

We Oblates, who, like our brethren of the cloister, believe that God is the better part and that He should be the first served, ought jealously to reserve the daily time for the *lectio divina*. Let us read the Fathers; let us read the old, solid mystical authors, those of our Order, those who shall be recommended to us by our Superiors and directors. After imploring light from on high, let us read them slowly, attentively, under God's eyes, stopping to reflect, to contemplate, to pray. We shall thus assimilate all that solid substance; we shall impregnate our life with the thoughts of the Saints.

The "divine reading" is at once *spiritual reading* and prayer. Still it is well to set a time for prayer properly so called. In other words, for example, in the evening we shall have our spiritual reading, which we may do before Compline, according to the monastic practice, and in which, before going to bed, we can find the matter of our last thoughts. And we shall place the time of prayer in the morning, after Matins if possible, at that time when there is some chance of not being disturbed.

---

[3] *Commentary*, p. 307.

[4] *All for Jesus* (Westminster, Md.: The Newman Bookshop, 1944), Chapter 8, pp. 354-455.

[5] *Commentary*, p. 307.

St. Benedict, as has been seen, knows no particular method of prayer. It is quite simply the fruit of the liturgy and of the sacred readings. Our morning prayer,[6] therefore, will feed at once on our readings and on the liturgical prayer we have just completed. Hymns, Psalms, lessons, mysteries, lives of the Saints, orations—we shall find there an inexhaustible source of reflection and contemplation. The Psalms in particular adapt themselves in a surprising way to the liturgical cycle and to our states of soul.

The mind which has contemplated the mysteries, followed Jesus Christ, Our Lady and the Saints, found its own needs in the petitions the Church addresses to God, makes a selection as if by instinct in the memories of those readings. All those things enlighten one another mutually. And while we pray and meditate, we are continuing to pray with the Church, to sing with her, to contemplate with her. The Church is our guide and our mistress. And the thoughts and resolutions she herself has prompted and inspired will be found as if brought to life again every time we take up our breviary during the day.

Prayer is not a little exercise apart, separated from the rest of our life by a sort of partition. On the contrary, it maintains a close contact with the Office and the *lectio divina*. And thus is realized in the interior life a unity more fruitful than the dispersion in which too many souls live, poorly enlightened on the close connection which ought to make a single whole of the Office, spiritual reading and prayer.

March 29—July 29—November 28

From the Calends of October until the beginning of Lent, let them apply themselves to reading up to the end of the second hour. At the second hour let Terce be said, and then let all labor at the work assigned them until None. At the first signal for the Hour of None let everyone break off from his work, and hold himself ready for the sounding of the second signal. After the meal let them apply themselves to their reading or to the Psalms.

On the days of Lent, from morning until the end of the third hour let

---

[6] We are not differentiating between meditation and prayer. The authors on spirituality make a distinction between them. The first is above all an operation of the mind, which considers a truth or a mystery in order to be convinced of it and permeated with it; the other is above all an operation of the will, which desires, asks and loves (cf. Dom Vitalis Lehodey, *The Ways of Mental Prayer*, pp. 13-14). In practice the two are confounded, although in advancing in the spiritual life the part of prayer ends by getting much the better of meditation's part.

them apply themselves to their reading, and from then until the end of the tenth hour let them do the work assigned them. And in these days of Lent they shall each receive a book from the library, which they shall read straight through from the beginning. These books are to be given out at the beginning of Lent.

But certainly one or two of the seniors should be deputed to go about the monastery at the hours when the brethren are occupied in reading and see that there be no lazy brother who spends his time in idleness or gossip and does not apply himself to the reading, so that he is not only unprofitable to himself but also distracts others. If such a one be found (which God forbid), let him be corrected once and a second time; if he does not amend, let him undergo the punishment of the Rule in such a way that the rest may take warning.

Moreover, one brother shall not associate with another at unseasonable hours.

COMMENTARY

The second period, for the organization of the work, begins with the Calends of October, that is on September 14, and goes to the beginning of the ecclesiastical Lent. It coincides, therefore, with the monastic Lent. The hours of the day are shorter and the nights longer. The great labors of the summer are completed. The work will be more in the interior of the monastery.

From Prime (6 o'clock) until the "second hour complete," that is until 8 o'clock, there will be *lectio divina*. The second hour being completed, Terce will be said. From Terce until None, namely 3 o'clock, manual labor. At the first sounding of None each one will leave off his work in order to be ready when the second signal sounds. From this we see that there is no more siesta. There is no longer any reason for one, since the nights are long enough from now on. We see also that mention is made of a second ringing for the Office of None. It was likely the same with the other Hours.

The Office of None is followed by the meal. Then until evening "the brethren apply themselves to their reading or to the Psalms." The Psalms, therefore, could furnish matter for the *lectio divina* if one wished.

With the ecclesiastical Lent begins the third and last period. St. Benedict is going to devote the whole following chapter to this holy time. Here he only indicates its general schedule. It is a period when, in union with the Church, prayer should be more frequent and fervor more ardent. A longer time, therefore, will be devoted to the sacred reading. They will apply themselves to it not merely "until the second full hour" as previously, but "until the third full hour," namely 9 o'clock. And the manual labor, which will not on that account be diminished, will end one hour later, that is at the tenth full hour. This schedule has been modified at different epochs, even among the Cistercians, who until the 19th century had tried to maintain it.

Something which is likewise special to Lent and which, unlike the previous point, has been maintained, is the distribution of books from the library to each monk. These books are to be read "consecutively and in their entirety," Our holy Father insists particularly on this attentive, connected reading. And so he wants one or two elders deputed to go about the monastery at the hours of reading and watch over the brethren. If they encounter (which God forbid!) any monk unoccupied, unprofitable to himself and harmful to the others, whom he is distracting from their occupation, he will be reprimanded once, and even twice if he repeats the offense. And if he does not amend his conduct, he will be subjected to the regular punishment. This rule, Dom L'Huillier points out, applies not only to Lent but to the whole year.

In this connection St. Benedict makes this remark: "One brother should not associate with another at unseasonable hours." From this we gather that there were regular hours when the monks could speak, in particular to ask for what they needed; yet those times when the silence was interrupted could not therefore be compared to recreations such as we understand them today.

APPLICATION

We shall have occasion to speak of Lent in the following chapter. Let us retain from this one what our holy Father teaches us about the way in which we should do our spiritual reading. He does not want us to read distractedly, to jump from one part to another, to devour superficially a stack of works on spirituality, to yield only to impulses of curiosity or to the vain desire to know everything. He wants us to take a book recommended by our Superiors, and by them judged capable of doing us good. This book must be read "right through from the beginning."

"This ordinance," says the author of the *Translation and Explanation*, " is very important both for virtue and for knowledge. For the reading done without order and without continuity, a mere skimming here and there of that which pleases us more, serves only to entertain our curiosity and the shallowness of our mind, favoring our concupiscence; besides which it is impossible in so doing to grasp well an author's meaning, which one cannot well understand and know except by examining all things step by step and trying to penetrate them, by comparing the end with the middle and the middle with the beginning, and attempting to relate all these things one to another."

This application is so much the more important when there is question of the things of God, of supernatural truths designed to feed meditation in us, to increase our knowledge and love of the Lord, to arouse our concern with the one thing necessary—all results which a distracted and superficial glance will never produce. Dom Étienne recalls these words of Palladius: "The beginning of our estrangement from God is manifested by the distaste for sacred reading." *Initium recedendi a Deo fastidium doctrinae est.* "The greater or lesser degree of relish felt in these letters come from heaven," he concludes, "is often the thermometer of the soul's health."

March 30—July 30—November 29

On Sundays, let all occupy themselves in reading, except those who have been appointed to various duties. But if anyone should be so negligent and shiftless that he will not or cannot study or read, let him be given some work to do so that he will not be idle.

Weak or sickly brethren should be assigned a task or craft of such a nature as to keep them from idleness and at the same time not to overburden them or drive them away with excessive toil. Their weakness must be taken into consideration by the Abbot.

COMMENTARY

Sunday is the Lord's day. Thus it is fitting that it be particularly sanctified. On that day there is no manual labor; all are to apply themselves to sacred reading, with the exception of those who are delegated to the indispensable offices.

There are brethren, however, who cannot be obliged to reading. Some of them are remiss or lazy. Although they know how to read, they are absolutely without intellectual curiosity and wholly incapable of application. Others are illiterate. For the former as for the latter, some useful occupation will be provided, so as to keep them from idleness. If the concern is with Sundays—for this regulation is probably of daily application—this work will be chosen from among the indispensable duties.

They must not be overburdened, however. St. Benedict has no intention of inflicting a punishment on them. He desires only that regard be had for their lack of understanding as well as for the weakness of their bodies. The idea is solely to protect them against the too often pernicious consequences of idleness.

APPLICATION

St. Benedict is anxious that the Sunday be truly the Lord's day. On that day, as we have seen, the liturgical Offices are longer and more solemn. But outside of the Offices the Sunday still remains the day of the Lord. With what should we be occupied if not with Him? St. Benedict sets our program for us: *Dominica die lectioni vacent.* Let us recall that *lectio* is reading, meditation, prayer. Let us not go looking for anything else but God.

Without speaking of those multitudes who have forgotten the way of the Church, how many Christians there are who consider themselves faithful, for whom the sanctification of the Sunday is summed up in an early morning Mass! For an Oblate of St. Benedict, if he is not a priest, Sunday means the parochial Solemn High Mass, it means Vespers, Compline, instructions, sacred readings, the whole fulfilled in the joy of feeling oneself more entirely at the Lord's service. By a stronger reason it means all that for the priest, charged with reminding the faithful of God's positive commandment.

Let us not give an hour or two to the divine Master and the rest to the world and to pleasures. We cannot be true Oblates, worthy of our holy Father, if we do not strive to be perfect Christians. How would we be such if, instead of living truly and fully the life of the Church, we were to delude ourselves, like too many Christians, by mistaking for a correct life a few religious practices sprinkled in an existence practically pagan? On Sunday more than on other days we are the workmen of God. Let us not cheat Him of any moment.

CHAPTER 49
On the Observance of Lent

March 31—July 31—November 30

ALTHOUGH the life of a monk ought to have about it at all times the character of a Lenten observance, yet since few have the virtue for that, we therefore urge that during the actual days of Lent the brethren keep their lives most pure and at the same time wash away during these holy days all the negligences of other times. And this will be worthily done if we restrain ourselves from all vices and give ourselves up to prayer with tears, to reading, to compunction of heart and to abstinence.

During these days, therefore, let us increase somewhat the usual burden of our service, as by private prayers and by abstinence in food and drink. Thus everyone of his own will may offer God "with joy of the Holy Spirit" (1 Thessalonians 1:6) something above the measure required of him. From his body, that is, he may withhold some food, drink, sleep, talking and jesting; and with the joy of spiritual desire he may look forward to holy Easter.

Let each one, however, suggest to his Abbot what it is that he wants to offer, and let it be done with his blessing and approval. For anything done without the permission of the spiritual father will be imputed to presumption and vainglory and will merit no reward. Therefore let everything be done with the Abbot's approval.

COMMENTARY

St. Benedict spoke of Lent in the preceding chapter. But this is a period of such importance that he deems it necessary to come back to it at length. We now know the material organization of Lent; the concern here will be with its spiritual organization. "At all times," says St. Benedict, "the monk's life ought to be conformed to the observance of Lent." Obviously our holy Father does not mean to signify here that the exterior mortifications peculiar to Lent ought to hold for all times; still less does he want to invite the monks to give themselves over freely to those mortifications outside of the prescribed period. Fasting does not constitute the essential element of Lent, which is rather the interior renewal of which St. Paul was speaking when he said: *In novitate vitae ambulemus.*[1]

---

[1] "Let us walk in newness of life."

310

During Lent that must be practiced which one should always have done: "guard one's life in all purity." He who so "guards" his life is detached from all that separates or turns him from God; that is, he is detached from the world. As soon as a thought of self-love, of pride, of sensuality, of hate, penetrates into the soul, the soul is less pure; it belongs less to God. God wants us to be all for Himself; and it is that total belonging, without holding back, without confusion, which ought to be a life-time condition. But *paucorum est ista virtus*; there are very few who maintain themselves in such a purity. The "holy" days of Lent have for their purpose to lead us back to that purity by "expiating all the negligences of other times."

There will be during Lent, therefore, a negative work and a positive work to be accomplished. The first consists in a general way in "renouncing all vices"; the second, in keeping oneself closely united to God.

But St. Benedict does not want to rest on general, vague, ideas. He specifies the principal works of Lent. They are first of all prayer, prayer full of faith, of fervor, of tenderness, going so far as to make compunction well up in the heart and tears in the eyes. Then more ardor for communal prayer, more frequency in "private prayers."

The sacred readings will be longer and meditated more. The holy Patriarch has already spoken to us of them in the preceding chapter.

Finally, the "abstinence" will be more severe. But here it seems evident that our holy Father does not reduce the scope of the word abstinence to the mere privation of food: "let him withhold from his body some food, drink, sleep, freedom of talking and enjoyment." But in this matter there is room to make a distinction.

There are a thousand little privations, a thousand little mortifications which may present themselves to us in the course of the day. It is well not to let pass "the light, discreet touch of the Holy Spirit" which "solicits to this good action, to this little mortification,"[2] No authorization is necessary for that.

But the case is quite otherwise with the mortifications which are out of the ordinary. There are souls who have a "gift" from God for this kind of penance, who are called to it, and who thereby do a work of love and of apostolate. But how frequent are the illusions on this point! Outward

---

[2] Dom L'Huillier, *Explication Ascétique et Historique*, Tome 2, p. 145

mortification is not always a sign of sanctity. It is sometimes encountered in union with immortification of the mind or of the will. Its extraordinary character constitutes a danger of pride, which causes one to suppose oneself more advanced than the others who are not doing so much, on this point at least; and consequently it causes one to delude oneself. Thus our holy Father wanted to take a wise precaution against dangers of that sort. Every resolution on this point should be submitted to the "spiritual father." Mortification is then found returning to obedience. And where it becomes truly meritorious is when, no longer having the attraction of an enthusiastic fervor which makes everything easy, it no longer presents anything but asperities. Then it is a true cross one carries out of obedience, and the reality of the suffering causes the temptations of pride to be forgotten. Finally, there is one sentiment which ought to dominate the whole of Lent: "the joy of the Holy Spirit." The soul that renounces itself, the soul that gives itself should do so joyously. Moreover, what does it renounce? Vanity and illusion. To whom does it give itself? To Him who is all Beauty, all Goodness, all Peace, all Joy.

But the joy of Lent takes a special coloring from the fact that one is going towards Easter. "With the joy of a spiritual desire," says St. Benedict, one must "look forward to holy Easter." Easter means the Lord revived and living among us. It means the climax of that renewal of a soul which has finally found its Savior again in full measure; it means the Light, symbolized by the Paschal Candle, which comes to illumine minds and hearts; it means the Alleluia which rings out in the whole city of souls. For the Christian there is no joy greater than that of Easter; and the thought that one is advancing toward that joy already throws a ray of light, as it were, on the penances and mortifications of Lent.

APPLICATION

For us Oblates this whole chapter is to be taken literally. Our holy Father is merely restating for his children what the pastors of souls in all ages teach their faithful. If he separates his children from the world, he does not separate them from that great current of spiritual life which circulates in Holy Church. Quite to the contrary, he wants them to be charged with it and to live by it. They should be perfect Christians. In penance they will be the most joyful. Is not the Church the mystical body of Jesus Christ, and are they not of those who have kept closest to the divine Master's footsteps?

CHAPTER 50

*On Brethren Who Are Working Far From the Oratory
or Are on a Journey*

THOSE BRETHREN who are working at a great distance and cannot get to the oratory at the proper time—the Abbot judging that such is the case—shall perform the Work of God in the place where they are working, bending their knees in reverence before God.

Likewise those who have been sent on a journey shall not let the appointed Hours pass by, but shall say the Office by themselves as well as they can, and not neglect to render the task of their service.

COMMENTARY

The case of those who would not find themselves at the monastery at the times of Office or of meals must certainly be provided for. Are they also bound by the Rule, and in particular by the obligation of the Office?

As a preliminary point St. Benedict establishes that certain absences can be legitimate and authorized by the Abbot. But such absences can only be accidental: an urgent labor in a "grange" or in an employment for which in a given circumstance hired labor happens to be lacking. It is not possible to return to the monastery for one of the little Hours; the whole time would be spent in going and coming. The monk will recite the Office, therefore, in the place where he is working, in fields or woods.

To characterize the manner in which he should then perform it, St. Benedict says that he is to do it "bending the knees in reverence before God." Certain commentators have understood that the Office recited by one monk or a little group of monks outside of the oratory was to be said kneeling. It is undoubtedly in virtue of this interpretation that the Maurists used to take that posture when they recited the Office privately. Today the commentators are agreed in admitting that in St. Benedict's intention the Office is to be said with "the customary ceremonial: bows, genuflections, prayers said kneeling or prostrate: *cum tremore divino flectentes genua*; which words do not mean that the whole Office is recited kneeling, but rather that the same rubrics are kept as in choir."[1]

The purpose of the words *cum tremore divino* is to remind us that God is present everywhere, and that even while reciting the Office far from the oratory we should none the less consider ourselves in His divine presence.

But the absence may be prolonged. The question here is no longer of an employment in a place somewhat removed, but of a real journey. St. Benedict wants the Office in such cases to be celebrated at the "appointed Hours." When the Hour came, the monk was to choose a propitious place, dismount from his horse and pray as he would have done in choir. The Cluniac custom dispensed with the kneeling and genuflections when the ground was snowy or muddy. Compensation was made by the recitation of the *Miserere*. St. Benedict suggests also that one must adapt oneself to the potentialities of the place: *ut possunt agant ibi*. Let us remember further that at St. Benedict's time there were no portable breviaries and that the monk had to be content with reciting by heart. He will do his best, therefore. The essential thing will be not to neglect rendering to God at the desired time "the task of his service."

APPLICATION

This chapter is of concern for us. Our holy Father does not conceive of the Office as recited otherwise than with the postures of the choir. In holding to them not only do we render the Lord the homage of our whole being, body and soul, but we also associate ourselves better with those who pray with the same postures in the monastery. As we have already said, such should be our ideal. We are the men of the liturgy, of the public prayer. Let us follow our holy Father's intentions to the best of our ability.

We have likewise spoken previously of the horarium. St. Benedict shows us here to what extent he insists on it. "St. Benedict would have been surprised at a monk saying Lauds, for instance, at sunset or bedtime."[2] Is it not through the schedule of Hours also that we associate ourselves more closely with our monastic family? After censuring those who without special necessity hurry, the first thing in the morning, to say all at one time what they ought to divide up in a day, as well as those who, through negligence, put off the whole duty until evening, Dom Morel remarked: "Is that to join one's brethren in spirit in order to honor God

---

[1] Dom Paul Delatte, *Commentary*, p. 323.

[2] *Ibid.*, p. 324.

with them from a single heart and a single mouth? Is it not rather to separate oneself from them, and in separating oneself to surrender all the delights and all the advantages of the Communion of Saints?"[3]

A propos of the words *ut possunt agant ibi* Dom Delatte reminds us also "that there are places which are less favorable to a pious and becoming recitation of our Office."[4] We should indeed take care to find a place where the occasions of dissipation or distraction are either absent or reduced as much as possible, and where we can readily consider ourselves, "with a divine fear," under God's eyes. "Of the place where we find ourselves," says Dom Morel, "we ought to make, as it were, a temple where we may perform this duty with a holy fear and a religious respect. He who has this fear changes the most profane places into holy temples; he who has it not, often profanes the most sacred places."[5]

---

[3] *Méditations*, p. 362.

[4] *Commentary*, p. 324.

[5] *Méditations*, pp. 360-361.

CHAPTER 51
On Brethren Who Go Not Very Far Away

April 2—August 2—December 2

BROTHER who is sent out on some business and is expected to return to the monastery that same day shall not presume to eat while he is out, even if he is urgently requested to do so by any person whomsoever, unless he has permission from his Abbot. And if he acts otherwise, let him be excommunicated.

COMMENTARY

St. Benedict is concerned here mainly with the meals. It happens that for some reason some monks have to journey more or less far. If they can complete their journey in one day, St. Benedict does not want them to accept a meal outside of the monastery, however earnestly they may be entreated or whoever may be the persons who entreat them. There are cases, however, in which an acceptance can be justified. It is the Abbot who is judge of them. Anyone who would dispense himself from asking for authorization shall be excommunicated. This probably means excommunication from table.

APPLICATION

We ought to be extremely reserved in the matter of worldly gatherings, banquets and so forth. We must not forget that we have chosen God for our portion, that we are to seek Him alone and that we do not find Him by behaving like bons vivants. It would not befit the profession which we have made and which unites us to the monastic Order, for us to be seen often at pleasure parties. The Oblate lives a family life; it is at his own hearth that he should especially take his pleasure, leading a simple and dignified life in the midst of those whom God has entrusted to him.

But it is to the priests that this rule may be more particularly applied. In most dioceses the Statutes remind the priest that he ought to frequent the table of lay people as little as possible. He may take for himself this passage from Dom Delatte's Commentary:[6] "The tables of layfolk were not made for us; neither their wines nor their talk suit us. Men sometimes

---

[6] P. 326.

employ the pretext of edification; but is not the edification much more real when we are only rarely seen? Would not people of the world be rather surprised that monks (or priests) should accept invitations so readily? If they eat and drink little, they will be suspected of hypocrisy; if they have good appetites and appreciate good wine, they will be charged with excess."

CHAPTER 52
On the Oratory of the Monastery

April 3—August 3—December 3

ET THE ORATORY be what it is called, a place of prayer; and let nothing else be done there or kept there. When the Work of God is ended, let all go out in perfect silence, and let reverence for God be observed, so that any brother who may wish to pray privately will not be hindered by another's misconduct. And at other times also, if anyone should want to pray by himself, let him go in simply and pray, not in a loud voice but with tears and fervor of heart. He who does not say his prayers in this way, therefore, shall not be permitted to remain in the oratory when the Work of God is ended, lest another be hindered, as we have said.

COMMENTARY

The word oratory comes from the verb *orare*, to pray. The oratory is the place consecrated exclusively to prayer. St. Benedict wants it to be nothing but that. It is not to be made at the same time a workshop, as with the monks of Tabennisi, who used to weave baskets during the psalmody; it is not to be made a storeroom; no other gatherings except liturgical gatherings are to be held in it.

Dom Haeften[1] points out that with certain hermits of Egypt there was a distinction between the church and the oratory.[2] For St. Benedict that distinction does not exist: the oratory is the monastery's church. The church is the house of God. In it, therefore, one should have "reverence for God" and keep strictest silence. We see what place it was to hold in the community. And so undoubtedly the monks who were craftsmen and artists were to consecrate to it the best of their efforts and their talents.

---

[1] *Disquisitionum Monasticarum Libri XII*, Proleg., 18, §4.

[2] See Cassian, Institutes, Book 3, Chapter 2; in C.S.E.L., Vol. 17, p. 34; in Nicene and Post-Nicene Fathers, 2nd series, Vol. 11, pp. 212-213. This passage is cited by Dom Haeften, although it does not explicitly mention an oratory separate from the church, but describes the custom the Egyptian monks followed of praying in their cells instead of coming together for the little Hours of the day. See also Rufinus, *Historia Monachorum*, Chapter 5; in P.L., Tome 21, cols. 408-409; in Herbert Rosweyd, *Vitae Patrum* (Antwerp, Moreti, 1615), p. 459.

From the application of this chapter have arisen those splendid monastic churches which elicit our admiration.

Public prayer has its place in the oratory, but also private prayer, the prayer said by the monk "by himself," St. Benedict, who had not yet concerned himself with private prayer, desires that nothing be upset in it "by another's importunity." There must be no talking, no noise, not even any outcries and loud sighings on the part of those who are praying.

And in this regard our holy Father gives a plan of private prayer. It has its place naturally outside of the Office. The monk, wholly impregnated, no doubt, with the thoughts poured into his soul by the liturgy, feels himself drawn to a more intimate conversation with the Lord. He betakes himself in solitude to the oratory; there reigns the greatest silence. In him also silence becomes more profound, a silence untroubled by any interior noise, any phraseology, any tumult of words. The Lord is there; it is the heart that speaks, and from it the prayer gushes forth with so much fervor, with so much love and compunction, that it is sometimes accompanied by tears.

One must surely be on guard not to distract those who pray thus. The best means to that end will be not to enter the oratory oneself except for prayer.

APPLICATION

We shall apply this short but important chapter of the Holy Rule if we have the respect and the veneration for churches which our holy Father demands. True respect is born of the spirit of faith. Is not the church the house of God? Is it not there that the Lord resides in His tabernacle? And even if the Holy Eucharist were not found there, would it not still be a place sanctified by so many fervent prayers, by so many graces granted down through the ages?

Every church is something sacred. How does it come about that so many Christians behave themselves there as if they did not believe, as if what they profess and teach were real only in certain circumstances or in certain ceremonies? Hence those churches are transformed into halls for so-called sacred concerts, nay even, alas, (we have seen it) into movie houses. How far we are, then, from the mind of St. Benedict and the practice of the Saints!

"St. Martin," his earliest biographer tells us, "conducted himself in church with so much reverence and devotion that no one ever saw him seated there, but always kneeling or standing, his face pale and trembling; and when someone would ask him why he was trembling, he would say: 'How shall I not have fear and how shall I not tremble, being before the face of my God and my Judge?'[3] It was a fear which certainly raised itself to love and made certain Saints appear as if sweetly ravished in the presence of the tabernacle.

The same thought of faith ought to instil in us a relish for the property of the churches, for their ornamentation, for the maintenance of everything that pertains to the divine worship. Is it not under the impulse of this thought that so many Sisters and Regular or Secular Oblate women devote themselves to the making of liturgical ornaments?

Dom Étienne finds still another teaching in this chapter. Commenting on our holy Father's words, "Let him go in simply and pray," he concludes: "There is in these lines an implicit invitation to what we call the visit to the Most Blessed Sacrament, and an expression which deserves to be meditated on carefully: intentione cordis, the application of the heart. It reveals the secret of true prayer. The formulas by themselves are not enough; the attention of the mind is difficult and fleeting; but the intention or the tendency towards God, not revoked—there is the force of prayer, the voice of the Holy Spirit."

---

[3] Sulpicius Severus, *Dialog* 8, Chapter 1. (Translator's note: In the editions available there are only three *Dialogs*, and the only part of the above quotation to be found is the following in Dialog 2, Chapter 1: *nam in ecclesia nemo umquam illum sedere conspexit*—"and, as to the church, no one ever saw him sitting there"; in C.S.E.L., Vol. 1, p. 180; translated by Alexander Roberts in *Nicene and Post-Nicene Fathers*, 2nd series, Vol. 11, p. 38.]

CHAPTER 53
On the Reception of Guests

April 4—August 4—December 4

ET ALL GUESTS who arrive be received like Christ, for He is going to say, "I came as a guest, and you received Me" (*Matthew* 25:35). And to all let due honor be shown, especially to the domestics of the faith and to pilgrims.

As soon as a guest is announced, therefore, let the Superior or the brethren meet him with all charitable service. And first of all let them pray together, and then exchange the kiss of peace. For the kiss of peace should not be offered until after the prayers have been said, on account of the devil's deceptions.

In the salutation of all guests, whether arriving or departing, let all humility be shown. Let the head be bowed or the whole body prostrated on the ground in adoration of Christ, who indeed is received in their persons.

After the guests have been received and taken to prayer, let the Superior or someone appointed by him sit with them. Let the divine law be read before the guest for his edification, and then let all kindness be shown him. The Superior shall break his fast for the sake of a guest, unless it happens to be a principal fast day which may not be violated. The brethren, however, shall observe the customary fasts. Let the Abbot give the guests water for their hands; and let both Abbot and community wash the feet of all guests. After the washing of the feet let them say this verse: "We have received Your mercy, O God, in the midst of Your temple" (*Psalm* 47:10).

In the reception of the poor and of pilgrims the greatest care and solicitude should be shown, because it is especially in them that Christ is received; for as far as the rich are concerned, the very fear which they inspire wins respect for them.

COMMENTARY

As we have already observed, St. Benedict wants his children to live by faith. It is in the light of faith that everything should appear to them; it is according to faith that they should judge and evaluate. Now faith makes us see God everywhere, but above all in the souls of those who are our brethren in Jesus Christ. In reality, there is something of Christ in them.

Substituting Himself for His own, did not Our Lord say in His Gospel, "I was a guest and you received Me"?

Guests, therefore, who frequently present themselves at the monastery gate and who are always presumed to be Christians, are to be received as Christ Himself. To this rule there will be no exceptions. "All" strangers will be the object of pious, devout attentions. Of course, the nature of these attentions will be proportioned to the persons. Though being equally affectionate and considerate, the attentions will be manifested differently, for example, to the rich and to the poor, to princes and to craftsmen.

There are two categories of guests, however, who are to be welcomed with quite special regard. The first are the "domestics of the faith." Some have thought, relying on texts from St. Paul where all the Christians are called "fellow-citizens of the saints" (*Ephesians* 2:19) and "domestics of the faith" (*Galatians* 6:10), that the concern here was with Christians in general, as opposed to infidels or Jews. But since in the sixth century the Christians must have represented almost the totality of the guests, the reason for such a distinction is not very easy to see. The concern is rather with those who are particularly consecrated to the service of the Lord, namely monks and clerics in general. The second category are the pilgrims.[1] These tire themselves out on the highways for love of God and of His Saints. Their fatigue is blessed; their needs are often greater than those of the guests. On these grounds they represent more particularly the Son of Man, who also traversed the highways of the world without having whereon to lay His head, entrusting Himself to the hospitality of pious souls.

A little later St. Benedict will speak also of a third category, the poor, whom he will join to the pilgrims. A too natural instinct prompts us through fear to render honor to the rich; sometimes it is even self-interest that guides us. And we might be tempted, on the other hand, to neglect or even to despise the poor as people of small consequence. St. Benedict cannot allow such a lack of the spirit of faith: "Let the poor and the pilgrims be received with a special care and solicitude, because it is principally in their person that Christ is received." As we can see, St. Benedict is wholly permeated with the Savior's words: "Come, you blessed

---

[1] The text says *peregrini*. Dom Guéranger translated merely by "travelers" (*voyageurs*) and later "strangers traveling" (*voyageurs étrangers*). With the majority of the commentators, the Farnborough translators keep the translation "pilgrims" (*pèlenns*).

of My Father ... I was hungry and you gave Me to eat; I was thirsty and you gave Me to drink; I was a guest and you welcomed Me; I was naked and you clothed Me; I was sick and you visited Me.. .. Truly, I tell you, whatever you have done for the least of My brethren, it is for Me that you have done it" (*Matthew* 25:34-40).

Our holy Father is not content to indicate in a general way in what spirit guests must be received. He specifies the method and, one might say, the ceremonial of the reception.

A guest is announced. As the case may be, the Superior or the brethren—that is to say some of them, those who have been assigned this function, and not, unless by exception, the whole community—come to meet him, as did Martha and Mary at the news that Jesus was coming.

For a few days the newly arrived will be associated with the family. The true union of Christians takes place in Christ. It is by prayer first of all, therefore, that the unity in the present case is going to be affirmed. The guest is conducted to the oratory. When the prayer is concluded, host and guest feel themselves truly brethren, members of the great family of Christ's Church. The devil cannot pray.

The newly arrived, therefore, is not a devil hidden under a human appearance. Then the kiss of peace is given him.

Here St. Benedict opens a parenthesis to go back to all that should precede the *osculum pacis*, the kiss of peace.

That kiss of brotherly peace is, in fact, the last act of the little scene which constitutes the reception. Let us go back, then, to the guest's arrival. He is welcomed first by a salutation full of humility, which is made, as the case may be, either by inclining the head or by prostrating the whole body. The guests, let us not forget, represent Christ. "It is the Christ received in them who is adored in them." Even before being confirmed against any diabolical illusion, one should assume as a preliminary attitude that this is so. It is then that one will conduct him to prayer, and will embrace him fraternally on coming out of the oratory.

Along with prayer, the communal table is the symbol most expressive of brotherhood. After the guest, tired out from his trip, has been led there, the Superior or the one whom he has appointed to care for guests will take his place next to the guest. He will read to him or have someone read to him a few passages from an edifying book; then the guest will be served "with all kindness."

Our holy Father's charity will not let the traveler eat alone. The

Superior or his delegate will eat with him, therefore, unless there be an ecclesiastical fast on that day. The guest, being himself obligated to such a fast, would not conceive of a monk's breaking the law of the Church.

It goes without saying that St. Benedict does not intend that the Abbot take a full meal with every guest who presents himself; it suffices for him to take with the guest a few mouthfuls "to break the bread of charity" and to give witness to the brotherly character of the welcome. There is an exception, to be sure, when the guests' meal takes place at the regular hour; for we shall see that as a general rule the Abbot eats with the guests.

The meal will be preceded by all the marks of charity customary in the ancient hospitality. The Abbot himself, as the Christ whose place he holds once did before the Last Supper, will pour water over the guest's hands and will wash his feet, soiled by the trip he has just made. The Holy Rule reads: "Let the feet of all the guests be washed both by the Abbot and by the entire community." Obviously, St. Benedict cannot want all the monks, one after the other, to wash the feet of each arriving guest. The guests would indeed have good reason to complain, remarks Dom Mège, "if they had to endure being washed and washed again as many times as there were monks." The text probably means, adds Dom Delatte, that all the religious "should fulfil this charitable office in turn."[2]

This act of charity, moreover, takes a little liturgical turn with the short formula of thanksgiving which concludes it. After the washing of the feet, the monks say this verse: "We have received Your mercy, O God, in the midst of Your temple."

It is the beginning of this formula especially which justifies its use in the circumstances. Animated by the spirit of faith, the monk wants to forget that he has devoted himself, that he has been merciful and charitable. He wants to remember only one thing: that, in the person of the guest, God Himself has visited him. And it is God who has truly shown mercy to him by thus coming to him and accepting his lowly services.

In this whole chapter the assumption is always that the person received is a man. No one would think of receiving women in the monastery. Besides, women scarcely ever traveled. But as the case could arise, there surely must have been a way of hospitality provided which would safeguard the monastic traditions. With St. Pachomius, as also later

---

[2] *Commentary*, p. 337.

on at Cluny, there were hospices outside of the cloister for women and children. It is probable that in St. Benedict's time the infrequent women travelers found welcome with the nuns established relatively close to the monastery or with those pious Oblate ladies who often lived in its shadow and occupied themselves in washing or mending the monks' clothes.

APPLICATION

A part of the ceremonial of hospitality has always remained. The prayer and the washing of hands always accompany the guest's arrival or his entrance into the refectory. The washing of feet is no longer necessitated by our modern style of dress; the prostration, to which St. Benedict did not obligate anyway, has likewise disappeared.

What remains above all is the Christian, brotherly cordiality which characterizes Benedictine monasteries. The fact is that hospitality is a Christian virtue strongly recommended by Jesus and by the Apostles. It was the desire to fulfil the Law of the Lord perfectly on this point that made the monks the originators of hospices and hospitals. Today the service of these houses has passed to the hospitaler Orders. But monastic hospitality is always ready. It is thereby that the monks' apostolate is realized in great part, which was surely in St. Benedict's mind when he asked that the guest "be edified."

The Oblate also should have the spirit of hospitality, therefore. Whether his guests be friends or strangers, rich people or poor, agreeable visitors or those disagreeable ones who are received more through duty than through affection, are they not always Christ? St. Benedict spares nothing that his guest be really welcomed and receive at the same time refreshment of the body and that of the soul. Let us recall Christ's words, which so impressed our holy Father; let us recall St. Paul's words, "Do not forget hospitality,"[3] and how the great Apostle took care to remind the Bishop as well as the Christian widow[4] that they should be hospitable.[5] The writings of the Fathers are filled with similar counsels.

This, no doubt, is a fitting place to speak of that diminutive of hospitality which consists in giving a good welcome to those who come to call on us. As a general rule, people rightly expect to be charitably

---

[3] *Hospitalitalem nolite oblivisci* (*Hebrews* 13:2).

[4] 1 Timothy 5:10.

[5] 1 Timothy 3:2.

welcomed by a priest or a person making profession of piety. It seems so natural that the Master's bounty be reflected in His servants.

We may do a great deal of evil by showing ourselves impatient, upset, or sometimes impolite in face of a visit which displeases us, either by reason of the person, who is by nature little suited to us, or by reason of the hour, which does not please us. Who knows whether that meeting was not the hour of God, or was not at least going to prepare for it? Our coldness, our impatience may have arrested on the lips the trusting avowal for which the person had come!

Let us remember that we are, or that we ought to be, filled with the spirit of Jesus, that for Him we ought to forget ourselves, and that those who come to us, even sinners, even wretches, also represent Jesus Christ. St. Benedict has taught us, in the chapter on the cellarer,[6] to whom he specially recommended "children, guests and the poor," that there is an amiable way of showing people out and of refusing them something. He has several times repeated to us his desire "that no one be troubled or vexed." Imperturbable goodwill towards all is a very meritorious form of self- denial, of humility, of charity to one's neighbor; it is often a discreet and effective means of procuring the good of souls.

April 5—August 5—December 5

Let there be a separate kitchen for the Abbot and guests, that the brethren may not be disturbed when guests, who are never lacking in a monastery, arrive at irregular hours. Let two brethren capable of filling the office well be appointed for a year to have charge of this kitchen. Let them be given such help as they need, that they may serve without murmuring. And on the other hand, when they have less to occupy them, let them go out to whatever work is assigned them.

And not only in their case but in all the offices of the monastery let this arrangement be observed, that when help is needed it be supplied, and again when the workers are unoccupied they do whatever they are bidden.

The guest house also shall be assigned to a brother whose soul is possessed by the fear of God. Let there be a sufficient number of beds made up in it; and let the house of God be managed by prudent men and in a prudent manner.

On no account shall anyone who is not so ordered associate or converse with guests. But if he should meet them or see them, let him

---

[6] Chapter 31.

greet them humbly, as we have said, ask their blessing and pass on, saying that he is not allowed to converse with a guest.

COMMENTARY

St. Benedict endows the monastery with three kitchens: that of the brethren, that of the sick, that of the guests and the Abbot. It is the spirit of charity which inspires him. He does not want to expose either the sick or the guests to a cuisine often improvised by chance cooks. And besides, since the arrival of guests is unforeseeable and frequent, it will be easier to offer them what is necessary if there is a special kitchen for them with permanent cooks. The latter will generally be two in number, appointed for one year. If there are many guests, they will be given helpers; if visitors are lacking, they will be employed elsewhere. We find here St. Benedict's principle of conduct for all the offices of the monastery.

To lodge the guests there will likewise be a special "cell," the location of which our holy Father does not indicate. Beds are always to be found there made up in sufficient number. With time, the "cell" was multiplied. There was the hostelry for the rich or well-to-do guests and the almonry for the poor, the sick, the pilgrims. This was the origin of the hospices and the hospitals.

In charge of the guest cell St. Benedict puts a brother of whom he requires certain particular qualities. He must be wise and must administer with prudence. His soul must be possessed by the fear of God. The fact is that his position is full of dangers: almost continuous contact with the world, temptations of vain curiosity, of gossip, of self-conceited kindness, and so forth.

If the guest master should guard himself from the dangers of association with worldly people, so much the more should the other monks, whose duties do not require ordinary relations with them. They will not associate with the guests; they will merely greet them in passing "and ask a blessing," that is, pronounce, according to the custom, the formula *Benedicite*, by which a person always marked his respect to a superior or an elder or a distinguished personage.

APPLICATION

In this passage St. Benedict appears to be occupied with two things: to insure all the necessary attentions to the guest; to prevent the guest's presence from being an occasion of dissipation.

It is to realize the first that he establishes a special kitchen. Obviously, the traveler does not come to the monastery to make good cheer; but he needs to refresh his strength, spent by the trip, and he must not be exposed to surprises.

Nowadays, in the French Congregation, a simpler solution has replaced the somewhat complicated arrangement of the early days. The monks' cook is appointed for an indefinite term, and the guests take their meals in the monastic refectory.

It is also to insure the necessary attentions to the guests that St. Benedict requires special aptitudes of the guest master. He wants to teach us thereby once more that in the exercise of hospitality we should treat those whom we entertain with all the attentions and all the politeness which true Christian charity inspires.

But our holy Father does not want the visit of the guests to be a source of dissipation. Is not that what we ought to guard against also in the exercise of hospitality? It would be regrettable indeed if those whom Providence sends us were to return disedified and leave us less recollected. We need not pose, obviously, or set ourselves up constantly as preachers. But there are ways of acting and subjects of conversation which we must know how to avoid. There are preoccupations in which it is not necessary that we take part, even if these are fashionable.

We may say of the priest, and particularly of the priest Oblate, what Dom Delatte says of the guest master:[7] "His conversation should never be worldly, under pretext of adapting himself to the mentality of some visitors. There are matters of which he may confess his ignorance; who expects him to have the information of a press agency?" And the scholarly commentator adds: "Nor is he required to set himself up as a permanent director and instructor." But if we strive to be truly what we ought to be, namely men of God, we shall radiate God, and our visitors will not ask us to be anything else. We shall be doing good to them even without preaching. As Dom Delatte says again: "Sometimes we teach by our words and sometimes by our books, but most of all do we teach by our lives." And that teaching is often the most effective.

---

[7] *Commentary*, p. 340.

CHAPTER 54
Whether a Monk Should Receive Letters or Anything Else

 N NO ACCOUNT shall a monk be allowed to receive letters, tokens or any little gifts whatsoever from his parents or anyone else, or from his brethren, or to give the same, without the Abbot's permission. But if anything is sent him even by his parents, let him not presume to take it before it has been shown to the Abbot. And it shall be in the Abbot's power to decide to whom it shall be given, if he allows it to be received; and the brother to whom it was sent should not be grieved, lest occasion be given to the devil.

Should anyone presume to act otherwise, let him undergo the discipline of the Rule.

COMMENTARY

In the preceding chapter our holy Father put his religious on guard against associating with strangers. Such association might disrupt their recollection. As Dom Bernard Laure remarks, it might put them in contact, by means of news from the outside, with the world they had given up. Moreover, the guests were sometimes bearers of letters or of *eulogiae* from the monks' parents or friends. That is undoubtedly what leads the holy Patriarch to speak of the letters and the *eulogiae*.

No one may, in any way or under any pretext whatsoever, receive letters, *eulogiae* or any little presents whatsoever from his parents or from other persons, without the authorization of the Abbot.

We have already spoken of the *eulogiae*; they were small objects—images, relics, little loaves, fruits, etc.— which used to be offered in token of friendship. St. Benedict does not forbid the brethren to receive these objects.

It was permitted, with St. Pachomius for example, that the parents might bring some to the monks.[1] But he wants everything to be done with the Superior's authorization. It is for him to judge whether the nature of the presents or letters, and the relations which they presuppose, are not apt to create some dissipation in the soul, or to make a little of the spirit

---

[1] Ladeuze, *Etude sur le Monachisme Pakhomien*, p. 292.

of the world re-enter there.

But it is not only with the outside that St. Benedict requires a control of the exchange of letters and of little gifts. He wants the same measure to rule the exchanges of the same kind between monks, whether of the same monastery or of different monasteries. It is possible that St. Benedict was thinking here of individual friendships, which are always prejudicial. It is more probable that he saw, especially in the exchange of gifts, an infringement on poverty. The monk has renounced all property. He has nothing of his own, therefore. What he would wish to offer is not his, but only for his use, and the offering is legitimate only in the measure in which it is permitted by "the father of the monastery," to whom he should look for everything.

For the same reason, a gift offered even by parents may not be accepted without the Abbot's being informed of it. It is he who, if he deems fit, will assign it to the one for whom it is destined. But he is still free to offer it to another. And the holy Father, thinking of the vexation which the monk will perhaps experience, deprived of what was intended for him, exhorts him not to abandon himself to that feeling. It is in view of his own good that such assignment has been made; and that vexation, if he gave himself up to it, could "give occasion to the devil"; that is to say, it could lead him to murmuring, to revolt, perhaps to some scandalous excess. As for anyone who might have received anything secretly, he will be subjected "to the regular discipline."

APPLICATION

In decreeing these rules, St. Benedict wanted to assure his disciple of the twofold detachment from the world and from worldly goods. He does not want the monk to be grieved if he is deprived of a good to which he might have laid claim had he been of the world.

This should show us that we ought to know how to stand being deprived of the things which would seem to be our due. We are obliged as Christians, *a fortiori* as Oblates, to the virtue of poverty. This virtue, says Dom Delatte, "leads us not only to fulfil our vow indifferently well, but to practice renunciation and privation with facility, promptitude, and joy."[2] If we see ourselves deprived of what we expected, let us not content ourselves with being resigned. On the contrary, let us bless the Lord, who

---

[2] *Commentary*, p. 345.

has perhaps dispensed us from one more attachment, however small it be, to some created object. He is our wealth; and if we really love Him, we are rich enough to be able to pass up many of the things here below.

Our correspondence also, if we do not watch it, may contribute to keeping us in the spirit of the world. Through it we may frequent environments from which our profession separates us; through it we may entertain relations which are nothing but worldly, and steal precious time from the duties of our state. For a priest, for an Oblate, there are precautions to be taken with regard to letters; and we can very well apply to ourselves what Dom Delatte observes on this chapter:[3] "Perhaps we write too many letters. Why can we not confine ourselves to those demanded by politeness, charity, and real utility?... We should drop not only all frivolous, trivial correspondence, but also such as is of a purely worldly character. Let us also remember the dangers of letters of 'direction.' And when we write, let it be always with sobriety, and moderation, and in a supernatural spirit."

---

[3] *Ibid.*, p. 343.

CHAPTER 55
On the Clothes and Shoes of the Brethren

April 7—August 7—December 7

ET CLOTHING be given to the brethren according to the nature of the place in which they dwell and its climate; for in cold regions more will be needed, and in warm regions less. This is to be taken into consideration, therefore, by the Abbot.

We believe, however, that in ordinary places the following dress is sufficient for each monk: a tunic, a cowl (thick and woolly for winter, thin or worn for summer), a scapular for work, stockings and shoes to cover the feet.

The monks should not complain about the color or the coarseness of any of these things, but be content with what can be found in the district where they live and can be purchased cheaply.

The Abbot shall see to the size of the garments, that they be not too short for those who wear them, but of the proper fit.

Let those who receive new clothes always give back the old ones at once, to be put away in the wardrobe for the poor. For it is sufficient if a monk has two tunics and two cowls, to allow for night wear and for the washing of these garments; more than that is superfluity and should be taken away. Let them return their stockings also and anything else that is old when they receive new ones.

Those who are sent on a journey shall receive drawers from the wardrobe, which they shall wash and restore on their return. And let their cowls and tunics be somewhat better than what they usually wear. These they shall receive from the wardrobe when they set out on the journey, and restore when they return.

COMMENTARY

Well before St. Benedict's time there were customs and traditions relative to the habit of monks. Cassian appeals to symbolic meanings in his commentary on those traditions. Let us recall that our holy Father received the habit of religion from the monk Romanus, a thing which would not be explained if monks had not had special clothes. Not that these clothes differed by their form from those of everyone else; but their

332

exclusive use, their simplicity, the mediocrity of their quality sufficed to distinguish a monk. They really constituted a uniform which allowed the wearer to be recognized, as each social category was recognized by the fashion of dressing.

St. Benedict leaves a certain latitude as to the application of the rule he is going to give; but this latitude applies less to the form than to the quantity and the quality of the clothes each one is to receive. "In cold regions more is needed. In warm regions, on the other hand, less is needed." It will be for the Abbot to judge.

The monk's clothes are: 1) the cowl, 2) the tunic, 3) the scapular.

The cowl is a hooded mantle enveloping the body after the fashion of the ancient chasubles, and consequently without sleeves. Cowls, not monastic, are found represented on the Roman monuments. The monastic cowls must have had that form. It is probable that the *melota* of St. Benedict which the little Placidus saw floating above his head was a little cowl of sheepskin.

In time the cowl evolved in different ways, according to the localities. Sometimes it was split down the sides and took the form of a large scapular. Such was the cowl of Cluny. In certain localities the two flaps were rejoined by straps or bands, also called "St. Benedict's stitches." The monks of Chezal-Benoît and the Carthusians wore the cowl in that style. Again, thanks to a double stitching, it was furnished with large sleeves, like the present cowl of the Benedictines and the Cistercians. Yet again there are narrow sleeves which have been added to it. It is thus that we see it on certain miniatures representing St. Bernard. Whatever the case may be, the cowl is the monks' choir vestment. St. Benedict wants it "woolly in winter, thin or worn in summer."

The tunic was a robe ordinarily of linen, worn next to the body, with sleeves to the elbow. It was held by a cincture of leather or cloth.

The scapular was worn during working hours. As its name indicates, it covered the shoulders and hung down in front and in back; much shorter, no doubt, than the present scapular, yet certainly at least to the knees, as is proved by the story of the monk of Ascalon told by the Abbot Dorotheaus.[1] It was probably furnished with a hood. It was, in fact, a reduced cowl. The scapular and the cowl have evolved in such a way as sometimes to resemble each other. The monks of Cluny wore no scapular,

---

[1] *S. P. N. Dorothaei Expositiones; in* P G., Tome 88, col. 1638.

but their cowl rather resembled one, and they covered it with a garment, an ample robe with long sleeves, which they might just as well have called a cowl.

On their feet the monks will wear *pedules*, a word which probably designates light slippers for indoors. The Farnborough translators say that they correspond perhaps 'To stockings or to gaiters, or again to slippers" (*à des bas ou à des guétres, ou encore à des chaussures*). That hardly helps us. The monks will likewise have *caligae*, work shoes similar, we suppose, to the military sandals which were fastened to the feet with straps and which might serve as well for the daily labors as for journeys. Unless, as some suppose, the *pedules* were nothing but stockings; in that case, the *caligae* would have been for constant use.

Of what color will the monks' clothes be? St. Benedict attaches no importance to this. "Of all these things," he says, "let not the monks complain." The colors chosen, no doubt, were austere and not flashy: white, black, gray, brown. Dom Mayeul Lamey thought the brown prevailed, being the color of the unbleached wool and consequently the simplest and least elaborate.[2] The white was hardly worn anywhere except in Egypt.

As to the quality, that will be the most ordinary and the cheapest that can be found in the territory. In the sixth century, observes Dom L'Huillier, the art of buying in quantities for a low price was unknown. What cost less was certainly coarser in make, but substantial. That was what St. Benedict desired, out of concern for poverty.

Our holy Father is concerned that the clothes be proportioned to the stature. The wearing of grotesque clothes, either ridiculously short or ridiculously long, will not be made an object of mortification. The Abbot will watch over this matter.

Each monk will have two tunics and two cowls. One will serve for the day, the other for the night or to replace the one that has to be washed. They slept, therefore, clothed with the cowl over the tunic.

St. Benedict does not want anyone to have reserves of clothes. Anyone who thinks one of the pieces of his wardrobe needs to be replaced is to bring it to the clothes-room. It will be used for the poor—a point which proves that the monks were not accustomed to dressing in rags, but that their habit, while quite simple and ordinary, still was always proper.

---

[2] *Oeuvres Choisies*, pp. 240 ff.

The religious on a journey will have a right to *femoralia* or drawers. On those occasions they will be given clothes "somewhat better than the ones they wear usually," and they will take care on their return to restore them to the clothes-room after having washed them.

APPLICATION

The application of this chapter will bring our attention to bear upon two points: 1) the monastic vestments assigned to the Oblates, 2) the clothes ordinarily worn.

The piece of monastic clothing which the Oblates wear and which joins them materially to the Order is the scapular. "Its shape and size are left to each one's good pleasure."[3] It is worn under the clothes. Consequently, when the form of the latter permits, it may have the dimensions of the scapular of the Regular Oblates, which hangs a little below the knees.. It may not be replaced by the so-called "scapular" medal.[4]

The wearing of the scapular has its importance. "The necessity of guarding this point of material contact with their Order," say the Statutes,[5] "will be for them a sweet obligation. At the very time when they would have to mingle with the world and its festivals, their habit will help them maintain in themselves the sentiments which the great martyr Cecilia had, of whom the Church tells us: *Cantantibus organis, Caecilia virgo in corde suo soli Domino decantabat, dicens: Fiat ... cor meum ... immaculatum, ut non confundar.*"[6] In order to become well permeated with the spirit in which we ought to wear our scapular, we may profitably meditate from time to time the beautiful prayers which accompany the investiture and which are borrowed from the ancient monastic ceremonial.

It appears to be well established that certain Oblates of the Middle Ages used to wear their religious habit so that it showed, as the Franciscan Tertiaries and others used to do. This is recalled particularly by a former

---

[3] "Les Oblats Séculiers," following *L'Église ou la Société de la Louange Divine,* p. 85.

[4] *Ibid.*

[5] *Ibid.*

[6] "While the musical instruments were playing, the virgin Cecilia sang in her heart to the Lord alone, saying: '... let my heart ... be undefiled, that I be not ashamed.'" First responsory at Matins of St. Cecilia, November 22; in *Roman Breviary in English* (New York: Benziger Brothers, Inc., 1950), Autumn Part, p. 741.

Council of Bayeux, reported by Dom Bessin.[7] It is mentioned also by the Fourth Lateran Council, in 1215, speaking "of the confreres who remain in the world and are offered to the Order by putting off the worldly garb."[8]

The Abbé Dubois tells in his history of the Abbey of Morimond[9] how the pious clergy of the neighborhood, moved by the example of the monks, put on their habit and followed the monastic Rule in their own houses as best they could. "Many cures," he says, "unable to resist such moving examples, regarded it as the greatest good fortune to be affiliated with the Order, had their heads shaved, took the monastic habit and lived like Cistercians in their presbyteries." This happened in the middle of the 12th century.

Today, canon law has decided all that. The exterior wearing of the monastic habit depends at the same time on the Abbot and on the Ordinary of the diocese to which the Oblate belongs, and is permitted under the conditions set by the holy canons.[10] In practice it is worn with the above- mentioned permissions only in certain monastic ceremonies in which an Oblate might be called upon to fulfil some function.

There is, however, an old traditional devotion relative to the monastic habit which the Oblates are invited to maintain. They may, say the Statutes, "if they so wish, be buried in the black monastic habit, scapular and cincture."[11] Thus the Oblate sleeps his last sleep, awaiting the resurrection, in the same habit as his brethren of the monastery. It attests his belonging to the monastic Order, even in the tomb.

Dom Louis Gougaud, who has studied the history of this custom, concludes his study with this observation: "The Third Orders, notably those of St. Francis and of St. Dominic, which quickly acquired a very great popularity, adopted among their customs this old medieval devotion. Thanks to them and thanks also to the Institute of the Oblates in the Order of St. Benedict, it has not completely disappeared from the Christian

---

[7] *Conci. Rotham Provinciae,* II, 59, 241.

[8] Labbe, Conc. L. XIII, col. 57, quoted by Dom L'Huillier, "*Coup d'Oeil sur l'Histoire des Oblats dans l'Ordre Bénédictin,*" in *Bulletin de S. Martin et de S. Benoît,* August, 1925, p. 246.

[9] p. 103.

[10] Canon 703.

[11] *Manual for Oblates,* p. 50, §39.

customs of our days."[12]

It stands to reason that there should not be a contrast between what our monastic scapular signifies and our ordinary clothing, ecclesiastical or secular. "They shall despise pomp," say the Statutes of the Oblates.

There is a discretion which justifies, for certain Oblates living in the world, especially in certain circumstances, the wearing of clothes befitting their rank and their station. They must nevertheless be on guard against finding in that necessity the justification of a certain luxury which would not be demanded by any convention.

For the ecclesiastical Oblates the question is much simpler. No pretext of situation justifies for them any elegance or luxury in clothing. Nothing obliges a priest to wear silken belts trimmed with fringes, or velvet collars or golden chains. He will always be seemly with the simplest clothes, provided they be, according to the recommendation of St. Benedict himself, proper and made to fit. It would be out of place, consequently, for an Oblate to deck himself out in such trifles. We have only to take literally our holy Father's recommendation: *De quarum rerum omnium ... grossitudine non causentur ... sed quales inveniri possunt in provincia qua degunt aut quod vilius comparari potest.*

And since we are speaking of the ecclesiastical habit, itself composed also of a tunic practically identical in form to the monastic tunic, it may be *a propos* to recall this passage from Dom Delatte's *Commentary:*[13] "Our habit guards us, is a part of our enclosure and completes it: it holds us in the sweet captivity of God. And perhaps we should not seek elsewhere for the motive of that disfavor, or rather hatred, which the religious habit encounters from the devil and his agents. It is a bad sign when a priest or a monk is eager and glad to return to what the liturgy calls The ignominy of worldly dress.' The cowl does not make the monk, but what service it renders him! There is a real relation between our dress and our state; there are things which we feel to be impossible, conduct which we shall never attempt, just because we wear the livery of God. Let us esteem and venerate it. ..."

---

[12] *Dévotions et Pratiques Ascétiques du Moyen Age,* collection "Pax" (Abbaye de Maredsous, Belgium, 1925), p. 139.

[13] P. 347.

April 8—August 8—December 8

For bedding let this suffice: a mattress, a blanket, a coverlet and a pillow.

The beds, moreover, are to be examined frequently by the Abbot, to see if any private property be found in them. If anyone should be found to have something that he did not receive from the Abbot, let him undergo the most severe discipline.

And in order that this vice of private ownership may be cut out by the roots, the Abbot should provide all the necessary articles: cowl, tunic, stockings, shoes, girdle, knife, pen, needle, handkerchief, tablets; that all pretext of need may be taken away. Yet the Abbot should always keep in mind the sentence from the Acts of the Apostles that "distribution was made to each according as anyone had need" (*Acts* 4:35). In this manner, therefore, let the Abbot consider the weaknesses of the needy and not the ill-will of the envious. But in all his decisions let him think about the retribution of God.

COMMENTARY

After the clothes, the bedding is considered. It constituted the monk's only furniture in St. Benedict's time. For we must remember that he slept in a dormitory.

The equipment of the bed was composed of *matta, sagum, lena* and *capitale.*

The *matta* was not exactly a mattress. It was perhaps a quilted straw mattress, or more probably a simple rushmat.

The *sagum* was, according to Dom Calmet, "a bed-covering ... thin and . . . light." It took the place of sheet and coverlet at the same time.

The *lena* was a thick covering, perhaps a fur. Dom Calmet thinks that it served only in winter, and was added to the *sagum* or replaced it.

The *capitale* or pillow was a large cushion or bolster stuffed with straw or hair, or perhaps even with feathers.

The bedding has varied more or less with time and with the Constitutions; it has always remained austere. But everywhere, in conformity with St. Benedict's spirit of discretion, the monks have received the number of covers which the climate or the season demanded.

The bed being the monk's only furniture, it was only there that a monk less faithful to his Rule might be tempted to hide some small objects of which he wanted to insure himself the possession, unknown to his Abbot. St. Benedict wanted to forestall the occurrence of such deeds, so little in conformity with the spirit of poverty. Thus he asks that inspections be made from time to time in the monks' bedding. He knows that even the very person who has renounced many things for love of God may let himself be fascinated by the most trivial objects. And so he demands that "the vice of property be cut out by the roots."

St. Benedict does not by any means consider "property" a vice in itself. In reality, it is neither good nor bad. It becomes harmful only in the measure in which a person sets his heart on it. It is always harmful in the person who has made a vow of poverty and who receives everything he needs from the "Father of the monastery," for it presupposes necessarily an excessive and unruly attachment to an object which is in no way necessary. St. Benedict proves, in fact, that this vicious ownership has nothing to justify it, since the Abbot is there to give everyone the necessities of life, "that is: a cowl, a tunic, stockings, shoes, a girdle, a knife, a pen, a needle, a handkerchief, tablets." Still, it is important that the Abbot himself give no occasion for the vice of property by showing himself too stingy in the distributions; he must give "to each one according to his needs."

And in this connection our holy Father has a sentence in which his wholly paternal soul is manifested once more: "Let the Abbot consider the weaknesses of those who have need and not the bad will of the envious." There are always sullen minds to judge that he is too liberal, too generous, too pliable for such and such a one. He must indeed be on guard against listening to them. He would be exposing himself to letting the weak suffer, through a sort of human respect. Has not St. Benedict reminded him repeatedly of the condescendance with which he must surround the weak? In these circumstances it is God alone whom it is important to consider, God to whom the Abbot will one day have to render an account of all his conduct.

In speaking above of that which the Abbot ought to assure to each of his monks, St. Benedict has furnished us a little inventory of the objects deemed indispensable. We already know several of them. The *bracile*, of which there had not yet been question, was supposed to have been, according to the translation used by the Maurists, the Abbé de Rancé and various commentators of the 17th century, a sort of drawers; the name was supposed to come from *bracca*, which "was a type of breeches" (*haut-de-chausses*). In reality, the concern is with a very large belt for daytime, which served as a pouch. From it was suspended the *cultellus* or knife which served in the refectory and for certain labors. In it also was put the *mappula* or handkerchief. Each monk had also a needle for mending his clothes. He also had tablets coated with wax and a stylus for writing. This last detail proves that the monks of St. Benedict's time were not, in the majority, illiterate, as is sometimes exaggeratedly affirmed.

APPLICATION

Commenting on this chapter of the Holy Rule, Dom Delatte writes: "A monk should be able to renounce many items of comfort."[14] It should be the same with the Oblate. In our bedding, in the objects for our personal use, is it not fitting to avoid all that would savor of luxury or favor sensuality? Nothing prevents us from putting into practice what the Declarations of the French Congregation prescribe concerning those objects for our brethren the monks. We read there: "The bed should be such that a person may satisfy the need of sleep on it, but not pamper softness."[15] And further on: "Let no one be permitted to decorate his cell with silken hangings, mirrors, gildings, but only with painted or sculptured images which prompt to piety. Let the chairs be simple, furnished with straw or reed."[16] And in another place: "Let every luxury and every superfluity disappear from the things necessary to life."[17]

It is to be understood that this element of austerity should be strictly personal with us, and that it would be indiscreet and even contrary to the mind of St. Benedict to want to impose it on our guests or on those who dwell under our roof. No one will require of us a luxury or an excessive refinement of comfort which would often be out of place; but there are certain niceties, certain attentions which are demanded by charity in general and by the duties of hospitality in particular.

---

[14] *Commentary*, p. 356.

[15] Declaration on Chapter 22.

[16] Declaration on Chapter 33. It is to be understood that the application of these prescriptions has to be made with a great deal of discretion, taking account of situations. The essential thing is to observe the spirit of them.

[17] Declaration on Chapter 33.

CHAPTER 56
On the Abbot's Table

April 9—August 9—December 9

ET THE ABBOT'S table always be with the guests and the pilgrims. But when there are no guests, let it be in his power to invite whom he will of the brethren. Yet one or two seniors must always be left with the brethren for the sake of discipline.

COMMENTARY

This little chapter has caused much ink to flow. Its obvious purport is this: the Abbot is to eat with the guests and the pilgrims. We have seen that these have a kitchen apart, which is, moreover, the Abbot's kitchen. It follows from the first phrase, *mensa cum hospitibus*, as well as from its comparison with several others, that this meal likewise had its place in a separate refectory and at a different hour from that of the community. The guests certainly could not be forced to wait until the Hour of None. And if, as has been seen, the Abbot does break the fast on account of the guests, this means that their meal precedes the canonical Hour.

This prescription of the Holy Rule was to lead sometimes to disastrous consequences. In those places where the Abbots were of lukewarm piety and worldly-minded, as happened in the ages of decadence, the meals with the guests readily took on the aspect of banquets.

Thus the great commentators of the 17th century shied away from the literal interpretation, and they have won some contemporaries over to their own interpretation. Dom Martène, Dom Mèe, Dom Ménard and more recently Dom L'Huillier have had to force the text in a clever and skilful way to make it signify that the Abbot ate with the guests, to be sure, but in the communal refectory and at the hour of the conventual meal.

On the other hand, the obvious interpretation is upheld by Bernard of Monte Cassino, Haeften, Perez, the Abbé de Rancé, Dom Calmet, Dom Ètienne, Dom Delatte and others.

"This rule is very holy in its origin," explains Rancé, "and it cannot be doubted that in so far as the Superiors preserved the spirit of their Fathers and dwelt in the holiness of their state, it was a great edification for the strangers to eat with them; they found men filled with the Spirit of God, living in mortification and penance, who were giving, by their example even more than by their speech, holy instructions to all those who came to see them." And the Abbot of La Trappe describes with pleasure those meals full of simplicity which recalled "the holy *agapes* of the first Christians."

It must have been so in St. Benedict's time. Since then, experience has made another procedure preferable. The guests, at least in the French Congregation, eat in the communal refectory. This is the application of the thesis upheld by Dom Martène and others. It is not entirely in conformity with the letter of the Holy Rule, but it is quite in harmony with its spirit.

APPLICATION

The historical commentary on this chapter, if we had the leisure to pause over it, would be full of austere lessons for us. It would show us what part excessive seeking of well-being, sensuality, love of feasting and of junketing have had in the decadence of institutions and in the loss of souls.

Our Lord, St. Paul and the Fathers often put the Christians on guard against the abuses of the table. They knew what manifold dangers accompany those abuses, and they did not consider them compatible with the profession of disciples of Jesus Crucified. Their teachings should not be lost on us. It is well that we avoid junketing, that we be not fastidious over our dishes, that we even do some little hidden mortifications rather often in our meals.

Let us remember also that we have made profession of detachment and of poverty. We are the Lord's "stewards," and our superfluity belongs to the alleviation of the poor rather than to the search for dangerous satisfactions. This is what St. Bernard wrote to Henry, Archbishop of Sens: "They cry, the poor who are naked! They cry, those who are hungry; they complain and they say: It is to us that what you waste belongs; it is from us that you cruelly snatch what you spend uselessly.'"

Moreover, for the Christian, as for the Abbot and his monks, the family table, simple, frugal, in an atmosphere wholly impregnated with affection, is what is most fitting.

The duties of hospitality themselves do not necessarily imply a profusion of victuals and of wines, which is always out of place, and is really shocking if the concern is with an ecclesiastic. Here again good taste, nicety, understanding, proprieties, born of a feeling of what one is and of what one owes to charity towards one's neighbor, will inspire in us the best way of acting. We shall have pleased, we shall not have disedified; perhaps we shall have done what our holy Father desired when he asked the Abbot to take a place in the midst of his guests: we shall perhaps have done some good to souls.

CHAPTER 57
On the Craftsmen of the Monastery

April 10—August 10—December 10

F THERE ARE CRAFTSMEN in the monastery, let them practice their crafts with all humility, provided the Abbot has given permission. But if any one of them becomes conceited over his skill in his craft, because he seems to be conferring a benefit on the monastery, let him be taken from his craft and no longer exercise it unless, after he has humbled himself, the Abbot again gives him permission.

If any of the work of the craftsmen is to be sold, let those through whose hands the transactions pass see to it that they do not presume to practice any fraud. Let them always remember Ananias and Saphira, lest perhaps the death which these incurred in the body (*Acts* 5:1-11), they themselves and any others who would deal dishonestly with the monastery's property should suffer in the soul. And in the prices let not the sin of avarice creep in, but let the goods always be sold a little cheaper than they can be sold by people in the world, "that in all things God may be glorified" (*1 Peter* 4:11).

COMMENTARY

The monastery was supposed to be self-sufficient. The talents of the brethren, therefore, were put to profit for the various labors necessary to assure the daily upkeep. Among them there might be carpenters, painters, sculptors, copyists, illuminators, and so forth. Some had learned their art in the world, other had been initiated into it in the monastery.

It naturally happened that the production surpassed the needs of the house. St. Benedict sees nothing wrong in drawing profit from that production. But what he is anxious about is that the success in a trade or an art and the consideration of the gains which the monastery draws from it do not lead the workman or the artist into temptation. They are to work by the order and under the good pleasure of the Abbot. They are to work also "in all humility." As the monk's soul is worth more than the money he earns or the advantages he brings, it is preferable to take him away from his work rather than let him succumb to vainglory.

St. Benedict calls the monastic craftsmen *artifices*, artisans. It would not be right by reason of that designation to take them for the first Lay

Brothers. They were monks like the others. St. Benedict did not know the present distinction between *chori* and *conversi*.

What seems probable enough is that besides these artifices there were workmen in the vicinity of the monastery who lent the monks their cooperation for certain labors. The passage of Chapter 48 where it is said that in poor monasteries the monks themselves might be obliged to gather the harvest, lets it be understood that in rich or well-to-do monasteries lay workmen were employed. A little further on, we shall see laymen employed likewise as intermediaries in the sale of the products.

Inevitably, those workers lived in a monastic atmosphere. It is evident that St. Benedict, whose apostolic soul was anxious for the salvation of the peasants in the neighborhood, must have been interested more particularly in those whose work put them in closer relation with the monastery. Attached to the monastic church by bonds perhaps not precise, but undergoing the attraction of the monastic piety, they ended by being considered as the "familiars" of the monastery, which incorporated them to a greater or lesser degree. This was undoubtedly the common origin of the Lay Brothers, who came to live a regular monastic life, and of the Secular Oblates, who under different forms were affiliated with the monastic Order.[1]

Thus the monastery assimilated in various degrees all that revolved around it. The creation of the Lay Brothers, which had its full development in the 11th century, permitted the classification into the educated monks on the one hand, whose principal function was the Divine Office, and the Lay Brothers on the other hand, charged with the material work. Below these two classes of religious, the monastic family then completed itself with the "perpetual servants," the Oblates and others whose situation varied according to the localities, and finally with those to whom had been accorded the "fraternity" and the union of merits and prayers.

In our Chapter 57 the "familiars" are in the background. The artisans are monks forming no special category.

The monastery may be called upon, therefore, to drain off the overproduction by sale. For that purpose, as we have seen, it will make use of intermediaries, designated by the words "those through whose hands the transactions will pass." To these St. Benedict recommends perfect

---

[1] Abbé Deroux, *Les Origines de l'Oblature Bénédictine* (Ligugé), P- 57.

honesty. Let them not permit themselves to deduct little occult benefits from the sale. That money is not theirs, it is the monastery's, therefore the Lord's. And our holy Father reminds them of the example of Ananias and Saphira, remarking that their case would be worse than that of those two unfortunates. The money of Ananias and Saphira was really theirs. They were too prudent according to the flesh, but they were not thieves. Thus they were punished only "in their bodies." The unfaithful intermediaries are truly thieves, and, what is more, thieves of the Lord's goods, for such are the goods of the monastery; and the Lord, thus injured, might well punish them "in their soul."

St. Benedict does not want his monasteries, under the pretext of selling the surplus production, to become houses of commerce, where great profits are reckoned. He enjoins particularly that "the evil of avarice do not creep into the prices." They will sell, therefore, at equal quality, a little less dear than the merchants are selling.

It has been pointed out that nowadays this lowering of the selling prices of the monastery's products below the selling price of the same products in commerce would hardly be possible because of the competition. But there remains one resource: to make large, from the gains, the part of the poor. The essential thing is that "God be glorified" through the generosity and charity of the monks. *Ut in omnibus glorificetur Deus.*

APPLICATION

This chapter contains a twofold lesson: lesson of humility and lesson of disinterestedness.

It is a very frequent temptation that prompts us to glorify ourselves over what we produce, whether the concern is with science, with art or even with manual labors. We attribute to ourselves an importance which we have not, and this vanity, at first more or less conscious, may end by encumbering our spirit and may prevent our soaring towards God. We are pleased with ourselves, we are somebody, we admire ourselves.

There is room, perhaps often, for examining ourselves on this point, nay even for consulting the guide which is our conscience. Who knows whether it will not be well for us, where the occupation in question is optional, to abandon it for a time if our director considers that necessary? Did not Our Lord say, "If your eye scandalize you, pluck it out and cast if from you" (*Matthew* 5:29)? In any case, a prudent guide will be able to indicate to us the means of maintaining ourselves in humility, or of returning to it if we have yielded to pride.

We have already spoken at length about detachment and poverty. St. Benedict does not want "avarice to creep" into his children's hearts. He does not want to see in them those financial preoccupations which very quickly end by becoming dominant in a soul if one does not guard against that. "Eagerness for the good (that is, for wealth)," says the Abbé de Rancé, "is forbidden all those who are Jesus Christ's and who serve Him, I say to those very ones to whom the use of wealth is permitted."

The best remedy will be the habit of generosity, which will inspire us to set aside from each gain a very large part for the poor and for good works. Nothing is more disedifying than to see a so-called pious person whose heart and whose purse are almost always closed. On the contrary, by reason of us, our God, who knows how to inspire charity and detachment in souls, must be blessed by those who will see that in the end it is from Him that the first thought of our acts flows.

The last clause of this chapter, 'That in all things God may be glorified," has become, with the word Pax, the motto of the Benedictine monks and Oblates.[2]

---

[2] "Statutes of the Oblates," in *Manual for Oblates*, p. 50, §41.

CHAPTER 58

On the Manner of Receiving Brethren

April 11—August 11—December 11

HEN ANYONE is newly come for the reformation of his life, let him not be granted an easy entrance; but, as the Apostle says, 'Test the spirits to see whether they are from God" (*1 John* 4:1). If the newcomer, therefore, perseveres in his knocking, and if it is seen after four or five days that he bears patiently the harsh treatment offered him and the difficulty of admission, and that he persists in his petition, then let entrance be granted him, and let him stay in the guest house for a few days.

After that let him live in the novitiate, where the novices study, eat and sleep. A senior shall be assigned to them who is skilled in winning souls, to watch over them with the utmost care. Let him examine whether the novice is truly seeking God, and whether he is zealous for the Work of God, for obedience and for humiliations. Let the novice be told all the hard and rugged ways by which the journey to God is made.

If he promises stability and perseverance, then at the end of two months let this Rule be read through to him, and let him be addressed thus: "Here is the law under which you wish to fight. If you can observe it, enter; if you cannot, you are free to depart." If he still stands firm, let him be taken to the above-mentioned novitiate and again tested in all patience. And after the lapse of six months let the Rule be read to him, that he may know on what he is entering. And if he still remains firm, after four months let the same Rule be read to him again.

Then, having deliberated with himself, if he promises to keep it in its entirety and to observe everything that is commanded him, let him be received into the community. But let him understand that, according to the law of the Rule, from that day forward he may not leave the monastery nor withdraw his neck from under the yoke of the Rule which he was free to refuse or to accept during that prolonged deliberation.

COMMENTARY

From this chapter to Chapter 66 inclusive, there will be question of the recruitment and of the good order of the community. It is the recruitment which is first given special attention.

Noviter veniens quis ad conversionem ... The candidate to the religious life is presented as a candidate for "conversion." According to recent critics,[1] *conversationem* would have to be read here, with the meaning of "religious life." But, as Dom Delatte observes, the word *conversio* "accorded with the ecclesiastical language of the time," and the expression "is very felicitous."[2] Let us add this observation, which seems important. In Chapter 63, speaking of the conventual order, St. Benedict declares that the monks are to take their places *ut convertuntur.* But *convertuntur* supposes *conversio* and not *conversatio.* Is there really cause to change *conversio* continually into *conversatio*? To be converted is to turn oneself away from the world in order to embrace a new life, turned wholly towards God; and in that sense the entrance into the monastery is indeed a conversion.

The one who presents himself to be converted must be "tested." Who knows whether his move really comes from God; whether it was not prompted by some illusion which will be quickly dissipated, or by some boldness which will have no tomorrow? It must be found out, therefore, whether the candidate has really been guided by the desire, or better the formal will, to give himself to God. And so he will be tested.

At St. Benedict's era, when many characters were still uncouth and gross, because of the mixture of the barbarians in the Roman population, and when also the faith was profound, the trials were really hard. The new arrival will be received without amenity. He will be left at the gate of the monastery; and if that is half opened, it will be to make him hear disagreeable things. This cooling reception will suffice to deflate superficial enthusiasms and to dissipate illusions.

The porter had to have a certain experience in order to vary the tests. These may last four or five days. Certain Fathers of the East used to go further. But if St. Benedict does not want to attract the newcomer by caresses and kindnesses which might be deceptive, still he is careful not to exasperate his good will. And if he holds out, if he persists in his request, the door will be opened to him and he will be brought into the guests' "cell."

We are not told what took place in that cell. Probably the postulant was employed at some labors, as were certain guests. Perhaps he lent his cooperation to the guest master. That permitted a more leisurely

---

[1] Dom Cuthbert Butler, *Sancti Benedicti Regula Monasteriorum*, pp. 149-151.

[2] *Commentary*, p. 367.

examination of him. Without specifying further, St. Benedict tells us that he remained there "a few days."

This brief period having elapsed, he is put into the "cell of the novices." For them there was a special quarter, therefore, where they could "meditate, take their meals and sleep." In other words, the novitiate had its refectory, its dormitory and no doubt also a common room where the novices gathered to study (that is the meaning of *meditetur*) and to receive the teaching of supernatural doctrine. For the Divine Office the novices evidently joined with the community.

St. Benedict tells us concerning the new entrants: "Let a senior be assigned to them who is skilled in winning souls, and let him examine them with the greatest attention." The obvious sense of the text[3] certainly seems to be that there will be a senior for each novice, although it does not exclude the hypothesis of two or three novices entrusted to the same senior.[4] We have not, consequently, a novice master properly speaking. That was in conformity with the tradition of the solitaries and of a certain number of monasteries of the East. But does that not also presuppose that the novices were frequently mingled with the community in such a way that they could be under the eyes of their guides? Or indeed must it be admitted that a group of seniors eminently fitted for forming the young dwelt constantly in the novitiate? Or must it rather be assumed that at certain hours the novices would go to find the senior in charge of them, to receive his teaching? Dom Delatte prefers to admit that there was in reality a novice master, and that St. Benedict's way of expressing himself is only a process of explanation. But does it not seem likely that if there was but one senior for all the novices St. Benedict would have written, not "let a senior be assigned to the novice," but "let the novice be sent to the senior"? The assignment of all the novices to a single senior would raise difficulties of the first order.

Our holy Father does not speak of taking the habit. This, indeed, was not done before the monk made his profession. But since the form of the

---

[3] Translator's note: The commentary throughout this paragraph is based on the received text, which has "him" (*ei* and *eum*), although the commentator's own translation at the beginning of the paragraph conforms rather to the reading accepted by Dom Benno Linderbauer and Dom Cuthbert Butler, namely *eis* and *eos*.

[4] Dom Benedict van Haeften, *Disquisitionum Monasticarum Libri XII*; and Dom L'Huillier, Explication *Ascétique et Historique*, Tome 2, p. 204.

secular clothes was not very different from that of the monastic clothes, the novices' habit was probably close enough to that of the monks. Nor was there any postulant period properly speaking.

The senior in charge of one or more novices had to have particular aptitudes: a great knowledge of souls and a certain perspicacity for discerning spirits. He needed also a zeal enlightened by faith, to instruct them, form them and win them to God. He will examine, therefore, "with the greatest attention" whether his novice "is truly seeking God." To seek God and not to seek oneself, to go towards God, to find Him and to seek Him still in order to find Him always more—such is the Christian life, of which the religious life is the whole perfection. The sincerity of this search for God will show itself under three aspects: zeal for the Divine Office, zeal for obedience, zeal for opprobriums.

The zeal for the Divine Office goes without saying, since that Office is the work *par excellence* of the monk, and since a good part of his life will be employed in it.

No one would conceive of a monk without zeal for obedience, since each one of his actions is to be done under the aegis of obedience.

The zeal for opprobriums is love of humiliations. Let us recall the place of humility in Benedictine spirituality. Obedience itself is but a degree of humility. Obedience and humility, those two virtues necessarily contain a notable share of renouncement and of sufferings. One will not fail, certainly, to show the novice the attractive sides of obedience and humility, but it will be useful and even indispensable to prepare him for the unpleasant things they offer. He will be made to know "all the hardships and trials through which one goes to God." This first teaching, therefore, continues the trials of the beginning under another form. Its purpose is not to discourage from the religious life the soul which seeks God, but to prepare it for the crosses it will have to carry all its life and to make it love them.

This first phase of the formation will last two months and will conclude, if the novice "promises to persevere in his stability," with a reading through of the Holy Rule, after which he will be told: "There is the law under which you want to do battle; if you can observe it, enter; but if you cannot, depart freely."

Then the formation will continue, with its teachings and its tests. At the end of six more months there will be a new reading of the Holy Rule.

Finally a last trial of four months, concluded by a third reading, will put an end to the novitiate. The latter will have lasted twelve months.

The nature of the novitiate as conceived by St. Benedict shows that our holy Father did not have numbers in view, but quality. He wants in so far as possible to have proven disciples, souls truly courageous in the search for God. The asperities of the welcome to begin with, then the commentary on the dura et aspera which will have to be encountered on the way, then the summons, "If you cannot, go away freely," eliminate little by little the souls too lazy or insufficiently suited to the monastery's life of obedience and humility.

The point is that there is question of a perpetual engagement in the service of God. The novice who persists at the third summons must know that, starting from the day of his profession, "it is no longer lawful for him to depart from the monastery." He no longer belongs to himself, he is the Lord's. That is the law of stability.

APPLICATION

This chapter is easily applied to Oblates. The Oblate, like the monk, is a convert. He has felt that God was calling him to a more perfect life, as nearly as possible approaching monastic perfection, and that in consequence he must break with the more slothful life he had led thus far. He then turned toward the monastery.

The monastery's greeting nowadays is not so formidable for the candidate to the monastic life or to the Oblature as it may have been in the sixth century. Nevertheless, we may be sure that even for the Oblature the monastic Superiors do not look to numbers and do not accept at first glance whoever presents himself. The Oblature, indeed, is not a league, a propaganda society or a protective association designed to bear weight by gathering many adherents; it is the individual adoption, made by a monastic family under certain conditions, of a Christian desirous of perfection, who will receive a participation in the spiritual goods of the monastery, of which in return he is "to promote, as far as lies in his power, the good,"[5]

The Oblates, therefore, will not necessarily be more than a relatively restricted number. Indeed, the monastery can admit to affiliation only the candidate whom it knows well, and whose life cannot do harm to the Benedictine name. That is what we are given to understand by this

---

[5] "Statutes of the Oblates," in *Manual for Oblates*, pp. 39-40, §1.

passage of the Statutes: "As it is the duty of Oblates to strive with perseverance to lead a more holy life, only those should be admitted to their number who are commendable for their good morals and good name. Moreover, no one under the age of 15 shall be accepted as an Oblate Novice."[6] Nowadays the entry into the religious life begins with the "postulantship." The postulantship is a creation of the Maurists, following the edict of March, 1768, forbidding religious profession before 21 years of age; it thus allowed acceptance of the candidates sooner. It lasted a year, and the postulants were not put in with the novices.

Today the postulantship is not obligatory for the choir monks, but it ordinarily takes place. The postulants wear the scapular, but they are put in with the novices. On becoming novices they will receive the cowl without sleeves which distinguishes the latter from the professed monks.[7]

For the Oblates there is a sort of discretionary postulantship, which may last three months: "About three months after the first application, or even at once if the perseverance of the candidates can be relied upon, they may receive the medal and the small black scapular of St. Benedict, the latter, from this time on, always to be worn under the ordinary garments."[8]

The Oblate Novice will be entrusted to a religious chosen by the Abbot, the director of the Oblates, who, from near or far, will guide him in his new life, will explain to him the nature of Benedictine spirituality, will indicate to him how to make the Holy Rule enter into his life. For the novice, as soon as he has put on the habit, will have to strive to penetrate that Rule so that it becomes a part of him, and to extract the wealth of spirituality contained in each one of its pages.

That is why on the day of his profession the following injunction will be laid on him, in almost the very terms indicated by St. Benedict: "Son, you have already sufficiently learned the Rule under which you wish to serve, not only by reading but also by a whole year of practice and experience as an Oblate Novice. You are, therefore, aware, under what conditions you are about to be accepted as an Oblate of St. Benedict. If, then, you are ready and willing to observe the salutary teachings of our

---

[6] *Ibid.*, pp. 40-41, §§4, 5. In the French Congregation the minimum age is 17.

[7] The above paragraph applies to the French Congregation. Some other Congregations follow a different procedure.

[8] "Statutes of the Oblates," in *Manual for Oblates*, p. 41, §6,

holy Father Benedict, according as your state in life permits, and are resolved to persevere in your holy resolution, you may now make your final Oblation; if not, then you may still freely depart."[9] During the novitiate, which will last one year, it is important to consider well what we want. We have come to ask St. Benedict to help us seek God. In fact, people must be able to say of us: *Vere Deum quaerit.* In order to seek God we must first of all "renounce the pomps and vanities of the world, being mindful of the words of Our Savior: 'You are not of the world.' "[10] Hence we must strive, following the Apostle's advice,[11] to have "our conversation ... in heaven."[12]

The concern here is not with an enthusiasm which will have no tomorrow, with a fit of devotion, with an urge of romantic sentimentality; the concern is with an engagement, a total gift without any taking back. We have to examine, therefore, the conditions of life which will be asked of us.

Do we love the Divine Office? For children of St. Benedict, it is the highest expression of the divine praise, the source and the food of the interior life.

Do we love obedience? It is through obedience that the gift of ourselves to God is realized, together with the renouncement of all that is not God.

Finally, do we love humility?

To seek God is to seek Jesus Christ, and Jesus Christ crucified. We shall have to renounce, therefore, certain habits, certain satisfactions, certain pleasures even though they be legitimate. We shall have to lead a more retired life. We shall have to accept on the part of those who do not understand us accusations, mockeries, perhaps persecutions. We shall have to undergo with love our trials, little or great. We shall have to subject ourselves to an austere Rule, according to our circumstances, faithfully, in a spirit of obedience, not only for a year or two, the time in which a "novice fervor" wears itself out, but always; not only in the joy and the transport of the soul, but in its dryness and fatigue. No one can find God here below without finding the Cross. We must look squarely in

---

[9] *Manual for Oblates,* pp. 234-235.

[10] "Statutes of the Oblates," in *Manual for Oblates,* p. 43, §12; cf. *John* 15:19.

[11] *Philippians* 3:20.

[12] "Statutes of the Oblates," in *Manual for Oblates,* p. 43, §12.

the face "the hardships and asperities through which we go to God."

Obviously, the idea is not to frighten ourselves, to cast ourselves into despair, but to consider what is asked of us by the God of love who wants us more perfect. To accept perfection is evidently to accept in advance some purifying crosses which we cannot foresee and which God alone knows, but it is to accept them while saying with the Apostle, "I can do all things in Him who strengthens me."

Note on the "conversio morum."—Dom Cuthbert Butler, who was perhaps the most competent scholar of our times in the critical study of the Holy Rule, considered himself obliged, in virtue of the textual critique itself, to suppress uniformly in the text the word *conversio*, "conversion," replacing it by *conversatio*, which signifies "manner of life."[13] The novice would simply be promising to "live as a monk," that is, in conformity with the Rule.

To that correction we shall object in the first place that, positively, St. Benedict always uses the word "to convert" to signify the entrance into the monastic life (cf. Chapter 2[14] and Chapter 63[15]), and that consequently there is equivalence for him between entrance into that life and conversion. Why forbid him to use the substantive, since he uses the verb?

Moreover, the ancient authors used to distinguish perfectly between *conversio* and *conversatio*, the second being the consequence of the first.[16] Why should we want St. Benedict to have known only the second, and why refuse him the use of the first? There is so much the less reason for doing so since, as Dom Delatte points out, going back to St. Augustine and to St. Caesarius, the formula *conversio morum* is in conformity with the ecclesiastical language of the time.[17]

Finally, the word *morum* after *conversatio*, as Dom Butler himself admits,[18] does not offer a very satisfactory sense, while it is quite natural

---

[13] *The Journal of Theological Studies* (Oxford: Clarendon Press), Vol. 9, October, 1907, p. 106; *Sancti Benedicti Regula Monasteriorum*, pp. 149 ff.;*Benedictine Monachism*, 2nd ed. (New York: Longmans, Green and Co., 1924), pp. 134 ff.

[14] *Non praeponatur ingenuus ex servitio convertenti.*

[15] *Reliqui omnes ut convertuntur ita sint.*

[16] Dom Ildefons Herwegen, *Geschichte der Benediktinischen Professformel*, p. 49, quoted by Dom Butler, *Benedictine Monachism*, p. 136.

[17] *Commentary*, p. 367, note 1.

[18] *Benedictine Monachism*, p. 137.

after *conversio*.

Dom Butler argues above all from the good manuscripts. But that argument is not of an absolutely probative force, since the resemblance between the two words always made possible a confusion on the part of the copyists. As the critics acknowledge, variants proposed by manuscripts which are otherwise of less value may very well represent the original reading.

Thus Dom Fernand Cabrol seems closer to the truth when he observes with regard to the expression "conversion of character" that St. Benedict "gives considerable importance" to these words, that they signify "a changing of life" and "the taking of a new direction," a meaning no longer found in the commonplace *conversatio*.[19]

April 12—August 12—December 12

He who is to be received shall make a promise before all in the oratory of his stability and of the reformation of his life and of obedience. This promise he shall make before God and His Saints, so that if he should ever act otherwise, he may know that he will be condemned by Him whom he mocks. Of this promise of his let him draw up a petition in the name of the Saints whose relics are there and of the Abbot who is present. Let him write this petition with his own hand; or, if he is illiterate, let another write it at his request, and let the novice put his mark to it. Then let him place it with his own hand upon the altar; and when he has placed it there, let the novice at once intone this verse: "Uphold me, O Lord, according to Your word, and I shall live: and let me not be confounded in my hope." Let the whole community answer this verse three times and add the "Glory be to the Father." Then let the novice brother prostrate himself at each one's feet, that they may pray for him. And from that day forward let him be counted as one of the community.

If he has any property, let him either give it beforehand to the poor or by solemn donation bestow it on the monastery, reserving nothing at all for himself, as indeed he knows that from that day forward he will no longer have power even over his own body. At once, therefore, in the oratory, let him be divested of his own clothes which he is wearing and dressed in the clothes of the monastery. But let the clothes of which

---

[19]   Dom Fernand Cabrol, Saint Benedict, p. 66. It is worthy of note that St. Gregory, who knew the Rule, used the word conversus in the "Life of St. Benedict" to indicate one who has entered the monastery. Cf. Dialogs, Book 2, Chapters 17, 18; in P.L., Tome 66, cols. 168, 170.

he was divested be put aside in the wardrobe and kept there. Then if he should ever listen to the persuasions of the devil and decide to leave the monastery (which God forbid), he may be divested of the monastic clothes and cast out. His petition, however, which the Abbot has taken from the altar, shall not be returned to him, but shall be kept in the monastery.

COMMENTARY

The novitiate has now ended. The novice is going to become professed. The engagement which he is going to undertake and which is going to introduce him completely into the monastic life will bear on three points: stability, conversion of morals, obedience.

We have already spoken of stability in the commentary on the first chapter. We have seen how St. Benedict combats gyrovagy through stability, and establishes his disciple in an environment and a Rule in which there will no longer be any play for his caprices and illusions. Without stability, nothing lasts; the work of sanctification is compromised.

Obedience is no less important; it is through obedience that perfect renouncement is realized, a renouncement which detaches the man from his own will in order to attach him to Jesus alone.

The conversion of morals is the religious life as a whole, the life of a soul which unceasingly turns away from the world in order to remain turned towards God. In fact the words *conversio morum* imply stability and obedience; and if our holy Father has wished to mention these latter specially, that is because of the capital importance he attributes to these two aspects of perfection.

St. Benedict has not indicated poverty and chastity by name. They also are contained in the *conversio morum.* How could a Christian be "converted" to God if he were still attached to the flesh and to the goods of this world? And since the present concern was with an engagement in the monastic life, the ideas of chastity and poverty, inseparable from that of the conversion of morals, drew from the circumstances a meaning quite precise indeed, which made any definition unnecessary. The Rule under which the new monk vowed the conversion of his morals implied, in reality, absolute chastity and poverty.

We have seen that Dom Cuthbert Butler relentlessly corrects the word *conversio* into *conversatio* wherever he meets with it. He has not failed to so do in this place, and the Farnborough translators render the passage thus: "The one who is to be received... binds himself... in the matter of his stability and of his *manner of living* and of obedience." At bottom the idea is the same, for the concern can be only with a virtuous manner of living. "The professed one cannot bind himself to anything but to live well, to maintain an exemplary conduct."[20] But the formula is much more vague than the one which has become traditional. And is the correction really justified?

The text of the promise will be drawn up on a paper called *petitio*, that is, request. On this paper will be indicated the names of the Saints whose relics are found in the oratory, as well as the name of the Abbot. If the monk is literate, he himself will write out the formula on the parchment; if he is unlettered, another will do it on his behalf. The text of the Holy Rule would seem to indicate that the paper was drawn up during the ceremony of profession itself. It is more probable, however, that it was written in advance and that nothing more remained but to sign it.

St. Benedict indicates only the outlines of the ceremony of profession. This takes place in the oratory, where the relics are exposed. The next chapter gives us to understand that the altar is covered with a cloth, something which was done only at Mass. The whole community has gathered together. The one to be received "pledges himself before all," that is to say, most likely, reads aloud the formula of his petitio. He then puts his name to it; the unlettered one will content himself with a mark. Then he himself lays it on the altar. Then begins the chant of the *Suscipe*: "Uphold me, O Lord, according to Thy word, and I shall live: and let me not be confounded in my hope." He chants it three times, and each time the choir repeats the chant. To the third repetition it adds the *Gloria Patri*. Finally, the new monk "prostrates himself before each one's feet, asking him to pray for him."

The first part of the ceremony is completed; the novice is incorporated; he is now going to take the monastic habit. It will be remembered that at St. Benedict's time and even long after, the novices kept the lay attire. The abandonment of their personal effects marks the rupture of the last tie with the world. It is the conclusion, the achievement of another rupture which has been decided in the preceding days, from the tie of property.

The monk must possess nothing. If he had goods, he had to abandon them completely, without the least reservation. He has given them to the

---

[20] *La Régle de S. Benoît*, p. 139.

poor, or else, by means of a formal deed, he has bestowed them upon the monastery. In that case the deed is probably laid on the altar also, since that often used to be done, as Dom Martène points out, in donations to monasteries. The word *solemniter* indicates, moreover, that the donation was effected formally and that it was read in the presence of witnesses.[21]

The new monk no longer has anything. He no longer has even "power over his own body"; that is to say, notes Dom Butler, that he is bound "to the observance of chastity."[22] Then he is stripped of all his effects and clothed with those of the monastery. The garments taken off are deposited in the clothes-room. They would be given back to him if, "by the devil's persuasion, he consented to leave." His monastic clothes would then be taken away from him and he would be cast out as an unworthy one, for he has not the right to break his promises. To be unfaithful to them is to mock God.

At the end of the ceremony the Abbot took the document of profession from the altar, and it was to remain in the Abbey's archives. Even in case the unfaithful monk should quit his monastery, it would not be given back to him; it would stay there, in witness of his perjury.

APPLICATION

After one year of novitiate the Oblate, like the monk, is called to make profession—that is, if the Superiors deem it fitting. This profession or Oblation, say the Statutes, "is a rite approved by the Church, by which anyone of the faithful living in the world, having been moved by a desire for greater perfection and by a special devotion to the Patriarch of Monks and to his Order, offers himself to God, to Our Savior, to the Blessed Virgin Mary, and to our holy Father Benedict. By this act, he spiritually affiliates himself with a Benedictine monastery and its community, in order thereby to lead a more perfect Christian life in the world according to the spirit of the Rule of St. Benedict; to share likewise in the spiritual treasures of the Benedictine Order and enjoy the special privileges granted by the Church to Oblates; and to promote, as far as lies in his power, the good of the monastery to which he is attached, and of the entire Benedictine Order."

"This Oblation," the Statutes add, "is not a vow, nor is it irrevocable,

---

[21] *Traduction et Explication Littérale*, p. 429.

[22] *Benedictine Manachism*, p. 39.

but as it is a deliberate resolve of the will made before God and man and confirmed by a sacred rite, it is worthy of high respect."[23]

Consequently, we may very well say of the profession of Oblature what Dom Delatte says of the monastic profession:[24] "It is pre-eminently a contract, a bilateral contract, between the novice on the one side, and God and the brethren on the other: I give myself wholly and forever to God and to the monastic Order, that God and the monastic Order may admit me to communion with them, may put me in possession of their life. It is adoption into God s family. . .

The ceremony of the profession of Oblates follows in outline the indications of the Holy Rule. Its prayers are borrowed from the ceremonial of the monastic professions. It takes place ordinarily in the church, and is presided over by the Abbot or a delegate of the Abbot. The Oblate Novice, standing before the altar, reads his formula of Oblation, then signs it with a cross and his name. He then hands it to the celebrant, who wraps it in the altar cloth. After which, kneeling with hands folded, he recites the *Suscipe*, but he says it only once.

The formula of monastic profession expresses, as we have seen, a threefold promise: stability, conversion of morals, obedience. In the formula of Oblation we read only: *Promitto ... conversionem morum meomm ad mentem Regulae ejusdem sanctissimi Patris Benedicti ...*"I do promise. . .the reformation of my life according to the spirit of the Rule of the same most holy Father Benedict...."[25] Of course, no one will imagine that it was desired to dispense the Oblates from stability and from obedience. We have explained above (Chapters 1 and 5) in what stability and obedience consist for the Oblates. But since that stability and that obedience find themselves included in the "conversion of morals" or "reformation of life," and are understood in an acceptation less precise than for the monks, it was not deemed necessary to express them.

The "conversion of morals," as we have already said, is the seeking after perfection, the seeking after God. That seeking has for its point of departure an engagement; it is the profession; we shall do battle under a Rule. And the whole of our activity, of our "morals," will tend toward a single goal: God. *Aversio a creaturis, conversio ad Deum.*

---

[23] *Manual for Oblates*, pp. 39-40, §§1, 2.

[24] *Commentary*, p. 396.

[25] *Manual for Oblates*, p. 238.

Dom Paul Chauvin in his conferences on *The Oblature in the Order of St. Benedict*[26] has written, in a chapter devoted to the conversion of morals, that "the monastic life and, by derivation, the Oblate life, is the total envelopment of the being by mortification." The one who tends to perfection, indeed, renounces all that is not God; all of that is to be dead for him; at least, he must strive to make it so. He mortifies the flesh, the love of pleasures, the love of riches, the love of honors, the attachment to his own will—that the Lord Jesus may be the sole Master in him. Is not that, moreover, what Our Savior has demanded of us: "Let him who will be My disciple carry his cross and follow Me"? St. Benedict wanted only to implement the Gospel; and by following in the footsteps of the holy Patriarch we are but following Christ with him, carrying our cross.

The religious profession has often been compared with the profession of Baptism. In fact, we may say that our Oblation is a pledge to live in conformity with our character as baptized persons and in the logic of our Baptism. Now the logic of our Baptism is the *conversion* of our morals towards God, it is perfection, it is sanctity.

There, then, is what we have pledged ourselves to. We could, no doubt, be tempted to say in moments of laxity: "That Oblation is not a vow.... Our Rule does not bind us either in its letter or in its spirit under pain of sin." The fact remains that on the day when we promised, we vowed ourselves to perfection, relying on efficacious means, approved by Holy Church. The day that we turn away wilfully from those means, it is certain that we cease to advance, that we are more lukewarm, that we withdraw somewhat from God. And the condition of our soul may be serious. Let us remember the words of St. Bernard: "In the way of perfection, he who does not advance, goes back." And to disclaim what we have promised is not only to stop advancing, it is positively to go back.

The beautiful prayer *Suscipe* which the Church puts upon the lips of the Oblate as upon those of the monk is, as Huysmans said, "the 'Open, Sesame!' of the monastic life." It can be made the object of profitable meditations. A pious Maurist, Dom François de Lamy, once devoted a whole dissertation to commenting on it.[27] "Our holy Father, who knew the

---

[26] *L'Oblature dans l'Ordre de S. Benoît*, p. 48.

[27] *Sentiments de Piété sur la Profession Religieuse Applicables à la Profession des Chrétiens dans le Baptême* (Paris: Pierre de Bats, 1697), 230 pp.

Psalter thoroughly," says Dom Delatte,[28] "found no more appropriate formula than this simple verse of the hundred and eighteenth Psalm. The novice is standing, in the presence of God. ... And the general sense of his prayer ... is undoubtedly that of a supreme affirmation of his sacrifice, but above all of a humble and trustful appeal for its acceptance. Having done all that is in his power, the novice begs God to fulfil on His side the engagements entailed in the contract. God has engaged to receive and accept; He has given His word; His fidelity is pledged. The novice is sure that God will not fail him.... He begs Him to let it be even so and to deign to accept him as His son. If we are unfaithful, the contract is violated and without fruit; God is mocked and we are disappointed and frustrated. Therefore, it is really against his own frailty that the novice wishes to fortify himself: *Suscipe me, Domine* ... Grant that I may be really 'given' and really 'received,' truly received because truly given, and that both of us may be able to keep our word. Both my gift and Yours rest wholly in Your blessed hands."

By our Oblation, indeed, we give ourselves to God, we give Him the whole nothing that we are. *Suscipe me Domine* ... We give ourselves to Him with complete confidence ... *non confundas me*. For He has made promises to us ... *secundum eloquium tuum*. In return He will give us His life, *et vivam*; His life, that is to say His grace, that is to say finally Himself living in us. May we never recant, never take ourselves back. We should then lose all, we should lose ourselves and we should lose the Infinite; we should lose God.

---

[28] *Commentary*, p. 398.

CHAPTER 59
On the Sons of Nobles and of the Poor Who Are Offered

April 13—August 13—December 13

 F ANYONE of the nobility offers his son to God in the monastery and the boy is very young, let his parents draw up the petition which we mentioned above; and at the oblation let them wrap the petition and the boy's hand in the altar cloth and so offer him.

As regards their property, they shall promise in the same petition under oath that they will never of themselves, or through an intermediary, or in any way whatever, give him anything or provide him with the opportunity of owning anything. Or else, if they are unwilling to do this, and if they want to offer something as an alms to the monastery for their advantage, let them make a donation of the property they wish to give to the monastery, reserving the income to themselves if they wish. And in this way let everything be barred, so that the boy may have no expectations whereby (which God forbid) he might be deceived and ruined, as we have learned by experience.

Let those who are less well-to-do make a similar offering. But those who have nothing at all shall simply draw up the petition and offer their son before witnesses at the oblation.

COMMENTARY

There has already been question several times of the presence of boys in the monastery. Chapter 59 is going to inform us on what conditions they are there. For a good understanding of this chapter we have to go back to the customs of the sixth century. "To appreciate the customs of antiquity," says Dom Delatte, "we need the antique soul; to appreciate Christian practice we need the Christian soul."[1] The Oblature is an act of the paternal power.[2] Among the Romans the *patria potestas* is absolute. The father, therefore, may pledge the future of his children in their own interest. But, notes Dom Calmet, "what is wrong with destining them for a profession where not only do they run no risk, but where they have infinitely more opportunities to work out their salvation than in any other

---

[1] *Commentary*, p. 411.

[2] Abbé Deroux, Les Origines de l'Oblature Bénédictine, p. 3. 435.

condition?"

But here the juridical action has a religious character. It is to God that the father gives his child; he gives him irrevocably. When the boy reaches adult age, it will not be for him to confirm or to break the bond contracted by the paternal will between himself and the monastery; his Oblation is a true profession.

To specify fully the conditions of that Oblation, St. Benedict will distinguish between the noble child and the poor child, not that before God and before the Rule the one is more than the other, but because, the one having goods and the other having nothing, certain precautions are to be taken with regard to the first in order to avoid temptations in the future to the "vice of property."

There is no age limit for the admission of a boy to the monastery. He may be "very young"; he may be somewhat bigger, like the little Placidus, or adolescent like the young Maurus. If he can write, he makes his petitio, like the monk; if he is too small, it is made by his parents.

This petitio is nothing else than a document of profession; that is why St. Benedict refers us back to the preceding chapter for its contents. It implies, therefore, the vows of stability, conversion of morals and obedience. This document the parents "wrap up, together with the boy's hand and the oblation, in the altar cloth." The oblation in question is most likely the bread and wine of the sacrifice, something which proves indeed that the profession took place at the Mass, probably at the time of the Offertory. The Abbé Deroux thinks that the *palla* of which St. Benedict speaks is not the altar cloth but rather the *mappula*, the corporal which served "to envelop the chalice and the paten containing the oblations destined for the altar."[3]

We have seen that at the time of the monk's profession he had to settle the question of his goods. The same has to be done for the little Oblate. To be sure, he possesses nothing, but his parents are rich or well-to-do; he must not some day be able to declare himself heir. The parents, therefore, must promise by an oath 'To give him nothing, either of themselves, or through an intermediary, or in any way whatever.' Every occasion of possessing must be avoided for him. No doubt this pledge also was the occasion of an act which was read at the ceremony, unless it figured in the document of Oblation.

---

[3] *Ibid.*, pp. 15-16.

St. Benedict is particularly anxious about this oath. He wants to avoid untoward incidents, of which he has already seen the sad consequences—*quod experimento didicimus*. When the boy grows up he must know that there is no longer any access to property possible to him, and consequently he must have no temptation from that quarter.

Still, there is a generous deed the rich parents can perform : to institute a donation in favor of the monastery which takes charge of their boy. That donation may be in money, it may be in real estate; and in the latter case the parents may reserve the income to themselves, if they deem fit. But from these goods the boys is to draw no special advantage. They will not be his, but the community's.

St. Benedict does not speak of the taking of the habit. But most likely it took place in the same ceremony. The boy was "given"; he had no need of a novitiate to examine his vocation. He was a little monk, entered there and then into the monastic life. We have seen more than once how the fatherly St. Benedict enjoins the taking account of the weakness of his age.

For the little poor boy whose parents possess nothing at all, there is no need of all those formalities. It suffices concerning the document of Oblation that the parents lay it on the altar, as above, in the presence of witnesses.

APPLICATION

In commenting on this passage of the Holy Rule, Dom Delatte makes this observation:[4] "With this chapter may be connected the question of 'adult Oblates'; internal Oblates, who give themselves to the monastery in order to live there the life of the monks and under a Rule, with or without a religious habit; external Oblates, who are, so to speak, the fringe of the monastic garment. Properly speaking, such Oblates do not form a Third Order; they belong, as do the monks, to the monastery of their profession."

What historical relation is there between the adult Oblates and the little Oblates of the Holy Rule? Is it a relation only of name? Or indeed has there been an evolution?

The origin of the adult Oblates is rather complex.

We have already spoken, *à propos* of the artisans, of those "familiars"

---

[4] Commentary, p. 412, note 2.

of the monastery who might well be the ancestors of the present Oblates.

The Abbé Deroux, who has devoted an important work to the question, believes that since the Church, with the development of ecclesiastical law, took away from the children's Oblation its value of formal pledge, the little Oblates when they arrive at the age of reason were permitted to confirm their profession freely. Some did so and remained monks; others reentered the world without contracting any bond with the monastery. But others again, "although not feeling a vocation, yet fearing the dangers of a worldly life for which their monastic education had scarcely prepared them, asked to remain as lay persons in the monastery, to live under the protection and under the direction of the Abbot, and thus swelled the number of the *famuli*."[5]

So it is that, under the influence of circumstances, here and there, and with divergencies according to the places, are constituted within the monasteries and around them, or in their spiritual environment, categories of Christians desirous of participating in the monastic life without taking a place either among the *chori* or among the *conversi*. The Oblates of today may claim them as their ancestors.

---

[5] Abbé Deroux, *Les Origines de L'Oblature Bénédictine*, p.89.

CHAPTER 60

On Priests Who May Wish to Live in the Monastery

F ANYONE of the priestly order should ask to be received into the monastery, permission shall not be granted him too readily. But if he is quite persistent in his request, let him know that he will have to observe the whole discipline of the Rule and that nothing will be relaxed in his favor, that it may be as it is written: "Friend, for what have you come?" (*Matthew* 26:50).

It shall be granted him, however, to stand next after the Abbot and to give blessings and to celebrate Mass, but only by order of the Abbot. Without such order let him not presume to do anything, knowing that he is subject to the discipline of the Rule; but rather let him give an example of humility to all.

If there happens to be question of an appointment or of some business in the monastery, let him expect the rank due him according to the date of his entrance into the monastery, and not the place granted him out of reverence for the priesthood.

If any clerics, moved by the same desire, should wish to join the monastery, let them be placed in a middle rank. But they too are to be admitted only if they promise observance of the Rule and their own stability.

COMMENTARY

Almost all the monks were laymen at the time of their entrance into the monastery. Nevertheless, it could happen that priests or clerics desirous of a greater perfection would ask admission. The priest is obliged by vocation to work at his personal sanctification. The Pontifical has reminded him of it: *Imitamini quod tradatis.* But the monastic profession, by establishing him in the organized perfect life, will be a powerful aid to him in that work. What procedure is to be followed with regard to a candidate coming from the priesthood?

St. Benedict does not refuse him. Because of the dignity with which the priest is clothed, it does not appear, though Dom Mège has supposed the contrary, that the holy Father subjects him, like the layman, "to insults and vexations," but he shows himself not too impressed; he subjects him to a more or less protracted period of waiting. For it is to be feared that this monk, clothed with the priesthood, in the midst of plain laymen, may consider himself superior to the rest. Perhaps he has been in a position which gave him the habit of commanding. Perhaps he arrives with more or less systematic ideas. There may be a danger there both for him and for the monastery.

St. Benedict puts a condition to his entrance, therefore: "Let him know that he will have to observe the full discipline of the Rule and that in nothing will it be relaxed for him." He will not have any prerogative or exception to count on, therefore, except by notice from the Abbot. And if he is tempted by any demon of vanity, he is to repeat the Gospel question: My friend, why have you come? Is it not to be a monk and nothing more?

Those wise precautions do not prevent our holy Father from thinking of rendering to the dignity of the priesthood the honor due to it. The Abbot will find in his spirit of faith the means of reconciling that honor with the integrity of the monastic life. St. Benedict suggests some ways. Instead of his rank according to conversion, he may be granted a place after the Abbot's. He may likewise be invited to give the regular blessings in the course of the Office and in the refectory.

Finally he may, says the text, *missam tenere*. The formula has brought forth varied commentaries. For some, such as Dom Claude de Vert, Dom L'Huillier and perhaps Dom Calmet, who is not very clear, the *missa* is the collect with which each Hour concludes. For the greater number, with Dom Mabillon, Dom Guéranger, Dom Delatte, it is the Mass. We know that the Low Mass did not exist at that time, and that there was High Mass only on Sundays and feast days. If there happened to be several priests in the monastery, and notably monks ordained at the Abbot's request, our priest who came last would not necessarily be called upon to celebrate Mass.

Whatever the case may be, the priest become monk has nothing to demand. On the contrary, he ought to give "examples of humility" to all.

Likewise, if an important office in the monastery comes to be vacant, and there is question of constituting someone in charge, let him not use the weight of his priestly character or even only the superior rank which has been conceded him. His true place, the one to which he has a right, is not that which he occupies, but rather that which he would have occupied if account had been taken only of the date of his profession.

What is said of the priest applies equally to the lower clerics. The Abbot may accord them a middle place, below that of the priests, somewhat above that of their entrance. But with the same conditions they are to pledge observance of the Rule and promise their stability.

APPLICATION

What our holy Father says of the priest monk can be applied likewise to the priest Oblate. In his admirable notes on "Le Prêtre et l'Ordre de Saint-Benoît," Dom Guéranger gave the priest Oblate the following advice: "He will keep himself on guard against a certain self-sufficiency which may easily arise when the distinction is not made clearly enough between what is due to the station in life and what is due to the man; a disposition contrary to humility which St. Benedict with his prudent experience had already observed and to which he opposes this forceful sentence addressed to the priests who gave themselves to him: *Magis humilitatis exempla omnibus det.*"

Those of us who are priests find in this chapter, indeed, our true program and, we might say, our chief prerogative as Oblates: to give to our brethren in Oblature and to others the example of a more entire practice of our Rule and of a more intimate assimilation of its spirit.

We are invited, therefore, to ask ourselves from time to time why we are Oblates. *Amice, ad quid venisti?* It is surely not to draw a sort of vanity from it and to think ourselves above others; it is much rather to take long steps in humility. And if some prerogative is granted us without our having sought it, then, remarks Dom Delatte, "we should put ourselves, before God, back into the place that is ours of right and which we know well: the last place, the place of nothingness."[6]

---

[6] *Commentary*, p. 417.

CHAPTER 61

How Pilgrim Monks Are to Be Received

April 15—August 15—December 15

F A PILGRIM MONK coming from a distant region wants to live as a guest of the monastery, let him be received for as long a time as he desires, provided he is content with the customs of the place as he finds them and does not disturb the monastery by superfluous demands, but is simply content with what he finds. If, however, he censures or points out anything reasonably and with the humility of charity, let the Abbot consider prudently whether perhaps it was for that very purpose that the Lord sent him.

If afterwards he should want to bind himself to stability, his wish should not be denied him, especially since there has been opportunity during his stay as a guest to discover his character.

COMMENTARY

At the age in which St. Benedict was writing his Rule, the monastic Order had not the unity it later had. The Rules changed with the monasteries, being usually nothing but the Abbot's will. There were at the most customs, general and traditional observances, which the Abbot would adapt to his particular conceptions.

There was no stability, either; and we may observe, with Dom Butler,[1] that St. Benedict, although imposing stability in his own Rule, does not censure even by implication the stranger monk who has left his monastery. The monk who was not finding in the direction of his Abbot the ideal of which he had dreamed, could go to try the experience with another. He could also, with the blessing of his Superior, undertake pious journeys, distant pilgrimages to the famous holy places or the great monastic centers. All of that was nothing abnormal, quite the contrary. In the Patriarch's time, continues Dom Butler, stability was "a Benedictine specialty."

Now it might happen that of those monks on a journey should present himself at the monastery. He would be fraternally received. He would mingle in the community's life, share its exercises and its labors. It would quickly be perceived whether the new guest was a holy man or not. There

---

[1] *Benedictine Monachism,* p. 125.

would be plenty of leisure to observe him. If he not only did not show an overly demanding nature nor cause any trouble, but, quite to the contrary, contented himself in all simplicity with the local custom, he would then be kept "as long as he desired."

Moreover, the one who had come to be edified might himself be a source of edification. He might have a long experience of the monastic life. And who knows whether it was not Providence that had sent him?

This holy monk would find himself led to make comparisons, and sometimes even to venture, with all the discretion desired, useful observations, if not remonstrances. Far from imitating the trouble-maker or the conceited person, he would not share his impressions with every comer, but with him alone to whom it belongs to direct the monastic family, with the Abbot. And in his overture he would put neither pride nor anger, but he would express himself "with the humility of charity." What could one do better than to listen to him with the same humility, to examine his sayings "with prudence" and to profit by them if they were justified?

And since this monk would not have the spirit of gyrovagy, but would be a true religious, it might happen that he should ask for his stability. He would be well enough known now; he could be evaluated. There would be no reason for refusing such a request.

APPLICATION

"Here assuredly," writes Dom Delatte in his commentary on this chapter,[2] "is one of those passages wherein is reflected most clearly the humble and discreet spirit of our holy Father, his intellectual docility. One may be very holy and very clever, and yet have something to learn from others. Moses was certainly more elevated in grace and more gifted than Jethro; yet he received good counsel from him (*Exodus* 18:13ff.). And our souls should be all the more open to the ideas of others, the more we cease to be observant of the details of our own life. Those who come from outside, who have had other experience and do not bear our familiar yoke

---

[2] *Commentary*, p. 419.

of custom, are more apt to discern our shortcomings."

How dear is our holy Father's soul made by this humility, this prudence, this distrust in himself! How they make us admire and love him! But also what a lesson they give to us, whom he wishes indeed to look upon as his children but who are so far removed from his perfection.

We have tried to adapt our life to his teaching and to his spirit. Our attempt is necessarily imperfect. Attracted by certain aspects, we perhaps neglect others, which do not fail, however, to have their importance. It may be that we carry about with us serious imperfections which we do not suspect. And we believe ourselves faithful disciples of our Father.

It may happen, it will certainly happen that, one day or other, Providence will put in our path some priest, some religious, some fellow Oblate or even someone who is no more than one of the faithful, who, more clear-visioned than we, will point out to us charitably that imperfection, that gap in our conduct. How far from perfect it would be to resist, to treat from the height of our illusions the one who believes that he ought to warn us! Our holy Father asks a quite different attitude of us. You see that this censurer is truly humble and charitable, that he has no desire at all to mortify you, that he is motivated by good intentions. Reflect seriously on his words, for fear of rejecting a counsel from heaven, *ne forte eum propter hoc ipsum Dominus direxerit.*

This great and useful lesson is, no doubt, the only one that may now be drawn from this passage. It is evident that this chapter presupposes a different monastic setup from what we have today. "A case identical to that presented by the stranger monk coming from distant parts with the desire and the freedom to establish himself in the monastery cannot be supposed in our days," as Dom Étienne points out. "In the sixth century it was quite different." The letter has grown old, but the spirit is always practical and life- giving.

April 16—August 16—December 16

But if as a guest he was found exacting or prone to vice, not only should he be denied membership in the community, but he should even be politely requested to leave, lest others be corrupted by his evil life.

If, however, he has not proved to be the kind who deserves to be put out, he should not only on his own application be received as a member of the community, but he should even be persuaded to stay, that the others may be instructed by his example, and because in every place it is the same Lord who is served, the same King for whom the battle is fought.

Moreover, if the Abbot perceives that he is a worthy man, he may put him in a somewhat higher rank. And not only with regard to a monk but also with regard to those in priestly or clerical orders previously mentioned, the Abbot may establish them in a higher rank than would be theirs by date of entrance if he perceives that their life is deserving.

Let the Abbot take care, however, never to receive a monk from another known monastery as a member of his community without the consent of his Abbot or a letter of recommendation; for it is written, "Do not to another what you would not want done to yourself" (*Tobias* 4:16).

COMMENTARY

The traveling monk was not necessarily a model of virtue. Perhaps he was nothing but a vulgar gyrovague, "exacting" and "prone to vice," exhibiting a veritable "wretchedness" of soul, capable of perverting some of the community. "He shall be politely told to depart." Even in this expulsion St. Benedict wishes charity to be shown.

We have seen the case of the monk asking for his stability. But it could come about that he would not ask for it and yet it would appear desirable. There was nothing amiss then, quite the contrary, in leading him to take up permanent residence in the monastery, or even in proposing it to him. Will he not serve there the same Master he has served elsewhere? For, "in all places it is one Lord alone whom one serves, it is under one King alone that one does battle." Perhaps he will serve Him better, this Lord and King, since he will be edified by the fervor of his new brethren, as he himself will edify them, through his advice based on experience and through his examples.

Moreover, this individual, who is presumed to be a picked individual, the Abbot may "place in a somewhat superior rank." He is not a novice in the monastic life. Account is taken, as it had been for the priest, of the time already passed in the special service of the Lord. At that time there was but one religious "order," with manifold variants. The question of the monastery was accidental, since, save with St. Benedict, stability was unknown.

All that has been said thus far applies to monks coming from distant lands, perhaps from that East so rich in monastic life. If there is question of someone coming from a nearby monastery, the procedure is quite different. It would be a lack of tact and of charity with regard to an Abbot whom one knows, to take one of his children away from him. "We must not do to another what we do not want done to us." The consent of that Abbot or letters or recommendation will be required.

APPLICATION

This passage has given rise to considerations of a canonical order and to considerations of an ascetical order.

Certain commentators bring in here the questions of transfer from one Order to another, from one monastery to another, questions which are regulated by canon law. With respect to the various religious Orders, the canonical situation of the Benedictine Oblates is the same as that of the Tertiaries. It is set forth in Canon 705. They cannot belong to several Orders at a time, as has sometimes been seen.

Each religious Order has its own spirit, its observances, its trends. By wishing to attach himself to two or three Orders, a person would run a strong risk of having the spirit of none of them. He would not know how to be at the same time a good Benedictine, a good Jesuit and a good Franciscan. There are different dwelling places in the heavenly Father's house, but the same person cannot occupy several of them.

Canon law, however, sometimes permits passage from one Order to another; but this must be *justa de causa*, "For a just cause." These transfers ought to be as rare as possible; that is why the entrance of the future Oblate into the novitiate has generally been preceded by three months of reflection, that one may be able, as the Statutes say, "to rely on the candidate's perseverance." The novitiate itself has the purpose of assuring that perseverance.

But a second question may be put, that of the passage from one monastery to another of the same Order or of the same Congregation. To resolve the question, we must keep well in mind that the Oblate belongs not exactly to an Order, as the Tertiary, but to a particular monastery, the Benedictines forming a federation of monasteries rather than an Order properly so called. We may consider each monastic family, as we have already observed, as being made up of its Fathers, its Lay Brothers, its Regular and Secular Oblates. It is to be expected that the passage from one family to another, although it is not forbidden by canon law, cannot be effectuated so easily as that provided by Canon 705 for the passage from one fraternity of Tertiaries to another fraternity. In the other Orders there are isolated Tertiaries who are not dependent on any one house; there is nothing of that sort in the Order of St. Benedict. The motives for the passing from one monastery to another will be left to the evaluation of the father of the family, namely the Abbot, and we may be sure that those transfers are not accorded easily.

Aside from the commentary of a disciplinary order, our reading for today admits of another, of an ascetical order. If it is profitable to follow the counsels of the experienced and virtuous people whom Providence has placed in our path, with what care on the other hand must we not avoid contact with that one who (which God forbid!) even among our fellow Oblates, would prove *superfluus et vitiosus*, exacting and prone to vice. This is the lesson drawn by Dom Morel in his *Meditations* on this chapter:[3] "Consider what kind of conduct it is for us to associate with people whom we can neither frequent without danger nor imitate without losing ourselves. Let us rather turn our eyes and our heart towards the good people; let us attach ourselves to the true servants of God, and let the love of our duty be the only good which attaches us to them; let us seek in their counsels, in their examples and in their prayers the lights, the models, the helps which we need. Let us truly love our Rule and all those who love it and who practice it; let our joy be in seeing it observed and in observing it ourselves; let us rejoice in their fidelity, and let us by our fidelity be a cause of joy to them."

---

[3] *Méditations*, p. 417.

CHAPTER 62
On the Priests of the Monastery

F AN ABBOT desires to have a priest or a deacon ordained for his monastery, let him choose one of his monks who is worthy to exercise the priestly office.

But let the one who is ordained beware of self-exaltation or pride; and let him not presume to do anything except what is commanded him by the Abbot, knowing that he is so much the more subject to the discipline of the Rule. Nor should he by reason of his priesthood forget the obedience and the discipline required by the Rule, but make ever more and more progress towards God.

Let him always keep the place which he received on entering the monastery, except in his duties at the altar or in case the choice of the community and the will of the Abbot should promote him for the worthiness of his life. Yet he must understand that he is to observe the rules laid down by deans and Priors.

Should he presume to act otherwise, let him be judged not as a priest but as a rebel. And if he does not reform after repeated admonitions, let even the Bishop be brought in as a witness. If then he still fails to amend, and his offenses are notorious, let him be put out of the monastery, but only if his contumacy is such that he refuses to submit or to obey the Rule.

COMMENTARY

A previous chapter spoke to us about those who, being clerics or priests already, wanted to become monks. The supposition here is a monastery not presently counting priests among its members. The case would be frequently met with in the fifth and sixth centuries. St. Benedict himself was not a priest. It is only conjectured that he was a deacon.[1]

The monks would then go in a body to the neighboring church for the

---

[1] Dom Benedict van Haeften, *Disquisitionum Monasticarum Libri XII*, Proleg., 18, pp, 33-35. Dom A. L'Huillier, *Le Patriarche Saint Benoît*, (Paris: Victor Retaux, 1905), pp. 267-270. In his *Saint Benoît, Essai Psychologique* (Paris: Pierre Tequi, 1922), pp. 278-280, Dom Hebrard has given his reasons for inclining strongly to the belief that St. Benedict was a priest, but the reasons are not convincing. [Translator's note: Ildefonso Cardinal Schuster adds other reasons for holding that St. Benedict was a priest, in his *La "Regula Monasteriorum," Testo, Introduzione, Commento e Note* (Turin: Società Editrice Internazionale, 1942), pp. 420-422.]

Holy Sacrifice of the Mass, which was not, moreover, celebrated every day; or else the Abbot would have a priest from outside come to the monastery. But was it not simpler to be self-sufficient and to set up a monastic clergy? It is this latter measure which St. Benedict here considers.

The Abbot, therefore, chooses a monk who may be "worthy of exercising the priesthood," and presents him to the Bishop. It is the Abbot himself who makes the choice, for the idea is to ordain a monk not for a ministry outside the monastery but for service inside. It even seems here that the vocation consists in the Abbot's choice, to the exclusion of all solicitation on the part of the candidate.

The ordination will necessarily place this monk in a privileged position. Our holy Father fears lest this be for some a source of danger—danger of pride or of disobedience. He reminds the new priest, therefore, that his ordination does not confer on him the right to occupy, outside of the sacred functions, any other place than that which agrees with the date of his profession. If the Abbot judged otherwise about it, that would be less because of the priesthood than by reason of the "merit of life" of him who is so honored.

St. Benedict reminds him also that his sacred character, far from putting him above the Rule, puts on him a strict obligation to be more perfect than the rest, and consequently more submissive and more obedient. And he will owe this obedience not only to the Abbot but to the Prior and the deans, to whom he might consider himself superior. The text of this passage, it is true, in the most authoritative manuscripts reads that he is to submit to the Rule established "for the deans and the Priors," *regulam decanis vel praepositis constitutam*; but the sense invites us rather to read "the rule established by the deans and the Priors," *regulam a decanis vel praepositis constitutam.*[2]

If the priest should prove to be proud and disobedient, he would be regarded as a rebel and frequently admonished. It seems certain that, out of respect for his priesthood, our holy Father wanted to spare him the rod; although, according to Hildemar, beating was practiced in parallel cases in the ancient French monasteries.

If the offender is incorrigible, the Bishop of the place is called as

---

[2] In favor of this correction *cf.* Dom Paul Delatte, *Commentary*, p. 428, and Dom Prosper Guéranger in his translation. Against it, Dom Cuthbert Butler, *Benedictine Monachism*, p. 177, and the Farnborough translators.

witness. *Episcopus adhibeatur in testimonium.* The Bishop is chosen undoubtedly because he is the one who ordained the offender, and also because his witness, being that of a man outside the monastic family and enjoying besides an incontestable importance, bears a fuller measure of impartiality in so grave a decision. The Bishop gives his opinion, therefore. It is not he, however, who expels the culprit in case that extreme measure is deemed advisable. The idea is to expunge an unworthy son from the family; and this can only be the deed of the father of the family himself, namely the Abbot.

APPLICATION

This whole chapter is one for priest Oblates to meditate. They will find here again a lesson already received in one of the preceding chapters. There may indeed be danger of their considering themselves, from the fact of their priesthood, freer with regard to the Holy Rule and its spirit than their brethren, the lay Oblates, as if its observance were good only for the common man. Our holy Father reminds us that the one who would so judge would be unworthy of the dignity with which he has been vested as well as of the monastic affiliation to which he has been admitted. His priestly character confers on him, among other things, an obligation, that of showing himself more perfect than others. It is he above all who ought to be as it were an incarnation of the monastic spirit in the midst of the world. Let him guard against self-exaltation and pride, therefore. Let him take for himself what Dom Delatte says of the priest-monk: "The special law of his life is advancement, a continuous progress toward that example of obedience and humility which Our Lord gives him at the altar: *Sed magis ac magis in Domino proficiat.*"[3] It is he, the priest, above all, who ought to be a model and a living Rule for his brethren; and his priesthood ought to furnish him "a powerful motive for more perfect obedience to the common Rule and the stimulant of an unceasing progress toward sanctity."[4]

Dom Guéranger has written some admirable pages for the priest Oblate, "truly attached to the monastic Order," pages which will have to be read often, and from which we shall take this passage as being able to illustrate this section of the Holy Rule: "Our priest will remember always

---

[3] *Commentary,* p. 427.

[4] Dom Étienne Salasc, *La Règle de S. Benoît Traduite et Commentée,* p. 562.

that he is given as a spectacle to the world, to the Angels and to men, and that if the deacon is enjoined to guard the *mysterium fidei* in a pure conscience, he, the priest, who works that same mystery, identified with the incarnate Word by his more sacred character, should be such that he may furnish to the heavenly Father the occasion of saying, because of the resemblance He will find in him with His Son: This is My beloved Son, in whom I am well pleased'."[5] Such, indeed, is the ideal toward which he ought always to tend. *Magis ac magis in Domino proficiat.*

---

[5] "Le Prêtre et l'Ordre de Saint-Benoît," in *L'Église ou la Société de la Louange Divine*, pp. 40-41.

CHAPTER 63
On the Order of the Community

 ET ALL keep their places in the monastery established by the time of their entrance, the merit of their lives and the decision of the Abbot. Yet the Abbot must not disturb the flock committed to him, nor by an arbitrary use of his power ordain anything unjustly; but let him always think of the account he will have to render to God for all his decisions and his deeds.

Therefore in that order which he has established or which they already had, let the brethren approach to receive the kiss of peace and Communion, intone the Psalms and stand in choir. And in no place whatever should age decide the order or be prejudicial to it; for Samuel and Daniel as mere boys judged priests.

Except for those already mentioned, therefore, whom the Abbot has promoted by a special decision or demoted for definite reasons, all the rest shall take their order according to the time of their entrance. Thus, for example, he who came to the monastery at the second hour of the day, whatever be his age or his dignity, must know that he is junior to one who came at the first hour of the day. Boys, however, are to be kept under discipline in all matters and by everyone.

COMMENTARY

Like any society, a community cannot exist without order. "Order," writes Dom Delatte, "is the law of every group or collective body: it exists in nature, it is found among the Angels, it is demanded by civil and religious society."[1] And so St. Benedict wanted to regulate in a special chapter the place of each one in the monastery. To determine that place he brings in three factors: the date of conversion, merit of life, the will of the Abbot.

The date of conversion (*conversionis*, or as Dom Butler will have it, *conversationis*)[2] fixes the monks' rank in general. Whether we must

---

[1] *Commentary*, p, 431.

[2] Let us note that a few lines farther on, St. Benedict employs the verb *converti* to express the same idea: *reliqui omnes ut convertuntur*. Is not that an argument in favor of *conversio*?

understand by "time of conversion" the date of entrance into the monastery or that of entrance into the novitiate, is something we shall see later on.

"Merit of life" indicates a supereminent virtue. Dom Delatte,[3] citing as reference the commentary of Dom Cal- met, supposes that "merit of life" can serve as a basis in this sense, that it "recommends" a monk "for some office or for the priesthood," something which will naturally be worth a higher place for him in the community. But that interpretation does not follow from the text, which seems to put the offices and the priesthood out of the question. Besides, there has been question of the latter in the preceding chapter. The concern is solely with the supernatural worth of the monk, considered in itself. It goes without saying that it is not for the religious himself to judge of his merit and of the rights it might confer on him. That would be contrary to the seventh degree of humility, which requires a person "from the bottom of his heart" to esteem and proclaim himself "lower and viler than all"; consequently, it would be a strange presumption. It is for the Abbot alone to evaluate.

But the Abbot's evaluation, especially in that which concerns the offices, may bear on something other than supernatural perfection. Certain natural talents, certain aptitudes may designate a monk for a superior place. Here again the Abbot is judge.

In all these things he will take care to avoid the arbitrary. He knows that he owes God an account of his judgments and his deeds.

Our holy Father enumerates some circumstances in which the order is to be kept more particularly: "the peace," that is to say, the procession of the monks, during the Mass, going to the altar to receive from the celebrant the kiss of peace; the Communion; the intonation of the Psalms; finally, the place in choir.

Will account have to be taken of age? Not in St. Benedict's opinion. Our holy Father had had with him youths of eminent sanctity, such as St. Maurus and the little Placidus. He knew through the Scriptures that Samuel and Daniel had judged the elders. The true age of the monks will be that of conversion and also that of sanctity, which confers on youth the maturity of old age.

It stands to reason that if the Abbot can make one go up, he can also, for just cause, make one go down, *degradaverit*.

---

[3] *Commentary*, p. 432.

Nor may it be forgotten that there are little boys in the monastery. Will they also take rank according to their day of conversion? It seems certain that St. Benedict is for the affirmative, since he does not wish account to be taken of age. Let us recall that in the first stages of the Benedictine institution, the Oblation constituted a real profession, and that these little Oblates were true monks. But in order to obviate any inconvenience, St. Benedict puts them, whatever be their rank, under the surveillance of all, and more especially perhaps of their neighbors.

Let us come now to the little problem indicated above: When does the *tempus conversionis* begin? The commentators are quite far from agreeing on this point.

Some, supporting their opinion by Chapter 58, where it is said of the monk who has just made his profession that "starting with this hour he is considered a member of the congregation," hold that the time of conversion begins with the profession. Dom Louis Quinet, Abbot of Barbery, sees in this view "some probability. . .since on that day the monk promises the conversion of his morals."[4]

Yet the same Dom Quinet avows that the other opinion is still more probable. Does not St. Benedict say clearly, "Let him who will have come to the monastery at the second hour of the day know himself to be the junior of him who has come at the first hour?" From which, continues Dom Quinet, "one can easily conclude that it is the entrance into the monastery to be received there which gives the rank, and not simply the profession, as the practice still is today in the Cistercian Order."[5] Dom Delatte, referring back to Dom Haeften, is of the same opinion: "The text of the Rule, if read without prejudice, would seem to be clearly in favor of the date of entry into the monastery."[6] Likewise Dom Étienne: "The terms of the Rule are of a clarity safe from all confusion."

Dom L'Huillier considers the problem of little importance. "The novitiate being of a set year," he explains, "outside of which there is no fluctuation except 'a few days' passed in the guest house, consequently outside of the monastery properly so called, the calculation according to the entry into the novitiate or according to the profession will always give the same result. And that is why the holy Patriarch refers ambiguously to

[4] *Éclaircissements sur la Règle de S. Benoît*, p. 307.

[5] *Ibid.*, p. 306.

[6] *Commentary*, p. 434.

the one and the other date."

Dom Quinet concludes wisely: "To resolve the question entirely, we must mind the custom of the place where we are ... because the immemorable customs which do not destroy the law take on the strength of the law and explain it sufficiently, wherefore they are called interpretative of the laws."

In practice, notes Dom Delatte, "according to monastic usage, almost universal and of long standing, every monk receives his rank in the community according to the date of his profession."[7]

APPLICATION

Strictly speaking, this passage might have its almost literal application in those places where groups of Oblates have been able to form in the shadow of the monasteries or in certain centers where the frequent contacts with the monastery make regular meetings possible. Still it does not seem that up to now, in general, the necessity of such an application has made itself much felt. But that could happen.

On the other hand, these lines have a general import. Order is willed by Providence. In the state, in the family, in the shop, there is necessarily organization and hierarchy. Each one ought to accept the role and the place in which God and his superiors and the nature of things have put him. If in that place he has to exercise a measure of authority, whether spiritual or temporal, let him take care to maintain order and peace. Commanding is neither a pleasure nor a satisfaction, and that man will have a hard accounting to make before the Sovereign Judge who "troubles the flock entrusted to him and acts unjustly in anything whatsoever." All his judgments and all his actions "will be weighed in the divine balance"; that is what he should think of "always." If, on the contrary, he is placed in the last rank, in the rank of those who have only to obey, let him rejoice over it, for that is the best part. Let him pray especially for those who have the formidable charge of guiding the rest and of assuring the peace of the flock.

April 19—August 19—December 19

The juniors, therefore, should honor their seniors, and the seniors love their juniors.

In the very manner of address, let no one call another by the mere

---

[7] *Ibid.*

name; but let the seniors call their juniors Brothers, and the juniors call their seniors Fathers, by which is conveyed the reverence due to a father. But the Abbot, since he is believed to represent Christ, shall be called Lord and Abbot, not for any pretensions of his own but out of honor and love for Christ. Let the Abbot himself reflect on this, and show himself worthy of such an honor.

And wherever the brethren meet one another, the junior shall ask the senior for his blessing. When a senior passes by, a junior shall rise and give him a place to sit, nor shall the junior presume to sit with him unless his senior bid him, that it may be as was written, "In honor anticipating one another (*Romans* 12:10).

Boys, both small and adolescent, shall keep strictly to their rank in the oratory and at table. But outside of that, wherever they may be, let them be under supervision and discipline, until they come to the age of discretion.

COMMENTARY

This passage has been called the code of monastic politeness. This politeness has the advantage over worldly politeness of being wholly impregnated with the spirit of faith. The formulas and the gestures in it correspond to the sentiments they express.

The young will honor the elders, and the latter will surround them with affection. This respect, as also this affection, exclude a certain out-of-place familiarity, which manifests itself in calling a person by the mere name. For the elders, the young will be "brothers"; for the young, the elders will be "*nonni*," a word probably of Egyptian origin, which signifies "paternal reverence." Dom Louis Quinet, who was writing in 1651, tells us that the word *nonnes* is "at present in use among the Benedictines and the Bernardines."[8] Today it has almost fallen into disuse; it has been replaced by "Dom," reserved for the professed who have attained the priesthood.

Among the ancient monks the term abba, abbot, designated not a Superior but "either an elder who had under his orders one or several disciples, or a monk whose age or exceptional virtues recommended a particular esteem."[9] St. Benedict reserves it to the Superior; for this word, of Syriac origin, means "Father," and the Abbot is really the Father of the monastic family. He will also be called *Domnus*, diminutive of *Dominus*, Lord. These terms of affectionate respect have their reason for being: "The

---

[8] *Éclaircissements*, p. 308.

[9] Dom Jean Martial Besse, *Les Moines d'Orient*, p. 168.

Abbot is believed to hold the place of Christ"; it is "for the honor and the love of Christ" that he is so called.

We know that the title *abbé* has passed by extension to the members of the secular clergy, largely on account of the system of commendatory Abbots, of unhappy memory. The remembrance of these latter has fortunately disappeared, and the titles of *Révérend, Pere Abbé* or *Révérendissime Père Abbé* permit the making of the necessary distinctions.

After the formulas come the gestures. These are inspired by the same intentions. When two "brothers" meet, the younger asks the blessing of the older. This blessing has been interpreted in various ways. Among the ancient monks of East and West, the younger would bow, saying *Benedicite* or *Benedic, Pater*, except at the time of the great silence. In asking the older one for his blessing, the younger recognized in him the presence of God, who, through him, was blessing. Dom Guéranger kept this formula in the Declarations he established for Sainte-Cecile. In the French Congregation they content themselves with a bow, removing the hood if the head is covered.

Dom Louis Quinet mentioned the variety of the aplications of this prescription of the Rule in his time: "As to the blessing mentioned in this chapter, of the elders with respect to the young, it is understood of an outward sign of respect, as a bow, a reverence, deference or other outward mark which shows the esteem the young man has for his elder, and not an actual genuflection or blessing such as all should receive from the Abbot when they go out from his presence or which they ask of him on meeting him."[10]

When a superior passes, the inferior rises and makes room for him to sit down, and he himself does not sit down again until after having been invited to do so. Obviously, the prescription does not apply if the elder is passing and repassing in the same place. St. Benedict concludes with some remarks on the children, remarks which repeat what he had already said previously.

---

[10] *Éclaircissements*, p. 309.

APPLICATION

"One could not meditate, appreciate and assimilate too much," notes Dom Étienne, "the sentiments of paternity and of filiation, of respect and of love which these few lines suggest, nor practice too much the external cult by which to manifest, conserve and increase those sentiments," Politeness and courtesy such as our holy Father demands are based on a profound sentiment of faith. Christ is everywhere and in everyone. Christ, head of the family and most loving Father, resides in the Abbot. The Abbot holds his place; this must be believed, *creditur*. Christ, brother and friend, resides in each member of the family. *Christus in eis adoratur*. If this formula applies to the sick (Chapter 36), to the guests (Chapter 53), to the poor and to the pilgrims (ibid.), by a stronger reason does it befit the members of the monastic family. This family constitutes a privileged one in the great family of the Church of Jesus Christ. We Oblates ought to rejoice at receiving the title "Brother" on our document of Oblation, and at having so signed it.[11]

But, living in the world, in the bosom of a family, of a parish, of any group whatsoever, we ought to bear there those same sentiments drawn from the school of St. Benedict. With regard to all our brethren, therefore, of whatever kind they be, we shall keep ourselves as far from out-of-place familiarities and from wrong standards as from mere worldly and verbal politeness. Enlightened by the spirit of our Rule, which is not other than that of the Gospel and of the Apostles, notably of St. Paul, we shall find it easy to practice those counsels which Msgr. Gay gave to persons consecrated to God: "Abound in reciprocal regards. There are those of speech, there are those of silence; there are those of accent, of expression, of look, of gestures. Do not lack any. Be prompt to render them all."[12]

A propos of this chapter the commentators, says Dom Delatte,[13] "take occasion of what is said here about sitting to observe that a monk should never sit in the loose and lazy manner of the worldling." *Cum sedes non superpones alteri cruri alterum crus tuum.*[14] The same recommendation has

---

[11] This title is not used on the document of Oblation in all the Congregations.

[12] *De la Vie et des Vertus Chrétiennes*, quoted by Dom Étienne Salasc, *La Règle de S. Benoît Traduite et Commentée*, p. 570.

[13] *Commentary*, p. 440.

[14] "Do not cross your legs when you sit."

often been made to ecclesiastics. Oblates should remember that they are not of the world, though living in it; that worldly, nonchalant attitudes are not becoming to them; and that to gain in their apostolate to the people of the world, they have only to put into their manners, their gestures and their words that reserve and that politeness which are the natural expression of a sentiment of reverence towards God present everywhere—present in us, present in our brethren.

CHAPTER 64
On Constituting an Abbot

April 20—August 20—December 20

N THE CONSTITUTING of an Abbot let this plan always be followed, that the office be conferred on the one who is chosen either by the whole community unanimously in the fear of God or else by a part of the community, however small, if its counsel is more wholesome.

Merit of life and wisdom of doctrine should determine the choice of the one to be constituted, even if he be the last in the order of the community.

But if (which God forbid) the whole community should agree to choose a person who will acquiesce in their vices, and if those vices somehow become known to the Bishop to whose diocese the place belongs, or to the Abbots or the faithful of the vicinity, let them prevent the success of this conspiracy of the wicked, and set a worthy steward over the house of God. They may be sure that they will receive a good reward for this action if they do it with a pure intention and out of zeal for God; as, on the contrary, they will sin if they fail to do it.

COMMENTARY

St. Benedict has already devoted Chapter 2 to the Abbot, and he has come back several times to this important question of the abbatial government. Here he completes or confirms his previous teachings.

The first part of this chapter is devoted to the election of the Abbot. In principle, the choice of an Abbot is reserved to the monks. "In most cases," writes Dom Delatte, "this is the safest and most equitable method, the monastic family being better informed and more directly concerned than anyone else."[1] But, as our holy Father points out, the election can give three results: 1) the whole community, acting "according to the fear of God," agrees in choosing a good monk; 2) there is not unanimity; 3) there is unanimity or nearly so, but in choosing an unworthy one.

The first case offers no difficulty.

As far as the second is concerned, our text is rather obscure: "That the one be made Abbot ... whom a part of the community, though it be small,

---

[1] *Commentary*, p. 443.

shall have chosen by a wiser counsel." And the commentators give the most varied explanations. This text, which must have been "very clear," notes Dom Étienne, "for the contemporaries of the Lawgiver, who possessed traditional notions on its application which we no longer have, is not without obscurity for their successors."

The common interpretation is this: If, on the one side, the majority favors one candidate, and, on the other side, a more fervent minority favors another, it is the elect of the fervent minority who is to prevail. Is that really what St. Benedict wanted? Does not every minority tend to consider itself more enlightened, more in the current of the community's true interests? Is not that a real nest of wrangling? And who will pronounce between the majority and the minority? An external authority? But St. Benedict does not speak of that at all for the preceding case.

Dom L'Huillier thinks the *pars quamvis parva* will have been chosen in advance by a prior election, and will form "electors of the second degree," or else that it will be formed naturally of those whom St. Benedict calls the elders, the spiritual elders. But in reality is not this to go out of the hypothesis proposed by St. Benedict or at least to render it useless? By recognizing the elective value of that pars parva, the community agrees in advance on the result of the vote; and consequently there is unanimity.

Dom Mège proposes an explanation that seems better. The votes are divided. If there is an absolute majority, it is that majority, which, however, is but a "part" of the community, that fixes the choice. If the votes are spread out.

St. Benedict does not want another ballot. They will trust in the relative majority, namely in that, *quamvis parva*, which forms the most numerous group. Still, this explanation does not absolutely account for all the data of the text, notably the qualification *saniori consilio*.

At present all those discussions have only an historical value, the method of election being fixed by canon law.

The third hypothesis which St. Benedict envisions, although with regret, *quod quidem absit*, but with his habitual sense of the possible realities, is that of a community in full decadence which agrees to fix its choice on a man to its measure, who will tolerate or favor its vices. Here, recourse must indeed be had to an authority outside the monastery, in an age when there is neither Congregation properly so called nor Superiors General. That authority will be the Bishop of the diocese, or else the Abbots of the monasteries in that locality, or even the influential lay persons of the neighborhood. There is undoubtedly an inquiry; the Bishop presides, the Abbots advise and the laics bring to their aid the support of the "secular arm." In the face of an evil so lamentable as that of a monastery abandoned "to its vices," it is a duty for all the Christian persons whose situation puts them in the way of intervening, to remedy the evil "with a pure intention and out of zeal for God." It would be a sin to let that evil exist.

Here again, canon law has specified and ruled definitively what was too indefinite or obsolete in the letter of the Holy Rule.

APPLICATION

All Christians are interested in seeing that those who have the role of guides, apostles, living examples in the Church, make themselves noticed "through merit of life and wisdom of doctrine," so closely is everything related in that Church of Christ. That is why, for example, the election of the Sovereign Pontiff, of a Bishop, of a Superior is always prepared for by fervent prayers. Those prayers even constitute the best guarantee of a choice according to the heart of God.

The Oblates, who, according to their Statutes, should "promote in so far as possible the good of the monastery to which they are attached and of the whole Order," would not be worthy of their affiliation with the monastic Order if they did not identify themselves, so to speak, with all the spiritual interests of the family which has opened its bosom to them. When that family has been deprived of its head, of its Father, they should unite themselves wholeheartedly and with all fervor to the supplications of their brethren, asking God to designate a new Father for them. The religious who have the grave duty of declaring themselves solely "according to the fear of God" have need of that aid. The role of the Oblates is found to be the same as that of the Lay Brothers, who do not take part in the voting but unite their fervent prayers to those of the community.

April 21—August 21—December 21

Once he has been constituted, let the Abbot always bear in mind what a burden he has undertaken and to whom he will have to give an account of his stewardship, and let him know that his duty is rather to profit his brethren than to preside over them. He must therefore be learned in the divine law, that he may have a treasure of knowledge from which to bring forth new things and old. He must be chaste, sober and merciful. Let his mercy always triumph over his justice, that he himself may obtain mercy. He should hate vices; he should love the brethren.

In administering correction he should act prudently and not go to excess, lest in seeking too eagerly to scrape off the rust he break the vessel. Let him keep his own frailty ever before his eyes and remember that the bruised reed must not be broken. By this we do not mean that he should allow vices to grow; on the contrary, as we have already said, he should eradicate them prudently and with charity, in the way which may seem best in each case. Let him study rather to be loved than to be feared.

Let him not be excitable and worried, nor exacting and headstrong, nor jealous and over-suspicious; for then he is never at rest.

In his commands let him be prudent and considerate; and whether the work which he enjoins concerns God or the world, let him be discreet and moderate, bearing in mind the discretion of holy Jacob, who said, "If I cause my flocks to be over-driven, they will all die in one day" (*Genesis* 33:13). Taking this, then, and other examples of discretion, the mother of virtues, let him so temper all things that the strong may have something to strive after, and the weak may not fall back in dismay.

And especially let him keep this Rule in all its details, so that after a good ministry he may hear from the Lord what the good servant heard who gave his fellow-servants wheat in due season: "Indeed, I tell you, he will set him over all his goods" (*Matthew* 24:47).

COMMENTARY

The words we have just read complete Chapter 2 and sometimes repeat it. We find here again our great Patriarch, with his discretion, his deep humility, his tenderness. This is an admirable passage, very personal, which brings to mind the text of St. Gregory sending us to the Rule for a good understanding of St. Benedict's soul, "for he acted not otherwise than he taught."

Our holy Father comes back to that thought which is very dear to him and which he wants to inculcate forcibly in his successors and in all those who will share with them any part of authority: The Abbot will have to render an account to God of his management; he is but the steward of God.

In his charge, he continues, he ought to consider not so much the dignity as the burden. He is not Abbot to receive honors, although honors be legitimately due him, but to serve, to be useful.

To that end he must realize certain conditions. He should be learned in the divine law, so as to be able to teach it to his monks. But to that theoretical teaching he should join the much more efficacious teaching of example. A Saint preaches much more by what he is than by what he says. That is why the Abbot should be "chaste, sober, merciful," etc.

St. Benedict insists particularly on mercy. The Abbot, he says, must "always make mercy prevail over justice," and that for several reasons. First, in his own interest. If he wants to obtain mercy from God, he should be merciful himself. Next, and especially, in the interest of him who is weak or sinful. Vices, obviously, must be hated, but the sinners, who are our brethren, must be loved. *Oderit vitia, diligat fratres.*

And what moderation, what discretion is needed to correct the vices of one's neighbor! Be fearful of breaking the vessel in being too anxious to scrape off the rust. You must punish, to be sure, but do not forget your own frailty. Do not break the already bruised reed. Who can doubt that vice should be punished? But put into the very punishment as much as you can of prudence, of charity. Strive "to be loved rather than to be feared."

"St. Augustine," observes Dom Delatte,[2] "gives the same counsel. So the ancients knew not that superfine spirituality which would have us guard against a warm attachment to our Superior, in order that we may obey with purer intention: which would make us distinguish carefully between the man and the Superior, so as to fortify ourselves against a too natural affection for the former."

The Abbot's conduct, therefore, will be full of discretion in everything. Discretion is "the mother of the virtues." It prevents one from being "turbulent and anxious, extravagant and obstinate, jealous and over-suspicious." The Abbot will strive to proportion all things, to exceed in nothing, to calculate the effort according to the work and the individual: "let him so temper all things that the strong may still have something to long after, and the weak may not flee." That will be the good means of bringing about observance of the Rule, which thus will not be too heavy for the one class and will appear to the others as an invitation to do still better.

It is by acting in that way that the Abbot will deserve, on the day of the rendering of accounts, the reward of the good servants.

---

[2] *Commentary,* p. 452.

APPLICATION

St. Benedict has been anxious to remind us that the Abbot's task is a heavy burden. The very discretion which is so sweet to those who are obeying is a difficult virtue for the one who is commanding. Does it not require a persevering control of himself? He must often be strong indeed in order to be gentle and merciful, as well as to be just.

Moreover, the fatherhood of souls is always a heavy charge. Some are fervent; that fervor must be sustained and directed. Others are weak and sinful; falls must be prevented, wounds healed, those who fall must be lifted up again. And, after all that, one day a strict account will have to be rendered to the Sovereign Master of the safety of all those souls. How we ought to pray for our spiritual Superiors of whatever kind, for our Bishop in particular and, as Oblates, for our Abbot!

Dom Bernard Laure, concluding the commentary on this chapter, makes this observation: "Not only the Abbot, but all those who have authority over others and are supposed to guide them, will find real profit in rereading this chapter often and in making it the object of their meditations."[3]

As we have already said, the present chapter constitutes with Chapter 2, of which it is the complement, an admirable pastoral treatise. The priest, who is charged with the care of souls and who will one day, like the Abbot, have to justify his administration at God's tribunal, will have everything to gain by assimilating our holy Father's teaching. It is of a perfect simplicity and clarity; and each one of its precepts, so luminous, so rich in doctrine, easily prompts beneficial reflections and fruitful resolutions.

---

[3] *Commentaire*, pp. 428-429.

CHAPTER 65
On the Prior of the Monastery

April 22—August 22—December 22

IT HAPPENS all too often that the constituting of a Prior gives rise to grave scandals in monasteries. For there are some who become inflated with the evil spirit of pride and consider themselves second Abbots. By usurping power they foster scandals and cause dissensions in the community. Especially does this happen in those places where the Prior is constituted by the same Bishop or the same Abbots who constitute the Abbot himself. What an absurd procedure this is can easily be seen; for it gives the Prior an occasion for becoming proud from the very time of his constitution, by putting the thought into his mind that he is freed from the authority of his Abbot: "For," he will say to himself, "you were constituted by the same persons who constituted the Abbot." From this source are stirred up envy, quarrels, detraction, rivalry, dissensions and disorders. For while the Abbot and the Prior are at variance, their souls cannot but be endangered by this dissension; and those who are under them, currying favor with one side or the other, go to ruin. The guilt for this dangerous state of affairs rests on the heads of those whose action brought about such disorder.

COMMENTARY

The Abbot can have himself assisted by a second. Perhaps that was the practice of certain monasteries in St. Benedict's time. Our holy Father gives him the name of *praepositus*, which could be rendered by "Provost." With Cassian, St. Basil, St. Gregory of Nyssa and others, the *praepositus* (in Greek *proestos*) is the Superior himself.[1] We have seen that the name "abbot" did not necessarily designate a Superior. On the other hand, with St. Caesarius and St. Macarius, *praepositus* has the same meaning as with St. Benedict.

Today the *praepositus* is the Prior. In St. Benedict the word prior had a rather vague sense; it designated the Superior as well as an elder, or just simply the one who presided at a function. Have St. Benedict's successors been influenced by the fact that he admits as with regret the sometimes

---

[1] Dom Jean Martial Besse, *Les Moines d'Orient*, p. 168.

necessary presence of the *praepositus*? The fact is that they have let the name drop, though not the function, and that today and for centuries back the Abbot's second is called "Prior."

There existed at the time of the holy Patriarch, at least in certain places, a custom whose fatal consequences he must have verified. The Prior, elected perhaps by the community or chosen by the Abbot—we do not know—would receive his "institution," his "ordination" from the Bishop (*sacerdos*) or from the Abbots who had ordained the Abbot himself. From which certain Priors would draw this conclusion: "If I have been chosen by my Abbot, still it is not from him that I have received my powers, but from those who ordained me. Therefore I do not depend on him, and he cannot deprive me of powers he has not given me."

St. Benedict has in view, then, those Priors "inflated with an evil spirit of pride" who stand up to their Abbots scandalously and refuse submission. He has seen "envies, quarrels, detractions, jealousies, dissensions, disorders"; he has seen the souls of the two antagonists in danger, and those of the poor religious "going to perdition." At that thought, at that memory, our holy Father protests. His style, generally so calm, so full of peace, becomes lashing, indignant: *Quod quam sit absurdum*—How absurd that is! But are not the guilty ones chiefly those who make such ordinations? *Qui talibus in ordinatione se fecerunt auctores.*[2]

We shall see later what should be the procedure, according to St. Benedict, in the choice and ordination of the Prior. Dom Delatte points out that, by an inexplicable singularity, the Congregation of Saint-Vanne, which was nevertheless an admirable monastic reform from other points of view, had entrusted to the General Chapter the duty of designating the claustral Priors. Was that not to fall back into the abuse condemned by St. Benedict? Still, there was perhaps a circumstance more than attenuating: did they not escape thus from the influence of the commendatory Abbots?

Let us note in passing that the Priors here in question are the claustral Priors. They must be distinguished from the "conventual" Priors, who have the same jurisdiction as the Abbots in certain monasteries not erected into an Abbey, or belonging to Congregations whose Constitutions do not embrace the abbatial title. The Benedictine Sisters of

---

[2] Translator's note: Dom Benno Linderbauer's text has a slightly different reading: *qui talius inordinationis se fecerunt auctores*—"who made themselves the authors of such disorder."

the Blessed Sacrament have only Prioresses, the Blessed Virgin being considered as the real Abbess. The claustral Priors must be distinguished also from the "simple" Priors, Superiors of small communities dependent on a larger one, which are like "a part of the mother house."[3]

APPLICATION

What St. Benedict desires for his children is peace, not only exterior but interior. The Benedictine soul ought to move in an atmosphere of peace. Thus everything that destroys peace is supremely hateful to it.

One of the great enemies of peace is "the evil spirit of pride," which is the very spirit of the devil. It is pride which, in the case envisioned, breathes into the Prior sentiments of conceit which will trouble his judgment and inspire him with sophisms to justify his revolt.

The spirit of pride rises up by instinct against lawful authorities. It pretends that they are rivals encroaching on our supposed rights. *Hinc suscitantur invidiae* ... Thence jealousies, hatreds, disorders.

St. Benedict has the highest idea of order, but he esteems it especially because it is a condition of peace and because the good of souls depends on it. When there are divisions among the children of one Father, "it is impossible that their souls do not find themselves in peril amid those divisions."

Let us not, therefore, believe ourselves easily hurt in our rights by our Superiors or our brethren. Let us not, by reasserting those pretended rights, destroy the peace of a soul which ought to be filled above all with God. Let us not, by our self-styled revindications, spread agitation and disorder about us. The good of souls, divine charity, peace are worth a hundred times more than everything that we want to pretend to.

In consequence, let those who have to fulfil some function involving more or less authority, under a spiritual or temporal superior, meditate the lessons of this chapter. "Consider," wrote Dom Robert Morel in his Meditations on the Rule of St. Benedict,[4] "that exaltation is to be feared for everyone, but it is especially disastrous for the ambitious, because it is always followed by their fall, God so permitting in order to punish their pride and to make them bear its penalty. The desire of their exaltation grows with their exaltation itself and causes their penalty and their

---

[3]   Dom Paul Delatte, Commentary, p. 456.

[4]   *Meditations*, pp. 422-423.

torture. They set no limits to their ambition, and their ambition gives them no rest. They want to dominate over everything, and do not want to be dominated by anyone. Oh, how important it is to be humble, in order to limit oneself and to live content!" How important it is to be humble, we shall add, for our own sanctification and for the true edification and the salvation of the souls for which we shall have to answer also before God.

Let us keep ourselves also, notes Dom Étienne, from destroying the just prestige which our superiors ought to enjoy, by a more or less conscious jealousy. That prestige also is a condition of peace. It is necessary to all legitimate authority; and for a soul truly animated with the spirit of faith, that prestige is at bottom the very prestige of God, in whom all authority has its source.

April 23—August 23—December 23

To us, therefore, it seems expedient for the preservation of peace and charity that the Abbot have in his hands the full administration of his monastery. And if possible let all the affairs of the monastery, as we have already arranged, be administered by deans according to the Abbot's directions. Thus, with the duties being shared by several, no one person will become proud.

But if the circumstances of the place require it, or if the community asks for it with reason and with humility, and the Abbot judges it to be expedient, let the Abbot himself constitute as his Prior whomsoever he shall choose with the counsel of God-fearing brethren.

That Prior, however, shall perform respectfully the duties enjoined on him by his Abbot and do nothing against the Abbot's will or direction; for the more he is raised above the rest, the more carefully should he observe the precepts of the Rule.

If it should be found that the Prior has serious faults, or that he is deceived by his exaltation and yields to pride, or if he should be proved to be a despiser of the Holy Rule, let him be admonished verbally up to four times. If he fails to amend, let the correction of regular discipline be applied to him. But if even then he does not reform, let him be deposed from the office of Prior and another be appointed in his place who is worthy of it. And if afterwards he is not quiet and obedient in the community, let him even be expelled from the monastery. But the Abbot, for his part, should bear in mind that he will have to render an account to God for all his judgments, lest the flame of envy or jealousy be kindled in his soul.

COMMENTARY

In order to avoid the evils of which there has been question in the preceding section, "in order to keep peace and charity," the Abbot ought to have full freedom to organize his monastery. Often he will be able to get along without a *praepositus* and have himself aided by the deans, as we have seen above in Chapter 21. That is a great advantage; for where a function is exercised by several persons, there is scarcely any chance for one to become proud rather than the others.

It may happen, however, that the necessity of having himself aided by a second, with whom he collaborates more closely, prompts the Abbot to place some monk above the deans. That will be the Prior. This Prior he himself will choose, after consulting with "brethren fearing God," and it is he who will ordain him: *ordinet ipse sibi* ... The Prior, therefore, will owe everything to the Abbot, both his choice and his institution. He will not even have the temptation to set himself up as a rival.

So established, the Prior is the Abbot's man. He should execute his orders faithfully, and no one should be more faithful than he to the precepts of the Rule.

And as he depends solely on the Abbot, the latter can demote him if he is proud or if he "despises the Holy Rule." Still, he will not come to that extremity until after four admonitions and the application of the regular discipline, as indicated in Chapter 28. Let us recall that the ordinary monks are warned only twice and the deans three times. St. Benedict shows a particular condescension for the Prior, therefore. If, despite all, he does not correct himself, it is only then that the Abbot will come to his demotion and even, if he persists in his bad dispositions, to his expulsion from the monastery.

Our holy Father feels the need, however, of recommending to the Abbot himself not to tyrannize. It would be regrettable for him, in face of a Prior who in good faith has won the esteem of the monks, to let "his soul burn with the flame of envy and jealousy." He will remember rather that he owes God an account of all his decisions.

APPLICATION

This chapter, like many others, has a general import. It is of interest to whoever, under a spiritual or temporal superior, is charged with fulfilling some function.

In the first rank we shall place the priests, enlisted in the hierarchy and serving in the ministry of souls. The priest is the collaborator of the Bishop and of the other Superiors placed over him by the Bishop. The priest Oblate, therefore, if he will be faithful to the spirit of his holy Father, will remind himself that his role is not only to cause the orders of his Superiors to be carried out, but to cause the Superiors to be respected and loved.

The same principle, moreover, should regulate the attitude with regard to the other authorities. Some people, for the more or less conscious purpose of making themselves prevail and of attracting all esteem to themselves, may be tempted to provoke by allusions, by insinuations, some disaffection or even some contempt towards those whom they represent. They imagine, no doubt, that they ought to draw benefit from a comparison between their ways of acting and thinking and those of the Superiors. What really inspires them is "the illusion of exaltation," the pride of which St. Benedict speaks.

We must always remember one thing: that when a function has been assigned us, our duty is to show ourselves worthy of the trust given us by being more humble, more obedient, more respectful, more devout than the rest. We should not be good Oblates in acting otherwise, and our holy Father could reproach us with "despising" the spirit of his "Holy Rule."

On the other hand, if we ourselves have subalterns, let us be on guard against treating them haughtily, against being jealous of their successes, against unjustly doing them harm. Let us not forget that we shall have to give an account to the Lord of every unjust measure in their regard.

CHAPTER 66
On the Porters of the Monastery

April 24—August 24—December 24

AT THE GATE of the monastery let there be placed a wise old man, who knows how to receive and to give a message, and whose maturity will prevent him from straying about. This porter should have a room near the gate, so that those who come may always find someone at hand to attend to their business. And as soon as anyone knocks or a poor man hails him, let him answer 'Thanks be to God" or "A blessing!" Then let him attend to them promptly, with all the meekness inspired by the fear of God and with the warmth of charity.

Should the porter need help, let him have one of the younger brethren.

If it can be done, the monastery should be so established that all the necessary things, such as water, mill, garden and various workshops, may be within the enclosure, so that there is no necessity for the monks to go about outside of it, since that is not at all profitable for their souls.

We desire that this Rule be read often in the community, so that none of the brethren may excuse himself on the ground of ignorance.

COMMENTARY

A single gate gives access to the monastery. If there is a secondary one, it is reserved for the servants, the workmen and the wagons. That is a tradition designed to safeguard the cloister. At this gate will be placed "a wise old man, who knows how to receive and to give a message, and whose maturity does not permit him to stray about."

The one who is appointed to serve as intermediary between the world and the interior must indeed be a man of silence and recollection, a man who loves the cloister and flees vain gossip. The nature of his functions demands that his cell be placed near the gate. He welcomes the visitors and the poor. He knows how to answer the former with tact and discernment, and the latter with charity and bounty.

His faith, which will make him see God in the person of the visitors, be they rich or poor, will sustain him in a task so delicate. So much virtue is needed in certain moments of pressure or with certain people, in order not to become impatient! The *Deo gratias* by which he greets the visitor will recall that thought of faith to him. This *Deo gratias* has remained in use with the monks when someone knocks at their cell. In the porter's speech a person ought to sense that meekness which the fear of God inspires and the earnestness given by the fervor of charity.

The function of the porter so understood demands dispositions so supernatural that among the Fathers of the East it was considered as one of the principal functions of the monastery. And Dom Calmet in his commentary insinuates that to entrust the office of porter to laymen is an indication of a lessening of the monastic sense.

In speaking of the porter, St. Benedict is thinking above all of guaranteeing the enclosure. It is that same thought which leads him to speak of the conditions in which the monastery ought to be disposed. Everything necessary ought to be found there, "water, mill, garden, bakery and various crafts," not that our holy Father is thinking of comfort, but because he wants to avoid as far as possible for his sons the occasions or the pretexts for wandering outside. "That," he says, "is not at all profitable for their souls."

The last sentence of this chapter appears to be without relation to what precedes. What our holy Father asks to be read over often is obviously not the chapter concerning the porter, but the whole Rule. This short text is regarded by many commentators as the conclusion of a first edition of the Holy Rule. The following chapters are supposed to have been added later. We have already spoken, in the commentary on the Prologue, of the conventual reading of the Rule. St. Benedict wants his children to be perfectly instructed in it, that they may not find an excuse for their irregularities in ignorance and that, on the contrary, they may be deeply penetrated with its spirit.

APPLICATION

The monk has renounced the world; and it is to maintain him in that renouncement that St. Benedict is concerned with assuring him, even materially, a real cloister. But every Christian should also renounce the world, in very virtue of his Baptism; and the Oblate's renouncement, despite the absence of material cloister, should approach the monk's as nearly as possible. In the ancient oration which was recited over us the day that we put on the Benedictine scapular, we were reminded that this habit was one "which the Fathers of old wished to be worn by those who renounced the world," *hoc genus vestimenti, quod sancti Patres ... ab renuntiantes saeculo ferre sanxerunt;*[1] and on the day of our profession we answered "I do," *Volo,* to this question which was put to us: "Do you renounce the vanities and pomps of the world?"[2]

By our habit and by our profession, therefore, we ought to be of those who, quite logically, with the pledges of their Baptism, put a separation between the world and themselves. St. Gregory says of our holy Father that "under the eyes of the divine Spectator he dwelt alone with himself," *habitavit secum.* It is for us to be the *ostiarii,* the porters of our soul. It must not be like a room open to every comer, and all sorts of thoughts must not come to wander about in it. We must not go out of ourselves, where we find God, to run after the vanities of the world. Our ministry, our situation, our profession, our apostolate may oblige us to more or less frequent contacts with the people of the world; they cannot oblige us to look for worldly associations and to take part in the joys of the world.

Nothing obliged us to become Oblates. If we have asked for "the mercy of God and brotherhood with you as an Oblate of our most holy Father Benedict," it is not to resemble just any ordinary Christians who think they can serve God and the world. In spirit we are monks (let us recall the etymology of the word); and if we have the honor of the priesthood, we are "churchmen." Let us have no ambition to be anything else. To frequent what is conventionally called the world, with its pleasures, its feasts, its futile preoccupations, is not befitting for true children of St. Benedict: *omnino non expedit animabus eorum.* It is our holy Father who tells us this.

In his *Moralia* on Job, St. Gregory explains to us what we ought to be from this point of view "when" (I sum up his ancient Benedictine biographer, Dom Denis of St. Martha), "distinguishing two kinds of solitude, the one merely exterior, the other interior, he says that if anyone engaged by body in the multitude of the people, in the troubles and the agitations of the world, finds himself nevertheless quite tranquil within, he should be regarded rather as solitary than as living in the city. While on the contrary, to be far in body from the company of men is not to be in solitude if one gives entrance into one's mind and into one's heart to worldly thoughts and desires."[3]

In his *Sermon 40 on the Canticle of Canticles,* St. Bernard says the same

---

[1] *Manual for Oblates,* p. 226.

[2] *Ibid.,* p. 236.

[3] *Histoire de S. Grégoire le Grand* (Rouen, 1647), p. 33.

thing in another way: "O holy soul, remain alone, so as to preserve yourself for Him alone, whom you have chosen to yourself from among all others.. . . Withdraw yourself, therefore; I do not mean in body, but withdraw in mind, in intention, in devotion, in spirit."[4]

Let us make up our mind to it, therefore. In order to assure our interior solitude and our separation, let us not willingly go out of our house, out of our parish, out of our works of zeal and of apostolate, to go and seek the world. Neither let us call it to ourselves. We belong to Jesus Christ. He alone should interest us, and the rest for love of Him.

Let the Oblate living in a family know that his true milieu is his family; his true cloister, the circle of those who live with him. Too often, the people of the world dream of only one thing, to get away from their home as often as possible, in search of pleasures elsewhere. The Benedictine spirit is essentially a family spirit. To be faithful to the spirit of the Rule, therefore, the Oblate to whom Providence has entrusted the care of a family should love his home and maintain there that profound union which can come only from supernatural charity, grouping all the souls, so to speak, in one and the same search for God.

Are we saying that in order to bear witness to our separation from the world, we must take on a frowning, stern air towards the people of the world with whom we shall find ourselves in contact? God forbid! St. Benedict would send us back to the brother porter, who, by situation, has to greet all kinds of people, and who nevertheless is to show himself ever filled "with the meekness of the fear of God" and with "the fervor of charity." The spirit of faith, of which our holy Father has repeatedly spoken to us, inspires a certain supernatural courtesy which makes virtue attractive and causes the worldlings themselves to feel all the inward peace and deep joy that exists in a life all for God, peace and joy which, if they take a good account of them, have nothing in common with their poor pleasures, so empty and so fleeting.

---

[4] In *P.L.*, Tome 183, Col. 983; translated by Samuel J. Eales in *Life and Works of Saint Bernard*, Vol. 4 (London: John Hodges, 1896), p. 254.

CHAPTER 67
On Brethren Who Are Sent on a Journey

ET THE BRETHREN who are sent on a journey commend themselves to the prayers of all the brethren and of the Abbot; and always at the last prayer of the Work of God let a commemoration be made of all absent brethren.

When brethren return from a journey, at the end of each canonical Hour of the Work of God on the day they return, let them lie prostrate on the floor of the oratory and beg the prayers of all on account of any faults that may have surprised them on the road, through the seeing or hearing of something evil, or through idle talk. And let no one presume to tell another whatever he may have seen or heard outside of the monastery, because this causes very great harm. But if anyone presumes to do so, let him undergo the punishment of the Rule. And let him be punished likewise who would presume to leave the enclosure of the monastery and go anywhere or do anything, however small, without an order from the Abbot.

COMMENTARY

There are cases in which it is necessary for some of the brethren to leave the monastery and go away on a journey. St. Benedict would have them at least, as Dom Delatte says, "surrounded and protected by a spiritual enclosure, so that the monastery may, as it were, accompany them continually."[1]

The brethren whom the Abbot has deemed fit to send outside recommend themselves before their departure to everyone's prayers. The text says *omnium fratrum vel Abbatis orationi,* word for word "to the prayer of all the brethren or of the Abbot." But the critics have often pointed out that with St. Benedict the particle *vel* is sometimes copulative. Nevertheless, certain commentators, as Bernard of Monte Cassino, Boherius and others, hold for the disjunctive sense. St. Benedict would mean that when those departing cannot take their leave of the whole community, it will suffice to present themselves before the Abbot. That explanation has been generally abandoned.

---

[1] *Commentary*, p. 468.

After the last prayer of the Office, continues the text, the monks will never fail to pray for those absent. This precept of St. Benedict is fulfilled at the end of the antiphon to the Blessed Virgin which follows each Office of the day and of the night. When the hebdomader has said the formula *Divinum auxilium maneat semper nobiscum,* "May the divine assistance always remain with us," all respond *Et cum fratribus nostris absentibus. Amen,* "And with our absent brethren. Amen."

Their journey ended, the brethren, on the very day of their return, prostrate themselves on the floor of the oratory at the end of each canonical Hour, to implore the prayers of all because of the transgressions they may have committed outside. These transgressions our holy Father enumerates: sight or hearing of bad things or vain talk.

The concern is first with faults of surprise: while they were passing amid the world, unedifying spectacles, unsuitable speech may have struck the senses and brought them some vain distraction. Besides, more or less fortuitous meetings may have led to unduly long conversations, banal, even somewhat frivolous, sometimes none too charitable.

From all that dust they must purify themselves on their reentry into the cloister. It is for that purpose that they ask the assistance of everyone's prayers. In present-day practice this prostration does not take place after each Hour, but only at the end of the one following the return.

If the monk, once he has returned, ought to deliver his soul from the sights and sounds of the world, so much the more should he guard against talking about them to his brethren and troubling them in turn. Would it not be an occasion of ruin for them, and has not many an example of that been seen? *Plurima destructio est!* Hence the offender will be subjected to the regular discipline.

The final sentence declares subject to the same discipline whoever goes out of the cloister without the Abbot's order. Here, notes Dom Delatte, we remark again the use of the vel copulative: likewise he who would presume to leave the enclosure of the monastery and (*vel*) to go anywhere and (*vel*) to do anything (understood: where he will have gone). That is to say, whatever be the purpose of his journey, however laudable or however insignificant it may be, he will be punished because he will have acted without the Abbot's order. In effect, his step will have been vitiated by that absence of permission.

APPLICATION

The lesson of this chapter is at bottom the same as that of the preceding chapter, but it is more explicit. We Oblates have not the advantage of the cloister; most of the time we do not even live in its shadow; we are, if not at heart at least in body, perpetual absent ones. We have therefore an urgent need of the prayer of our brethren of the cloister; and in fact they desire indeed to count us in the number of those "absent brethren" for whom they pray several times a day, according to the precept of our common Father: *commemoratio omnium absentium fiat.*

It is we above all who need to establish around our soul and our senses a spiritual enclosure. The thought of our monastery, with its vision of fervor and peace, contributes to this. In the midst of the world we tell ourselves: I am the brother of the monks, I belong to the monastic Order; I am no longer of the world.

St. Benedict shows us where especially the danger lies. It is in the surprises of sight. If we are not on our guard, if our glances wander to this side and that, there are certain objects on which they will light and of which the sight and the memory can disturb us directly or unconsciously, and sometimes deeply. It is the same with the surprises of hearing. They are little stains which will register with us almost without our knowing it.

And what shall we say about the conversations, about the *otiosi sermones*? Vain conversations in which we wound charity, in which we seek notice, in which we sift again our little animosities, and so forth. We carry all those impressions with us; they rise up in our prayers; they turn us away from the thought of God; they make our fervor languish; they "resuscitate," as Dom Delatte remarks, "matters to which we are dead, and which, by God's help, are dead to us: 'The world is crucified unto me, and I unto the world'."[2]

For those of us who are priests engaged in the service of the Lord, the less we go out into the world, the less we leave our rectory, our parish, our customary life with its everyday duties, its habits of piety and its sanctifying environment, the better that will be for us. It is not good that we run after worldly spectacles, public celebrations, and so forth; they are not made for those who "renounce themselves to take the Cross of Christ." We do ourselves no good there, and we carry away nothing but evil.

---

[2] *Ibid.,* pp. 470-471.

And are the duties of the Oblate living in a family so different? Does he not know that there are surroundings in which if he is truly Christian, a Christian tending to perfection, he would be entirely out of place; surroundings to which it behooves him not to lead his family if he desires, as is his duty, to inculcate in them the seriousness of the Christian life? There are family joys which are blessed by God, but the Christian sense permits him to distinguish them from the futile, unwholesome joys of the world.

If we do not seek the world, it can come to us, not only in the form of visits, but also in the form of newspapers, more or less serious magazines which insinuate into our mind their dangerous maxims and their pernicious ways of thinking. We give them access to us under the pretext that we must "keep up with the world." A grave illusion, a certain cause of "many ruins."

This is undoubtedly the place to mention a monastic practice rather widespread among the clergy: the recitation of the *Itinerarium* before leaving on a journey. It is an excellent shield against the surprises of the evil one. To the ordinary prayers the Benedictine Breviary adds after the last oration that of St. Benedict, *Intercessio*, taken from the Common of Abbots, with the mention: *beati Patris nostri Benedicti*.

When they take their weekly outing, the Benedictine monks have also the custom of reciting at their departure and their return, before the Blessed Sacrament if possible, some traditional prayers found in the Monastic Breviary. It is quite natural that we should recite them also when we go out for some pastoral round, some visit to the poor or some outing.

Let us not forget, either, the *Et cum fratribus nostris absentibus* at the end of the Hours. It will be the response of the absent brethren to those who pray for them in the shelter of the family house.

CHAPTER 68
If a Brother Is Commanded to Do Impossible Things

F IT HAPPENS that difficult or impossible tasks are laid on a brother, let him nevertheless receive the order of the one in authority with all meekness and obedience. But if he sees that the weight of the burden altogether exceeds the limit of his strength, let him submit the reasons for his inability to the one who is over him in a quiet way and at an opportune time, without pride, resistance, or contradiction. And if after these representations the Superior still persists in his decision and command, let the subject know that this is for his good, and let him obey out of love, trusting in the help of God.

COMMENTARY

The commentators are agreed in recognizing that the "impossible" things of which there is question here have no relation to certain paradoxical obediences imposed by some of the desert Fathers. Neither is there question of things materially possible, but impossible for a righteous soul because they directly wound justice or charity. The concern is above all with things psychologically impossible, or at least apparently so because they are in formal contradiction with our tastes, our tendencies, our aptitudes. The effort required in order to accomplish them seems to us insurmountable. "A species of delusion which is only too natural"[1] makes it appear evident that we shall really be unable to do the thing.

Our holy Father desires first of all that the order be welcomed "in all meekness and obedience." There must be no recriminations, but on the contrary a real desire to obey if one can. The thing seems impossible to you? Try first, and it will be seen afterwards.

But even after a first attempt, fulfilled in these good dispositions, "the burden seems wholly to exceed the strength." In that case, go and find your Abbot. Avoid a tone of impatience. Choose the opportune moment. Let there be in your speech neither pride nor a spirit of resistance nor contradiction. Simply set forth your reasons.

Then either the Abbot will be persuaded and obedience will be saved,

---

[1] Dom Paul Delatte, *Commentary*, p. 473.

or else he will see that you are deluding yourself and he will persist. Be assured that he is right. The thing required is truly possible; it is only strength of will that fails you. You love God; entrust yourself to Him. Since He loves you also and is witness of your good will, He will give you the strength, and with Him you will be able to do everything.

APPLICATION

Everything is to be retained by us in this little chapter. "It is almost always," notes Dom Morel,[2] "for want of faith and love that we find difficulty or impossibility in the things we are commanded to do. If we believed and loved as much as we should, everything would appear possible and easy to us, because our love would smooth out all the difficulties for us and our faith would obtain for us the strength we lack. ... Let us love, and we shall obey without any trouble." Dom Delatte expresses the same thought in other terms. "The incapacity of men," he says,[3] "often arises from sloth or pusillanimity. They too often forget the simple truth that if a thing is to get done we must do it. And when we have spent long hours in contemplating, in a spirit of false and foolish self-pity, the real or pretended difficulties of our duty, we have not changed the reality of things one whit: our duty is always our duty, and the will of God abides: we have only succeeded in weakening ourselves. 'Fortune favors the brave': in this case fortune is the grace of God."

And how could that grace fail us? Who indeed commands us? Someone in whom our faith makes us see Christ. It is Christ, therefore, who wills this thing so hard for our nature. And since it is hard, it is therefore a little of His cup of bitterness which He presents to us who for us was "obedient unto the death of the Cross." *Potestis bibere calicem*? Can you drink this chalice? How could we refuse it?

Our experience, moreover, teaches us about those pretended impossibilities. How many times that which at first glance had appeared insurmountable to us has seemed easy once we have resolved to set ourselves to it with our heart full of charity! "Was it only that?" we say. It was only that indeed, because the Almighty was with us and because His divine love, once we have entrusted ourselves to it, is always strong enough to make us love even what we find repugnant.

---

[2] *Méditations,* p. 428.

[3] *Commentary,* p. 475.

CHAPTER 69
That the Monks Presume Not to Defend One Another

CARE must be taken that no monk presume on any ground to defend another monk in the monastery, or as it were to take him under his protection, even though they be united by some tie of blood-relationship. Let not the monks dare to do this in any way whatsoever, because it may give rise to most serious scandals. But if anyone breaks this rule, let him be severely punished.

COMMENTARY

It is obvious that St. Benedict is not here forbidding anyone to make known humbly to his Abbot, in certain cases, the attenuating circumstances of the offense of some brother, or certain conditions which he may not know about and which modify the nature of an act or of a situation. Those are quite legitimate things, which can render service at once to the Superior and to the one who has been reprimanded or punished.

What St. Benedict has in mind are other cases, from which may arise "a very grave occasion of scandal." A monk has been justly punished by his Abbot. He has relatives in the monastery; and these, blinded by affection, do not want to see the gravity of the fault. They consider the Superior too severe; they arouse the offender; they urge him on to revolt, and instead of helping him charitably to accomplish as best he can that obedience which is difficult for him or to support that regular satisfaction which has been inflicted on him, they inspire in him the spirit of disobedience. If they could, they would even form little clans and thus destroy the peace in the house of God.

As the commentators point out, there is a kinship more subject to caution that that of blood; it is, according to Dom Delatte's expression, "the relationship of choice,"[1] that is to say, the particular friendships which always blind those who give way to them. They also are grave sources of division. St. Benedict desires that every attempt at coterie be severely punished.

---

[1] *Commentary*, p. 476.

APPLICATION

The cases envisioned by our holy Father may be encountered everywhere. Wherever there is grouping and authority, there is a tendency to little societies apart, to coteries. A person wants to be distinguished, he wants to have his particular group; and if any authority has to intervene against one of the members of the clan, he protests, he recriminates, he provokes resistances.

At other times, he takes voluntarily "under his protection" whoever has been censured or punished, to attract him to himself, to show his own importance, to make his Superiors feel that he is really there. He thus throws suspicion on the authority, forgetting that it represents the Lord; and that is the ruin of charity.

The associations of piety or good works, "fraternities," parishes sometimes suffer from these little maneuvers, excited by little clans more or less closed, always turbulent, always "against," whose plots sometimes degenerate into scandals.

The true child of St. Benedict should be the man of enlightened charity, of peace, of humility, of justice, of obedience. Neither kinship nor, *a fortiori*, particular friendships, which are always to be shunned, should sway his judgments; and he can never be too much on guard against what his holy Father points out to him as "very grave occasions of scandal."

CHAPTER 70
That No One Venture to Punish at Random

April 28—August 28—December 28

VERY occasion of presumption shall be avoided in the monastery, and we decree that no one be allowed to excommunicate or to strike any of his brethren unless the Abbot has given him the authority. Those who offend in this matter shall be rebuked in the presence of all, that the rest may have fear.

But boys up to 15 years of age shall be carefully controlled and watched by all, yet this too with all moderation and discretion. Anyone, therefore, who presumes without the Abbot's instructions to punish those above that age or who loses his temper with the boys, shall undergo the discipline of the Rule; for it is written, "Do not to another what you would not want done to yourself" (*Tobias* 4:16).

COMMENTARY

The concern here is not with those who would let themselves go at random to acts of violence, but with those who would permit themselves to inflict supposedly regular punishments. These punishments in St. Benedict's day are either excommunication or the rod. The Abbot alone has the power of them, or he who has received command of them from the Abbot. Outside of those conditions, every correction or excommunication is forbidden.

The sentence which follows, and which is taken from the first Epistle to Timothy (5:20), offers difficulties: *Peccantes autem coram omnibus arguantur, ut ceteri metum habeant.* Dom Guéranger translated: "Those who commit faults shall be reprimanded before everyone" (*Ceux qui commettent desfantes seront repris devant tout le monde*). So rendered, the first words are indeed vague. What faults are in question? And moreover, has not the Rule established that, in general, faults will be the occasion first of all for secret warnings?

Others connect *peccantes* with what precedes. The concern here is with those who sin against this point of the Holy Rule. Dom Delatte believes this explanation should be rejected. "Such a development of the text," he

413

says,[2] "is apt, but why did St. Benedict omit the few words needed to make the sentence clear, and say absolutely, without formal reference to what precedes: 'those that sin'? Moreover, St. Benedict presently specifies the punishment which he reserves for those who correct without authority—viz., the degrees of the regular discipline; and the regular discipline implies something other than public rebuke."

Dom Delatte thinks the translation must be: "Those who sin before everyone, shall be reprimanded." The difficulty is that this punctuation is not that of the Epistle to Timothy. Besides, if in this interpretation the word *peccantes* takes on a more exact meaning, it is to the detriment of *arguantur*, which becomes too vague.

In our humble opinion, *peccantes* is sufficiently determined by the context: they are indeed those who fail in this point of the Rule. To be sure, they will be "subjected to the regular discipline"; but besides, into the censure which he will put upon them before the community, the Abbot will know how to put such vigor that no one will be tempted to imitate the offender. The whole interest of the sentence bears, in reality, on the ending: "that the others may thereby conceive fear."

The boys, namely those who have not passed 15 years, are under the surveillance of all and subjected equally to the direction of all. Not arbitrarily, however. If anyone thinks he should punish any boy, this must be "with all measure and reason."

Whoever, concludes St. Benedict, permits himself to punish without mandate any one of his brethren or to chastise a boy without discretion will be subjected to the regular discipline. "We must not do to another what we would not want done to ourselves," St. Benedict likes this formula, which he has already used and which forms the ninth instrument of good works.

APPLICATION

St. Benedict forbids two things: 1) to excommunicate; 2) to strike.

To excommunicate, as we have seen previously, is to separate anyone from the communal life, to cut off a member of the family. Now, aside from disciplinary excommunication, there is another of a moral order, too widespread, alas, in the world.

All our brethren, ransomed by the blood of Jesus Christ, have a right

---

[2] *Commentary*, p. 480.

to our charity. It is in that charity that the communion of souls is established. Now, what does hate do? It excommunicates, for hate separates more than anything else in the world.[3] St. Benedict so detests hate, even in its mildest forms, that he prescribes, as we have seen, that at the end of the Office of Lauds and of Vespers the *Pater* be chanted, that enmities may thereby disappear. Is it not natural that we should enter fully into these sentiments of our holy Father, which are also those so much recommended by the Lord, and that we should excommunicate no one from the charity we owe to all?

Hatreds and animosities ordinarily beget violence, sometimes physical, too often moral. One strikes one's brother, as St. Augustine says, "with the sword of the tongue." There are people, remarks Dom Cuthbert Butler,[4] "not officials but officious, who think they have a roving mission to set things right ... in season and out of season." These are benevolent justices of the peace with whose service a person would willingly dispense. Let us guard against arrogating such a role to ourselves. On the other hand, if our situation sometimes puts on us the necessity of reprimanding and correcting, let us know how to do so at once with the spirit of justice and the spirit of charity.

"Speaking generally," writes Dom Delatte,[5] "all correction should fulfil the three following conditions: the corrector should have power to correct, the cause should be just and reasonably adequate, and the punishment should be proportioned to the fault. The effect of correction will be much jeopardized, if it is manifest that we are yielding to impatience, or to natural antipathy, or to irritability of temperament: let us keep our antipathies for our own faults." These counsels are worth meditating. In reality, they will often have their application, whether in family life or in our relations with our inferiors, or with the neighbor in general.

The duties of correction with regard to children in particular are always of delicate application. St. Benedict indicates to us the conditions which will render them profitable: a mixture of kindness and severity, patience, justice, discretion and, above all, a great deal of charity.

He puts us on guard against natural antipathies, which may sometimes

---

[3] The application is that given by Dom Columba Marmion, *Christ, the Ideal of the Monk*, pp. 78-79.

[4] *Benedictine Monachism*, p. 204.

[5] *Commentary*, p. 481.

provoke acts of violence, and which would be painful to us too if we felt that others held similar antipathies against us.

CHAPTER 71
That the Brethren Be Obedient to One Another

April 29—August 29—December 29

OT ONLY is the boon of obedience to be shown by all to the Abbot, but the brethren are also to obey one another, knowing that by this road of obedience they are going to God. Giving priority, therefore, to the commands of the Abbot and of the Superiors appointed by him (to which we allow no private orders to be preferred), for the rest let all the juniors obey their seniors with all charity and solicitude. But if anyone is found contentious, let him be corrected.

And if any brother, for however small a cause, is corrected in any way by the Abbot or by any of his Superiors, or if he faintly perceives that the mind of any Superior is angered or moved against him, however little, let him at once, without delay, prostrate himself on the ground at his feet and lie there making satisfaction until that emotion is quieted with a blessing. But if anyone should disdain to do this, let him undergo corporal punishment or, if he is stubborn, let him be expelled from the monastery.

COMMENTARY

Obedience is necessarily due to the Abbot, who represents Christ; but its practice constitutes such a good and is so effective in destroying conceit and pride, those two great obstacles in the search for God, that it is good to spread its practice as much as possible: "Let the brethren obey one another." There will be, therefore, besides the obedience due to the Father of the monastery and to the officers commissioned by him, a sentiment and a constant tendency, as it were, for mutual obedience.

The concern here obviously is not with orders given by just anyone, but with an habitual attention inspired by "charity and solicitude." Every occasion of satisfying the legitimate desires of a brother is a good fortune for the monk; for, remarks Dom Delatte, "each act of submission removes a portion of his self-love and gives him more of God."[1] That is indeed quite the contrary of the spirit of "contention" which leads one to answer back everything done by others, to oppose them, to find fault with them. The

---

[1] *Commentary*, p. 482.

spirit of contention separates, the spirit of obedience unites effectively in charity.

St. Benedict is so concerned for that active brotherhood, manifested by a real eagerness, that he does not allow it to be destroyed even for a short instant. He who causes trouble should be corrected. .Our holy Father does not say how; undoubtedly by public reproaches or the regular correction.

The second part of this chapter envisions not so much obedience in itself as one of the consequences of the spirit of mutual disobedience, namely disunion. The concern of the Superiors in watching over the application of the Holy Rule, and the practice of giving corrections, may provoke in the one who is not supernatural enough more or less animosity, a little momentary antipathy and, in certain violent natures, temptations to hatred. In the Superior even—and it is of him that St. Benedict seems to be thinking especially—there may have been an emotion, even slight. That he was right is always to be presumed; the idea is not to contest in order to know who is wrong or who is right.[2]

The concern is above all with the mutual charity which is injured; it is that which must be reestablished. A child ought to take it hard to think that his father is somewhat irritated with him. What to do? Quite simply, go and prostrate oneself at the feet of the angered or contradicted Superior and await his blessing. The Father who blesses has no more power to be discontented; in a moment all is pardoned, all is forgotten, and the divine peace reenters into the hearts.

This "satisfaction" is so necessary that our holy Father makes of it not the object of a counsel, but a point of Rule, which he imposes under pain of bodily chastisement and even of expulsion. Whoever willingly dwells in hatred no longer has his place in a family where the peace of Christ should reign.

APPLICATION

Obedience is considered by our holy Father as a good: *bonum obedientiae*. To the possession of this good he attaches the greatest importance. A person could not pretend to be truly his child, therefore, if he did not work to procure this good for himself. The *bonum obedientiae* is imposed on the Oblate, then, as well as on the monk.

It is important, consequently, to grasp well what St. Benedict wants

---

[2] Dom Cuthbert Butler, *Benedictine Monachism*, p. 204.

from us. Assuredly he would not allow anyone to content himself with an obedience wholly material. What he demands is not only acts of obedience but the spirit of obedience. Appearances could not suffice. The spirit of obedience should penetrate the heart of his children, should be like the atmosphere in which the soul moves, should impregnate the whole activity. It is at once humility, charity, renouncement; it is above all a spirit of faith.

"It is by this way of obedience," says St. Benedict, "that the brethren go to God." God is always the unique and last term, the One whom we seek beyond creatures. St. Benedict has taught us to find Him in our Superiors, of whatever sort they be, in our pastors, in our Abbot, in our brethren of the parochial or monastic family, in the sick, in the poor, and in all Christians generally.

Now this view of faith ought not to be reduced to an abstract, Platonic conception. If we really see Christ in our brethren, logically we ought to experience for them habitual sentiments of deference, a sincere desire to serve them and to show kindness to them. Our brother is good and virtuous; how sweet it ought to be to serve him, for Christ is more apparent in him. He is imperfect or even sinful; the love of the Christ humiliated in this sinner, of the Christ who would live in him and whom we should desire to see live there, will put into our conduct a discreet note of zeal and of apostolate. Our attitude, our speech, our ways of acting will breathe that inward "charity" and "solicitude"; for we do not serve Christ as He wants to be served by taking "a bored and skeptical attitude,"[3] by having the air of doing a favor, by admiring ourselves inwardly or by seeking to make ourselves admired.

Obedience so understood, in its broadest acceptation, is quite the opposite of that spirit of the world to which our holy Father wants us to be completely foreign. The spirit of the world is made of pride and egotism: it tends to the exaltation of the ego. The individual considers only his rights, his advantages, his pleasures, his interests. Society is a juxtaposition of egotisms. The spirit of St. Benedict is the spirit of the Gospel. All are united in the living Charity which is God. The very greatest exist only to serve the rest. The Abbot applies himself more "to being useful than to dominating," and the Sovereign Pontiff is "the servant of the servants of God."

---

[3] Dom Paul Delatte, *Commentary*, p. 483.

To keep this obedience, sacrifices, mortifications of a spiritual order are sometimes necessary. To dissipate the clouds and reestablish concord, one must know how to humiliate oneself. In the same spirit as the monk who without dispute goes and casts himself at the feet of his Abbot, we shall always find in the refinement of our faith and our charity the words, the attitudes, the manners of proceeding which are suitable for maintaining or revivifying in our relations with our brethren in Jesus Christ, whether Superiors or inferiors, that veritable spirit of obedience such as our holy Father understands it.

CHAPTER 72
On the Good Zeal Which Monks Ought to Have

April 30—August 30—December 30

UST as there is an evil zeal of bitterness which separates from God and leads to hell, so there is a good zeal which separates from vices and leads to God and to life everlasting. This zeal, therefore, the monks should practice with the most fervent love. Thus they should anticipate one another in honor; most patiently endure one another's infirmities, whether of body or of character; vie in paying obedience one to another—no one following what he considers useful for himself, but rather what benefits another—; tender the charity of brotherhood chastely; fear God in love; love their Abbot with a sincere and humble charity; prefer nothing whatever to Christ. And may He bring us all together to life everlasting!

COMMENTARY

There is a close connection between this chapter and the preceding ones. The mutual obedience just spoken of is one of the most apparent effects of good zeal. Dom Delatte thinks, moreover, that this passage might be considered "as a synthesis of the entire Rule."[1] St. Benedict, he continues, "condenses the whole science of monastic perfection into a few short and pithy sentences, which have the brightness and solidity of the diamond. Although the points of doctrine, and even the forms of their expression, are already partly known to us, their selection and grouping give them a new value."

Zeal is a certain interior warmth of the soul tending towards an end, good or bad. There are two kinds of zeal.

There is an "evil zeal of bitterness" which separates from God and leads to damnation. St. Benedict does not define it in any other way. It is the zeal of the miser who runs after riches, the zeal of the epicure who is consumed in the pursuit of pleasures. This evil zeal produces fruits of corruption. There exists a sort of apostolate of the evil zeal; for evil, like good, has its adherents and its defenders. The vicious person wants to be justified before himself and before others, and he scarcely finds any means more efficacious than to render others evil like himself.

---

[1] *Commentary*, p. 486.

Good zeal is quite the contrary; it "separates from vices and leads to God." St. Benedict wants it very ardent. It has been said that the obedience of which we spoke previously is "charity in action."[2] Good zeal is charity in full activity. This it is, in reality, which inspires the mutual kindnesses, which helps in supporting with a peaceable and affectionate patience the neighbor's faults of character and his bodily infirmities. It renders obedience easy. It triumphs over the egotism which seeks itself by making us prefer to what is useful to us that which is so to another. Without good zeal the virtues are somewhat constrained, forced; sometimes they are not even anything but the appearances of virtues. But the soul which forgets itself through the effect of good zeal can only love with a "chaste affection." And in mentioning that chaste affection, notes Dom Chauvin,[3] St. Benedict transports us, we might say, into heaven itself, where the elect "like the Angels of God" love one another with a tenderness uniquely supernatural.

The common text of this passage of the Holy Rule is punctuated thus: *Caritatem fraternitatis casto impendant amove. Deum timeant.* A certain number of critics propose, according to the manuscripts, to read rather: *Caritatem fraternitatis caste impendant. Amove Deum timeant.* This is the reading admitted by the Benedictines of Farnborough in their translation of the Holy Rule, where we read: "Let them render to one another chastely the charity of brotherhood; let them fear God out of love" (*Qu'ils se rendent chastement la charité de la fraternité; que d'amour ils craignent Dieu*). And Dom Chauvin finds "more savor" in this reading.

Indeed this punctuation, which appears to be the most ancient, fits in better with the context. Good zeal puts chastity into fraternal charity; it puts love into the fear of God. The service of God in fear alone would have something of an obligatory pressure; fulfilled with the fervor of good zeal, it makes fear disappear in love.

Good zeal realizes something analogous in the relations with the Abbot. For the monk enlivened with good zeal, the Abbot is not the necessary master and the indispensable organ of order; he is much better: he is the Father. Abba, Pater. "Let them love their Abbot," says St. Benedict, "with a sincere and humble charity."

Good zeal can arrive at all these results only by the fact that it proceeds

---

[2] Dom Étienne Salasc, *La Règle de S. Benoît Traduite et Commentée*, p. 613.

[3] "Le Bon Zele," in *Bulletin de S. Martin et de S. Benoît*, June, 1926,, p. 163.

from Christ and leads to Him. It is born, propagates itself and acts in a soul only by the fact that that soul has put Christ above everything. The soul gives itself to the neighbor because it gives itself to Christ, whom its faith shows it in the person of all its brethren.

APPLICATION

"This chapter," writes Dom Bernard Laure, "is one of those which a person could not reread and meditate enough."[4] It is also, notes Dom Chauvin, one of those "which have contributed the most to give to the Benedictine family its mark of distinction." Every one of its sentences imposes itself on us, every word is wholly penetrated with doctrine. The soul of our holy Father, our teacher and our model, appears to us here in all its radiant beauty and in all the fervor of its piety. He is truly the *pius pater* of the Prologue, of whom it is sweet to call oneself the child.

On its import Dom Cuthbert Butler[5] has written pointed observations. Here, he says, "St. Benedict gives his formal precepts for the community life, which indeed are golden rules for regulating the life of any family, natural no less than monastic. ... These are, indeed, nothing else than the everlasting principles of the practice of the family virtues and the discipline of family life."

In the first place there is this one, which dominates and from which flow all the rest: "Let them prefer absolutely nothing to Christ." Jesus Christ alone sought, loved, contemplated, and nothing but Him. We do not have two parts to make in our soul and in our life, that of Christ and that of the world or, what comes back to the same thing, of our self-centered ego. Jesus wants all: "He who is not with Me is against Me." We do not have to balance, therefore. We must be His.

But, wonderful thing, having renounced everything for Him with a true renouncement, we are going to find everything again! Let us open our eyes, as our holy Father told us in the Prologue, "to the deifying light" and let us look. Every creature is transparent to the eyes which

---

[4] *Commentaire*, p. 464.

[5] *Benedictine Monachism*, pp. 204-205.

contemplate God. It is He whom one finds again in the creature, it is He whom one wants to see there always more living and more beloved.

There is the principle of the apostolate under all its forms. Supernatural charity, since it is Christ who is sought, and since charity comes from Him; sincere charity, since He is witness of it and since He is not content with appearances; humble charity, because it implies a certain reverence for that in our brethren which is of God. Universal charity, which excepts no one, but still goes out of preference to those who surround us and are more specially, according to the flesh and according to the spirit, our relatives and our brethren.

For love of Christ we shall love those whom He has entrusted to us, those to whom He has entrusted us, those to whom He has united us: our pastors, our faithful, our Abbot and our brethren of the monastery, our family, our poor, our friends, our enemies; serving them, devoting ourselves to them and praying for them as best we can. The more we increase in this supernatural charity, the more we shall be assured of realizing the great precept of our Father: That nothing, absolutely nothing be preferred to Jesus Christ! And vice versa, the more we grow in the unique love of Jesus, the more we shall love our brethren also.

EPILOGUE
On the Fact That the Full Observance of Justice Is Not Established in This Rule

May 1—August 31—December 31

NOW we have written this Rule in order that by its observance in monasteries we may show that we have attained some degree of virtue and the rudiments of the religious life.

But for him who would hasten to the perfection of that life there are the teachings of the holy Fathers, the observance of which leads a man to the height of perfection. For what page or what utterance of the divinely inspired books of the Old and New Testaments is not a most unerring rule for human life? Or what book of the holy Catholic Fathers does not loudly proclaim how we may come by a straight course to our Creator? Then the Conferences and the Institutes and the Lives of the Fathers, as also the Rule of our holy Father Basil—what else are they but tools of virtue for right-living and obedient monks? But for us who are lazy and ill-living and negligent they are a source of shame and confusion.

Whoever you are, therefore, who are hastening to the heavenly homeland, fulfil with the help of Christ this minimum Rule which we have written for beginners; and then at length under God's protection you will attain to the loftier heights of doctrine and virtue which we have mentioned above.

COMMENTARY

All the commentators have admired in this last page of the Holy Rule our holy Father's spirit of humility. He does not end on a cry of triumph. He does not proclaim, like the ancient poet:

Exegi monumentum aere perennius.[1]

On the contrary, he concludes on words of a modesty so evidently sincere as to move us deeply. He has written this Rule in order that "we might show, in some manner at least, the uprightness of our characters and a beginning of religious life." Without any doubt, St. Benedict does not mean to say that he has written his Rule for lax people, who will not

---

[1] "I have built a monument more durable than brass."

425

be capable of great perfection and will find themselves satisfied with ordinary virtue. God forbid! Quite to the contrary, it is evident that he has drawn it up for the benefit of souls which are still imperfect, but which he wants to urge on towards perfection.

It will adapt itself, therefore, to their present weakness, but not to leave them in it. It will open before those souls unbounded vistas of perfection, it will raise them even to the point where 'The heart, enlarged, having run with an ineffable sweetness of love in the way of the commandments" (Prologue), is established in that "perfect charity which casts out fear" (Chapter 7).

To help itself in this direction, the soul is going to draw on those same sources which have sustained and enlightened the holy Patriarch. These are the Holy Scriptures, Old and New Testaments, which offer themselves to us first of all with the prestige of "divine authority." They are the "holy Catholic Fathers," whose writings raise us directly to our Creator. Does not their teaching represent that catholic tradition which brings to us the true sense of the Scriptures? There are, again, "the Conferences of the Fathers and their Institutes and their Lives." St. Benedict has in mind here, evidently, the works most familiar to the monks of his time, those which contained the monastic tradition, the *Collationes* and the *Instituta Coenobiorum* of John Cassian, and the *Vitae Patrum.*[2] There is finally "the Rule of our Father St. Basil," who was then regarded as the greatest legislator of the cenobitic life.

These are so many "instruments of virtue" for the monks who want "to live well and to practice obedience."

In enumerating this small but precious library of the true religious, St. Benedict cannot help thinking about the great examples which it recalls. He sees rising in his memory the lofty figures of such men as Anthony, Pachomius and the Abbots mentioned by Cassian. And this sight wrings from him a new cry of humility. By comparison with those heroes of asceticism what are we if not "inert," "evil-living," "negligent" men, who ought "to blush with confusion"?

But the holy Father cannot leave us with this sorrowful feeling of our wretchedness. The Fathers were men like us, and they have attained the

---

[2] See *The Wit and Wisdom of the Christian Fathers of Egypt*, translated by E. A. Wallis Budge from the Syrian version of the *Apophthegmata Patrum* (Oxford University Press, 1934), 445 pp.

"summits." Let us try to follow them, supporting ourselves on "this little Rule for beginners." We are not alone; Christ is there to help us. And this Rule, so humble in appearance, provided we observe it as well as we can, will lead us as high as those whose memory fills us with admiration.

Is there any need to add that St. Benedict's foresight was perfectly accurate? His Rule, in which the extremes of certain Eastern desert Fathers are no longer found, his Rule so balanced, so full of discretion, has led multitudes of souls even to the highest degrees of sanctity.

APPLICATION
We have gone through the whole Rule written by our holy Father. We have been able to see what treasures of spirituality are found enclosed in it. It is a mine that we can always dig with profit. When we have read it for the first time, we have observed in it, as the Prologue promised us, "nothing harsh, nothing heavy." We have admired the suppleness with which it adapted itself to our weakness.

But the more we have meditated it, the more we have understood that to practice it is not to remain in one place. We must "run" in the way of the commandments, we must detach ourselves from the world, we must renounce ourselves, annihilate our own will, combat pride and raise ourselves through self-denial and the Cross even to the perfection of love. Those are goals which no one can attain without an unceasing struggle and a great deal of courage. The day that we stop running, that we feel too tired to go forward in detachment from the world and adherence to Christ Jesus, on that day we shall no longer be truly, but only in name, sons of St. Benedict, since we shall have ceased following our Father to the summits to which he wants to lead us.

To arouse and sustain our courage we have the divine words of the Holy Writ, which we must meditate. The liturgy, with its Psalms, its Epistles, its Gospels, each day offers to us the most inspiring passages. To these we should join a regular, consecutive reading, not with the state of mind of critics who see only the human side, but with that of the Christian who, as St. Augustine says, "seeks Jesus in the books." To this reading we shall join, as St. Benedict recommends, that of the Fathers and the Doctors. There we shall find a fertile spirituality and very sure guides. How much time certain Christians lose, not only in profane and futile readings, but in reading those little books of "popular" devotion, where one finds so little doctrine and so much sentimentality!

But we should not forget that we are attached to the monastic Order. The holy monks of the past are our spiritual family. The desert Fathers in particular are our authentic ancestors. The reading of their lives has always been dear not only to the religious but to the fervent Christians of the great religious ages. It is good for us Oblates to familiarize ourselves with their doctrine, set forth in various writings, notably those of Cassian, especially recommended by our holy Father. At the thought of so many wonderful examples of strength, of renouncement and of divine love, at the meditation of those sentences expressing an intimate experience of grace, we ourselves will feel more ardent and more desirous of following with them the paths of Christ.

"We are the children of the Saints." Aided by the examples, the counsels and the intercession of our heavenly family, we shall make our own the spirit of the Holy Rule; we shall observe it according to our means and our opportunities. Those who have gone before us will recognize us as brothers; and, after having guided and sustained us here below, they will welcome us, with the Father of the immense Benedictine family, on the threshold of the heavenly home.

—FINIS—